International Law, New Diplomacy and Counterterrorism

This interdisciplinary book explores how terrorism is meant to target a government's legitimacy, and advocates for sounder defensive measures when countering international attacks.

The dramatic increase in global cooperation throughout the twentieth century—between international organisations and their state missions of diplomats, foreign officers, international civil servants, intelligence officers, military personnel, police investigators, judges, legislators, and financial regulators—has had a bearing on the shape and content of the domestic political order. The rules that govern all of these interactions, and the diplomats engaged to monitor and advocate for compliance, have undergone a mushrooming development following the conclusion of each world war. This dramatic growth is arguably the most significant change the international structure has experienced since the inception of the state-based system ushered in with the Peace of Westphalia in 1648.

International Law, New Diplomacy and Counterterrorism explores the impact of this growth on domestic legitimacy through the integration of two disciplines: international law and political philosophy. Focusing particularly on the cross-border counterterrorism actions launched by the United States, the author investigates how civil societies have often turned to the standards of international law to understand and judge the legitimacy of their government's counterterrorism policies reaching across international borders. The book concludes that those who craft counterterrorism policies must be attentive to defending the target of legitimacy by being wholly mindful of the realms of legality, morality, and efficacy when exercising force.

This book will be of much interest to students of international law, diplomacy, counterterrorism, political philosophy, security studies, and IR.

Steven J. Barela is an Assistant Professor at the Global Studies, Institute and a member of the Law Faculty at the University of Geneva, Switzerland.

Routledge New Diplomacy Studies
Series Editors: Corneliu Bjola
University of Oxford
and
Markus Kornprobst
Diplomatic Academy of Vienna

This new series will publish theoretically challenging and empirically authoritative studies of the traditions, functions, paradigms and institutions of modern diplomacy. Taking a comparative approach, the New Diplomacy Studies series aims to advance research on international diplomacy, publishing innovative accounts of how "old" and "new" diplomats help steer international conduct between anarchy and hegemony, handle demands for international stability vs international justice, facilitate transitions between international orders, and address global governance challenges. Dedicated to the exchange of different scholarly perspectives, the series aims to be a forum for inter-paradigm and inter-disciplinary debates, and an opportunity for dialogue between scholars and practitioners.

New Public Diplomacy in the 21st Century
A comparative study of policy and practice
James Pamment

Global Cities, Governance and Diplomacy
The urban link
Michele Acuto

Iran's Nuclear Diplomacy
Power politics and conflict resolution
Bernd Kaussler

Transatlantic Relations and Modern Diplomacy
An interdisciplinary examination
Edited by Sudeshna Roy, Dana Cooper and Brian Murphy

Dismantling the Iraqi Nuclear Programme
The inspections of the International Atomic Energy Agency, 1991–1998
Gudrun Harrer

International Law, New Diplomacy and Counterterrorism
An interdisciplinary study of legitimacy
Steven J. Barela

International Law, New Diplomacy and Counterterrorism

An interdisciplinary study of legitimacy

Steven J. Barela

Routledge
Taylor & Francis Group

LONDON AND NEW YORK

First published 2014
by Routledge
2 Park Square, Milton Park, Abingdon, Oxfordshire OX14 4RN

and by Routledge
711 Third Avenue, New York, NY 10017

Routledge is an imprint of the Taylor and Francis Group, an informa business

First issued in paperback 2015

British Library Cataloguing in Publication Data
A catalogue record for this book is available from the British Library

Library of Congress Cataloging-in-Publication Data
Barela, Steven J., 1971 author.
International law, new diplomacy and counter-terrorism : an
interdisciplinary study of legitimacy / Steven J. Barela.
    pages cm. – (Routledge new diplomacy studies)
    Includes bibliographical references and index.
    1. Terrorism (International law) 2. Terrorism–Prevention–Law
    and legislation. 3. War on Terrorism, 2001–2009. I. Title.
    KZ7220.B37 2014
    344.05'325–dc23
                                                        2013035370

ISBN 978-0-415-70835-7 (hbk)
ISBN 978-1-138-18364-3 (pbk)
ISBN 978-1-315-88604-6 (ebk)

Typeset in Baskerville
by Wearset Ltd, Boldon, Tyne and Wear

To Margaret and her piano

Contents: overview

Preface: from flight attendant to academia   xiii
Acknowledgments   xv
List of abbreviations   xvii

Introduction:
the Genii of the City   1

1 Conceptualizing legitimacy as a target   12

2 International counterterrorism and a legitimacy deficit   56

3 Through the lens of legality:
detention without judicial review   102

4 Through the lens of morality:
just war and public diplomacy   148

5 Through the lens of efficacy:
torture on suspicion   194

Conclusion:
jeopardizing legitimacy and drones   251

Bibliography   265
Index   284

Contents: detailed

Preface: from flight attendant to academia   xiii
Acknowledgments   xv
List of abbreviations   xvii

Introduction:
the Genii of the City   1

1   **Conceptualizing legitimacy as a target**   12
     I Introduction 12
     II Political violence and legitimacy: social science and philosophy 17
       a Sociologist Max Weber 19
       b Philosopher Jürgen Habermas 21
     III Erosion of power relations: social scientist David Beetham 24
     IV Coerced obedience and action in concert: political theorist Hannah
       Arendt 27
     V An uncoerced pull toward compliance: international jurist Thomas
       Franck 30
     VI Legitimacy as a target: historian Guglielmo Ferrero 31
     VII Exposing the Genii of the City: legal philosophers Ost and
       Kerchove 36
       a Formal validity: legality 40
       b Axiological validity: morality 42
       c Empirical validity: efficacy 44
     VIII An intersection of laws and morals: legal philosopher
       H. L. A. Hart 49
     IX Overlap and application 54
     X Conclusion 55

2   International counterterrorism and a legitimacy deficit   56

I Introduction: destruction, not construction, of legitimacy 56
II Terrorism as tactic and strategy 59
    a   Terrorism as tactic 61
    b   Terrorism as strategy: revenge, renown, and reaction 63
III International law as the framework 72
    a   Detention through the lens of legality 76
    b   War-making through the lens of morality 81
    c   Interrogation through the lens of efficacy 84
IV A legitimacy deficit and causality 88
    a   New diplomacy and domestic civil society 91
    b   Pertinent judicial decisions 93
    c   Further civil dissent 94
    d   Military dissent 95
    e   Causality 98
V Conclusion 100

3   Through the lens of legality:
detention without judicial review   102

I Introduction 102
II The US and international law 107
    a   Transnational judicial dialogue and the US Supreme
       Court 107
    b   International norms: a framework for dialogue 111
III The Rasul *decision: stimulating the dialogue 113*
    a   A realignment of precedent 114
    b   Human rights norms and the Ahrens *dissent 117*
IV The onset of dialogue and the Hamdan *decision 120*
    a   The Geneva Conventions as part of the UCMJ 122
    b   The Application of Common Article 3 124
    c   Common Article 3 and the military commissions 126
V The continuation of dialogue and the Boumediene *decision 128*
    a   The Military Commissions Act of 2006 128
    b   The constitutional right to habeas corpus 130
    c   Deficiencies of the DTA and the Unconstitutionality of MCA,
       §7 134
VI Further exchange on detention under Obama, but without
   moderated dialogue 136
    a   Detention without judicial review beyond Guantánamo 138
    b   "Meaningful review" 140
    c   NDAA 2012 141
    d   The closing of Guantánamo? 143

VII Conclusion: detention and diplomatic implications 144

4 **Through the lens of morality:**
just war and public diplomacy 148
I Introduction 149
II Anticipatory attacks and the just war doctrine 153
  a The classic doctrine 155
  b Transition to the modern era: a telling bifurcation over
    "just feare" 158
    i The humanist tradition and holy war 159
    ii The scholastic tradition and a secular doctrine 163
  c The dawn of international law 165
  d Following the lineage: Pufendorf, Vattel, and Kant 169
III The Bush Doctrine: preemptive or preventive war? 172
IV Last resort and a moment for deliberation 176
V Right authority and the UNSC 182
  a Chapter VII and Iraq 185
  b Humanitarian intervention in Iraq 189
VI Conclusion: diplomatic implications, and the Obama
Doctrine 191

5 **Through the lens of efficacy:**
torture on suspicion 194
I Introduction 194
II Legality: the torture memos 200
  a The Bradbury memos 202
  b Pushback from the legislature and the judiciary 204
  c A flawed attempt at efficacy for legality 205
III Efficacy: six high-profile suspects 211
IV Ibn al-Shaykh al-Libi: casus belli *213*
V Abu Zubaydah: the pivotal moment in torture policy 215
  a The clash between the FBI and the CIA 216
  b Authorizing further ill-treatment and torture on suspicion 220
  c The apex of the waterboard and its eighty-third
    application 222
  d Erroneous suspicions 226
VI The "dirty bombers": the insidious nature of torture 229
  a José Padilla 230
  b Binyam Mohamed al Habashi 231
VII Mohammed al Qahtani: destroying the endgame 236
VIII Kahlid Shaykh Mohammed: correct suspicions and efficacy 239

IX Torture on suspicion: clarifying the moral argument 243
X Conclusion: remedy, redress and diplomatic implications 247

Conclusion:
jeopardizing legitimacy and drones   251

Bibliography   265
Index   284

Preface
From flight attendant to academia

In 2001, I was working as a flight attendant for United Airlines. The night before the attacks of September 11, I had just returned home to Denver (via SFO) after working an international flight from London. My wife, who was also a flight attendant, dragged me out of bed that Tuesday morning, speaking animatedly about airplanes and tall buildings. Since the events were beyond explanation, she insisted that I shake off the jet lag and see what was happening for myself. Since that moment I have been unable to divert my attention from those attacks and what they spawned.

The events of that morning had an enormous impact upon my country and upon my life, and I reacted to them by pivoting to study terrorism and counterterrorism all the way up to the doctoral level. My intention in this preface is to briefly trace the path I have followed to the publication of this book, which in itself provides a rough outline of my understanding of the anatomy of global terrorism today.

When I was a new flight attendant, I was based out of Newark, New Jersey, and had thus worked with some of the crew who were the victims of the box-cutters even before the planes had become deadly projectile weapons. I count myself enormously fortunate not to have lost any loved ones that day, having both family and friends in the industry. Since two out of four of the hijacked planes belonged to United Airlines, my company took a particularly big hit in the depressed economy that followed, and the job of flight attendant changed considerably as cuts in both the workforce and in pay ensued.

As a result, I decided to return to university while still working. Studying the phenomenon of terrorism and my country's reaction to it understandably drew my interest in the International Studies program in which I enrolled at Denver University. It was through my studies there that I came to regard the disciplines of international law and political philosophy as being best suited for illuminating the central issues. To further pursue the marriage of these two branches of learning, I left my job as a flight attendant to accept a position as a doctoral assistant at the University of Geneva.

After nearly a decade of living in Geneva, I have come to call this city my home, and there is no doubt that its people, history, and the celebrated "Spirit of Geneva" have had a direct impact upon my work. The fact that it is a prominent home for international law and public diplomacy contributed greatly, with the city serving as the European offices of the United Nations, housing the seat of the UN High Commissioner of Human Rights, and the long-established home of the International Committee of the Red Cross. In addition to this, long before the city became host to international organizations, Geneva had been eloquently and properly described by eighteenth-century English visitor George Keate as a place where one would find "Scenes of Academic Silence, where Philosophy is more studied than the Sword" (as cited in Roberts 2006: 54).

It is in this setting that I have researched and studied the attacks of 9/11 and the "war on terror" to complete my doctoral work. In order to accomplish what I felt was necessary to suitably address this subject, I simultaneously completed an LL.M. degree in the laws of war and human rights. This provided me with the background and training to analyze the applicable norms and codified laws governing cross-border violence, detention, the use of force, and ill-treatment. Integrating this field with political philosophy led me to conceptualize the legitimacy of a government as a target in asymmetrical conflict.

It is well known that individuals choosing the dastardly tactic of targeting noncombatants are much weaker than their government adversary, and so they clearly wish to upend the conventional battlefield. To do so they pursue a *strategy of provocation* in order to goad a government into doing injury to itself that could never be achieved by non-state actors: that is, jeopardizing its own legitimacy.

More than a decade after 9/11 it is not difficult to see the overreaction that was provoked. By engaging in counterterrorism policies that run into problems of legality, morality, and efficacy, a government falls into the legitimacy trap laid by its foes. As we now know, this is a bipartisan mistake that can be made by both Republican and Democratic administrations.

Once we understand that the actions of government in response to terrorist acts are often directly related to the legitimate exercise of authority, and consequently central to the conflict, the need for more thoughtful counterterrorism policies becomes imperative.

Much of the past decade of my life has been spent contemplating, investigating, and conceptualizing the pertinent questions in the hope that we can better develop a counterterrorism policy that reduces the damage we do to ourselves. This work is my response to the attacks of that fateful day in 2001, and it is meant to help us understand and defend the target of legitimacy.

Steven J. Barela
Geneva, June 2013

Acknowledgments

As noted in the Preface, this book represents the final destination of a long academic road through various disciplines to arrive at a Ph.D. in law at the University of Geneva. Without a doubt, there has been one person who must stand out in these acknowledgments due to his extremely deft hand at guiding me through this not so obvious interdisciplinary path: Alexis Keller. In addition to his more bureaucratic expertise (a skill never derided by anyone who has navigated the elaborate halls of academia), Alexis Keller also opened my eyes, right at the pivotal moment in the development of my theory, to the work of Guglielmo Ferrero, who sits at the center of this study of legitimacy. If only for these two significant contributions (there are countless more), he sits atop this long list.

Next, a heartfelt extension of gratitude goes to the co-director of my doctoral thesis, Maya Hertig. She stepped in to help ensure the rigor of my legal argumentation and scholarship, not to mention assisting me in avoiding pitfalls in one of my most challenging chapters. Additionally, I had the very good fortune of assisting in the "University Forum 2005–8: Democracy and Terrorism" project when I first arrived at the University of Geneva. In particular, it was the remarkable work of the international lawyers involved in this forum that inspired me to pursue an LL.M. degree. The clarity and thoroughness of this discipline shone through brightly in this project; thus, sincere appreciation must be expressed to these scholars. This leads me to the Geneva Academy of International Humanitarian Law and Human Rights. My experience there was so positive and foundational that I cannot leave out any of the outstanding professors who all merit tribute: Paola Gaeta, Marco Sassòli, Louise Doswald-Beck, Robert Kolb, and Andrew Clapham. In addition, I would like to express my sincere gratitude to two jury members who helped strengthen this interdisciplinary work with their insightful comments and questions: US law professor David Cole of Georgetown Law, and professor of legal philosophy François Ost of Saint-Louis University, Brussels.

Before coming to Geneva, the genesis of this project goes back to my work at the University of Denver, Graduate School of International Studies (now the Korbel School). Although every single course I followed there provided a valuable piece of the intellectual formation that lead me down this path, I would be remiss not to mention two names in particular. The first is former Dean Tom Farer, who was the original international lawyer who piqued my interest in and fascination with the discipline. In addition to this early awakening, Tom Farer monitored my route through all of the studies I undertook in Geneva and was always available for encouragement or counsel. Finally, this brings me to Alan Gilbert. During my time in the program I enrolled in every course offered by Alan. This is an indication of both his keen intellect as well as his ability to connect with students during some of the most difficult to comprehend political times. Most importantly, it was his course on Theories of Non-Violence that initiated the philosophical stirrings that undergird this book.

Abbreviations

ABA	American Bar Association
AP-I	Additional Protocol I to the Geneva Conventions
AP-II	Additional Protocol II to the Geneva Conventions
AUMF	Authorization to Use Military Force
CAT	United Nations Convention Against Torture and Other Cruel, Inhuman or Degrading Treatment or Punishment
CBW	Chemical and Biological Weapons
CIA	Central Intelligence Agency
CSRT	Combatant Status Review Tribunals
DOD	US Department of Defense
DTA	Detainee Treatment Act of 2005
ECtHR	European Court of Human Rights
EITs	Enhanced Interrogation Techniques
FLN	Front de Libération Nationale
FBI	Federal Bureau of Investigation
GCs	Geneva Conventions
GSS	General Security Service (Israel)
HRC	Human Rights Committee
ICC	International Criminal Court
ICCPR	International Convention on Civil and Political Rights
ICISS	International Commission on Intervention and State Sovereignty
ICJ	International Court of Justice
ICRC	International Committee of the Red Cross
ICTY	International Criminal Tribunal to Ex-Yugoslavia
MCA	Military Commissions Act
NAFTA	North American Free Trade Agreement
NSS	National Security Strategy
OLC	Office of Legal Counsel
OPR	Office of Professional Responsibility
PCIJ	Permanent Court of International Justice
POW	Prisoner of War

SERE	Survival, Evasion, Resistance, and Escape
UCMJ	Uniform Code of Military Justice
UNSC	United Nations Security Council
UNSCOM	UN Special Commission

Introduction
The Genii of the City

An international lawyer should no longer write for rulers alone (who may or may not heed his words); he ought to write mainly for ordinary citizens: he should offer them parameters by which to judge international affairs, and analytical mechanisms for examining the intricacies of the world community.

(Cassese 1989: viii)

If society withdrew its obedience, the commander's rule was at an end. Even Clausewitz, let us recall, was of this opinion, for he understood that military victories were useless unless the population of the vanquished army then obeyed the will of the victor.

(Schell 2003: 221)

On September 11, 2001, the population of the United States of America began their day with news that four civilian aircraft had been commandeered to become deadly projectile weapons. The crashing of two of these airplanes into the World Trade Center in downtown Manhattan was caught on film and broadcast as the population sat in awe before their television sets, watching the destruction of a national symbol. The spectacular terrorist event thus became a vivid image etched into the psyche of a nation. Using terrorism expert Brian Jenkins' assessment that "terrorism is theatre" (1975: 16), we can see the event as theater *par excellence.*

Working with the concept of terrorism as theater, one can begin to see that, of all the tools implemented in orchestrating the tragedy of that day (including, e.g. box-cutters, airplanes, and skyscrapers), it was the television that proved to be the most strategic. The fact that the most destructive portion of the event was caught on film and repeatedly broadcast over the airwaves served Al-Qaeda's overarching interests of destabilizing the US Government in the hope of jamming its operation. The reason that this shared potent image is so important is because it successfully drew the audience, specifically the American public, directly into the conflict as participants. The diffusion of the events of that day must simply be recognized as a part of the nature of US media and democracy, and these violent and destructive images brought a citizenry full of ire directly into the fold for the creation of counterterrorism policy.

It is the reaction to these terrible events that will primarily concern us in this book. This is because terrorist groups involved in asymmetrical conflict are trying to shift the field of battle away from a conventional military encounter where they are clearly at an enormous disadvantage and instead use a "strategy of provocation" to further their goals (Laqueur 1977: 81). This baiting is a challenge which the victim state must carefully consider when crafting its counterterrorism policy since it has considerable hard power to wield should it choose to do so.

While it is rare that there is a completely coherent idea of what response their deeds will produce, a central motivation of those who employ terrorism is to incite some type of reaction from their government adversary. In this book, it will be the response of the "war on terror" that will drive our analysis and serve to provide the evidence of legitimacy as a target of terrorism. By more fully conceptualizing legitimacy, and by analyzing the reaction to 9/11 through its lenses, this basic element of societal structure will become elucidated as an essential factor in such conflict. Thus we will see the need for legitimacy to be placed at the center of the analysis of counterterrorism: policy that cannot be disentangled from the terrorism that provokes it.

There is no doubt that 9/11 was a violent attack on innocent civilians in flagrant transgression of the principles of humanitarian and human rights law that should be properly recognized and deplored. The "violation of established norms" is in fact one of the characteristic features of a terrorist act (Laqueur 1977: 3) and is a reason why it often triggers such a vehement and powerful response.

Democracies tend to be particularly susceptible to such provocation since the spectacular nature of violent attacks makes good television coverage for a free press, a fact with which terrorist groups are familiar. Imagery and coverage of terrorist acts intensify panic and fear within the targeted society, which generally leads to an insistence upon clear and bold action to ensure security. The short democratic election cycle helps to foster a rapid and forceful response since politicians wish to be seen as attentive to security concerns. Yet it has been keenly pointed out that while "[s]peed and force are both critical elements in a successful military campaign; it is far less clear that they are necessary ingredients of a successful counterterrorism policy" (Richardson 2006: 101). Thus, it is the tension created between bold and legitimate action that we will see played out in this book.

One of the distinctive characteristics of this particular terrorist attack is that it was an act of cross-border violence. The reason why this feature of the strike is so crucial is that the counterterrorism response was thus inevitably subjected to the rules of international law to help assess its legitimacy. In this circumstance, international laws are the most clear and obvious standards available to citizens to judge the legitimate use of physical force by their governments.

Along with the mass proliferation of media forms which make the theater of terrorism much more dramatic, the twentieth century has also seen an exponential growth of international law. An important part of that expansion has been in rules protecting individuals from abuses by government. In this way a valuable metric has developed, by which citizens have become able to measure their government's legitimate exercising of physical force, especially when it is done against or over foreign nationals. Because international humanitarian law and human rights treaties, along with the UN Charter, have framed the questions pertaining to the legal nature of the responses to these terrorist strikes (seen most clearly in internal government documents), international law will serve as the framework for this book.

To classify this work it is also necessary to recall the intimate relationship between international law and diplomacy. Of course, it is commonly recognized that a diplomat "must be conversant with the principles of public international law" since they are directly within their scope of operation (Chatterjee 2007: xxi). As international obligations expressed through treaties represent the duties states recognize to one another, they provide the foundation for the language and communications used by the representatives of those states in their relations. Building on this premise, this book will work particularly with the concept of *new diplomacy*.

In 2002, Harold Pachios, Chairman for the Advisory Commission for Public Diplomacy, gave a series of lectures for the US State Department discussing what he described as *new diplomacy*, and he saw it comprised of two primary components. In his speech he spoke of a renewed attention to diplomacy that was borne of the attacks of 9/11, and he indicated that this must be met with a renewed focus on *public* diplomacy (Pachios 2002). In other words, a greater effort should be made to explain the values and principles of the US to citizens in other countries. It had customarily been the case that exchanges between states were largely carried out behind closed doors and hidden from the public eye. However, in the second half of the twentieth century this has changed dramatically, with a move toward courting the general publics of other countries. Of course, this shift has tracked the major development of international organizations and the sweeping rise in multilateral treaties.

Second, the conduct of international relations has been significantly altered by the Internet, which has given ordinary citizens instant access to news of government actions across borders, international conventions meant to govern those activities, and data analyzing compliance. This technology also brings with it the ability for individuals to connect and organize with like-minded people within their own country or across the globe. Thus, the second facet of this phenomenon discussed by Pachios was labeled as *information age* diplomacy. The piece that becomes particularly relevant in this book, and which is suggested as an important feature of *new diplomacy*, is that the Internet renders the division between domestic and foreign publics purely theoretical since both have access to the same freely available information (Zaharna 2004). Pachios identifies these two elements of diplomacy, open and widely disseminated in today's world, as central to defining *new diplomacy*, and they likewise construct the understanding here.

Capturing extremely well the connection between international law and *new diplomacy* are the sentiments expressed by the renowned international jurist Antonio Cassese in the first epigraph to this introduction. Cassese's contention that international lawyers must address common citizens and offer them methods and structures for analyzing the actions of states was germane two and a half decades ago, and is now all the more compelling in consideration of the expansive growth of information age and public diplomacy. In short, *new diplomacy* acts as a figurative conduit for the flow of international law to ordinary citizens.

The specific tactics that will be analyzed in this book are detention, war-making, and interrogation, with a closing remark on drone killing. On the three primary issues, the policies of the "war on terror" reached beyond reasonable justification, no matter how well positioned the authorities were who drafted interpretation of the state's legal duties. When aggressive policies were forced into the open and explanations were demanded by courts, international bodies or the public, we will find that they failed to meet the basic requirements of *legality*, *morality*, and *efficacy*. Counterterrorism policies overreached and did not succeed in meeting the codified obligations of domestic, international, and constitutional law, a moral standard of reciprocity, and an empirical criterion of effectiveness. These critical failures all came with a cost to the government's legitimacy.

By the end of his second term, President George W. Bush, whose signature policy was indeed this global war against terrorism, found himself embattled, beleaguered, and in what can be termed a "legitimacy deficit." Because the mandate of the original architects of the "war on terror" has come to a close, our primary attention will be on these initial policies. Ample documentation exists in the public sphere and has been augmented by numerous leaks from concerned administration officials over the years. These leaks themselves indicate that a legitimacy deficit was suffered since such disclosures represent a lack of pull toward compliance with authority. Thus, for purposes of analytical clarity, much of the focus will be on the policies of the administration which suffered such a deficit in its second term.

Nonetheless, even though President Barack Obama was swept into office on a campaign emphasizing "change," we find that some of his counterterrorism policies have not departed in a significant way from those of his predecessor. In a move that was meant to live up to this campaign promise, on his second full day in office President Obama signed executive orders that indicated a noteworthy adjustment. Yet there has been continued legal struggle over detention policy and the failure to close the Guantánamo facility as promised. Additionally, there has been a shift in preferred tactics as detention and interrogation became severely questioned by both domestic and international audiences. As such, the Obama policies and their diplomatic implications will be analyzed at the end of each related chapter, with a look at the drone program in the conclusion to the book. Distressingly, we will find that the historical research found in Chapter 4 on imminence as the minimum trigger for the use of force will continue to be entirely relevant as the Obama administration has also chosen to redefine this indispensable standard for anticipatory action. If we consider that the diminished pull towards compliance primarily occurred in President Bush's second term, it is an appropriate time to take note of some of the similar seeds of illegitimacy that have been sown.

Interdisciplinarity is employed in this work in three distinctive ways. At the outset, on a conceptual level, this work represents a conscious integration of two primary disciplines: political philosophy and international law. Of course, this marriage is not novel. The noted scholar Martin Wight has described the 400 years of international theory leading up to the surge of its study in the twentieth century as a partition "between philosophically minded international lawyers and internationally minded political philosophers" (1992: 3). Thus, this work simply reaches back to this deep tradition and filiation of thought on international society to present a text that cannot be simply classified into today's disciplinary categories.

The intention behind using the intersection of these two disciplines is to formulate and investigate one specific impact of today's changing international environment on the internal political climate of individual states. The dramatic increase in global cooperation throughout the twentieth century—between international organizations and their state missions of diplomats, foreign officers, international civil servants, intelligence officers, military personnel, police investigators, judges, legislators, and financial regulators—has had a bearing on the shape and content of the domestic political order. The rules that govern all of these interactions, and the diplomats engaged to monitor and advocate for compliance, have undergone a mushrooming development following the conclusion of each world war. This dramatic growth is arguably the most significant change the international system has experienced since the inception of the state-based system ushered in with the Peace of Westphalia in 1648. Here we explore its impact upon domestic legitimacy.

The reasoning for fixing our gaze on international legal obligations will be best illuminated through the discipline of political philosophy. Specifically, we will look at the question of what maintains an authority as legitimate—that is, what actually generates and preserves the *will to obey* the authority who has the *power to command?* To explore this question, we will next employ interdisciplinarity as a tool of construction. Various specialists on the question of legitimacy will be brought together from different fields to engage in an "interdisciplinary dialogue" in order to construct a theory applicable to political struggle involving state and non-state actors. This interchange will be used to erect the concept of *legitimacy as a target*, and it will bring us to one particular author whose work undergirds this study.

In 1942 an Italian historian, Guglielmo Ferrero, wrote a valuable work of political philosophy entitled *The Principles of Power*, in which he explores the subject of legitimacy. Ferrero cogently explains that a government is "legitimate if power is conferred and exercised according to principles and rules accepted without discussion by those who must obey" (1942: 135). He makes clear that the structure of every society is based on the intersection of command and obedience. Put another way, the authority in command at the top of a community must be bestowed with legitimacy through compliance from below. Without the convergence of these two elements a collection of people cannot act in concert or work together toward shared goals. No doubt there has been significant attention on the top-down aspect of authority since it is much easier to identify, track, or even target. However, it is the elusive bottom-up component of legitimacy that will concern us here.

The conventional military method of engaging in armed conflict has been to focus one's forces on the enemy's command structure and military to "disarm the enemy" (Clausewitz 2000: 266–267). Yet this approach to and thinking about warfare has been shifting. Throughout the twentieth century there was a particularly curious development in the line of attack concerning political conflict, namely a conspicuous increase in the use of guerrilla warfare, nonviolent active resistance, and terrorism to attempt, sometimes successfully, to wrest power from an authority. Fittingly, the second epigraph here comes from an enormously valuable work by Jonathan Schell, which explores these contemporary developments in warfare and highlights the imperative of obedience (2003). One important element that each of these tactics has in common is that they are all means employed by non-state actors, even if the approach to the use of violence in each case differs significantly. It is hypothesized that each of these methods places a target on the legitimacy of a government, even if the scope of this particular investigation will only encompass terrorism.

Ferrero's work also provides an appropriate title to this introduction. While he identifies an element of society that often goes unnoticed (the uncoerced pull toward compliance), what constructs this force is said to be unknowable. He labels the content of legitimacy "the Genii of the City" and proposes that, although this obedience is ever-present in all communities acting in concert, it is unseen and without shape. Ferrero explains that "[b]ecause they are invisible, men are too often apt to be unaware of their presence and even of their existence. And yet these invisible Genii rule our entire existence" (1942: 17). Despite this coy proposal that the content of legitimacy cannot be known, it is the intention of this work to expose the Genii of the City. While such a project must certainly be undertaken with humility, it is also one that is demanded by the logic pursued in naming legitimacy as a target.

Thus, in the second half of Chapter 1 we will turn to the legal philosophers François Ost and Michel van de Kerchove's work on legal validity, which posits an integrative theory. They suggest that there are three primary conceptual spheres that intersect, overlap, and interact to create the strongest compliance pull. These legal philosophers put forward that this unseen pull is constructed by formal, axiological, and empirical validity, and the three concepts constructing legitimacy for our own model will be encapsulated in the shorthand of *legality, morality,* and *efficacy.* None of these spheres dominate or prevail over the others in the model as this theory is meant to be integrative in order to capture the interdisciplinary nature of legitimacy.

To begin Chapter 2, attention will be drawn to the fact that those who employ terrorist acts have the intention of damaging or destroying an existing legitimacy, but hold little interest in constructing a new one in its place. To illuminate this point most clearly, an examination will be carried out of the 2006 US Army Field Manual 3–24, *Counterinsurgency,* overseen by General David Petraeus, who was to step into a very prominent military and political role largely due to the doctrine found in this document. The manual's authors identify and return repeatedly to the idea that "[p]olitical power is the central issue in insurgencies and counterinsurgencies: each side aims to get the people to accept its governance or authority as legitimate" (US Army 2006: §1–3).

We will then put forward the major characteristics of terrorism, which can be largely summed up as public and politically motivated violence against noncombatants. Moving beyond the description of terrorism as a mere tactic, there will be the presentation of the three primary strategic goals of terrorism as revenge, renown, and reaction (Richardson 2006: 71–103). Most importantly, the focus will be on the objective of provoking a reaction. Indeed, it is the overreach that prompted the assertion that it was not the attacks of 9/11 that changed the world, but "[r]ather it was our [the US] reaction to September 11 that changed the world" (Richardson 2006: 167).

Next will be the presentation of the international legal framework that the US administration faced when confronting detention, war-making, and intelligence-gathering for its "war on terror." No doubt, the dimension and extent of the reaction of the US to the attacks of 9/11 has taken a form that has been noticed and felt worldwide. One reason for this is the fact that the response has run up directly against international treaties that the state has ratified, customary international law, and *jus cogens* obligations—all of which fall within the direct purview of diplomats.

In Chapter 3, we will look through the lens of *legality* and put forward an analysis of three landmark decisions handed down by the US Supreme Court on the question of wartime detention at the military facility in Guantánamo Bay, Cuba. It has traditionally been the case that courts in the US have demonstrated a great amount of deference to the executive in times of armed conflict. Consequently, the fact that the Supreme Court stepped into the fray to strike down the detention policy of the executive on three consecutive occasions, the last instance relating to policy created in conjunction with the legislature (a historic first in times of armed conflict), is important to note. In this context, the highest court in the land employed an emerging judicial tool to push back against overreaching by the other branches of government in a measured, patient, and resolute manner so as to eschew the traditional deference exercised by the Court.

Importantly for our purposes, the Supreme Court used international humanitarian law in its *Hamdan* decision of 2006 to bolster its mounting of a judicial ladder and place the international laws of war on the front pages of newspapers and as the leading story of nightly news broadcasts. The Guantánamo detention facility became a real diplomatic problem for the administration due to its contention that there were no applicable legal protections for those detained in the "war on terror," and the Supreme Court decisions striking this lawlessness down reinforced the international assertion that legal protection indeed existed. To complete this chapter we will look into what the Obama administration, the legislature, and the lower courts have done in the silence that followed the Supreme Court's original willingness to moderate a dialogue between the branches of government.

In Chapter 4, the next instance of international law impacting domestic political views on the legitimacy of the government will be explored through the high-profile and well-publicized debate in the UN Security Council over the invasion of Iraq in 2003. Here we adjoin the lens of *morality* and gaze through it to distinguish a clear overlap with *legality*. To reveal the importance of this intersection we will trace the matter of anticipatory attacks through the just war doctrine to discover that there was a telling bifurcation on this precise question in the seventeenth century.

The widely broadcast diplomatic debate at the UN had at least two consequences. The first was that the discussion had the effect of demonstrating that the US had options other than invasion because there was indeed a "moment for deliberation." This is precisely what the debate represented, and the moment was amplified by the unprecedented six to ten million people in the streets worldwide on February 15, 2003, protesting a war that had not yet begun.

Second, the fact that the US was legally obliged under Chapter VII of the UN Charter to go before the Security Council in pursuit of an authorization for the use of force against Iraq compelled an open and explicit reasoning for invasion. The US had to make a public case in a diplomatic forum that could and would be tested by citizens and the media from that moment forward. The most vociferous reasoning for the need to invade the nation of Iraq put forward before the Security Council was based on Iraq's possession of weapons of mass destruction and the state's connections with the Al-Qaeda organization. The fact that both of these claims turned out to be patently false underlined the reality that the military incursion was an unjustified use of force, and thus it failed on both the moral and legal standards emanating from the just war doctrine.

In Chapter 5, we will peer through the lens of *efficacy* to find that it shares a crucial point of overlap with *morality* and *legality* on the question of torture. Thus, for the final example of how international law has affected the domestic order of the US we will investigate the United Nations Convention against Torture (CAT). Under Article 4(1), the treaty requires that "[e]ach State Party shall ensure that all acts of torture are offences under its criminal law." It was signed by President Reagan and then ratified by the Senate, creating a binding legal duty in 1994. As it was explained in the infamous "Bybee memo," legislation was passed on torture to meet this requirement: "Congress criminalized this conduct to fulfill US obligations" (Bybee 2002b: 182). Thus, when speaking of torture, the domestic legal order had been directly altered by international law.

As a result, the authors of the "torture memos" were forced to directly confront the international legal prohibition of torture. While the "Bybee memo" explicitly states that it is "obvious" that "Congress intended Section 2340's definition of torture to track the definition set forth in CAT" (Bybee 2002b: 183), its authors proceeded to put forward a definition that certainly does not match the standard found in that treaty. Lawyers from the Office of Legal Counsel (OLC) went beyond the treaty language and counseled the President that for the criminal act of torture to occur a higher threshold had to be met. The memo read

> [t]he victim must experience intense pain or suffering of the kind that is equivalent to the pain that would be associated with serious physical injury so severe that death, organ failure, or permanent damage resulting in a loss of significant body function will likely result.
>
> (Bybee 2002b: 183)

The treaty speaks of "severe," but the memo's authors upped the ante with "so severe that." This manufactured standard of "death or organ failure" rippled through the public sphere and caused such a political uproar that the memo was retracted within a week of being leaked. Although the memo was a legal document, and thus by definition not meant for laymen, pain and suffering is something absolutely everyone can understand, even though very few have actually experienced organ failure and no one can explain how death feels.

Information concerning the torture and ill-treatment of detainees has continued to stream into the public sphere, particularly concerning those who were considered high-value detainees. The most significant abuse—torture, by its legal definition—has been documented and released to the public. Through our legal investigation of the "torture memos," an exploration of the effectiveness of the abusive treatment by way of the empirical data available on six of these detainees, and demonstration of how this clarifies the moral question on torture, we will find that this policy of ill-treatment fails each of our three tests of legitimacy.

As seen, we will apply the three lenses of legitimacy sequentially, adding one lens at a time. By applying the lenses of *legality*, *morality*, and *efficacy* in this manner, the intention is multiple. First, by beginning with the lens of legality it will be possible to see how these policies of the "war on terror" came into direct contact and conflict with the international legal obligations of the US. Next, the structure of our work will draw attention to the public aspect of *new diplomacy* in an information age, and this will demonstrate how international law became a direct part of the discussion about the legitimate exercise of physical force by the government.

Finally, by adjoining each lens successively we will see the intersection of and interplay between the three conceptual spheres. This represents the third facet of interdisciplinarity to be applied in this book. As each sphere or lens embodies a different approach to academic investigation (i.e., formal, axiological, and empirical validity), the intention is to explore how they interact without devolving into an analytical mush in which each component becomes largely indistinguishable.

A commanding authority is inevitably balanced upon how legitimately it exercises the physical force with which it has been bestowed. The pillars of *legality*, *morality*, and *efficacy* that sustain this legitimacy come under attack when an asymmetrical foe employs terrorist tactics to provoke an overreaction by the government. As will be seen throughout this work, the most difficult part of confronting such an enemy lies in distinguishing combatants from noncombatants, and making a distinction between the two is the very first rule of customary international humanitarian law. As was put forward in the authoritative study directed by the International Committee of the Red Cross, "**Rule 1**. The parties to the conflict must at all times distinguish between civilians and combatants. Attacks may only be directed against combatants. Attacks must not be directed against civilians" (Henckaerts and Doswald-Beck 2005: I, 3). This standard is essential to the conduct of legitimate warfare, and there is no doubt that it becomes an extremely arduous and demanding task in the case of asymmetrical conflict. By implementing policies that are illegal, immoral, and ineffective, directly stemming from using suspicion to meet the challenging requirement of distinction, a government runs the risk of alienating its citizens and destabilizing the structure of its own society.

To be sure, many who confront terrorism begin with the premise that one must focus on killing or vanquishing the enemy: offensive strategy. That is not the intention here, nor is it believed to be the correct starting point. By identifying a target at which terrorists aim, this book looks instead at defensive strategy. In doing so it promotes the building of resilience to deal with modern threats while not jeopardizing legitimacy. Thus, this investigation provides indications of where a society would want to fortify its defenses when facing an asymmetrical adversary using terrorism.

Diplomats defending, or foreign diplomats confronting, overly aggressive policy in the twenty-first century find themselves under growing pressure from citizens all over the world. Over the past six decades there has been a mass proliferation of international institutions and diplomatic personnel, along with nongovernmental organizations engaging them as representatives of an international civil society, all governed by international law. To suggest that this immense growth has not affected the domestic legal order or the mental framework for how citizens judge the obligations of their own government in an information age is to deny the shifting terrain. The pertinent question is just how much change has come about, not whether any change has actually occurred. As a result, this work represents a view on the impact of international law and *new diplomacy* that is worth noting, if only for crafting counterterrorism policy to better defend the target of legitimacy.

1 Conceptualizing legitimacy as a target

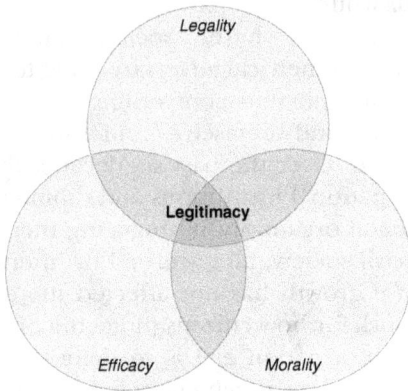

We can no longer have any illusions on the nature of the principles of legitimacy: they are human, that is empirical, limited, conventional, [and] extremely unstable. Any philosophical hack can demonstrate their absurdity; any dictator, at the head of a gang of cutthroats, can suppress them. Nevertheless, they are the condition of the greatest good that mankind, as a collective being, can possess—government without fear.

(Ferrero 1942: 314–315)

I Introduction

An essential dimension of political struggle, whether armed or unarmed, will inevitably revolve around the *power to command* and the *will to obey* since their establishment is what organizes a society. How this is instituted and exercised remains a central and oscillating question for any body politic, and it is surely necessary for a government to manage both elements in order to be defined as functioning. For a community to operate as a unit, decisions and plans must be fixed and then put into action. This clearly requires both command and obedience. Yet, while a commander can be targeted and destroyed with dominant strength, obedience is more elusive and volatile because it is inevitably up to each citizen to exercise this through her own individual will.

As a result, obedience is an element that cannot always be easily explained through the conventional prism of force. There is little doubt that the use of force has commanded compliance time and again. Nevertheless, today it has become clear that access to more powerful weaponry has faded as the primary deciding factor in every political struggle. It is therefore necessary to move beyond notions of pure force to investigate how some tactics applied by the less powerful in armed conflict are intended to achieve victory. Thus, this work will instead examine how the strategic goals of those who utilize terrorist acts might actually be achieved. That is, the aim is to achieve their goals through the provocation of a reaction deemed to be illegitimate since they are clearly not employing overpowering conventional force.

At the beginning of the twentieth century, German sociologist and political economist Max Weber put forward a definition of the state that has become central to Western political thought. Weber described the defining concept of the state as "a human community that (successfully) claims the *monopoly of the legitimate use of physical force* within a given territory" (Weber 1946: 78; original emphasis). The thesis of this work will build on what is considered here to be an essential element of this valuable definition: *legitimacy*. While much attention has been focused on the aspect of physical force found in this definition, the notion of its legitimate exercise is particularly useful for illuminating the line of attack charted by the asymmetrical tactic and strategy of terrorism.

Moreover, it should not go unnoticed that Weber emphasized the exercise of force by a state as the key function tied to its legitimacy. Likewise, this will serve to construct the thesis of this work, as the US wartime authority exercised in the "war on terror" was at times overreaching and in turn became damaging to the legitimacy of the government. Although it is important to recognize that it is extremely difficult to validate any legitimacy claim, one particular moment at which legitimacy comes into sharp focus is when a state's use of force is challenged. One historical example that has been pointed out is the legitimacy deficit that the US suffered during the Vietnam War. To be sure, many groups that have employed terrorism have raised the legitimacy of the use of force against the people they claimed to represent as central to their grievance against the perceived enemy government (Cook 2003).

Following this same line of thought, the US Army Field Manual 3–24 *Counterinsurgency* (2006) highlights the centrality of legitimacy over and over again in discussing modern warfare. While this army manual is focused on the use of the US military in foreign territory, and thus at first glance might not seem applicable in this broad conflict of the "war on terror," one should remember that Al-Qaeda has indeed engaged the US in its own asymmetrical conflict. This means that it is certainly appropriate to classify this group as insurgents attempting to undermine the US government, and, as such, the lessons of counterinsurgency are directly applicable to our discussion. The manual instructively explains,

> [i]llegitimate actions are those involving the use of power without authority—whether committed by government officials, security forces, or counterinsurgents. Such actions include unjustified or excessive use of force, unlawful detention, torture, and punishment without trial. [...] Any human rights abuses or legal violations committed by US forces quickly become known throughout the local populace and eventually around the world. Illegitimate actions undermine both long- and short-term COIN [counterinsurgency] efforts.
>
> (US Army 2006: 1–24, §1–132)

As we analyze the policies of the "war on terror" in this work, we will find that the exact same examples cited—i.e., the "unjustified [...] use of force, unlawful detention, torture and punishment without trial"—became part and parcel of that very policy. The fact that this military doctrine guiding US forces in their overseas campaigns claims that "legitimacy is the main objective" (US Army 2006: 1–21) lends credence to our own theory posited here, and both the coincidence and the divergence will be explored in the next chapter. Once we understand that the actions of government in response to terrorist acts are often directly related to the legitimate exercise of authority and are consequently central to the conflict, the need for more thoughtful and defensive counterterrorism policies becomes imperative.

This concept of legitimacy will be central to our analysis because the exercise of the "*legitimate use of physical force*" ultimately bears upon obedience to command. It will be posited that those who employ terrorist attacks attempt to achieve their strategic goals by driving a wedge between command and obedience within the enemy society. By provoking an overreaching reaction from a government to deal with the terrorist threat, or by triggering a response that is considered to be outside of the confines of the government's authority, the intention is that the citizenry of the rival society will deem the actions carried out to be an illegitimate exercise of physical force. If the determination of illegitimacy pertaining to a policy or government becomes widespread—that is to say, that citizens no longer orient their actions in accordance with the authority—then that society is significantly destabilized because it cannot function or move as a unit.

Even before such a drastic state of affairs occurs, a government that has a diminishing pull toward compliance with its authority encounters difficulties. That today's predominant purveyors of terror wish to immobilize and disorient their enemy to help reach their strategic goals is hardly controversial. In some measure, this will be an explicit conceptualization of what has been broadly suggested by other analysts.

Most importantly, however, the objective of this work is first to illuminate the manner in which non-state actors that employ terrorism attempt to reach their overarching goals through a "strategy of provocation" (Laqueur 1977: 81) meant to target legitimacy. Next, to enrich the discussion of legitimacy, we will present a distinctive way to conceptualize the specific content of legitimacy so that it can be applied as a series of lenses, or tools of analysis, for viewing and discussing this issue. In doing so, it will be possible to highlight the critical role that international law and diplomacy have played in evaluating the overreach in the "war on terror." With this clarified understanding of the enemy's strategy for reaching its objectives, we can have a valuable conversation about how a government attacked by terrorism can best defend itself.

To begin our discussion of legitimacy as a target, it is first necessary to explain the structure of this chapter. Partly because of its interdisciplinary nature, it is suggested that the sometimes rigid disciplinary lines of academia have not fostered sufficient attention on legitimacy during times of political struggle. Nonetheless, there are important works that can be utilized collectively as solid building blocks to construct our theory. The question of what makes power legitimate has been of concern for a whole host of professional groups (legal experts, political and moral philosophers, historians, and social scientists, to name but a few) who have approached the subject from diverse perspectives, primarily using their own professional expertise. Yet offering a single disciplinary perspective on the concept of legitimacy can skew and distort this topic of deep complexity. It is therefore preferable to employ an integrative methodology that sheds light on this multifaceted concept so as to overcome a narrower approach. To do so, we will present the pertinent work on legitimacy in a way that recognizes, grapples with, and illuminates the interdisciplinary nature of this concept.

To start, it is helpful to discuss some of the different terms used to describe a research project that is meant to bring together and integrate various disciplines in order to resolve a question too complex to solve through only one field of study. In general, there are three primary terms used to express this type of approach. *Multi*disciplinarity looks at a topic from the perspective of several disciplines at one time, but makes little attempt to join together their insights and thus is often dominated by the home discipline of the researcher. *Inter*disciplinarity brings together a collection of viewpoints from various disciplines and then draws on the diverse insights by finding ways to integrate them. The third term, *trans*disciplinarity, is meant to capture "that which is at once *between* the disciplines, *across* different disciplines, and *beyond* all disciplines" (Repko 2012: 20–21; original emphasis).

One useful way to think about these terms is to use the analogy of a jigsaw puzzle. Multidisciplinarity is about bringing differing points of view to the table as separate pieces of a jigsaw puzzle and making a modest effort to see how they might fit together. Interdisciplinarity is when one tries to assemble these puzzle pieces by comparing them, looking for the concave and protruding portions so as to find how they might usefully interact and join together. Transdisciplinarity is meant to describe when the pieces of a puzzle have been fitted together in a way that produces a whole new image. While it is important to recognize that this metaphor is imperfect because the outcome of a jigsaw puzzle is predetermined and the way disciplinary data comes together is much more fluid and supple, it is still a worthwhile analogy that communicates well the objective in looking outside of one discipline for answers to a complex question.

Thus, the first part of this chapter will be organized as a piece-by-piece construction of differing ideas on legitimacy put forward by the most pertinent intellectuals from different disciplines. In this way, it will be possible to see the logic and reasoning for the conceptualization of legitimacy as a target. While there are certainly various scholars who have discussed the concept of legitimacy, its meaning and application have been quite varied. Therefore, there is a limited number of works that are directly germane to our discussion here. As such, we will present the pertinent ideas from authors from different disciplines and allow them to come together in this chapter in what is meant to be an *interdisciplinary dialogue.*

Sections II–VI will explore the most relevant authors to have treated the concept of legitimacy relative to the context of political struggle. We will start by exploring the literature on the joining of political violence with legitimacy to arrive at the classical works on the subject by sociologist Max Weber and philosopher Jürgen Habermas. Then social scientist David Beetham's work on legitimacy will be investigated to expose his valuable discussion on power relations and their deterioration. Next, political theorist Hannah Arendt will provide highly beneficial insights on the idea of coerced obedience and its limitations, along with the definition of power as *action in concert.* The work of international legal scholar Thomas Franck will then present us with constructive language and vocabulary for better understanding the concept of an uncoerced pull toward compliance. With this we will arrive at the historian Guglielmo Ferrero, who will offer an indispensable discussion and imagery that will allow us to put forward our own unique conception of legitimacy as a target of terrorism.

Section VII will then present the logical and necessary next step. That is to say, it will expound on the work of legal philosophers François Ost and Michel van de Kerchove to hypothesize a structure and content for understanding legitimacy in our context presenting *legality, morality,* and *efficacy* as the interactive components being targeted by those who employ violent attacks on noncombatants. Next, Section VIII will discuss how the interplay and overlap of these elements can be understood through the work of legal philosopher H. L. A. Hart, along with presenting how the model will be applied in this book in Section IX.

II Political violence and legitimacy: social science and philosophy

There has been general recognition by some social scientists that legitimacy is an important part of the struggle when there is a clash between a government and a group that uses violent actions as their means to engage them politically. In the philosophical literature there have certainly been some attempts to define legitimacy. However, there has infrequently been an attempt to marry legitimation and terrorism in a way that would illuminate the analysis.

Martha Crenshaw edited the volume *Terrorism, Legitimacy and Power*, which brings together a variety of political scholars to investigate the consequences of terrorism. Of interest for us is that several of the contributors, including the editor, agree that "legitimacy is the key to a successful response to terrorism" (Crenshaw 1983: 147). One contributor focuses particularly upon the tension that is created by terrorism because a government needs to maintain and strengthen its own authority while at the same time diminishing the legitimacy of the terrorists. Hence both effectiveness and the legitimacy of policies are discussed as necessary elements for doing so (Quinton 1983: 52–64).

Accordingly, we find an approach throughout Crenshaw's book that dovetails with our own judgment that the legitimacy of the policies instituted to deal with a terrorist threat must be constructed with the understanding that overwhelming force without limits can backfire. This is especially the case when all of the culprits responsible for a violent act of terrorism are difficult, if not impossible, to distinguish, track down, and bring to justice. Yet, even though there is recognition in this edited work that "[a]ctions against the terrorists must be scrupulously legal," combating the threat using similar methods in retaliation is "morally abhorrent," and that "[e]fficiency and legitimacy [...] are closely related" (Crenshaw 1983: 33–35), there is a disappointing lack of effort aimed at giving any real shape to the concept of legitimacy.

Overall, this work by Crenshaw represents the type of attention that the social-science community has given to investigating terrorist attacks in the context of the legitimacy of a regime. One major difficulty for this discipline is that, as recognized by Crenshaw, the legitimacy of a regime is a normative concept and, as such, lacks any scientific metrics, or statistical data, by which it can be adequately measured. Recognizing this truth also means that it is not possible to simply assume that states under attack by terrorist actions, even democratic ones, are to be automatically deemed clearly and perpetually legitimate. This is not meant to suggest that those who employ terrorism have a just cause; it is only an unsophisticated binary framing of the conflict that would lead toward such a conclusion. Rather, it is to point out that the legitimacy of every regime is always in flux and change, and it can indeed be directly affected by terrorism and counterterrorism. Yet beyond this recognition of legitimacy as a normative concept, and pointing to the important connection between political violence and legitimacy, "most social scientists have rarely bothered to discuss the issue at any length" (Cook 2003).

One article that explicitly links terrorism and legitimacy is a piece by the philosophy scholar Deborah Cook, entitled "Legitimacy and Political Violence: A Habermasian Perspective" (2003). The reason she puts forward for writing her article is that "[s]ince political violence today often revolves around the issue of legitimacy, this issue requires much closer scrutiny than it has received in the existing social scientific and philosophical literature" (2003). In Cook's article, one gets a real sense of how much uncultivated territory lies between the phenomenon of terrorism and the concept of legitimacy. She explains,

> because legitimacy is a controversial and complex notion, involving not only legal and political matters, but also more strictly moral considerations, it is probably not surprising that social scientists usually avoid dealing with the issue once they have identified legitimacy as pivotal in the conflict between states and terrorist organizations.
>
> (Cook 2003)

This being the case, in her article Cook does a superior job of outlining the *problématique*. She identified the current lacuna in the literature and then moved the discussion forward by offering an insightful and pertinent analysis of the work by Max Weber and Jürgen Habermas on legitimacy. In doing so, she places it in the context of terrorism. Therefore, what is necessary for our work here is to highlight the most salient portions of Weber's and Habermas's work.

An investigation of Weber and Habermas on the issue of legitimacy presents us with two different approaches that have important impacts upon its treatment. It is necessary to begin by explaining the shortcomings of Weber's approach, and at the same time justifying the decision to instead follow Habermas on this issue. What we will find is that Weber offers a view of legitimacy that is not amenable to proof, or cannot be tested, because he sees it as based on unspecific subjective beliefs without identifiable content. On the other hand, Habermas adopts the position that the legitimacy of a regime can be accepted or rejected on rational grounds which actually rest on verifiable content that can indeed be tested. As will be seen throughout this book, while legitimacy is multifaceted and ever-shifting, there are some broad lines that can help us come closer to understanding and exploring its essence, even if we cannot know its precise contour lines at all moments and in all circumstances.

a Sociologist Max Weber

Max Weber's work on legitimacy has achieved classical status in the literature of political science and political sociology, even if it is incomplete. As noted above, the widely diffused definition of the state today comes from Weber when he spoke of "a human community that (successfully) claims the *monopoly of the legitimate use of physical force* within a given territory" (Weber 1946: 78; original emphasis). In the same "Politics as a Vocation" speech in which he put this classification forward, Weber stated and then asked,

> [l]ike the political institutions historically preceding it, the state is a relation of men dominating men, a relation supported by means of legitimate (i.e., considered to be legitimate) violence. If the state is to exist, the dominated must obey the authority claimed by the powers that be. When and why do men obey? Upon what inner justifications and upon what external means does this domination rest?
>
> (Weber 1946: 78)

Weber goes on to put forward three broad typologies as the "inner justifications" or "basic legitimations," in an attempt to answer the questions presented here. He presents these as *traditional, charismatic,* and *legal* authority: *traditional* authority is based on a belief in the legitimacy of what has always been known to exist and creates a pull toward obedience out of custom; *charismatic* authority rests upon the personal magnetism or pull created by the charisma of the person giving the order; and *legal* authority is based on the propriety of formally enacted rules and statutes. The motivations for recognizing orders or an authority as legitimate will vary, and in individual cases the stimulus to obey will sometimes be combined in differing ways.

However, the thrust of Weber's argument is that legitimacy is based upon belief. Looking at *traditional* and *charismatic* authority, it is quite easy to understand their basic components as subjective beliefs. At the same time, *legal* authority in Weber's scheme is at first meant to rest on "rational" grounds, giving a more stable foundation for the critical aspect of the *will to obey* underpinning a societal structure. Yet further investigation reveals that these "rational" grounds are themselves based upon belief. In his discussion of the three pure types of legitimate authority in *The Theory of Social and Economic Organization,* similar to what is found in this speech, Weber speaks of "[r]ational grounds—resting on a *belief* in the 'legality' of patterns of normative rules and the right of those elevated to authority under such rules to issue commands" (1947: 328; my emphasis). As such, Weber simply assumes that this belief is rational and gives no evidence or support for his argument. Therefore, whether a rule or command is genuinely legal is not determinative in Weber's scheme, since it is in fact the "*belief* in the legality" that truly matters.

As further evidence of subjective belief buttressing Weber's understanding of legitimacy, we can look to where he discusses "The Concept of a Legitimate Order" in this same book. Weber launches the entire discussion, with his own emphasis on the specific word in question, by explaining that "[a]ction, especially social action which involves social relationships, may be oriented by the actors to a *belief* in the existence of a 'legitimate order'" (1947: 124; original emphasis). So it can indeed be verified that for Weber legitimacy rested upon "belief."

Also of importance, Weber makes clear that sheer obedience is not enough to signify that the legitimacy has been bestowed from below. Not only must there be identifiable compliance, but this obedience must be willingly given. As Weber explains, "[t]he merely external fact of the order being obeyed is not sufficient [...]; we cannot overlook the fact that the meaning of the command is accepted as a valid norm" (1954: 328). Just as we will see in our discussion of coerced obedience and Arendt's exploration of how violence can at times undermine political goals, Weber too makes the important distinction that to obey out of fear or expediency would not coincide with the concept of legitimacy as discussed here.

Interestingly, Weber follows his discussion of the legitimacy of an order with a section entitled "The Concept of Conflict" (1947: 132–135). Yet although it makes good sense that the legitimacy of a regime would have a direct bearing on the type, frequency, and intensity of social conflict, Weber does not connect the two. He discusses conflict as a battle to impose one's will that is met with resistance, which can be either peaceful or violent, but he does not address the issue of legitimacy in this discussion. Cook expresses the absence of any deliberation as such,

> [t]his omission is all the more surprising because there may be a direct connection between conflict and the belief in legitimacy: when the vast majority of citizens believe in a state's legitimacy, they will be unlikely to engage in civil or uncivil disobedience. Conformity to laws will generally prevail. Conversely, the weaker the belief in legitimacy, the greater is the potential for conflict. When individuals do not believe that a state's laws are binding or legitimate, they will be less likely to orient their actions in accordance with these laws, and conflict may ensue.
> (Cook 2003)

For whatever reason, Weber does not concern himself with linking conflict to legitimacy.

While it is certainly understandable that Weber would interpret the complex notion of legitimacy as being supported primarily by belief since it is the sum of often tacit actions of many individuals oriented in one general direction, it leaves one wanting more. What is the content of this belief? Is it completely unknowable? Can one count on uncoerced obedience for future order? Perhaps most importantly for this analyst, is there any way to talk about legitimacy with more detail and form? Due to these important questions being left unanswered, Weber's work on fleshing out the details of legitimacy is not particularly useful when it comes to analyzing it in reference to terrorism.

b Philosopher Jürgen Habermas

German sociologist and philosopher Jürgen Habermas holds the very pertinent view that since the grounds of "rational" authority rest on reason, it is indeed possible to test them discursively. That is to say, Habermas believes that not only is it possible to examine the truth claims of a regime's assertions of legitimacy, citizens in democratic states today do in fact engage in such testing, proceeding by reasoning or argument rather than intuition and belief. This is of direct importance for our analysis since what is being put forward in this book is that legitimacy does have an empirical shape, or a form that is testable with facts, which can be discussed and investigated. Thus, the position of Habermas on this point will be presented here and will then serve as the philosophical basis of moving our work forward on how terrorism targets the legitimacy of a government's actions in response to the act of terror.

Habermas overtly identifies that it was Weber who was responsible for igniting the debate at a sociological level over the "truth-dependency of legitimations" because of its ambiguity (Habermas 1976: 97). As noted, Weber felt that legitimacy was based on an individual's subjective belief in a regime's order or authority, and it was precisely this point that Habermas found to be problematic; if this belief is conceived to be without any inherent relation to truth, then it is only of psychological significance to an individual and not amenable to the testing of rational justification. In other words, the manner in which Weber presented this belief made the motivation to bestow legitimacy of importance only on an individual level, and not something that could be examined by an entire society on the grounds of logic or reason. There can be (and surely are) individual reasons for granting obedience to a regime and orienting one's behavior in accordance. However, this conception of legitimacy leaves a large swath of intellectual territory that cannot be investigated, and Habermas keenly zeroed in on this shortcoming. To resolve this flaw he instead suggested that the grounds upon which legitimacy rests must be linked to their logical status, and thus they are criticizable because they either do, or do not, "*motivate rationally*" (Habermas 1976: 98). As Habermas explained it,

> every effective belief in legitimacy is assumed to have an immanent relation to truth, the grounds on which it is explicitly based contain a rational validity claim that can be tested and criticized independently of the psychological effect of these grounds.
>
> (1976: 97)

Most importantly, Habermas feels that not only is the belief in legitimacy correlated directly to truth, in democratic societies today it is increasingly the case that citizens indeed submit the claims of a regime to rational testing. That is, the general public requires more and more that the claims and exercising of authority meet the constitutional "catalogue of basic rights, strongly immunized against alteration," in part because the respect of these fundamental rights "has legitimizing force" (Habermas 1976: 101).

It is suggested here that there are also times when international law can represent this same type of constraint upon a regime because of both international and domestic legal reasoning and because of the fundamental nature of individual protections that can often be easily understood by a population. If we look at the actions identified to be illegitimate in the Army Field Manual overseen by General Petraeus—"unjustified [...] use of force, unlawful detention, torture and punishment without trial" (US Army 2006: 1–24, §1–132)—these are extremely important prohibitions which can be found in both humanitarian and human rights law. Additionally, we find these standards frequently discussed in the public diplomacy of the information age. While there is no doubt that there are still hurdles to be cleared for international norms to be generally utilized by citizens in order to discursively test a regime's legitimacy, this basic practice of legitimacy verification through similar means is relatively recent in human history (Habermas 1976: 86–88). As such, we can understand that the rising use of this tool of holding a government accountable for living up to its constitutional and international obligations surely has ramifications for the policies of counterterrorism. To defend itself against terrorism that is taking aim at legitimacy, a government must take into account the manner in which citizens bestow this uncoerced pull toward compliance.

As such, we find that Habermas takes the salient step beyond Weber to posit that the basis of legitimacy is indeed informed with discernible content. While Weber was satisfied to identify legitimacy as being required by every regime to exercise its authority, he did little to conceptualize it as analyzable, and even less so in the context of political violence that challenges the authority of a government. While Habermas has not delved deeply into studying terrorism in relation to legitimacy problems, he has palpably moved the study of legitimacy and terrorism forward by making their link feasible and reasonable. The two primary forms in which this is accomplished are, first, with his conclusion that "every effective belief in legitimacy is assumed to have an immanent relation to truth" (Habermas 1976: 97) and, second, his finding that citizens (particularly in democratic societies),

> as participants in a practical discourse test the validity claims of norms and, to the extent that they accept them with reasons, arrive at the conviction that in the given circumstances the proposed norms are

"right." The validity claim of norms is grounded not in the irrational volitional acts of the contracting parties, but in the rationally motivated recognition of norms, which may be questioned at any time.

(Habermas 1976: 105)

Both of these conclusions are critical for understanding the approach of this book. Like Habermas, we will assume (1) that the legitimacy upon which a regime rests has specific and knowable content; and (2) that citizens can and will test a government's claims to legitimacy.

It is also valuable to note that this Habermasian approach is being applied at a transnational level by a significant number of social constructivists and theorists of global governance. The work of Ian Johnstone explores the power of legal argumentation within international society and points to the influence of non-state actors as a reason why international law and diplomacy should draw more attention for understanding the operation of the international realm. He also puts forward that the power of the discourse which uses international law and its interpretation is keenly felt "in bilateral and multilateral diplomatic interaction," and thus we can see how the theory put forward here is useful for diplomats (Johnstone 2011: 8).

There is, nevertheless, one important element put forward by Weber concerning legitimacy that will be central to this study. The particular tack for studying the content of legitimacy claims will be directly related to Weber's contention that a state is defined by its "*monopoly of the legitimate use of physical force.*" That is to say, the manner in which the US government exercised its monopoly on force in the "war on terror" as the response to 9/11 will be used as our point of departure.

Although it is very difficult to validate any legitimacy claim, Cook was surely correct in suggesting that legitimacy can become a particularly important issue when a state exercises its use of force or violence. As she explained,

> [i]n principle, and to paraphrase Habermas, a state's claim that its laws and policies—in this case, those authorizing the use of force—are morally justified must be redeemed discursively by citizens. In practice, states have been obliged to demonstrate to their citizens, to other countries, and to the international community at large, that their use of force has been, and continues to be, constrained by just laws, polices, and practices. Where they have failed to do so, their legitimacy has been compromised, sometimes seriously.
>
> (Cook 2003)

III Erosion of power relations: social scientist David Beetham

David Beetham wrote on the subject of legitimacy in his book *The Legitimation of Power*, and his work offers a perspective that is particularly pertinent to our study. Beetham explores the manner in which a rule or ruler attains and maintains the *will to obey* and affirms our central contention that study of legitimacy "helps explain the erosion of power relations" (Beetham 1991: 6). This includes both striking breaks in political authority as well as the less dramatic moments of weakness or a diminished degree of cooperation that can be experienced by an authority.

Beetham astutely points out that legitimacy is not an all-or-nothing quantity because it can be "eroded, contested or incomplete" and, therefore, "judgements about it are usually judgements of degree" (Beetham 1991: 20). Thus, when speaking about legitimacy, we are most often discussing the degree of cooperation or the quality of performance. As Beetham explains, "[w]here the powerful have to concentrate most of their efforts on maintaining order they are less able to achieve other goals; their power is to that extent less effective" (1991: 28). Subtle shifts in power frequently occur and might often be explained in other ways. But this does not mean that the dramatic breaches of political and social order, such as riots, revolts, and revolutions, are the only forms of social change related to legitimacy. Put another way, the high level of drama that accompanies such events does not mean that they are the only shifts in power that are worth analyzing and discussing in the context of legitimacy. It is certainly useful to be able to look at and discuss other erosions of legitimacy that occur before there is no longer an intersection between command and obedience. Beetham elucidates the matter by explaining that "[a]s with so much else about society, it is only when legitimacy is absent that we can fully appreciate its significance where it is present, and where it is so often taken for granted" (1991: 6). In full agreement with Beetham, this should not mean that legitimacy can only be discussed when it is absent.

Also of importance is the fact that, although Beetham dons the cap of both social scientist as well as political philosopher and recognizes that both perspectives are valid and treat the issue of legitimacy, in his work he has chosen to approach the subject from the standpoint of the former. Part of the reasoning for this decision is based on his belief that social science has suffered from great confusion on this topic. Thus he wishes to help rescue it from the impact of Max Weber, whose "influence has been an almost unqualified disaster" (1991: 8). As a scholar who has written a treatise on Max Weber, this statement is by no means meant to malign his work or to diminish his large influence on twentieth-century social science.

Instead, Beetham takes issue with the definition of legitimacy that Weber provides in an attempt to avoid making a judgment on its existence in the manner of a philosopher, but instead to present a more scientific report on what is. Beetham, in agreement with what has been discussed above, reduces Weber's approach to defining legitimacy as a people's belief in legitimacy. The reasoning for such an understanding is generally thought to be based on a desire to place social scientists at an analytical distance from their subject and not to stand in judgment of a policy or power.

However, the result of basing legitimacy on belief was to make it an individual issue upon which comment was vague or useless for any broader analysis of a society. Beetham strongly disagrees and dissects the impact that Weber's "belief in legitimacy" has had on social science. Even if it has the laudable goal of insulating the analyst from judging or taking a position,

> the whole Weberian theory of legitimacy has to be left behind as one of the blindest of blind alleys in the history of social science, notable only for the impressiveness of the name that it bears, not for the direction in which it leads.
>
> (1991: 25)

To help recover from this impediment that Weber has left as his legacy on the topic of legitimacy, Beetham proposes constructing a tripartite structure of legitimacy that includes differing disciplinary approaches. Beetham is in agreement that the key to comprehending the concept of legitimacy is in recognizing "that it is multi-dimensional in character" (1991: 15). As an attempt to address this manifold concept, Beetham posits that it is necessary to manage its analysis with tools from legal experts, moral philosophers, and social scientists. In so doing, he posits that his framework will allow one to undertake two different tasks. The first is to carry out a systematic comparison between different forms of legitimacy found to be appropriate in varying historical types of social and political systems. Second, the structure hypothesized by Beetham allows the analyst to assess the approximate level of legitimacy present in a given context to help explain the behavior of those involved. Since this second task can be correlated to the gauging of the validity of counterterrorism policy and its effect on a government in relation to its citizens, the fundaments of Beetham's model are surely worth consideration.

The three primary aspects deemed by Beetham to be the essence of legitimacy can be classified into the realms of the legal, the moral, and the political. Beetham described these categories as operating cumulatively, and on different levels. He explained,

> [t]here is the legal validity of the acquisition and exercise of power; there is the justifiability of the rules governing a power relationship in terms of the beliefs and values current in the given society; there is the evidence of consent derived from actions expressive of it.
>
> (1991: 12)

The extent to which these factors are present determines the level of general obedience within a society, and the degree to which they are absent will allow us to explain why and how the *will to obey* a government or regime has eroded. Together these criteria provide the grounds upon which citizens are pulled toward an obligation to comply with what is laid down by those in charge.

One of the most useful consequences of Beetham's contribution is that he moves the analyst's focus of attention away from the consciousness of single individuals. The Weberian approach not only distorted the nature of legitimacy, but it also led to the corrupting of methodological processes of investigation. That is to say, it proposed a flawed research strategy for determining whether a power is legitimate: enquiring whether it is believed to be so. Beetham rightfully insisted that, when it comes to speaking about and analyzing legitimacy, "the evidence is available in the public sphere, not in the private recesses of people's minds" (1991: 13). If we are to ask the right questions about the acquisition and exercise of power, it is possible to give shape to legitimacy-in-context, and we are not left attempting to compile the opinions of citizens who may or may not understand what legitimacy even means.

Nonetheless, there is one particular criticism of Beetham's factors of legitimacy. The idea that the *power to command* must act within rules and processes that have been formally codified and tested through adjudication if necessary is the legal realm that is widely accepted by scholars of legitimacy, including Weber. As well, the view that the rules governing the power relationships within a community and the exercise of power must be found to be justifiable on axiological grounds is also philosophically sound.

However, the theory that the third leg of legitimacy is to be found in actions of consent by the subordinates in a society seems to suffer from the very same flaw of which Beetham accuses Weber; it misdirects our attention away from those who wield power and toward those who are beholden to it. There is no doubt that the actions of citizens, administrators, and military commanders can demonstrate an acceptance of legitimacy. It is even conceivable that these actions are indicative of the fact that the legitimacy of a regime or policy has maintained a certain level that is worthy of note. Nevertheless, it does not speak to the content of targeted legitimacy which we are seeking so as to be able provide an assessment of counter-terrorism policies. The "expressed consent" by subordinates does not offer any substance by which a policy or regime can be tested. Therefore, we will need to continue forward in search of this third piece to the puzzle of legitimacy. Yet for the moment we will set aside this further search for its contents while we provide additional shape to the concept of legitimacy itself in the context of political conflict.

IV Coerced obedience and action in concert: political theorist Hannah Arendt

There is indeed a tendency, and a very natural one it would seem, for us to be drawn toward the understanding of obedience in its coerced form as the most prevalent. Many believe that obedience is often compelled by the threat of sanction that is held over someone to get them to orient their action in a desired manner, if not by overt violence being exercised upon that person or his or her peers. The reason for this leaning is not exactly clear. Perhaps it is the fact that it is not easy to notice, or even to speak about, an uncoerced orientation of actions because when it is occurring we do not usually notice or mention it. However, when mass numbers of individuals are drawn to diverge from the demands of law and authority, we cannot help but realize it, remark upon it, and even become frightened by the chaos that ensues. When the legitimacy of an authority is no longer in existence, everyone knows it. Even so, all those who have sought power indeed yearn for such an unspoken, and if possible uncoerced, pull to obey their command.

The pertinent question is, then, what is the exact relationship of violence to obedience? To begin answering this question it is necessary to first recognize that obedience is directly related to power itself because it is an essential component of its construction. This is also the astute contribution of one particular political theorist who sheds valuable light on violence and its effectiveness as a political tool. Hannah Arendt ventured into well-trodden territory in her essay "On Violence" to extract an essential insight into power and violence that implicitly recognizes obedience as crucial for power to exist (Arendt 1970). Thus, her work will serve us well in this interdisciplinary dialogue.

Arendt's survey of the literature finds that political theorists have generally agreed that violence is the most blatant expression of power. Violence has been traditionally seen as the most reliable and obvious way to get others to do what we wish of them. She cites Voltaire affirming that "[p]ower consists in making others act as I choose," and Weber contending that power exists whenever it is possible "to assert my own will against the resistance" of others (Arendt 1970: 135). Clausewitz's classic definition of war should also be remembered here: "an act of force to compel our adversary to do our will" (2000: 264). Bertrand de Jouvenel split the concept of power into two vital components (reminiscent of Ferrero), and in so doing employed language already seen in this work. Jouvenel wrote that "to command and to be obeyed: without that, there is no Power" (1949: 96). The *power to command* and the *will to obey* have been highlighted here as an essential dimension to all political struggle since "there [is] in every society a centre of control" and "[a]t all times and in all places we are confronted with the phenomenon of civil obedience" (Jouvenel 1949: 17).

However, in her work "On Violence," Arendt focused on distinguishing violence from power because it was something she identified as having been largely overlooked, or unnoticed, by previous theorists. While most authors saw power and violence as nearly one and the same, Arendt saw the need to explicitly and definitively separate the two concepts from each other. In doing so, Arendt offered a definition of power that greatly helps to explain the manner in which this subject will be approached in this work. Arendt asserted that "[p]ower corresponds to the human ability not just to act but to act in concert" (1970: 143).

This straightforward framing of a term that is at times discussed without enough reflection has enormous implications. Most importantly, it removes the need for the use of weapons or coercion for power to exist. Conventionally understood, this approach is certainly an anomaly. Arendt herself presents Mao Tse-tung's definition of this term: "power is what grows out of the barrel of a gun" (1970: 113). For Mao, weapons, violence, and power were almost or completely synonymous. But if we are willing to take the philosophical step with Arendt, we can appreciate the difference between the weapons themselves and the intent behind their use. From a societal point of view, it is nearly always the case that arms are employed, or violence threatened, to force a specific behavior from a group of people—that is, political violence is meant to produce a desired behavior. However, it is the end, not the means, that matter here. The end is for people to act together in some desired way, while the means are employed to coerce them to do so. In this way, it is not a leap to arrive at a definition in which the deeds achieved by a group of people working together to the same end are, in fact, the point of employing force. For Arendt, power is expressed when people simply "act in concert." The critical element that this definition provides is an allowance for traditional understandings to be fully encompassed, yet it simultaneously offers a space in which a sometimes seemingly contradictory idea can be included. In other words, both the force of weaponry and massive nonviolent action can be defined as forms of power.

To a certain extent, this analysis of Arendt relocates power in the hands of those who grant their obedience, rather than simply with the officials that command. This is certainly not the case in every circumstance, but we must understand it as a part of the political equation. This is surely why a pull toward compliance with an authority is to be prized. The possession of such legitimacy by a leader is a precious commodity, just as its revocation can be termed a calamity. And this misfortune is not just for she who loses the power to command, for it is not always clear how the will to obey can be restored if it is lost or nonexistent. Of course, the problem of reestablishing a legitimate authority is enormously arduous, whether its dissolution came about via conventional hard power from abroad or as a result of overreaching force by the local government.

It was this conception of power that allowed Arendt to conceive of the downfall of the Soviet Union through its exercise of military force to quell dissent in Eastern Europe. This particular part of her work was a specific commentary on the events of 1968, known as the Prague Spring, in which the nonviolent resistance of the Czech people was met with tanks from the USSR and its Warsaw Pact allies. Arendt saw these events as a direct collision of violence and power, and, despite the immediate outcome of a crushed opposition, she arrived at the conclusion that this demonstrated a loss of overall power rather than an augmentation of it. It should be pointed out that there were very few analysts, pundits, or political scientists who foresaw the fall of the USSR, or even a discernable structural crack in its edifice. It was only after the fact that scholars started to point to the Solidarity Movement in Poland and the Charter 77 open association of peoples in Czechoslovakia as organizations which made a major contribution to bringing about the collapse of an empire without the use of arms (see, for example, Ackerman and Duvall 2000: 113–174).

In a more stark demonstration of causality, the Rose Revolution of 2003 in Georgia, the Orange Revolution of 2004 in Ukraine, the Tulip (Pink or Lemon) Revolution of 2005 in Kyrgyzstan, and the Cedar Revolution of 2005 in Lebanon brought about political changes without tanks, planes, or guns. Additionally, what has been called a "democratic wave" or Arab Spring in the Middle East in 2011 can also be classified into a similar category of people willing to "act in concert" without weapons or being coerced. Clearly, one must be careful about using too broad of strokes to describe the events in that region due to the very different cases of Libya and Syria, along with what has followed. Yet there were concrete events that defy many common tools of analysis. Arendt's definition of power and the limits it imposes on effective political violence begin to shed new light on how we might better understand them.

It is important not to misinterpret Arendt's point of view on this pivotal issue and to arrive at the conclusion that hers was an attempt to advocate a kind of political pacifism or that there is no place for the effective use of force in domestic or international politics. Arendt herself supported the death penalty for the man sometimes referred to as the "architect of the Holocaust," German Nazi Adolf Eichmann. This would clearly demonstrate a belief in the exercise of political violence in certain circumstances. The intention here, which follows directly from Arendt's point of view and work, is to clarify that the use of coercion can at times become counterproductive, and there are moments when it will in fact undermine the *will to obey*. What is simply put forward in the above quotes by Arendt is that violence can indeed be used to restore rule, or to command immediate and momentary compliance, but an assured enhancement of power it is not. Now that coerced obedience has been explicitly ruled out as a component of legitimacy as discussed here, we will turn to putting forward the most succinct and clear definition of legitimacy as it is understood in our work.

V An uncoerced pull toward compliance: international jurist Thomas Franck

International legal scholar Thomas Franck has also spoken to this concept in his book *The Power of Legitimacy among Nations* (1990). This work investigates the noteworthy phenomenon of significant obedience to international rules even though they are not enforced by a unitary system. While this remark may at first seem counterintuitive since there is so much attention on the violations of international law, this observable fact certainly merits much more attention. Many investigators of international law often ignore this important difference between the domestic and international legal systems and attempt to explain the latter with analogies with the former. However, Franck contends that glossing over this difference misses a fundamental characteristic of the international system that should be recognized and further investigated. He has aptly pointed out that the international realm provides an extremely fertile environment for investigations into legitimacy precisely because of this lack of an enforcement mechanism to ensure obedience. Thus, to whatever extent rules are obeyed in the international system, it is the product of a dynamic other than the threat of compulsion that exists in the domestic circumstance.

In this very useful discussion of legitimacy and the international system, there are at least two points of particular import. First, there is the strong and clear description of legitimacy as being marked by an uncoerced "pull towards compliance" (Franck 1990: 24). Second, Franck presents four indicators of the legitimacy of a rule or a rule-making process: (1) determinacy; (2) symbolic validation; (3) coherence; and (4) adherence. While Franck's phrasing and definition will serve us well in this work, these four indicators will be shown to be ill suited for our investigation.

Throughout the work, Franck makes it clear that he is speaking to an orientation toward the observance of rules that is not brought about by the use of force or threats. At the same time, he is well aware of the fact that this approach calls into question the dominant idea in legal philosophy that coercion is inherent to all valid law and adherence. However, Franck's intent is to show that this idea is of limited use and that it misses an important part of modern society since a notable part of functioning law is that it does not require constant force. Franck explains "[t]hose who claim to have identified one or more non-coercive factors in the engendering of obedience generally use the term *legitimacy* and its variant, *legitimation,* to enclose some or all of the additional or alternative (non-coercive) requisites of obedience" (1990: 16; original emphasis). Hence we see an insistence on the absence of force.

Adding to this basic component of legitimacy, Franck follows up by formulating a definition: "*a property of a rule or rulemaking institution which itself exerts a pull towards compliance on those addressed normatively*" (1990: 16; original emphasis). This meaning aligns well with what has already been put forward, even if it is particularly crafted so as to meet the task of defining what Franck is investigating. It is our intent to do just the same and to highlight the portion of this definition that fits our purposes, without changing its meaning. The particularly valuable pieces are that of a "pull toward compliance," and such a draw is without the aid of coercion. Thus we will combine the two most pertinent portions of Franck's definition in order to put forward *an uncoerced pull toward compliance* for our own primary definition. This coincides perfectly with the *will to obey* already suggested and adds valuable vocabulary for describing the concept under discussion.

Second, if we are to look at the taxonomy of legitimacy that Franck puts forward, we find that it is ill suited for the type of analysis that this particular work requires. There is surely nothing wrong with the four indicators of a rule's legitimacy for his purposes; however, this is not what we are addressing here. Our placement of legitimacy at the center of our analysis of asymmetrical conflict deals with the legitimacy of a government or a policy, not a rule or rule-making institution. And when examining international laws in this work, the focus will not be on the compliance of the state to a legitimate rule (in fact, the US did not comply with certain provisions), but rather that the content of the rule was a standard which citizens accepted as a valid norm for constraining the government. Therefore, we will not be speaking to the pull toward compliance of the rule itself, but rather what the policy that did not comply with certain international norms did to the status of the government in the eyes of a noteworthy portion of the population. Simply stated, we will address the content of what creates a pull toward compliance on individuals within a society rather than on states within the international realm.

Nonetheless, the idea of *an uncoerced pull toward compliance* precisely captures the basic societal ingredient of legitimacy, particularly relevant during political conflict, which we are conceptualizing in this work as a target of terrorism. To further explore the relationship of obedience to command we shall now turn to the historian Guglielmo Ferrero.

VI Legitimacy as a target: historian Guglielmo Ferrero

During the devastating upheaval of World War II, an Italian historian attempted to explain what he saw as the tragic dissolution of legitimate regimes in Europe. Guglielmo Ferrero finished the book *The Principles of Power* in Geneva in 1941 to put forward his own explanation. It is an extremely insightful text that parses out what he considers to be the central components of power and delves into the idea of legitimacy as a forgotten cornerstone of any organized society. In the beginning pages, Ferrero initiates his inquiry by posing the question (one that reminds us of Weber's similar query), "why then do some men have the right to command and others the duty to obey?" (1942: 22). His response is that the answer lies in the principles of legitimacy, and he explains that a government is legitimate, "if the power is conferred and exercised according to principles and rules accepted without discussion by those who must obey" (1942: 135).

Unfortunately, Ferrero did not expand upon what exactly produces this *will to obey* in a citizenry as he instead refers to the specific elements as the invisible "Genii of the City" (1942: 13–19). They are not necessarily knowable since most people are not even aware of the existence of this pull toward compliance. However, once we have explained exactly how legitimacy can be understood as a target of terrorism, the next objective of this work is to expose these "Genii of the City."

Of most importance, Ferrero provides an enormously useful discussion of the concept of legitimacy itself. He explains that when government is operating smoothly, there is an organized chain of command. It is clear whose orders are to be complied with, and to whom these designated few may direct obligations. Regardless of the structure of the specific arrangements, what is most significant is that there is a shared understanding amongst the people themselves.

Ferrero explains that in a democracy the people are sovereign and elect the leaders who they perceive to be in closest alignment with their own beliefs and who are conceived to be the most competent due to their training and experience. In a monarchy, the hereditary principle determines who is to rule from one generation to the next, and thus preparation from birth can ensue for the prince who is to take the throne. In an aristocracy, the elite class will inevitably have a number of gifted youth with access to education, and hence it will be possible to prepare a cadre of capable civil servants to hold the reins of power. In each case, a certain social understanding has triumphed and provides a logic for the arrangement of government, and the population accepts such administration.

However, Ferrero suggested that "the rational element in principles of legitimacy is purely accidental" (1942: 26). Inside each of these different societies, no matter its form, there is a reasoning that dominates and produces sufficient obedience within the general population and those in the upper echelons of society so as to allow the community to move as a single unit. Yet it is Ferrero's contention that this logic is neither etched in stone nor unchangeable. It is important to recognize this because it makes the legitimacy upon which a government rests susceptible to agitation and destabilization.

When legitimacy has been established, it appears stable and thus we expect it to prevail in perpetuity. However, Ferrero warns that we must not be overtaken by the impression that the past experience of legitimacy will always serve to predict what is to follow. As cited in the epigraph to this chapter, one of the vividly expressed conclusions on legitimacy was that legitimacy is entirely human and thus only as stable as our free will. Its absurdity can be easily demonstrated, and it can be suppressed by violence.

This should be understood as fundamental to the concept itself. Legitimacy is best described as amorphous over time, at least partially because it is a subjective human construction and thus fluid and malleable. Hence, it cannot be presented in what one would recognize as a traditional scientific framework based on falsifiable evidence. As Ferrero explained of this unpredictability, "[c]ollective reactions seem even more capricious and difficult to foresee than individual reactions" (1942: 309). The core of human relations, free will is an element that cannot be removed from any equation involving conscious beings, and thus complete objectivity and predictability will be inevitably elusive.[1] Thus Ferrero clarified that this precise element is

> why no science of the mind and of history analogous to the science of matter and nature has been formulated; one is even forced to consider whether the word "science" can be applied in the same sense to the physical and intellectual life of men, to the chemistry and history of societies.
>
> (Ferrero 1942: 309)

This conception of the state based on an unspoken agreement between the governed and those who govern is certainly one that can be traced back for centuries. While coerced obedience must not be discarded out of hand as a form of rule, and has certainly been used to dominate many a society, there is indeed a deep historical filiation in political theory of those who have conceived of government as dependent upon a tacit social contract in which both parties have rights and duties. Those who have conceived of government in this form have been described as "contractualists" and can be traced back at least as far as the Protestant and Catholic *monarchomachi*, or king-killers, in the sixteenth century, who contemplated the limits of government power with their resistance theory (Hopfl and Thompson 1979).

One of the other important aspects of legitimacy to which Ferrero draws our attention is a manner for visually understanding how its interaction with command is what constructs the basic configuration of power in any society. Indeed, he skillfully articulates the fundamental organization of society, which provides very useful imagery for our purposes. By outlining the place from which command and obedience emanate and how they interact with one another, we can better comprehend where the gaze of the analyst should be fixed in asymmetrical conflict. Ferrero cogently posited,

> [i]f, in democracies as in monarchies, the authority comes from above, in monarchies as in democracies legitimacy comes from below, since only the consent of those who must obey can create it. In every regime, therefore, the plenitude of the state is realized at the

intersection of two lines—one descending, which is authority, and the other ascending which is legitimacy.

(Ferrero 1942: 171)

One important aspect of this citation is its integration of a top-down approach with a bottom-up approach. Rather than promote one element at the expense of the other, there is a clear recognition of the existence of each and how we can understand their interaction in a simple form. So, if we are to sketch what Ferrero is describing when he speaks of the "plenitude of state," the result would look something like Figure 1.1.

With this schematic we have a visual tool that will help to further explain the theory that is being put forward in this work. As a starting point, we can identify authority as the general target in conventional warfare, in that it is an attempt to destroy the power structure from the top of this edifice. In the modern state, this authority is most clearly expressed and exercised through the military, which is authorized to exert force with the approval of the head of state. In this case, the military can be seen as a veritable appendage of the head of the government. The authority and its military arm are targetable in the sense that they are specific objects that can be placed in the crosshairs, literally or figuratively, of a weapon or military unit. In addition, its destruction can be empirically verified.

A clear example of this approach can be evidenced by the fact that the first bomb dropped in Baghdad in 2003 to commence the military operation of invading Iraq was programmed with coordinates from a satellite phone intercept for a mobile device that was said to belong to Saddam Hussein (Human Rights Watch 2003: 17–18). Although this intelligence proved to be incorrect, the thinking was that to "decapitate" the regime at the outset of hostilities would bring about an immediate, or rapid, collapse of the Iraqi military and thus an end to the fighting before it began. When the capture of Baghdad did not bring a desired end to armed resistance as it then morphed into an insurgency, the US military continued to target what was thought to be the commanding authority. It tried to hunt down Saddam Hussein, as well as to pursue his sons, Uday and Qusay, in an attempt to destroy the command structure they thought was leading the

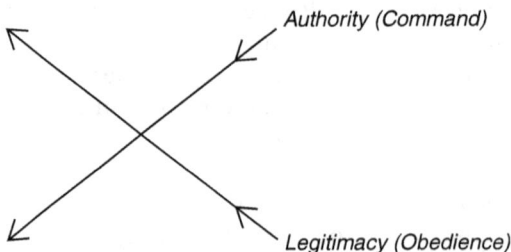

Figure 1.1

resistance. Eventually, Saddam Hussein was captured, hiding in a one-man foxhole near Tikrit, looking more like a destitute man than a leader, and his sons were killed in a safe-house in Mosul. So, the conventional military targeting meant to end the fighting can be clearly discerned, even though neither of these events had the strategic effect upon the insurgency that had been hyped and hoped for in advance (Packer 2005).

However, the theory being put forward in this work is that terrorism in fact attempts to attack a society not at the top point of authority, but from the other side of this schematic. That is to say, those who employ terrorism are attempting to target the legitimacy of the enemy government so as to knock it off balance and to weaken the enemy, if not to render it unable to operate as a coherent unit. Those employing terrorist tactics clearly do not have the means to topple a government through the use of weaponry aimed at the authority and its military arm. Hence, it makes more sense to conceive of the individuals who are engaged in battle with a government through targeting noncombatants as having redirected their efforts toward the *will to obey* of the population.

Our hypothesis is that if it is possible to provoke a response that brings about a shared belief within a large enough portion of the population that the regime suffers a legitimacy deficit or has become delegitimized because it has abused its authority, then the enemy government and society will stumble and perhaps even cease to function collectively. When commands are not followed because they are no longer deemed legitimate, then dysfunction becomes a serious problem, rendering a society inert. Let us remember that a command, even if properly directed by an official in her appropriate realm of authority, is only words into the wind if the *will to obey* has shifted and compliance can no longer be secured. In this way, non-state actors utilizing terrorist tactics are attempting to shift the terrain upon which a battle is waged.

Another vital piece that emerges in the above quote from Ferrero is that authority cannot stand alone as the only element in the analysis of power. There is little doubt that much attention is directed toward this top end of the hierarchy because of its effectiveness in revealing the structure and operations of a society. However, command cannot be understood as offering a complete description of a functioning society because of its dependent nature. Adding to the difficulty of analyzing this phenomenon is the fact that directing one's attention to legitimacy presents a natural stumbling block because a population's *will to obey* is often tacit, mixed, and complex, and therefore it is extremely problematical to track or quantify. Yet, despite this impediment, legitimacy cannot be ignored without a cost to the strength of one's analysis.

One unique and manifest intention of this work is to highlight this idea of tacit and active endorsement, or legitimacy, as the bull's-eye on the target of attacks conducted by actors employing terrorism. As such, it is necessary and possible to again draw up how this understanding of

terrorist attacks would look when applied to the imagery of power provided by Ferrero. To begin, a target should be placed on the bottom-up
element of legitimacy since this is where terrorist acts are better understood to be directed. At the same time, when such violence is successful in
goading a reaction that oversteps the bounds of authority considered valid
by the population, then we must also illustrate how that reduced legitimacy would appear in our diagram (see Figure 1.2).

What should also be noticed about this schematic sketching of how a
legitimacy deficit, or weakness, might be visualized is that it also indicates
what a further reduction in legitimacy might portend. In other words, in
this drawing we see that there continues to be an intersection between
command and obedience, signifying that while an authority still maintains
enough compliance to steer a society, there is a point (and a not-too-
distant one) at which this would cease to be the case. The "plenitude of
state" would no longer exist, and a community would be caught immobile.
Such a circumstance is what has also been described as a power vacuum,
in which no central authority has sufficient authority to command compliance from a large enough portion of the population.

What becomes clear in examining this above schematic is what is additionally necessary. That is, it is crucial to conceptualize the components that
construct the concept of legitimacy itself. Providing a hypothesis for what
can be considered to be the pillars required to maintain legitimacy is indeed
compulsory to take this work to its logical next step.

VII Exposing the Genii of the City: legal philosophers Ost and Kerchove

As we have now established that there is valid and logical reasoning for
understanding legitimacy as a target, and that following a Habermasian
view this target has a content that can be tested rationally, it is now necessary to put forward a manner for investigating legitimacy. In other words,
the intent is to expose Ferrero's "Genii of the City," which construct
legitimacy.

To do so, we will present and defend the use of a model of legal validity
from contemporary legal philosophers which will serve to give shape to

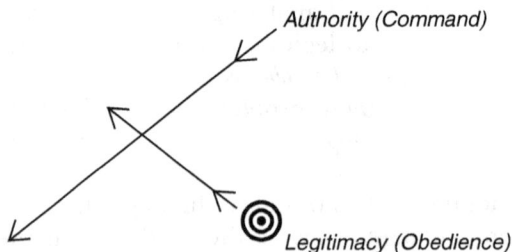

Figure 1.2

our own understanding of the taxonomy of legitimacy. Because of the inherent interdisciplinary nature of the concept under investigation, we have seen that it has been necessary to research the work of scholars from various disciplines to get us this far in our understanding of legitimacy. It is still necessary to continue in this vein, and thus the model to be put forward here will help to unravel some of this complexity with an approach that best integrates the most valuable features of differing philosophies and methods.

To expose the "Genii of the City" and thus promote more substantive discussions and investigations of this multifaceted concept that is being targeted by terrorism, we shall look to legal philosophy. As we have seen, legitimacy has been investigated from diverse disciplinary perspectives since it touches almost all those that deal with human relations, albeit in slightly different ways. Social scientist David Beetham explicitly recognized that legal philosophy indeed had a perspective that corresponded directly to his own study on the legitimation of power when he stated that "legitimacy is equivalent to *legal validity*" (Beetham 1991: 4; original emphasis). The manner in which we can describe this direct correlation is that both concepts are searching for what creates the elusive uncoerced pull toward compliance. While legitimacy deals with the pull toward obeying the commands of an authority, legal validity treats the attraction to an observance of codified rules.

The work on legal validity that will provide shape to the model to be used here is that of the Belgian legal philosophers François Ost and Michel van de Kerchove in their book *De la pyramide au réseau?* [*From the Pyramid to the Network?*] (2002). To introduce their work, Ost and Kerchove discuss two images that capture the essence of what they wished to accomplish. Most important for our purposes is the valuable conceptual thinking behind their move away from the conventional idea dominating legal philosophy: the notion that it is necessary to settle on just one philosophy for understanding legal validity.

The first image comes from the well-known frontispiece of a founding work of both legal positivism and modern political theory. Thomas Hobbes published *Leviathan* in 1651, and the decorative illustration facing the title page included the depiction of an all-powerful allegorical figure which symbolized the republic. This figure, whose body is constructed of the compilation of hundreds of other tiny bodies representing the population of the state, is holding the symbol of temporal power in one hand (a sword) and the symbol of spiritual power in the other (a crosier). We can discern that, seen together, these two representations of authority begin the outline of a pyramid, a symbol of top-down power. Considering Hobbes's conception of the state and his advocacy for an absolute sovereign, this interpretation of the frontispiece coincides with his superior work of political philosophy found inside the text.

The image is of the sovereign, the title holder of undivided and absolute power. This pyramidal structure is that of a linear and vertical hierarchy, leaving no doubt as to the source of law and authority. This figure of power was once represented and exercised by the divine right of kings, which later transformed into a sovereign crowned by universal suffrage, and can today often be understood as being embodied in technocrats. And just to clarify any uncertainties as to the meaning of the image, the Leviathan is found beneath a quote from the book of Job, "*Non est potestas Super Terram quae Comparetur ei*" ["There is no power on earth to be compared to him"] (Hobbes 1991: xciii).

The second illustration that Ost and Kerchove discuss comes from the graphic artist M. C. Escher, known for his portrayals of mathematical relationships among shapes, figures, and space. In Escher's work *Relativity*, it is initially difficult to orient oneself so as to comprehend what is occurring in the image, but the confusion slowly transitions into an distorted orderliness. People ascend and descend on stairs and in directions that appear to be incoherent, while doors and windows open from all directions onto the stairwells. Upon reflection, we begin to discern three separate worlds which are each perfectly logical in their own right, but which seem to converge into an absurdity when contemplated together.

Eventually we can conclude that what we are viewing are three coexistent hierarchies with none of them dominating the others. If we insist upon imposing one perspective as absolute, we are left with the irrationality of the whole image together as one. However, if we adopt a perspective without a gravitational pull in only one single direction, where one view is not privileged over the others, it is possible for our minds to arrive at something comprehensible.

Ost and Kerchove pose the question of whether our legal world today has shifted away from the monolithic hierarchy suggested by Hobbes, and instead leans toward "[a] world where political sovereignty would be relative, citizenship shared, multiple rationalities, a plurality of values ... a networked world" (2002: 8; my translation). It is certainly not within the scope of this work to delve into this complicated philosophical legal question. Nonetheless, the three dimensions of legal validity and their interaction that Ost and Kerchove put forward will certainly serve us well in this study. In part, this is due to the fact that what they propose, as seen here in the discussion of these images, is meant to move beyond the traditional pyramidal legal structure without rejecting its usefulness. Since legitimacy must certainly be treated from multiple and integrated perspectives, this thoughtful work on the subject of an uncoerced pull is most welcome.

To begin, for the discussion of legal validity it is first necessary to establish the material existence of a binding law. For some jurists, such as John Austin or Hans Kelsen, simply establishing the material existence of a rule would be sufficient for determining its validity. However, more recently legal philosophers of high repute, such as H. L. A. Hart, have observed that there is not necessarily a direct link between the existence of and the validity of a legal rule. Hart makes the valuable point that it is important to distinguish the difference between "validity" and "existence," "if only because failure to do this obscures what is meant by the assertion that such a rule *exists*" (1994: 109; original emphasis). As such, this work will first establish the material existence of the binding international rules that are indeed applicable to the "war on terror" in Chapter 2 in order to clear this first hurdle, and in doing so fix the first lens of *legality* into place.

Most importantly, Ost and Kerchove defend three primary criteria of legal validity. They are composed of three tests that are decisively multiple and interactive: formal validity, empirical validity, and axiological validity (2002: 309). These criteria are also expressed by Ost and Kerchove as *légalité*, *effectivité*, and *légitimité*. Once again, the imagery utilized by these authors is extremely useful: in this case, it is the use of the Venn diagram to help grasp the intersection of ideas they put forward since it will also provide the shape for our own concept of legitimacy; they conceptualize legal validity as three converging and overlapping circles of "*légalité*," "*effectivité*," and "*légitimité*" (Ost and Kerchove 2002: 352).

Since the third term of *légitimité* cannot be repeated since this is the central topic of this study, it is necessary to look for alternative terminology. The philosophical idea that grounds this particular criterion is sound, and thus it is unnecessary to reconceptualize the model; rather, we can simply replace the chosen language. In their discussion of axiological validity there are two clear guide posts that can help lead us to a substitute term. The first is that Ost and Kerchove tell us that this validity was favored by the proponents of natural law who advocated the use of reason to analyze human nature and deduce binding rules of moral behavior. Second, an axiological test is going to indicate the use of values and ethics for determining validity. Since we will reposition legitimacy to the center of our schematic, where there is an overlap of all three circles, it is not a substantive modification to simply exchange the word "*légitimité*" in Ost and Kerchove's arrangement with the term "morality." To transition our diagram to the form in which it will be applied in this work we will present the tripartite structure of legitimacy, or in other words its content, as *legality*, *morality*, and *efficacy*. With this slight and appropriate adjustment we can now conceive of our model of legitimacy as shown in Figure 1.3.

As seen in David Beetham's work, he also posited that part of the nature of legitimacy could be found in the concepts of legality and morality. Therefore, it is not surprising that we find these same two elements present in the conceptualization of legal validity by Ost and Kerchove. As such, it is reasonable to conclude that *legality* and *morality* do indeed construct part of legitimacy's content.

Additionally, the third sphere presented in the Ost and Kerchove's model—*efficacy*—does not quite translate directly to our purposes either, although it does point us in a positive direction. Below we will explain how it is presented by Ost and Kerchove, along with the manner in which its concurrent soundness will be extracted and applied in our work. Before

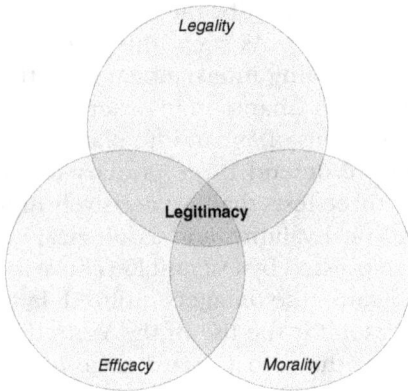

Figure 1.3

this, however, we shall first discuss formal and axiological validity in order to explain the understandings of legality and morality for our purposes. Because each one of these three spheres rests on a different current of thought in legal philosophy, we will also briefly present the currents of positivism, natural law, and legal realism respectively.

a Formal validity: legality

At the close of the eighteenth century, an important development took place in legal philosophy. The progression consisted of a deliberate step away from morality as the dispositive factor of legal validity and toward a theory of legal positivism in which the content of the law was not prescribed by natural or divine authority. At this historical moment, prominent legal scholars Jeremy Bentham and John Austin (in part known for their role in founding this legal philosophy) theorized and staunchly defended the premise that for analytical purposes the substance of law must be distinctly separated from any normative requirements. As Austin notably expressed it, "[t]he existence of law is one thing; its merit and demerit another. Whether it be or be not is one enquiry; whether it be or be not conformable to an assumed standard, is a different enquiry" (1954: 184).

Of importance for legal philosophy and the structure of the modern Western state, the positivist approach played a central role in conceptualizing legislation as the principal and technical instrument of governance, rather than a marginal one as it had been previously conceived. One reason why this laudable feat was achieved must certainly be credited to Austin's object of identifying "the distinguishing characteristics of positive law and so to free it from the perennial confusion with the precepts of religion and morality which had been encouraged by natural law theorists" (Hart 1954: x).

At what is widely recognized as the inception of this legal theory, one of the primary concerns of Bentham and Austin was to confront and dispute the writings of well-known jurist Sir William Blackstone. Their accusation was that Blackstone continually confused legal and moral analysis in his *Commentaries* by interpreting laws in the way he believed they *ought* to be, by affirming laws to be invalid if they were contrary to the laws of God, and by claiming that all laws gain their validity only from God's superior law. Bentham and Austin found these formulations to be dangerous because they opened the door to resistance to the authority of law and the state, and they were based on quite subjective grounds since ethical views will indeed vary at times. Furthermore, this also created a risk that some reactionaries would claim that a codified law clearly and automatically carries moral authority simply by its categorization as law. As such, these legal philosophers set out to clearly demarcate the difference between legal and moral authority that was found to be blurred by Blackstone. With this as their aim, Bentham and Austin primarily asserted two very simple principles: first, they affirmed that the mere fact that a law breaches a standard of morality does not strip it of its status as authoritative law; second, that a directive was considered to be of moral importance did not automatically render it a legal rule.

However, these two basic premises upon which Bentham and Austin insisted certainly did not foreclose the inclusion of morality within the framework of a functional legal system. Although legal positivism has been largely based upon this separability thesis, which aims to disconnect law from morality, some scholars from the school of legal positivism have worked consciously at clarifying what was *not* meant by their resolve and have concluded that "they certainly accepted many of the things that might be called 'the intersection of law and morals'" (Hart 1958: 597). It was readily accepted by them, as a historical fact, that each sphere had a strong influence on the other, and that there was indeed, as Austin put it, "frequent coincidence of positive law and morality" (1954: 162). While there has been much attention focused on the veracity of this claim of separability in legal positivism, and the case has certainly been made in a terminology that indicates a definite cleavage between law and morality, this has unfortunately "obscured the fact that at other points there is an essential point of contact between the two" (Hart 1958: 600). The fact that this partition has proved useful in unraveling two tangled ideas has sometimes clouded the notion that legal positivism has at no time insisted that morality is completely irrelevant. As such, one important point of coincidence will be discussed at further length below when dealing with the issue of overlap to demonstrate and emphasize that the three spheres constructing legitimacy are indeed interactive.

Nonetheless, our first aim is to describe and explain the formal validity that grounds the sphere of legality. It is important to recognize that the structural development of the state in Western societies has led to a bolstering of the philosophical logic of positivism. There are two circumstances in particular that can be identified as pertinent to this buttressing: one is the ever-increasing technicality and complexity of legal doctrine and its applications; the other is the wide acceptance and deliberate use of law as a steering mechanism for society. Due to at least these two evident and undeniable developments, there is good reason to endorse much of what legal positivism offers as a philosophy.

There is also little doubt that at the end of the eighteenth century there was solid reasoning for this philosophical development and the analytical desire to present a clear demarcation between the two vital and often tangled concepts of law and morality. The historic entanglement of the law and religion, particularly in Europe before the Enlightenment, certainly demonstrated the need for such extrication so as to have a clearer understanding of each concept in its own right.

The US government, which will serve as our point of analysis in this study of counterterrorism, is clearly a system saturated with rules and laws, creating a massive network of regulation and institutions. Thus the issue of formal validity is one that will have significant importance to this study. Since this form of validity signifies a direct affiliation to a judicial system, the procedures of adjudication are of primary importance here. The classic rule of law is pyramidal in form, and those who manage this legal hierarchy are the judicial authorities. As explained, "[c]ontrol of constitutionality, of legality and of conventionality have long been the only official tests of validity of rules, confirming the impression that validity is reduced only to formal legality" (Ost and Kerchove 2002: 327; my translation). It will therefore be necessary to take a look into the participation of and rulings by courts of the US as they were related to policies of the "war on terror." To carry out this task in the application of our model, Chapter 3 will look at the Supreme Court and its jurisprudence in dealing with detention without judicial review at the military facility in Guantánamo Bay.

b *Axiological validity:* morality

The axiological sphere covered under our heading of *morality* bears a strong relationship to the conception of natural law. This theory has notably stretched over at least 2,000 years of Western philosophy. Classical theories of natural law emphasized that its principles were of divine origin and could be exposed through human reason. Of great significance for the orthodox application of this legal theory, man-made law must conform to these principles handed down by God in order to be considered valid, or "*lex iniusta non est lex.*" The philosophy of natural law was thus built and maintained on the idea of an indivisible bond inevitably linking these two concepts.

There is little doubt that over the many centuries that natural law has been argued to be the proper and clearest lens through which we can view the human relationship with law, it has been put forward in differing forms. A look at some of the initiators of international law who tried to flesh out exactly how a natural law would create rules between states reveals many substantive differences. As such, to briefly clarify just what is being invoked when the term "natural law" is employed in this text, it is proper to look further.

The moral theorizing of Thomas Aquinas has played a central role in its foundation and development. Therefore, his primary tenets of "divine providence" creating the moral framework within which natural law operates and the fact that these contours are "rationally knowable" to all humans are our two principal elements giving meaning to the term. It was conceived that natural law had a celestial meaning and grounding but could at the same time be discerned through human reason.

However, much of the theological terminology, along with a great deal of metaphysics, that have been infused into this theory over the centuries have made for a problematic resonance within the contemporary intellect. This is certainly one reason why natural law has fallen from favor in comparison to legal positivism. However, what is meant by the invocation of the term of "natural law" today is less lofty. Much of the current meaning is that there are a few rudimentary principles of human conduct that can be reduced to certain elementary truths of importance and which are basic enough to be considered essential in any and all societies. For example, the concept of *self-preservation* has been identified by proponents of natural law, such as Grotius, Hobbes, and their followers, as "a paramount principle, and the basis for whatever universal morality there was" (Tuck 1999: 5).

It is important to remember that none of the original founders of international law who intended to ground it in natural law were speaking only to narrow legal issues but were, rather, putting forward broad treatises of politics, religion, and philosophy. The reason why this is of import is because it is useful to understand that this body of law at its origin was not based upon black letter law at all, but instead upon a broader notion that indeed nurtured a connection with morality. What this means for our discussion is that there is something to be found in the ideas of a universal morality which can be described as aligning more closely with coherence than incoherence. In accordance with one of the most prominent contemporary advocates of natural law, it is agreed that "coherence and goodness have more affinity than coherence and evil" (Fuller 1958: 636).

Nonetheless, it is necessary to provide further clarification of how exactly this axiological validity will be applied in Chapter 4 of this work, as coherence is certainly only a broad starting point. As such, there will be

two frameworks here that provide the appropriate tests of axiological validity: (1) just war theory, and (2) reciprocity. The former tradition is a
complex body of ideas that has grown out of a variety of religious and
secular sources and provides a framework by which we can approach the
moral constraints that are to be applied to the launching of war. Theologians, philosophers, and jurists have expounded upon the meaning of the
"legitimate" use of force in the international arena for centuries, and this
body of work will serve us well to investigate the boundaries of anticipatory
defense in historical perspective.

We will also arrive at exploring reciprocity in the work of the well-
respected moral philosopher Immanuel Kant. It will be seen that Kant's
categorical imperative for the formulation of the principle of morality is
particularly useful because its high level of abstraction allows for its
application in various circumstances. To solidify it as universally applicable, like many of his brethren of the Enlightenment, Kant found that its
inviolability was due to its coherent reasoning, which was to be expressed
through individual volition or will.

We can also find a correlation between Kant's categorical imperative
and at least two other noteworthy places. The first is Rawls' original position and the veil of ignorance. There is even enough of a coincidence for
Rawls himself to assert that "[t]he notion of the veil of ignorance is
implicit, I think, in Kant's ethics" (1999: 121). Second, it can be correlated
to that of the Golden Rule or the ethic of reciprocity, a tenet found in the
scriptures of all major religions (Armstrong 1993). Of course, there are
some who contend that the two concepts are not comparable because
Kant based his conclusions of moral good solely in reason, while the
Golden Rule has been said to conform to one's own standard. There is
surely a difference that exists here, but to delve too deeply into the subtle
differences of these concepts would quickly transplant them out of a
general and widespread understanding and into a more profound philosophical discussion that would remove everyday people from wielding the
ability to judge and determine the legitimacy of their own government.
Our contention will be that morality can in fact be straightforward and
knowable in many circumstances. As Kant put it, "we only, like Socrates,
direct their attention to the principle they themselves employ; and that,
therefore, we do not need science and philosophy to know what we should
do to be honest and good, yea, even wise and virtuous" (2010: 220).

c *Empirical validity:* efficacy

While at first glance one might consider the realm of efficacy to be rather
straightforward, Ost and Kerchove properly point out that this sphere "is
extremely complex, and deceptively simple" (2002: 329; my translation).
Perhaps most significant, these authors broach the important difficulty
that arises out of the fact that there are many different ways to construe

how this notion is to be understood and measured. Therefore it is necessary to put forward some of these differing interpretations so that they can be distinguished and clarified; doing so will allow us to address how we will treat the question of *efficacy* in this book.

To begin, the idea that a political policy must perform or function in the best possible manner with the least amount of waste of time and effort can be classified under the label of "efficiency." This particular approach, largely addressing the question of cost/benefit (but not reduced simply to it alone), is grounded in legal realism. One perspective on this philosophical school suggests that "rules should be viewed teleologically, as but means to the achievement of social ends" (Rumble 1965: 549), and, as such, it shares an important connection to sociological jurisprudence. What this means in the end is that the focus turns toward analyzing and judging the measured outcome of a law on society.

The manner in which Ost and Kerchove speak of this realm of *l'effectivité* is indeed different. They explain "[i]n the first analysis, we would say that *l'effectivité* relates to the capacity of a rule to produce the behavior desired by the legislator in those to which it is addressed" (2002: 329; my translation). While this is a more useful interpretation for our purposes, and certainly echoes the idea that we are trying to capture in our overall discussion of legitimacy, there continues to be an important problem. In this particular case of counterterrorism we are tackling the issue of security. One could say that security laws are addressed to criminals and are meant to produce the desired behavior of forbearance through deterrence. While this may indeed be the case in some instances, it is very difficult to argue that international laws are based on the concept of deterrence since there is no uniform enforcement mechanism.

There are at least two important points to keep in mind when contemplating these interpretations of effectiveness. The first is that we are here intending to direct our attention toward how it is that citizens evaluate the policy or regime of a government. The legitimacy of a government is based upon the reasoning and perceptions of its citizens, and therefore our particular question revolves around the effectiveness of the authority in charge. In both of the definitions put forward above there is an implicit understanding that the laws under scrutiny are addressed to those within the society. Therefore, each suggest that what is to be tested or analyzed is the impact that a law has on the general public.

However, our investigation is centered on the "*monopoly of the legitimate use of physical force,*" and thus our gaze is fixed in the other direction. This is indeed an important reason explaining the chosen framework for this study. Human rights law and humanitarian law are legal duties undertaken by governments directing the constraints under which they are to treat their own citizens and, many times, those who fall under their effective control. At the very same time they can be used as standards of assessment by citizens, just as suggested by Cassese in the opening epigraph to this book. They are not judging the society, but rather whether government is exercising its monopoly on force legally and/or legitimately. Therefore one could say that in this case the lens of analysis is inverted.

The second point that should not be forgotten is that the goal that is meant to be achieved in counterterrorism is that of increased security. Of course, even if this laudable objective is one that every government undertakes with certainty and assurance, realizing the safety of the members of a society is not nearly as obvious as might be assumed. Most importantly, the concept of security is based on perception and subjective belief. While empirical studies can be carried out and presented to citizens, very few people base either their sense of well-being or danger on these reviews. This is a significant feature of security that has been spotlighted at least as far back as the eighteenth century by Montesquieu when he suggested in Book XII of *The Spirit of Laws* that "[p]olitical liberty consists in security, or, at least, in the opinion that we enjoy security." Therefore, it is critical to remember that measuring effectiveness in our case suffers from an inherent difficulty of subjectivity.

As such, the term we will apply in our model is that of *efficacy*, and our working definition comes from its direct derivative: efficacious. That is, a policy should be judged by the Oxford English Dictionary definition of the term: "that [which] produces, or is certain to produce, the intended or appropriate effect." Since this meaning certainly opens the door to many different tools of measurement for arriving at an empirical validity, particularly depending upon the specific policy under review, it is not proper to pretend that there is but one applicable instrument that can be put forward. Hence what will be done here is to discuss the manner in which courts of different jurisdictions have broached this important question of *efficacy* in matters concerning counterterrorism policy. In doing so, this will provide an overview of how it has been treated in recent rulings so as to understand its relevance in this context.

Nonetheless, Ost and Kerchove do provide clues on how to invert this lens so that it can offer a view onto the legitimacy of a government. As mentioned, the notion of efficacy can equally apply to the policies of a government, just as the effective achievement of social ends can be evaluated. Therefore, this term is surely valid even if it needs to be transposed for our investigative purposes. Ost and Kerchove point out that the legal criteria of efficacy or effectiveness "has experienced a spectacular rise in importance over the last decades" (2002: 328; my translation). It is a term that has found currency in current legal terminology even though it was once reserved for sociological analysis. For example, in the International Covenant on Civil and Political Rights, Article 2(a) obliges countries that are a party to the Treaty to, "ensure that any person whose rights or freedoms as herein recognized are violated shall have an *effective* remedy." The European Court of Human Rights (ECtHR) used such language in its rulings: "[t]he Convention is intended to guarantee not rights that are theoretical or illusory but rights that are practical and *effective*" (*Airey* v. *Ireland*, §24; my emphasis). Additionally, Article 57(2)(c) of the First Additional Protocol to the Geneva Conventions requires that an "*effective* advance warning shall be given of attacks which may affect the civilian population." So, we can find that the terminology has indeed found its way into codified international humanitarian and human rights law.

Also, major judgments from high courts in differing jurisdictions, along with extrajudicial writings, indicate the recent influence that this leaning toward assessing the efficacy of policies has had within the legal world. This is not to say that courts have charged into the field of policy-making and rendered judgment on the work of the political branches; rather, this is simply an assertion that there are times and places when different high courts have found ways to enter into an evaluation of the efficacy of policies, most often by utilizing judicial tools such as "reasonableness" and "proportionality." As these legal devices for treating *efficacy* are implemented differently in various jurisdictions, even when bearing an important resemblance, it is not within the scope of this work to single out one test as superior or more applicable. This is especially the case considering that our intention in this work is to speak to *efficacy* as a component of legitimacy, meaning that citizens are unlikely to make such distinctions either.

One place where we can find evidence of assessments of efficacy in judicial decisions is in the 1999 ruling handed down by the Israeli Supreme Court on the methods of interrogation of the General Security Service (GSS). The Court found that it was not necessary to enter into an in-depth inquiry of the law of interrogation since they were simply dealing with the power under administrative authority. Therefore, the oft-repeated word for what was found to be required of such an interrogation is that it should be "reasonable." When the opinion discussed some of the details of what this was to mean, it entered into a discussion of efficacy and expounded that:

> a reasonable investigation is likely to cause discomfort. It may result in insufficient sleep. The conditions under which it is conducted risk being unpleasant. Of course, it is possible to conduct an *effective* investigation without resorting to violence. Within the confines of the law, it is permitted to resort to various sophisticated techniques. Such techniques—accepted in the most progressive of societies—can be *effective* in achieving their goals. In the end result, the legality of an investigation is deduced from the propriety of its purpose and from its methods.
>
> (*Public Committee against Torture in Israel* v. *The State of Israel* [1999], 23–24; my emphasis)

Also, when treating the specific techniques, the Court found that the "shaking" of an individual during the interrogation process "surpasses that which is necessary," and that forcing a detainee to crouch on her tiptoes "does not serve any purpose inherent to interrogation" (24). Overall, in its decision to rule against the government the analysis was meant to fit into the standard found by the Court that "[a]ll these limitations on an interrogation [...] flow from the requirement that an interrogation be fair and reasonable" (29). And, at one point, the Court even expressed that the ruling against the specific techniques was handed down because "[i]t does not fall within the scope of the authority to conduct a fair and *effective* interrogation" (27, my emphasis).

If we look into the extrajudicial writings of the former Israeli Court President, Aharon Barak, we find an explanation of the philosophy that underlay his decision-making process when he was President of the Court. The primary point that concerns us here is his discussion of the idea of "reasonableness." As we saw in the opinion Barak authored on methods of interrogation, this judicial tool allowed him to step in to evaluate the efficacy of government policy. Yet it was acknowledged by Barak himself in a law journal article in 2003 that "[i]ndeed, the efficiency of the security measures is a matter that is in the proper jurisdiction of the other branches of government" (2003: 138). However, this is not without limit. The political branches of government were required to stay within certain legal parameters, and the manner in which Barak established those parameters was with the tool of "reasonableness." In the same article, he explained that "[a]s long as the other branches are acting within the framework of the 'zone of reasonableness,' there is no basis for judicial intervention" (2003: 138).

Another clear example of the use of efficacy for the rendering of a prominent provision of a law passed in the wake of the 9/11 terrorist attacks outside the bounds of legality comes from the *Bundesverfassungsgericht,* or the German Federal Constitutional Court in 2006 (Lepsius 2006: 761). The Court examined the high-profile Air-Transport Security Act, which was passed in 2004 and which included a provision that empowered the minister of defense to order a passenger airplane to be shot down if it could be determined that the aircraft would be used as a projectile weapon against others and if this was the only means of preventing such a disaster. The German Constitutional Court examined this particular provision, clearly passed with 9/11 in mind, and struck it down as unconstitutional.

The decision handed down is largely known for employing Kantian moral reasoning through the legal principle of human dignity, and found that the persons inside the aircraft could not be used as mere means and sacrificed. However, the decision also employed a "proportionality test" to examine the facts and to determine that the presumed efficacy of such a policy was patently false and therefore could not be legal. Most pertinent to our discussion, the Court ruled that, "[t]he statute, simply, could never achieve what it pretended to pursue" (Lepsius 2006: 774).

Thus, we find that there is a persuasive argument for this notion of inverting our lens to judge the policies of government since we can see that it has found a foothold within legal minds at the highest levels, and thus is surely relevant for those who exercise their *will to obey*. While it must be recognized that international courts usually refuse to enter into discussions of efficacy when it comes to torture, in discussing legitimacy it becomes necessary to do so here because it is a question that common citizens will indeed take into consideration.

VIII An intersection of laws and morals: legal philosopher H. L. A. Hart

Since the model for legal validity put forward by Ost and Kerchove, transposed here for use in analyzing the content of legitimacy, is based on the interactivity of the three poles of *legality*, *morality*, and *efficacy*, it is necessary to clarify what is meant by this notion of integration (see Ost and Kerchove 2002: 341–351). What does it mean for these poles to stand not in juxtaposition, but rather in interaction with each other? For our purposes, we will focus on the notion of overlap between the spheres where we can see an interplay of the differing methodological approaches to validity. To demonstrate this point, we will flesh out one of the places of overlap here so that it can be understood in more specific detail. To do so, we will explore a particular place of coincidence between legality and morality that will serve as the major point of overlap for Chapter 4 on warmaking.

As has been noted above, there has long been an analytical tension between legality and morality and, although separating the two has often seemed advantageous, it has not been so easily achieved. Just where one ends and the other begins has not been something that has been resolved easily, if at all. For an example which demonstrates the longevity of this struggle over the attempt to separate law from morality, one can look to an ancient text by Xenophon. Interestingly, it is possible to find an implicit reference to an "uncoerced pull toward compliance" in this dialogue as Alcibiades asks Pericles to teach him what law is. Alcibiades steers him towards the question of tyranny and the dialogue ensues:

PERICLES: Yes, anything which a tyrant as head of the state enacts, also goes by the name of law.

ALCIBIADES: But, Pericles, violence and lawlessness—how do we define them? Is it not when a stronger man forces a weaker to do what seems right to him—not by persuasion but by compulsion?

PERICLES: I should say so.

ALCIBIADES: It would seem to follow that if a tyrant, without persuading the citizens, drives them by enactment to do certain things—that is lawlessness?

PERICLES: You are right; and I retract the statement that measures passed by a tyrant without persuasion of the citizens are law.

ALCIBIADES: And what of measures passed by a minority, not by persuasion of the majority, but in the exercise of its power only? Are we, or are we not, to apply the term violence to these?

PERICLES: I think that anything which any one forces another to do without persuasion, whether by enactment or not, is violence rather than law.

ALCIBIADES: It would seem that everything which the majority, in the exercise of its power over the possessors of wealth, and without persuading them, chooses to enact, is of the nature of violence rather than of law?

> To be sure (answered Pericles), adding: At your age we were clever hands at such quibbles ourselves. It was just such subtleties which we used to practise our wits upon; as you do now, if I mistake not.
>
> To which Alcibiades replied: Ah, Pericles, I do wish we could have met in those days when you were at your cleverest in such matters.
>
> (Xenophon 1994: 26–27)

What we find in this dialogue demonstrates that the attempt to separate law and morality is certainly not new to humanity. Nonetheless, we still cannot characterize this tension as being resolved today after significant efforts of legal positivists since the close of the eighteenth century. Nevertheless, we have seen above that the initiators of legal positivism did in fact admit to a regular coincidence of positive law and morality. Since even the originators of legal positivism did not rule out a coincidence at certain points, we will therefore accept its existence and demonstrate that one indispensable place of this overlap is the exclusion of the use of free, unconstrained violence.

To assist in tackling this issue we shall turn to the prominent positivist legal scholar and philosopher H. L. A. Hart. His book *The Concept of Law* is considered to be one of the most influential in contemporary jurisprudence, and it is here that he lays out and develops his own sophisticated view of legal positivism within the framework of analytical jurisprudence. After disputing Austin's theory that law can be described as the command of a sovereign backed by the threat of punishment, and contributing his innovative theory on primary and secondary rules, Hart delivers two chapters on the relevant topic: "Justice and Morality," and "Laws and Morals." In these chapters Hart highlights the enormous importance of maintaining *equity* within a legal system. He claims that this can be evidenced by the frequency with which words such as "fair" and unfair" have been invoked in criticism of law. The standard that is to "treat like cases alike" and "different cases differently" is so deeply embedded in our contemporary thought that it is near unanimous that blatant discrimination must be met with at least lip-service toward denunciation. Thus it has become less and less acceptable to overtly defend barefaced distinct treatment based on such natural human characteristics as color or gender.

Most importantly for our discussion, Hart directly correlates this concept of equity with a protection from wanton injury or death. He wrote that,

> [s]uch a structure of reciprocal rights and obligations proscribing at least the grosser sorts of harm, constitutes the basis, though not the whole, of the morality of every social group. Its effect is to create among individuals a moral and, in a sense, an artificial equality to offset the inequalities of nature. For when the moral code forbids one man to rob or use violence on another even when superior strength or cunning would enable him to do so with impunity, the strong and cunning are put on a level with the weak and simple.
>
> (Hart 1994: 164–165)

In this quote we see that Hart understands that the basic security for all within a society starts with a reciprocal forbearance, and he puts this forward as an essence of all forms of morality. As proponents of natural law posited before him, Hart saw that the shared interest of survival, or self-preservation, demands an agreement upon such restraint in order for humans to be able to coexist together. Yet what we will also see is that Hart does not view this as simply a moral standard. Rather, it is, for the very same reasons, an indispensable legal norm to boot.

A confusion that is often present in the debate over law and morals is the lack of a precise definition of morality as it would be applied over different circumstances. While codified law can always be directly referenced, and its exact formulation can be ascertained and documented with little quarrel, morals do not share the same quality. The fact that the exact contours of morality have changed over time (certainly within Western culture) and the fact that there is now an unavoidable interface of a vast range of cultures the world over, with each possessing their own view on human perfection, have both contributed to a difficulty in understanding morality as universal.

However, it is possible to clarify what is intended when the word "morality" is invoked by drawing a distinction between a "morality of duty" and a "morality of aspiration" (Fuller 1964: 3–32). These two categories represent opposite ends of the same scale, and the issue of where one leaves off for the other to begin has long dominated moral argument. A "morality of duty" starts at the bottom and "lays down the basic rules without which an ordered society is impossible" (Fuller 1964: 5), whereas a "morality of aspiration" is at the top end of this scale and is about human excellence or the fullest realization of our humanity. The difficulty in specifying with exactness all the forms of a "morality of aspiration" as we mount this scale does not mean that some of the more basic requirements of a baseline "morality of duty" are unknowable or incomprehensible. In other words, it is indeed possible to "know what is plainly unjust without committing ourselves to declare with finality what perfect justice would be like" (Fuller 1964: 12). This wide scope that morality can cover, from the most obvious demands of social living to the highest reaches of human aspiration, often leads to confusion over how morals might have any sort of uncomplicated relationship with law. Yet our discussion of legitimacy is concerned with the more discernible bottom end of this scale.

It is the teleological view of humanity that Hart disputes most forth-rightly and also that which relates to the top end of this scale (1994: 189–191). It should be recognized that the teleological conception of the human race—that we are perfectible and (perhaps even more dubiously) that we can know what this perfection looks like—most closely coincides with the "morality of aspiration." This belief that an identifiable purpose for humankind exists, and can even be legislated into being, can quickly lead to irresolvable disputes that badly muddy the waters of the relationship between law and morals. However, Hart properly draws our attention to the fact that even this teleological view can be applied narrowly enough to suit his purposes for legal theory and to account for the overlap we wish to spotlight here. Hart explains,

> [i]t will be rightly observed that what makes sense of this mode of thought and expression is something entirely obvious: it is the tacit assumption that the proper end of human activity is survival, and this rests on the simple contingent fact that most men most of the time wish to continue in existence. [...] This simple thought has in fact very much to do with the characteristics of both law and morals, and it can be disentangled from more disputable parts of the general tele-ological outlook in which the end or good for man appears as a specific way of life about which, in fact, men may profoundly disagree.
>
> (Hart 1994: 191–192)

This disentanglement is crucial to Hart's conclusions. By making this distinction from the teleological view and then underscoring the one remaining universal truth of human life (that we wish it to continue), he is able to straddle the two primary legal philosophies under discussion here. While the theories of legal positivism and natural law are often presented as mutually exclusive, Hart made sure to point out that there is indeed a place of coincidence.

It is for this reason that Hart arrives at the conclusion that the legal philosophy which has served as the general starting point via rejection for his own legal theory does in fact have a piece worth salvaging. He called this retrievable piece the "minimum content" of natural law and describes it as "universally recognized principles of conduct which have a basis in elementary truths concerning human beings, their natural environment, and aims" (Hart 1994: 193). From a renowned legal positivist, the recovery of this idea and its integration into his own theory is certainly worthy of note. It is this notion that Hart has used to conclude that there is indeed a moment when the actual content of law is prescribed. As he puts it,

> [i]n considering the simple truisms which we set forth here, and their connection with law and morals, it is important to observe that in each case the facts mentioned afford a *reason* why, given survival as an aim, law and morals should include a specific content. The general form of the argument is simply that without such a content laws and morals could not forward the minimum purpose of survival which men have in associating with each other.
>
> (Hart 1994: 193; original emphasis)

To help substantiate his conclusions, Hart researched and worked on the genesis of legal positivism by way of Bentham and Austin in his article "Positivism and the Separation of Law and Morals," published in 1958 within the pages of the *Harvard Law Review*. In it, much of the same reasoning is applied and similar conclusions reached. Hart specifically attempts to correct the point that Bentham and Austin saw no intersection at all between law and morals; rather, they believed that even if there were identifiable coincidences it was conceptually necessary to make the distinction for analytical purposes. For instance, even if it might only be the nascent form of the same argument that he himself made, Hart calls our attention to Austin's recognition that there are "resemblances between different systems which are bottomed in the common nature of man" (Austin 1954: 373; cited in Hart 1958: 620). Thus, such an acknowledgment would indicate that Austin was aware of at least a partial truth to be found in natural law. Thus Hart concludes that even the founders of positivism would deem there to be certain provisions necessary in a legal system. By sketching the hypothetical scenario that humans were somehow to become invulnerable to attack and could obtain sufficient nourishment through the breathing of air that could not rot nor spoil, Hart points out that all legal systems would no longer necessarily need minimum rules forbidding the free use of violence and theft. However, under our human conditions as we know them,

> such rules are so fundamental that if a legal system did not have them there would be no point in having any other rules. Such rules overlap with basic moral principles vetoing murder, violence, and theft; and so we can add to the factual statement that all legal systems in fact coincide with morality at such vital points.
>
> (Hart 1958: 621)

IX Overlap and application

An important quality of this model of legitimacy is not only that it aims to capture the tripartite structure of the content of legitimacy, but also that it presents a manner in which we can understand the interactive nature of the three elements of *legality*, *morality*, and *efficacy*. In other words, these poles are not in juxtaposition, but rather there is a place of overlap between these three philosophies or validities. This is part of the reason behind the introduction of the Escher image demonstrating three different poles coexisting and functioning simultaneously. It will therefore be important that the application of our model does not simply present just one pole of legitimacy, independent of the others, by treating one policy per sphere. Nor is it desirable to analyze each of the three policies of detention, war-making, and interrogation through all three of the spheres of legitimacy since it would create a redundancy at the expense of clarity. Additionally, it is felt that such repetition would serve little purpose in demonstrating and discussing overlap. Thus, this work will be organized in a way that tries to capture the utility of the three spheres of legitimacy and their overlap, while avoiding unwarranted duplication.

To accomplish our task, Chapter 3 will begin our analysis by peering solely through the lens of *legality* to the issue of detention without judicial review at Guantánamo so as to ascertain the manner in which formal validity was fleshed out by the US Supreme Court. Then, in Chapter 4, we will adjoin the lens of *morality* to analyze war-making policies in the "war on terror." Although the primary lens for this chapter will be that of *morality*, the focus of our attention will in fact be on the overlap with *legality* discussed above. Finally, in Chapter 5, we will affix the lens of *efficacy* to the other two so as to analyze the use of abusive interrogation techniques for the aim of gathering reliable and timely intelligence. While we will be gazing through the lens of *efficacy* in this chapter, the focus once again will be on the space where it overlaps with *legality* and *morality*. So, by adding the lenses one by one and concentrating upon the point at which there is overlap between them in the discussion of the three different policies, our intention is to gain substantive analysis of each issue while illuminating the interactive nature of the three poles of legitimacy.

In the end, this sequential application will also allow for a continuation of the use of interdisciplinarity throughout this work. This will first allow for fixing in place the lens of *legality*, which is believed to provide a useful and necessary setting of the parameters to begin. Additionally, as each lens of this analytical tool represents a different methodological approach to investigation (formal, axiological, and empirical), this sequencing will also help avoid a devolution into a type of analytical purée in which each the differing methods becomes indistinguishable from the others.

X Conclusion

Because the *power to command* and the *will to obey* are a vital part of the structure of any society, if enemies can find a way to disrupt or stress Ferrero's intersection of authority and obedience, then real damage can be done to a society. Through an interdisciplinary dialogue we have demonstrated that there is strong reasoning for bringing together the ideas of political violence and the legitimacy of a government. Due to its nature, the uncoerced pull toward compliance with an authority of the state has been, and throughout this work will continue to be, explored from different disciplinary perspectives.

We have also been able to hypothesize a general shape of the content of legitimacy in an attempt to expose the "Genii of the City." We have constructed a philosophically sound model by reasoning through the work of scholars treating legitimacy in the context of conflict and have put forward that the content of legitimacy consists of three overlapping spheres representing *legality*, *morality*, and *efficacy*.

With these analytical tools, and an emphasis on where they coincide, it will be possible to provide a valuable investigation and evaluation of the policies that were instituted in the counterterrorist response to the attacks of September 11, 2001. Not only is this possible for the response initiated by the Bush administration, but, as we will also see, these tools of analysis provide a worthwhile means for investigating the policies of the Obama administration that followed.

Notes

1 It should be acknowledged that there is a part of this argument that reminds us of what was put forward by Max Weber—that is, the notion that the rational component of legitimacy is accidental echoes the idea that it is solely based in subjective beliefs. However, as we have discussed above, it should be remembered that over the second half of the twentieth century, after Ferrero first published his work, there has been an exponential growth in standards that can be used to rationally test the legitimacy of a government. This helps explain our reasoning for following Habermas's view that the rational reasons for bestowing legitimacy have been becoming explicit and knowable. Most importantly, it should be clearly understood that the idea of legitimacy being testable by citizens and scholars does not equate with it being scientifically falsifiable. There is indeed a great distance between the two.

2 International counterterrorism and a legitimacy deficit

Rather, they seek either to cause the enemy to overreact and thereby permit them to recruit large numbers of followers so that they can launch a guerilla campaign, or to have such a psychological or economic impact on the enemy that it will withdraw of its own accord. Bin Laden called this the "bleed-until-bankruptcy plan."

(Richardson 2006: 6)

The government must function in accordance with law.
There is a very strong temptation in dealing both with terrorism and with guerrilla actions for government forces to act outside the law.... Not only is this morally wrong, but, over a period, it will create more practical difficulties for a government than it solves.

(Thompson 1966: 52; cited in Roberts 2008: 20)

I Introduction: destruction, not construction, of legitimacy

Attempting to understand the reasoning behind flying a hijacked commercial aircraft, filled with civilians, into symbolic buildings occupied by more noncombatants so as to build an Islamic caliphate indeed causes an analytical short-circuit. There is more to be understood about the "strategy of provocation" of terrorism, and thus we must look further.

The fact that Al-Qaeda crossed international borders to carry out its attack had a direct impact upon where the US administration focused its attention for interpreting the constraints it would be required to heed for counterterrorism policy: international law. At the same time, the international character of this conflict also helps to explain that while Al-Qaeda attempts to target US legitimacy, it has little intention of reconstructing a new legitimacy to later occupy that territory. It is important to understand that the aims are primarily related to destruction and not to construction, because this further promotes the need to fortify defenses around legitimacy where the attack is largely focused.

To flesh out this first point, it is most useful to look into a work that has been given significant credence by the US government itself. At the end of

2006, nearly four years after the invasion of Iraq, President Bush was under significant pressure to change course in that country. This was largely due to significant losses by Republican candidates at the polls in November 2006, along with the release in December of that year of a highly anticipated report by the Iraq Study Group (a bipartisan commission appointed and given a mandate by Congress) which began its recommendations by describing the situation as "grave and deteriorating" (Baker and Hamilton 2006: xiii).

At this critical juncture, the President appointed General David Petraeus to lead US troops in Iraq and to oversee the so-called "surge" strategy, which was based primarily on the US Army Field Manual 3–24, *Counterinsurgency*. General Petraeus was later promoted to head the US Central Command, and President Obama appointed him as the Commander of US forces in Afghanistan and then as the head of the Central Intelligence Agency (CIA). This meteoric rise certainly speaks to the relevance of the line of thinking found in the Army Field Manual drafted under his supervision.

The document was developed and written by military thinkers, and thus it is not surprising that they are primarily looking at the overseas operations launched by politicians to deal with the threat posed by terrorism. It is meant for use abroad and thus does not contemplate a legitimacy deficit at home, even if such a discussion would be most welcome. The strategy of provocation certainly manifests problems for the society and government that has been directly attacked, but the focus here is on the adversaries found abroad and the foreign theaters of operation.

Most pertinently, throughout the Field Manual there is an explicit recognition that legitimacy is the central front of the conflict at hand. This is first made clear in the very definition of the conflict: "an insurgency is an organized, protracted politico-military struggle designed to weaken the control and *legitimacy* of an established government, occupying power, or other political authority while increasing insurgent control" (US Army 2006: 1–1, §1–2; my emphasis).

Here, we see very clearly that the drafters of the manual are keenly aware that insurgents are attempting to weaken a government by targeting its legitimacy, and it is filled with similar references. It can thus be said that they saw the legitimacy of a government as the primary target of attack in the case of an insurgency, just as posited here. Demonstrating this point most clearly is the fact that there is an entire section that discusses this idea as central, falling under an unambiguous heading:

Legitimacy Is the Main Objective

The primary objective of any COIN [counterinsurgency] operation is to foster development of effective governance by a *legitimate* government. Counterinsurgents achieve this objective by the balanced application of both military and nonmilitary means. All governments rule through a combination of consent and coercion. Governments described as "*legitimate*" rule primarily with the consent of the governed; those described as "illegitimate" tend to rely mainly or entirely on coercion. [...] A government that derives its powers from the governed tends to be accepted by its citizens as *legitimate*. It still uses coercion—for example, against criminals—but most of its citizens voluntarily accept its governance.

(US Army 2006: 1–21, §1–113; my emphasis)

Of course, it is certainly debatable whether legitimacy can be so easily summarized, then taught to a military force so as to pass along a legitimate government to an occupied territory. Furthermore, traditional humanitarian law assumes that occupying powers should respect the existing laws and economic arrangements and therefore raises questions about the validity of transformative military occupation (Roberts 2007).

The notion of what constitutes a legitimate government and how that is to be achieved has been profoundly and hotly debated for centuries by political philosophers from Machiavelli to Hobbes to Locke to Rousseau. Therefore, it can come across as hubris to suggest that such a pivotal aspect of society's functioning has been resolved and can be moderated and manufactured by an uninvited outside military force. This is surely why foreign military operations aimed at the construction of legitimacy must be understood as nation-building, and perhaps as being beyond the capabilities of even the most powerful militaries. Consequently, before politicians commit troops to invasions abroad it should be understood that while "regime removal" is within the military's capacities, "regime change" is far more complex, and is yet to be fully understood by humanity.

Nonetheless, from the perspective of this work, what is most important is that all of the attention here is on constructing legitimacy outside of the US, not on the attempts to weaken or destroy the legitimacy at home. Therefore, it is valuable to recognize that the idea of focusing on the destruction of legitimacy, rather than on its construction, is a less complicated task. That is not to say that undermining and weakening the legitimacy of a government is easy and obvious. Rather, as with nearly all things known in this world, destruction is less difficult than construction.

Of course, this is not entirely surprising in the context of terrorist movements. In general, there have been only vague outlines put forward for the future world which they wish to create. Al-Qaeda speaks about the establishment of a caliphate ruled by Sharia law, but tends to fall short on any detail. Even after all of its carefully managed publicity campaigns, Al-Qaeda and its leaders "appear altogether more interested in the process by which the present system will be destroyed than in the functioning of the new system" (Richardson 2006: 85). One notable result that follows from not possessing a coherent vision of the future is that there are far fewer constraints on the means employed. If one is concentrated only on the destruction of the enemy because this is believed to be the sole obstacle to deliverance, then the methods chosen are irrelevant and public attacks on noncombatants become more easily seen as a viable option.

This is not uncommon for leaders of terrorist organizations in general, and of Al-Qaeda specifically. David Aaron, a diplomat who compiled a manuscript of the writings of extremists willing to target civilians, explained that:

> One of the curious things about jihadism is the notable lack of articulated political or social goals beyond implementing shari'a law. [...] Even such jihad writers as Sayyid Qutb focus their analyses on the shortcomings of other ideologies rather than explicating how their philosophy would translate into government structures and economic and social policy. As one jihadi notes, [...] it is as if they are not really interested in governing, but only in waging jihad. Bin Laden's only evident policy impact on the Taliban was in persuading them to blow up the historically priceless Bamiyan Buddhas.
>
> (Aaron 2008: 109; internal citations omitted)

As a policy prescription, destroying historic religious artifacts is undoubtedly limited and patently intolerant. Yet our work is meant to focus attention at the point of attack: the US political authority. In other words, we will posit how Al-Qaeda meant to weaken or destroy the legitimacy of its enemy's government through a strategy of provocation.

II Terrorism as tactic and strategy

Terrorism is not a new phenomenon. The term "terror" begins to appear in dictionaries and is used in writings in reference to the French Revolution, and in this context the term referred to political violence used as a tool by the state. The Jacobins were said to occasionally use the term "terrorism" or "terrorist" in a positive sense when writing about themselves, according to a French dictionary published in 1796 (Laqueur 1977: 6). The idiom contemporaneously migrated across the channel and into the English language, where in 1795 we find Edmund Burke referring in a famous passage to "those hell hounds called terrorists" unleashed onto the people of France (1999: 315).

Historian Guglielmo Ferrero provides a plausible theory for understanding the origins of this "reign of terror" that was let loose in 1789 (1942: 82–101). His hypothesis brings us back to the central issue of legitimacy for all organized societies. Ferrero reminds us that all aspects of the apparatus of state (i.e., laws, police, courts, and jailers) rest on the idea of an uncoerced pull toward obedience to command. Any government would become instantly and completely paralyzed if all subjects came to the simultaneous agreement to withhold their obedience. While Ferrero claims that man's existence is relatively ordered because this could seemingly never happen, there was in fact one such moment that he found in his historical research. On July 14, 1789, the Bastille, the infamous royal jail in Paris, was stormed by a crowd while a substantial number of nearby Royal Army forces did not come to defend the *ancien régime*. Ferrero highlights this moment as the complete collapse of legitimacy. A frightening chaos thus spread throughout all of France. Ferrero explains,

> It is less familiar that this victorious uprising was followed, for the first time in history, by the event which we held, not without reason, to be impossible: All over France, for six weeks, as soon as the news from Paris was heard, all the people—peasants, workers, lower middle classes, officials, upper classes—as at a signal after a secret agreement, refused to obey.
>
> (Ferrero 1942: 82–83)

Thus, it is Ferrero's theory that it was the absence of any legitimate authority that spawned this particular state terror epitomized by the thousands of public beheadings at the guillotine. This is certainly not to suggest a justification for the "reign of terror" that followed in an effort to impose order on a society without any recognized commanding authority, nor is it to launch into historical disputes over the events of that time period. The point is to underline the manner in which legitimacy rests at the center of struggles to steer any society.

Unfortunately, the frailty of human memory has meant that more recent events involving attacks by non-state actors have been regarded by many to be a novel phenomenon in our history. Most important during its long existence as a tactic is the belief that such political violence must be at least public, if not spectacular. Therefore, it is not new that such political violence is a spectacle in search of an audience. Consequently, terrorism expert Brian Jenkins spoke very aptly when he stated that "terrorism is theatre" (1975: 16).

The modern employment of terrorism can be said to have an enhanced political effect which can be attributed to more recent changes that have occurred within our societies. Here we highlight two significant transformations that have directly shaped the effectiveness of terrorism as both tactic and strategy. The first is the widespread proliferation of cameras, mass media, and information-sharing tools. Hence, when Margaret Thatcher spoke of publicity being the "oxygen" on which terrorists depend she was addressing a historical fact long understood as being tied to the phenomenon (Thatcher 1985). At the same time, she was identifying an experience of modern times that has continued to increase appreciably since the statement was first made.

The second important factor that has enhanced the impact of terrorist tactics is the notable rise during the twentieth century in international acceptance and explicit codification of detailed laws of war and legal treaties enshrining the idea that each and every individual has inviolable human rights. The development of such laws to protect individuals has been accompanied by a growth in cadres of diplomats, international military tribunals, and human rights monitoring bodies to debate and oversee implementation of these laws. While these enforcement mechanisms fall far short when compared with domestic law and governing institutions, such developments also represent giant steps forward when seen in an historical perspective.

International law protecting individuals has undoubtedly become more conspicuous in our human consciousness over the previous decades. That is to say, its development since the end of World War II represents a palpable change in the tools that citizens can use to evaluate and scrutinize their own government's protection of individual rights—protection to which the government is obligated by its legal commitments made to other states. And this is where *new diplomacy*, both public and widely disseminated, is having an intensified impact. Counterterrorism policy today is under a new type of microscope which frames and structures the scrutiny of a state that attempts to confront terrorist groups. As will become clear in what follows throughout this work, international law provides metrics for the public to employ to evaluate their own state's exercise of force. We will see that while the increased media sources have provided a drastic increase in credible facts distributed to the citizenry about abuses by the government, international law has offered analytical tools that can and have been applied in evaluating this increased empirical data.

a Terrorism as tactic

Before exploring terrorist groups' primary short-term strategic goals, it is first necessary to present the major characteristics of the tactic of modern terrorism. As a starting point, this work will take terrorism to mean public and politically motivated violence against noncombatants. However, there is no universally accepted definition of terrorism in international law (and even within some domestic jurisdictions), although there has been much debate and negotiation for decades. Notably, this discussion of a definition has taken place within both the legal community and academic literature.

The first aspect of terrorism that is widely accepted to characterize such acts is that it is *politically* motivated. If these acts are not so motivated, they can simply be understood as ordinary criminal activity. Therefore, a terrorist act is not only illicit, but is also meant to specifically challenge the authority of a regime by attempting to bring about a change in policy. Second, *violence* against persons, or the threat thereof, must be employed. Partly because the term "terrorism" has recently become so prevalent, it has been used promiscuously and has been applied to a variety of acts that do not fall into the same category (e.g., eco-terrorism and cyber-terrorism). Third, the specific chosen target often has symbolic significance because a message is being sent to a larger audience and not to the victims of the violence themselves. In the simplest terms, a terrorist act is *public*. Because the point of terrorism is that the impact is more psychological than the actual physical act itself, the choice of a more symbolic target attracts more of the vital "oxygen" of publicity. Looking at these widely accepted characteristics of terrorism, it is not difficult to see how the use of public and political violence is aimed not at the security forces or the state representatives of a regime, but instead at the legitimacy of its command.

Next are the more divisive features of modern terrorism, which have been stumbling blocks for the arrival at a commonly accepted international legal definition of this phenomenon, deemed by the United Nations Security Council (UNSC) to be a "threat to the peace" (Resolutions 1368, 1373, 1377). The two major obstructions have been whether terrorism must be committed by a *non-state group* (can a state commit terrorist crimes?) and whether the "targeting of innocents" includes attacks on the *security forces* of a democratic regime. Although it is in conflict with the original use of the term "terror" in the context of the French Revolution, for analytical clarity and, of greater importance, due to the understanding of legitimacy as being the primary battleground of this type of conflict, it makes most sense here to limit the terrorist designation to non-state actors and only those instances when their actions target civilians without a status within the government.

As to international legality, there already exist thirteen international conventions treating specific assets or persons believed to be current or future targets of terrorism. However, although the international community has been able to create conventions to deal with the hijacking of aircraft, the taking of hostages, terrorist bombing, illicit acts against the safety of maritime navigation, crimes against persons protected internationally (including diplomatic agents), the financing of terrorism, nuclear terrorism, etc., there has not been agreement on a general antiterrorist convention. Perhaps more widely known is that this also means that there is not one single, and widely accepted, definition of terrorism in international law.

Nevertheless, this fact should not confuse us into believing that there is insufficient agreement that the most abhorrent public and political violence is an international crime. As the former President of the UN International Criminal Tribunal for the former Yugoslavia (ICTY) Antonio Cassese expressed it, "[t]o my mind a definition of terrorism does exist, and this phenomenon also amounts to a customary international law crime" (2004: 214). Of relevance here is the fact that, as the Special Tribunal for Lebanon Appeals Chamber's Presiding Judge, Cassese took part in a historic decision where, for the first time, an international tribunal confirmed a general definition of terrorism under international law (2011).

There are times when the identification of those who are not armed and not engaged in defending a regime in an official position is indeed possible to ascertain, at least to a much more reasonable degree. As just one obvious example, we can look to 9/11. There is no doubt that the flight attendants, pilots, and passengers onboard all four aircraft that day were incontrovertibly civilians. One might suggest that the American Airlines Flight 77 airplane, flown into the US military headquarters of the Pentagon in Virginia, was aimed at a non-civilian target. However, the other two projectile weapons, filled with noncombatants and enough fuel for an almost six-hour transcontinental flight, were deliberately, publicly, and violently pummeled into the symbolic World Trade Center buildings in New York City which were occupied with civilians by any measure. The death toll from that day was 2,977 people of fifty-five different nationalities (excluding the nineteen hijackers), and all were civilians except for the fifty-five military personnel out of the 125 deaths at the Pentagon.

The UNSC reacted with astounding speed in passing Resolution 1368 just one day after the attacks, affirming that it

> *Unequivocally condemns* in the strongest terms the horrifying terrorist attacks which took place on 11 September 2001 in New York, Washington, DC and Pennsylvania and *regards* such acts, like any act of international terrorism, as a threat to international peace and security [original emphasis].

As such, it is indeed possible to identify certain acts as undoubtedly public and political violence by non-state actors directed against civilians, i.e., terrorism.

b Terrorism as strategy: revenge, renown, and reaction

While some are drawn to conclude that terrorism is senseless or irrational violence, it is important to understand that those who employ it do in fact have goals they are trying to achieve. Even though at times those who commit acts of terrorism can get so wrapped up in their violent actions that they sometimes miss the point themselves, this does not mean that strategic objectives do not exist. To understand why violence might be directed against unarmed bystanders who do not themselves have the capacity to direct any change, it is first necessary to recognize that there is nothing conventional about this type of combat. Those who choose such tactics are not trying to capture or hold any territory or to destroy the enemy's forces, nor do they have the level of weaponry needed to engage the military of a state on a traditional battlefield. Terrorists do indeed kill, and in a fashion that may at first seem wanton, but, as Brian Jenkins put it, "[t]errorists want a lot of people watching, and not a lot of people dead" (1975: 15). However, it should be acknowledged that the number of people dead surely has a direct impact upon the number of people watching.

With that said, a credible threat can be preferable to actually carrying out the deed since provoking a reaction is based upon the sentiments, or terror, induced. Having the enemy believe in an existing menace can circumvent the need to act and can therefore avoid failure or exposing weakness. Thus, inspiring and manipulating fear for political reasons through the purposeful public targeting of noncombatants can be described as the means, or tactic, of terrorism.

To get closer to understanding the tactic of terrorism as a means for accomplishing strategic goals, some of the most persuasive analysis comes from Louise Richardson in her book *What Terrorists Want* (2006). Richardson's expertise on the subject is impressive. She possesses the traditional scholar's familiarity with the literature that comes from the greater part of a professional life dedicated to the investigation of this age-old political phenomenon. In addition, to better understand their motives, means, and ends, she has interviewed insurgents, reviewed accounts of interrogations and interviews, and studied the statements of those who have purposely targeted civilians.

One of the most interesting elements that Richardson brings to the discussion of terrorism is what she refers to as the three Rs: Revenge, Renown, Reaction. She addresses the issue of the effectiveness of terrorism and sees no clear cases being proven. Instead, she presents a much more constructive way to get at the motivations of those who attack noncombatants, sometimes in a manner that sacrifices the terrorists' own lives. Richardson explains that "[a]ll terrorist movements have two kinds of goals: short-term organizational objectives and long-term political objectives requiring significant political change" (2006: 75). It is imperative to distinguish between the two if we are to get closer to understanding the dramatic and immoderate choice of employing the type of violence under discussion here.

The grand goal of reestablishing the Islamic caliphate has been avowed by prominent leaders of the Al-Qaeda movement. This immense political change would require a redrawing of international borders throughout the Middle East, northern Africa, and even a portion of the Iberian Peninsula in Europe. However, to present only this objective as what motivates members of Al-Qaeda to carry out their violent acts misses the more short-term immediate intentions.

While violence may serve as a means to achieve a specific aim, one must remember that the objective cannot be too far in the future for its sense to be truly understood. Though reestablishing the Islamic caliphate is the long-term goal that appeals primarily to the leadership of the Al-Qaeda movement, we know that groups who employ terrorism have been singularly unsuccessful in bringing about such grandiose goals. Thus, understanding that the near-term strategic goals motivating many followers are revenge, renown, and reaction is of importance in analyzing terrorism as a strategy. Of course, both objectives can be pursued simultaneously so the divergence can be kept limited and undamaging to the organization.

Revenge

The ubiquity of the theme of *revenge* is so prevalent in terrorist literature and discourse that it is almost superfluous to point it out. The theme of revenge illustrates the predominance of the idea of collective punishment found in many terrorist groups, as guilt is attributed with a very wide brush. Bin Laden clearly attempted to tap into this sentiment of a desire for revenge for perceived injustices in order to recruit followers and soldiers for a jihad against both the US and its allies. A catalog of reasons for vengeance indeed runs deep in bin Laden's rhetoric. In his 1996 *fatwā*, or religious opinion meant to be based on Islamic law, bin Laden wrote,

> It should not be hidden from you that the people of Islam had suffered from aggression, iniquity and injustice imposed on them by the Zionist-Crusaders alliance and their collaborators; to the extent that the Muslims blood became the cheapest and their wealth as loot in the hands of the enemies.
>
> (bin Laden 1996)

Just as intended, the list of grievances did not remain static. Following the Al-Qaeda attacks of 9/11 the US responded by invading Afghanistan within less than a month, and then Iraq in early 2003. These two wars launched in reaction to the terrorist attacks provided additional reasons for bin Laden to call for revenge against his enemies. Shortly after the invasion of Afghanistan, a challenge to the West and a rallying cry to Muslims to take up arms was broadcast on Al-Jazeera and attributed to bin Laden. In the recording bin Laden spoke of the bombing of the innocent people of Afghanistan and jumped on the language of "crusade" used by President Bush. Bin Laden hammered at this theme of retribution by emphasizing the grave slip of referencing the Crusades:

> After the US politicians spoke and after the US newspapers and television channels became full of clear crusading hatred in this campaign that aims at mobilizing the West against Islam and Muslims, Bush left no room for doubts or the opinions of journalists, but he openly and clearly said that this war is a crusader war. He said this before the whole world to emphasize this fact.
>
> (bin Laden 2001)

The reason why this is directly pertinent to our discussion of calls for revenge is that images of the atrocities of the war in Iraq, such as would occur in any form of high-tech or low-tech military operation, were indeed widely circulated throughout the Muslim world. Hence, a direct confrontation with US power at its most coercive and violent was faced by the people of Iraq and Afghanistan and spread extensively through television broadcasts to the 1.5 billion Muslims across the globe. One example of how bin Laden referred to such activity, which most assuredly served his purposes of inciting a desire for vengeance, was in his 2004 video known as "Message to America," in which he drew a direct correlation between what he considered to be atrocities of the past and how they seamlessly continued into the present:

> This means the oppressing and embargoing to death of millions as Bush Sr did in Iraq in the greatest mass slaughter of children mankind has ever known, and it means the throwing of millions of pounds of bombs and explosives at millions of children—also in Iraq—as Bush Jr did, in order to remove an old agent and replace him with a new puppet to assist in the pilfering of Iraq's oil and other outrages.
>
> (bin Laden 2004)

Any successful counterterrorism program must surely bear in mind this dangerous spiral of *revenge* and retribution.

Renown

The second short-term goal motivating groups that employ terrorism is the desire to achieve an elevated status, within one's own community or on the greater international scene at large. In this case, militants attempt to attain *renown* through exposure for their actions. But there is more at play than just the simple publicity that has been discussed. It is the concept of glory for attempting to redress what is considered by some a humiliation suffered. Because glory on a local or, increasingly, global stage is particularly important to the leaders of such movements, the recent revolution in information-sharing tools has had an acute impact on this phenomenon. One analyst has explained that in Iraq this has had a particular impact because "[f]or propaganda purposes, they create their own videos of virtually every terrorist attack, often at great risk to themselves and their operations" (Aaron 2008: 268). However, unlike revenge, which terrorists take for themselves, renown is something that must be bestowed by others, and this can come from a complicit community or from their enemies.

In looking into the writings and orations of Al-Qaeda, one indeed finds a focus on this issue of media coverage. Most important is an attempt to characterize a very small group of dedicated and zealous attackers as engaged in a real confrontation with the most powerful military of the world and its government. By portraying the struggle in these terms it certainly demonstrates an effort to cloak themselves in the "glory" of standing up to the oppressor. One of Al-Qaeda's top strategists, Abu Ubeid al-Qurashi, portrayed the struggle as such:

> In the media, the United States has failed to market its crusade. The US propaganda machine has been unable to defeat feelings of hatred toward the United States. It has not even managed to dispel the doubts within the United States. The immensity of the Western propaganda apparatus did not prevent its defeat at the hands of Shaykh Usama. The cameras of CNN and other Western media dinosaurs undertook the task of filming the raid [9/11] and sowing fear in its aftermath. It didn't cost al-Qa'ida a cent. Moreover, the "terror" tapes that CNN showed later demonstrated the mujahidin's increased capabilities and endeared them to the Islamic community.
>
> (Al-Qurashi, quoted in Aaron 2008: 270)

Speaking of the media outlets that address the Muslim population in the Middle East, al-Qurashi continued by explaining the value of the exclusive videotapes being broadcast, which brought worldwide notoriety to the Islamic community and the entire world. Al-Qurashi also demonstrates a sophisticated understanding of the use of the Internet to transmit their own propaganda to the media outlets that cover the interaction between the two parties, as well as how these outlets operate.

So, what we see is a small band of criminals willing to attack noncombatants to publicize their grievances, viewing itself as actively engaged with the mammoth entity it considers its enemy. This belief is not completely absurd. Perusing newspapers, magazines, television news coverage, and bookshelves on the subject of terrorism would certainly bolster this argument. Yet it should be recognized that non-state actors have not often seized the full attention and activity across the institutional spectrum of a state so thoroughly. Thus, these words from one of Al-Qaeda's leading members do not seem far off the mark. Al-Qurashi also explained the significance of the 9/11 attacks in comparison with the killing of Israeli athletes at the 1972 Olympics in Munich by saying that "The September 11 [operation] was an even greater propaganda coup. It may be said that it broke a record in propaganda dissemination. [...] With few exceptions, the entire planet heard about it" (quoted in Aaron 2008: 271).

Reaction

It must be pointed out that what sort of response is developed and carried out by a state is within its own hands, and not in those of the terrorists. In other words, although there are indeed political forces at play when it comes to setting counterterrorism policy, a state's *reaction* is of its own making and is most certainly of the highest importance. As has been astutely pointed out by one scholar, "governments have choices in how to combat terrorism—choices that can be key determinants of the outcome" (Crenshaw 1983: 31).

Those who choose to employ terrorism can be described as action-oriented groups. Yet although this is the modus operandi of an adversary, this certainly does not mean that confronting it on the same grounds is advantageous to those who are defending themselves from such attacks. Hence, because the terrorists want to provoke a reaction, one must carefully contemplate exactly how to respond to such public and political violence.

Democracies are especially susceptible to this type of provocation. They are often structured in a way that causes tension between the different branches of government over interpretation of the established constraints on their response (see generally Bianchi and Keller 2008). It is not an option for a state, nor would it be preferable, to refrain entirely from a response, as there is a legal and philosophical duty to protect citizens from such violent attacks. Of course, providing security has long been accepted as the first duty of government. Also, it is an international legal human rights obligation for states to protect individuals under their jurisdiction from terrorist attacks. However, the difficulty that arises in a democracy is that the free press and a short-term election cycle combine to push politics to the fore, and often into overreaction.

The spectacular nature of terrorist acts is meant to grab the attention of the press and to generate as much media attention as possible. Even though it is rarely the case that the press coverage produced is in any way sympathetic to the cause or plight of terrorist groups, the publicity gained relating to the event is indeed what they are seeking. With the collective eyes of a society fixed on the tragedy, the demand for an immediate and conspicuous response flows directly into the political process of a democracy, establishing a competition for who will best provide security. Unfortunately, this competition can skew and distort cool-headed reasoning since advocating swift and overwhelming force is often politically advantageous.

Many terrorist groups have promoted the use of attacks on civilians to incite a repressive reaction from the government because repressive action helps demonstrate that the ruling regime is unconstrained by limits. This can both push sympathizers to the side of the non-state actors in the psychological battle, as well as cause a government to overstep constraints that raise doubts about its legitimacy to its own citizens. As Richardson insightfully explains, "Part of the genius of terrorism [...] is that it elicits a reaction that furthers the interests of the terrorists more often than their victims" (2006: 101).

Michael Ignatieff echoes this in his book on modern terrorism and its effects on political ethics. He explains "it is the response to terrorism, rather than terrorism itself, that does democracy the most harm," and this damage is "exactly what a certain kind of terrorism intends" (Ignatieff 2004: 61). He continues:

> [s]uccess depends less on the initial attack than on instigating an escalatory spiral, controlled not by the forces of order but by the terrorists themselves. [...] Since a state will always be too strong for a cell of individuals to defeat in open battle, it must defeat itself.
>
> (Ignatieff 2004: 62).

The conclusion is that this challenge is indeed the nemesis of liberal democracies; they must not fall into this trap of provocation and abandon law altogether.

This idea of provocation of excessive reaction is unsurprisingly prevalent in the writings of Al-Qaeda strategists and leaders, and is thus found repeatedly in David Aaron's compilation of writings from Muslims who have taken the moral step of unabashedly and violently targeting noncombatants in an effort to promote their cause. Aaron deduces that

> [m]any of the jihadi statements in this book would achieve their desired effect if they exaggerated the threat and provoked an American overreaction. Such overreaction is a principal strategic objective of jihadi "raids." It makes the jihadis appear more powerful and threatening, which attracts recruits and enhances the message that the success of jihad is inevitable.
>
> (2008: 302)

We also find that the idea of driving a wedge between the citizens of the US and their government is considered to be strategically important by these groups. Al-Qurashi, specializing in strategy, has clearly studied the subject of insurrection and understands the nature of the conflict that has been engaged in by Al-Qaeda. He recognizes the limits inherent in the military dominance that the US possesses and seeks to capitalize on those limitations:

> Militarily, the 11 September raid is a great threat to the United States' current military standing. The asymmetric strategy that al-Qa'ida is pursuing entails the use of means and methods that the defender cannot use, recognize, or avoid. They rendered the United States' tremendous military superiority useless and reduced the effectiveness of US military deterrence internationally.
>
> (Al-Qurashi, quoted in Aaron 2008: 201)

Al-Qurashi was evidently quite pleased with the fact that the US military had become fully engaged in this battle, showing no concerns that

Al-Qaeda faces its awesome hard power in Afghanistan; we can gather that this is indeed a part of the plan.

In 2002, coalition forces in Afghanistan uncovered at least two letters from Osama bin Laden to Mullah Mohamed Omar, the spiritual leader of the Taliban movement and the de facto head of state of that country from 1996 to 2001. The two men were reported to have had a relationship that went back as far as the resistance to the Soviet occupation in the 1980s, and in these letters we can find further strategic explanations for the battle that Al-Qaeda wages against the US. Since the media is the means through which this publicity occurs today, it is not surprising that bin Laden identifies the media as the central front. He even goes so far as to say that "it is obvious that the media war in this century is one of the strongest methods; in fact, its ratio may reach 90% of the total preparation for the battles" (bin Laden 2002).

In another letter of a similar nature, cited by President Bush in a speech made in 2006, a key strategic disclosure is found. Bin Laden explained that Al-Qaeda was intending to launch "a media campaign to create a *wedge* between the American people and their government" (bin Laden 2006; my emphasis). The idea of a *wedge* being driven between a government and its people coincides directly with our premise that legitimacy is a primary battleground and a target of terrorism in that the intent is to disrupt the *will to obey* those who have the *power to command.*

Osama bin Laden also presented himself as a shrewd and cunning leader when he drew a comparison with the conflict undertaken with the Soviet forces in Afghanistan and the conflict in which the US now found itself engaged. He clearly believed that it was his forces' use of guerrilla warfare that led to the downfall of the Soviet Union in this south-central Asian country. His description of the event is that they "bled Russia for 10 years, until it went bankrupt and was forced to withdraw in defeat" (bin Laden 2004). He envisioned the current conflict with the US as taking place on this same battleground and spoke specifically about "bleeding America to the point of bankruptcy" (bin Laden 2004). While bin Laden appeared to be speaking primarily in economic terms, it is equally conceivable that this bankruptcy is figurative. An absence of funds would certainly lead to the need for military withdrawal, but, at the same time, a moral bankruptcy, or insolvency of legitimacy, would lead to the same result. Therefore, Al-Qaeda's strategy of provocation, or a "bleed until bankruptcy" plan, should be understood as both literal and metaphorical.

Furthermore, in the speech delivered in his "Message to America" video, bin Laden extolled Al-Qaeda's success in inciting the US to twice engage its military in this struggle in two different countries:

> All that we have mentioned has made it easy for us to *provoke and bait* this administration. All that we have to do is to send two mujahidin to the furthest point east to raise a piece of cloth on which is written

al-Qaida, in order to make the generals race there to cause America to suffer human, economic, and political losses without their achieving for it anything of note other than some benefits for their private companies.

(bin Laden 2004)

What can also be found in this citation is reference to the *wedge* mentioned above. We see that bin Laden draws an explicit distinction between the people of the US and the "private companies" that have profited from the government's policies.

Shortly thereafter bin Laden made a statement, directed to US citizens just before their presidential elections, that even more explicitly alluded to creating a rift:

It is true that this shows that al-Qaida has gained, but on the other hand, it shows that the Bush administration has also gained, something of which anyone who looks at the size of the contracts acquired by the shady Bush administration-linked mega-corporations, like Halliburton and its kind, will be convinced. And it all shows that the real loser is . . . you.

(bin Laden 2004)

With this unambiguous tying of the Bush administration to the private military corporations that had received contracts to assist in the war-making activities related to the "war on terror," we can clearly see a wedge being driven between the people and their government. If we think about Ferrero's explanation of the basic societal structure, we can easily see how the attempt to cause a division between command and obedience would put us directly on the battlefield of legitimacy.

For nearly two decades (particularly when considering human rights and counterterrorism), UN bodies have consistently highlighted that one of the aims of terrorism is the "destabilizing [of] legitimately constituted Governments."[1] Additionally, one of the scholars who has identified legitimacy as a critical issue in the investigation of terrorism has pointed out that "[b]oth the history of the results of terrorism and the analysis of its relationship to the legitimacy of regimes support the proposition that tolerating a right-wing counterterrorism reaction, [...] is destabilizing" (Crenshaw 1983: 33). As such, a major goal of this work is to flesh out exactly how it is that terrorism is "destabilizing" to a society since this is clearly an important consequence of terrorism.

It is therefore proposed that this destabilization occurs as a result of the *reaction* chosen by the affected government. Accepting Weber's widely acknowledged definition of the state as "a community that claims the *monopoly of the legitimate use of physical force*" means that every government runs the risk of pushing too far in its efforts to curb political violence if it steps beyond what is deemed to be legitimate. This is precisely the reason why counterterrorism is so critical; it cannot be disentangled from the terrorism that provoked it.

This brings us to the crux of the question as we have posed it here: how do we determine the *legitimate* use of physical force to counter against terrorism?

In their writings we have seen examples that Al-Qaeda strategists understand the constraints that exist for a government trying to combat terrorism or any other political violence. Of course, we cannot expect to find in these writings an in-depth legal analysis of US counterterrorism policies. Nonetheless, the approach of utilizing international law as a form of criticism in the propaganda or media war that has become an important part of armed conflict today has been identified as a trend in warfare. It has even been described with the term (meant to be pejorative), *lawfare* (Dunlap 2001).

As one example of Al-Qaeda's recognition of these limits on the US government specifically because of its explicitly expressed commitment to certain international standards, one can again turn to the strategic thinker al-Qurashi:

> As soon as the first real crisis hit the United States in the form of the September attacks, the United States embraced the opposite of all the principles it espouses: such as respect for freedoms and human rights. The detention camp at Guantanamo, which the United States wanted to use to terrorize Muslims, was a shameful stain on US "democracy." The unjust arrests that affected thousands of members of the Muslim community in the United States, and which violated the detainees' most basic civil rights, forever sullied the rosy image that the United States painted of itself. The US model for justice became arrest without a specific charge, a refusal to disclose the names of detainees, pressure and torture, claims without proof, widespread monitoring of telephone conversation and e-mail, the disclosure of individual bank accounts, and secret military courts that try cases by presidential order and do not allow defendants to appeal their sentences (including death sentences).
>
> (Al-Qurashi, quoted in Aaron 2008: 220)

Although it should not be anticipated that the Al-Qaeda group, steeped in its own minority interpretation of religious doctrine, would put forward a legal analysis, this certainly represents a good understanding of the issues at stake for the legitimacy of the US government.

III International law as the framework

The cross-border nature of the conflict in which the US administration found itself had the direct effect of compelling the government to construe its own rights and duties through the framework of international law. At every turn, we find that the administration in charge of directing the global campaign of the "war on terror" was confronted with constraints of international humanitarian and UN Charter law, along with human rights laws that had been growing in quantity and specificity throughout the twentieth century.

Though there were indeed consequences for doing so, they were of a very different nature than normally supposed. By goading its adversary to overreact and to step outside the bounds of its legitimate authority, those who employ terrorism hope to inflict injury by bringing about a discernible legitimacy deficit, delegitimation, or, if possible, full illegitimacy. In this particular case, a president whose signature policy had significant problems with *legality*, *morality*, and *efficacy* (and their overlap) ended up whittling away at his own legitimacy.

There is no doubt that international law does not hold the same status as domestic law, and the absence of a unified sanctioning mechanism can certainly raise doubts in the common citizen's mind about its validity. Columbia Law School Professor Louis Henkin has even pointed out that international lawyers "have often had to defend the very existence of International Law" (cited in Slomanson 2003: 1). Thus, at first glance, it might seem odd to put international law forward as a measuring stick by which citizens judge the legitimacy of their government.

However, there is one distinctive element of 9/11 that gave it the character that must shape the way we think about and analyze this terrorism and the response to these attacks: these were cross-border terrorist attacks. Non-state actors stepped across international boundaries to conduct public and politically motivated violence against noncombatants within the foreign territory of the US. Thus, when citizens of the victim country, and even more critically the official members of the state itself, attempted to understand the rights and duties related to its response, which was inevitably to reach outside of its domestic borders, international law was the most logical and concise (not to mention the most legally fitting) framework.

It should also be remembered that the response of the "war on terror" was indeed the signature policy of the administration that was to lead the nation for the more than seven years that followed. Not only were the terrorist strikes and their aftermath caught on film and stamped into the memory of the nation's people, in reaction there were two wars launched against Afghanistan and Iraq with the US military and coalition forces, complete with embedded journalists traveling with selected military troops. Additionally, a rhetorical and real military campaign was introduced under the umbrella term the "war on terror," which seized the attention of the people who were meant to be protected by its initiation.

The very evening of September 11, 2001, President Bush addressed a grieving nation and made a commitment that the government's response would indeed be international when he stated "We will make no distinction between the terrorists who committed these acts and those who harbor them" (Bush 2001b). Within days, Congress also responded by passing the Authorization to Use Military Force (AUMF). Not only did the legislation explicitly state that the president could use military force against "nations" determined to be responsible, it also included nations that harbored the individuals or groups responsible for the attacks. Some type of international conflict was certainly at hand. On October 7, 2001, the President announced that, on his orders, the US military had begun to strike against Al-Qaeda terrorist training camps and military installations of the Taliban regime inside Afghanistan.

There were both political and legal implications to labeling this response a war. One political consequence was that the operation was given the high-profile status of a monumental clash of peoples, a grand engagement of historical importance in which the survival of the political community was at stake. This served a domestic political goal by elevating the ruling government and by making it more difficult for the opposition party to challenge it at the polls. But at the same time it propelled the tiny group of enemy terrorists onto the global stage, giving them the glory and renown they desperately sought while empowering them psychologically, and thus aiding in their efforts to recruit new members. This bellicose framing of the conflict also opened the door to the large financial outlays and institutional concentration on the military instruments needed for conventional warfare.

When an effective counterterrorism policy depends on differentiating between the guilty and the innocent so as to avoid exacerbating the conflict, feeding these emotions at home can be counterproductive as it can be extremely difficult to quarantine soldiers who are tasked with making these critical distinctions. However, making this distinction between combatants and noncombatants is the very first rule of customary international humanitarian law (Henckaerts and Doswald-Beck 2005: I, 3).

This principle of distinction between civilians and combatants is one that goes as far back as 1868, when, in the St. Petersburg Declaration, it was declared that "the only legitimate object which States should endeavour to accomplish during war is to weaken the military forces of the enemy" (cited in Henckaerts and Doswald-Beck 2005: II, 15). This is an accepted rule of both international and noninternational armed conflict and establishes the meaning behind war as a distinct concept separate from civilian violence. The US has certainly been one of the abundance of countries affirming this principle over many decades. This essential distinction first appeared in the Lieber Code of 1863, a directive signed by President Abraham Lincoln during the American Civil War, which dictated to Union forces how to conduct themselves in the armed conflict. Hence the claim that this principle of distinction represented a "cardinal" rule, made by the International Court of Justice (ICJ), certainly had deep roots (1996: 257, §78).

At the same time, very important legal implications arose from calling the campaign against terrorism a war. This legal framing meant that certain norms of international law would need to come to the center of the administration's counterterrorism policy. To understand the extent to which this impacted the "war on terror" policies, one only needs to look at the legal advice directed from the Office of Legal Counsel (OLC) to the President of the US. A young, prominent academic named John Yoo, with an expanded view of executive power, found himself in a position at the Justice Department to draft legal opinions for what is "effectively an advance pardon for actions taken at the edges of vague criminal laws" (Goldsmith 2007: 96–97).

Just two weeks after 9/11, in an opinion that was to set the tone for the counterterrorism actions to come by the Bush White House, Yoo asserted that statutes passed by Congress cannot

> place *any* limits on the President's determinations as to *any* terrorist threat, the amount of military force to be used in response, or the method, timing, and nature of the response. These decisions, under our Constitution, are for the President alone to make.
>
> (Yoo 2001; my emphasis)

In other words, it was asserted by the OLC that the President was not legally bound by the laws enacted by Congress when it comes to war. This unrestrained view of the presidency certainly helps explain why John Yoo has been called a "godsend" for an executive that was deeply concerned by any legal impediments to its action (Goldsmith 2007: 98). At the same time, while this first memo dealt primarily with the Congressional and Constitutional limits the president needed to respect (i.e. none, in the case of war), this would also have a direct and profound effect on how international legal obligations were viewed by the administration and its lawyers.

It is not uncommon for practitioners and scholars to specifically highlight the respect for a legal framework as a critical element of an effective counterterrorism campaign. In the context of the "war on terror," that legal framework would be international law. If we consider again Weber's contention that the modern state is defined by the "*monopoly of the legitimate use of physical force*," to posit no limits whatsoever would raise a significant problem even if we are speaking of force applied outside the territory.

Sir Robert Thompson, one of the key figures involved in the British military and police operation against "Communist Terrorists" in Malaya after 1948, spoke specifically of this principle when distilling the basic tenets for similar cases: "The government must function in accordance with law" (Thompson 1966: 52; cited in Roberts 2008: 20). As seen in the epigraph to this chapter, doing so was not only a moral imperative, but one that had direct implications for the effectiveness of the operation as well. In this context, that law emanates from international treaties and customs, which does not change the need for the governed to feel as though the government exercises force legitimately.

Over the past half-century, international law has grown remarkably. The number of actors on the international stage has expanded from the original fifty-one founding members of the UN in 1945 to 193 member states as of 2011. The number of codified legal instruments has also increased markedly. In addition, there has been a significant increase in the number of international organizational bodies built by legal agreement and served by diplomatic state missions, which are often mandated to collect and analyze information relating to the fulfillment of the accords. At the same time, international law has also greatly developed as a valid global structure in the minds of diplomats, civil servants, and common citizens. Therefore, it is not surprising that the administration tasked with responding to the widely televised international terrorist attacks would feel obligated to legally justify its policies within this body of law.

As the "war" proceeded constraints materialized from surprising sources. Legal requirements were imposed by the interpretation of applicable law by the US Supreme Court. The UN Charter obligation that the UNSC authorize the use of force between states (other than for self-defense) forced a public debate in the world's most prominent diplomatic forum. And even before the inception of this conflict, there was the passing of a domestic law on torture which grew out of a duty found in the UN Convention Against Torture. Thus, this work will specifically address these controls found in international legal duties on the three contentious issues of detention without judicial review, the limits on international war-making, and the prohibition of ill-treatment in interrogation.

a Detention through the lens of legality

As the war in Afghanistan began in October 2001, it quickly became necessary for the Commander in Chief of the US forces to address the issue of where and under what legal authority to detain the persons being captured in that armed conflict. On November 13, 2001, Vice President Dick Cheney brought a four-page text, which had been drafted in strict secrecy by his lawyer, to a private lunch with the President. This document meant to strip foreign terrorism suspects of access to any court. By the end of the lunch, the document had the President's authorizing signature, and at the end of the day it became an official military order. The order was designed to remove any role whatsoever from the courts (civilian, military, or international), to allow for indefinite confinement, and to restrict proceedings, if there were to be any at all, solely to closed military commissions created by the President. The document, which was to lay out some of the most important groundwork for the detention, treatment, and trial of suspects in the "war on terror," was so tightly controlled, and passed through so few hands on the way to gaining the President's signature, that

Secretary of State Colin Powell and National Security Adviser Condoleezza Rice were said to be astonished to learn about the presidential order from the television news that evening (Gellman 2008: 162–168).

This critical legal document was drafted by Cheney's lawyer, David Addington, who modeled it on the military commissions created by President Franklin D. Roosevelt to deal with saboteurs from Nazi Germany in World War II. In doing so, an issue would arise that plagued the whole legal framework of the "war on terror." Legally speaking, there was an enormous problem with relying on a six-decade old model and the 1942 Supreme Court ruling upholding it when there had been a host of intervening treaties ratified, international institutions created, and domestic law enacted. The UN Charter, the Geneva Conventions, and binding human rights law are the most obvious international examples, while a newly built Uniform Code of Military Justice (UCMJ), the War Crimes Act, and the US Torture Statute are the domestic parallel. Radical changes had occurred in both the international and domestic legal obligations, along with the expectations of citizens for their government to respect them.

The next step in constructing what has been called a "legal black hole" by a prominent judge in another jurisdiction (Lord Steyn 2004) was the December 28, 2001, memorandum drafted by Patrick Philbin and John Yoo of the OLC. They found that if the administration should choose to open a detention center at its military facility in Cuba, "the great weight of legal authority indicates that a federal district court could not properly exercise habeas jurisdiction over an alien detained at [Guantánamo Bay, Cuba]" (Philbin and Yoo 2001: 29). It is here that we begin to see the first direct recognition of the manner in which such a policy course would create legal exposure to the law of nations, since it would indeed be these laws upon which the authority is based to hold them in detention and thus allow a detainee to challenge his status and treatment under international law. Thus, the administration and its lawyers were explicitly aware of the fact that the "war on terror" would be running smack into the state's international humanitarian law obligations.

What needs to be understood is that those combatants being captured by the US and the coalition forces in the armed conflict of Afghanistan were of at least two categories: first, members of the Taliban fighting on behalf of the ruling government of the state; second, members of the non-state group Al-Qaeda found in the country and fighting since they had previously installed military training camps in territory. This is significant because it means that we are talking about two different types of armed conflict (international v. non-intentional), each of which has its own legal regime.

The first armed conflict was regarded as necessary on account of the fact that the Taliban, as the effective government of Afghanistan, refused to expel the Al-Qaeda elements found within its borders, and thus the conflict can be defined as a traditional international armed conflict falling under the legal regime of the Hague Regulations and the Geneva Conventions, as well as customary international humanitarian law.

The second armed conflict against Al-Qaeda is theoretically (albeit contentiously) not limited to the territory of Afghanistan. As non-state actors they are not a party to the Geneva Conventions, nor do they have any international legal personality. However, this does not mean that there is no law applicable to the captured members of Al-Qaeda. Under a traditional interpretation, members of the Taliban would merit the status of prisoners of war (POWs) under the Third Geneva Convention, and members of Al-Qaeda would be protected by Common Article 3 found in all four of the Geneva Conventions and, in more detail, by Article 75 of the First Additional Protocol of 1977, both as customary law.

However, in what would eventually cause an extended public uproar and rise all the way to the US Supreme Court in three landmark decisions from 2004 to 2008, this was not the legal approach taken by the Bush administration. On January 9, 2002, John Yoo co-authored another OLC memo in which the explicit discussion of international law began: "Application of Treaties and Laws to al Qaeda and Taliban Detainees" (Yoo and Delabunty 2002). Anyone who has studied international humanitarian law can immediately recognize the form of legal analysis, the questions addressed, and the references cited, demonstrating the extent to which the administration went to justify its policies within this body of law. Nonetheless, the conclusions arrived at truly test the limits of honest and professional legal analysis. The determination that there was no applicable law whatsoever to the detainees comes across as a predetermined assumption meant only for expediency.

In this OLC document, it is advised that not only are members of Al-Qaeda not covered by the Third Geneva Convention as POWs (a reasonable conclusion), but that neither are they covered by Common Article 3, which has been called the "minimum yardstick" in armed conflict by the ICJ (1986: 114, §218). What this means is that international humanitarian law has become understood as offering minimum legal protections (i.e., freedom from torture and ill-treatment and an arbitrary loss of life or punishment) to absolutely everyone held in detention in an armed conflict, regardless of that person's nationality or combatant status.

Although the authors do explicitly recognize that there has been a discernible development in the laws of war since the adoption of the Geneva Conventions in 1949 (explicitly citing the *Nicaragua* v. *United States* by the ICJ and the well-known *Tadić* case of the ICTY), the authors dismiss this "recent trend," which would confirm Common Article 3 as "a catch-all that establishes standards for any and all armed conflicts not included in common Article 2 [international armed conflict]" (see Yoo and Delabunty 2002: 46). Remarkably, the authors chose to set aside the jurisprudence of the highest courts created by the UN Charter (the ICJ) and a UNSC Resolution (the ICTY) on the exact question at stake because "the result was merely stated as a conclusion, without taking account either of the precise language of Article 3 or the background to its adoption" (Yoo and Delabunty 2002: 46, note 19). According to their argument, two lawyers in the OLC are meant to have a more authoritative interpretation of the law, its history, and its scope than either of these high courts.

Legally speaking, this assertion holds no water. Although we often think of lawyers as zealous advocates for one side of an argument, this does not describe the status or role of lawyers in the OLC. This understanding of a lawyer's role is based upon the courtroom setting, where a judge has the mandate to determine the validity of each opposing argument (which is exactly what the ICJ and the ICTY carried out in this circumstance). The lawyers of the OLC, however, are called upon to prepare legal briefs that present the requirements of the law as authoritatively understood at that time. To set aside court rulings on the specific law in question is to ethically overstep into the realm of advocacy (Clark 2005: 463–469) and carries no legal weight.

The OLC also produced a memo detailing its legal assessment of the Status of Taliban Forces under Article 4 of the Third Geneva Convention of 1949 (Bybee 2002a). In this document we see administration lawyers digging into the nitty-gritty of international humanitarian law in order to justify the exclusion of any legal protections pertaining to anyone captured in Afghanistan. The OLC lawyers had argued that al-Qaeda members were excluded from POW status and the basic protections of Common Article 3. The specifics of this particular text argue for the same result, although through a different legal provision, for Taliban forces defending the state of Afghanistan.

Article 4 of the Third Geneva Convention lays out the criteria for determining whether a member of a militia who has fallen into the hands of the enemy is entitled to POW status. It provides the scope for determining who is to benefit from the entire Third Geneva Convention, designed to protect POWs. Most importantly, the OLC concluded that "the President possesses the power to interpret treaties on behalf of the Nation," and thus that his reading of the facts would effectively remove any "doubt" that would give rise to a tribunal hearing required by Article 5 to determine the status of a detained individual. In other words, this memo found that the president's own conclusions on the facts obviate the need for any courts to become involved to check this determination of status.

The document categorizes members of the Taliban as a "militia," thus holding them responsible for fulfilling the four conditions found in Article 4(A)(2). Those conditions are:

1 falling under a command structure;
2 having a distinctive sign recognizable at a distance;
3 carrying arms openly;
4 conducts operations within the laws of war.

What is found here by the OLC is that the Taliban "militia" meet only the third condition, but this "is of little significance because many people in Afghanistan carry arms openly" (Bybee 2002a: 138). It is denied that there was a command structure organizing the Taliban (and, when this did occur, it was often Al-Qaeda who was in charge); that they wore no uniforms or clothing that would distinguish them from civilians; and that they did not follow the Geneva Conventions or any other body of law. Additionally, the OLC concluded that these four conditions, at a minimum, must be met by all members of armed forces in order for them to be legally entitled to POW status.

It should not go unnoticed that there were some within the administration who explicitly argued against the adoption of this policy. Secretary of State Colin Powell wrote a noteworthy memo opposing this course of action. In presenting the "cons" to following this advice, the retired four-star general pointed out that such a decision would not fall in line with the long-standing precedent that had been set: "It will reverse over a century of US policy and practice in supporting the Geneva Conventions and undermine the protections of the law of war for our troops, both in this specific conflict and in general" (2002: 123). As well, the highest-ranking diplomat of the nation warned that "It has a high cost in terms of negative international reaction, with immediate adverse consequences for our conduct of foreign policy" (2002: 123). On both counts, he was correct. Powell clearly understood the law and the exigencies of public diplomacy.

Nevertheless, President Bush signed an official determination on February 7, 2002, that can be considered as one of the most critical documents tracing the framework for the detention and treatment of those captured in the first military action of the "war on terror." The document, "Humane Treatment of al Qaeda and Taliban Detainees," accepted the reasoning Bush received from his lawyers in the OLC regarding international treaty obligations and instituted their conclusions as policy (Bush 2002a). The most remarkable result of this decision is that the captured detainees were to be protected by *absolutely no laws*. The administration's lawyers had directly engaged with international law, yet their conclusion was that there was no applicable law. This eventuality had been preemptively addressed most succinctly in the Commentary to the Geneva Conventions: "nobody in enemy hands can be outside the law" (Pictet 1960: Vol. IV, 51)—that is, there is no gap through which a person may slip entirely unprotected. Through the investigation of the *Rasul, Hamdan,* and *Boumediene* cases in Chapter 3 dealing with this very question, it will be possible to grasp more fully how this particular point of international law had an impact upon diplomatic relations and the legitimacy of the government.

b War-making through the lens of morality

Jus ad bellum, or the use of force in international law, underwent a significant transformation in the twentieth century when there became a shared understanding among states that military action was not an unrestricted prerogative. While theologians, philosophers, and jurists have expounded upon the contours of the "legitimate" use of force in the international arena for centuries, the Kellogg–Briand Pact of 1928, signed by more than sixty nations, was the first explicit "renunciation of war as an instrument of national policy" (1928). Also at this time, an attempt to modify the right to wage war can be found in the treaty of the League of Nations and the Permanent Court of International Justice (PCIJ). It is certainly well known that neither of these treaties stopped states from plunging into a second devastating world war. However, there is no doubt that they represent a palpable legal shift in the understanding among nations about the justifiable use of force.

When the drafters of the UN Charter met in San Francisco in 1945, the intention was to build upon the prohibition of war that had begun with the Kellogg–Briand Pact and to address some of its shortcomings. The starting point pivots on Article 2(4) of the Charter: "All Members shall refrain in their international relations from the threat or use of force against the territorial integrity or political independence of any state, or in any other manner inconsistent with the Purposes of the United Nations."

While much of the international legal literature criticized the Kellogg–Briand Pact because it referred only to "war" specifically, and thus it was thought to leave unregulated all other uses of force short of war, this provision in the new charter was meant to transcend this narrow and ambiguous term. This provision must be read in conjunction with the preceding Article, which articulates that all members "shall settle their international disputes by peaceful means," clearly laying out the first step along the path envisioned to meet the goal expressed in the Charter's Preamble of saving "succeeding generations from the scourge of war."

However, the Charter provides for two exceptions under which the use of force can be legally exercised in the international realm. The first exclusion is when force is exercised with the authorization of the UNSC under Chapter VII to address a threat to the peace, a breach of the peace, or an act of aggression. This power is granted by Article 39 of the Charter. The second exception is derived from Article 51, which deals with the "inherent right of self-defense" in the case of armed attack.

There are various points of debate and discussion on the proper interpretation of these two exceptions found in the Charter and on the use of force in general. However, the prohibition of the threat or use of force between states found in the UN Charter has indeed had an impact upon what is considered to be the legitimate use of force in international society. At the same time, it should be admitted that there is solid ground supporting the claim that these detailed limits contained in the Charter never became legally operative, or that even if initially operative they lost their legal authority over time through widespread practice of noncompliance. Yet even this acknowledgment does not mean that states are left with an unfettered discretion in using force, otherwise debate and discussion of such matters would not occur at all at the UNSC.

Regardless of this unsettled controversy, it would be disingenuous to assert that this legal transformation did not somehow have an effect upon—if not in fact emanate directly from—the devastated and threatened grassroots communities of the globe after World War II. No matter where one pinpoints its genesis, the twentieth century witnessed a distinct development in the metric tools available to peoples to measure the justifiability of military actions taken by their own governments.

However, one should not lose sight of the fact that the shared beliefs of a community concerning the difference between right and wrong, or morality, play an important role in both law and legitimacy. While the moral filiations of the use of force in the international arena can be traced back over many centuries, it has only been in more recent times that states have taken the steps to codify them as legal restraints. The relationship between morality and law has been a major piece of this age-old discussion on the use of force.

The presentation of our argument in this manner should not be misunderstood as a blunt assertion that international law is simply the formulation of some kind of universal morality. Such confusion might be expected since there was a long tradition of conceiving law as the extension of a moral code within the theory of natural law. However, what is posited here is that the specific normative nature of the arguments for the invasion of Iraq opened the door to both a moral and legal criticism of the action, and this intersection is not inherent to all international legal disputes.

The central argument for the invasion of Iraq was based on an extension of the traditional understandings of international legal limits so that an anticipatory war could be waged against a *perceived* future threat. It was this theory of a war mislabeled as "preemptive" that patently failed a moral analysis. Moreover, this doctrine became further exposed as morally vacuous when the presumption, or knowingly false assertion, that Iraq possessed weapons of mass destruction was found to be demonstrably inaccurate (Iraq Survey Group, 2004). Indeed, the intelligence for such an allegation was misrepresented to US citizens during the brusque national debate over the need for an invasion (US Senate Select Committee on Intelligence 2008). As a result of this moral and legal deficit for the invasion of Iraq, further damage was done to the legitimacy of President Bush's signature policy of the "war on terror."

The intent of this work is certainly not to confront all the realist arguments against this understanding, so it will suffice to spotlight that war between states is a very public affair. Although there is no international police force, the possibility of violence being carried out by one state upon another in some kind of private action allowing the aggressor to escape unnoticed by others is simply not a possibility given the proliferation of cameras, both of the mainstream media and otherwise, and the international forum of the UN where 193 states sit with an open panoramic view on such action. This is not to suggest that wars will no longer be fought as a result of these optics, but to clarify the point that in today's international community war must be justified, launched, and waged in plain sight. In this regard, the public nature of diplomacy has become a fait accompli.

As one particularly glaring example of the incongruent interpretation of international law put forward by the US administration, we can look to the preventive war doctrine that was advanced in the National Security Strategy (NSS) of September 2002. In it, there was what was to become an infamous discussion of anticipatory military action. The government claimed that "The struggle against global terrorism is different from any other war in our history," and thus required that the US "adapt the concept of imminent threat" (The White House 2002: 5, 19). By attempting to redefine "imminent threat" as a danger that is no longer on the brink of causing violent injury but is instead pushed temporally further out to mean a menace in the undefined future, the US administration wished to infuse the expression "preemptive attack" with the recognized meaning of "preventive war."

As a result, there is a mixing of offense and defense that has long been considered an essential distinction in just war doctrine. As it was oddly put in the 2002 NSS, "we recognize that our best defense is a good offense" (The White House 2002: 6). Considering the language of an "inherent right of self-*defense*" found in Article 51 of the UN Charter, this unambiguous contradiction is a real problem.

As to the other exception for the use of force, that of a UNSC-approved exercise of military force to address a threat to the peace, the US indeed brought its case before the Council to seek such a Chapter VII authorization in one of the most public displays of international diplomacy in contemporary times. In late 2002 and early 2003, there was a high-stakes and high-profile debate which was closely followed in the US television and print press. This UNSC discussion made clear that the launching of military action against Iraq was not a last resort, and this dialogue among the major powers explicitly demonstrated that there was undeniably a *moment for deliberation*. Additionally, the US and UK's final argument for proceeding to invade Iraq without explicit authorization from the UNSC turned on attributing to themselves the power to unilaterally bypass the "right authority" of that body. Considering that a strong majority of the population of the US initially believed that the country should only invade Iraq with UN approval and allied support (Kull *et al.* 2003/2004: 569, note 1), the decision to invade regardless of such a UNSC resolution could not have had a negligible effect upon legitimacy.

c Interrogation through the lens of efficacy

To begin to talk about the stark international illegality of ill-treatment in interrogation, one can first look to the Geneva Conventions, where we find the laws that govern armed conflict. A detainee who qualifies for POW status is required under Article 17 of the Third Geneva Convention "to give only his surname, first names and rank, date of birth, and army, regimental, personal or serial number, or failing this, equivalent information." In other words, such detainees are not obligated to provide any intelligence information whatsoever. The provision clearly states that:

> No physical or mental torture, nor any other form of coercion, may be inflicted on prisoners of war to secure from them information of any kind whatever. Prisoners of war who refuse to answer may not be threatened, insulted, or exposed to any unpleasant or disadvantageous treatment of any kind.

However, it must be understood that this Article applies only to those who qualify for POW status. This is exactly why the discussion found above in dealing with the status of detainees is also critical to the issue of interrogation. As pointed out, the presidential determination of February 7, 2002, found that neither the Taliban nor Al-Qaeda members were to qualify for POW status.

Of equal importance was the determination in this same document that neither group of detainees was covered by Common Article 3 of the Conventions. This Article, which has been upheld by the highest international courts as "the 'quintessence' of the humanitarian rules found in the Geneva Conventions as a whole" (ICTY 2001: §143) also contains an explicit prohibition on the ill-treatment of detainees. Not only are cruel treatment and torture banned, but so too are outrages upon personal dignity, particularly the use of humiliating and degrading treatment. As such, the determination that there was no applicable law for members of the Taliban or Al-Qaeda meant that none of these rules would govern their interrogation.

Douglas Feith, a high-ranking official inside the Bush administration who has taken credit for formulating this legal analysis, has spoken of the calculation that was occurring behind the scenes. According to Feith, the reasoning was based on his work going as far back as 1985 when he argued that those who did not follow the Geneva Conventions should not be allowed to take refuge in those rules. When it was pointed out to him that such interpretation meant that there would be no law controlling interrogation, he boldly responded "that's the point" (Sands 2008: 35). So, not only did this determination of the laws of war not covering captured detainees in the "war on terror" have a direct impact upon their detention at Guantánamo, it also explains the manner in which international law was employed for the questions of interrogation.

Beyond international humanitarian law, human rights law has pon-
derously and methodically placed a tightly woven web of illegality over
torture as a means for gathering information or punishing anyone
detained in custody. Torture is a form of treatment that has been excluded
in both customary and treaty-based international law in all social contexts,
and no exceptions have been made for emergency or geography. The laws
of war, the Universal Declaration of Human Rights, the International
Covenant on Civil and Political Rights, and regional human rights treaties
all provide for an absolute prohibition of the use of torture and other
cruel, inhuman, or degrading treatment in even the most difficult of
circumstances.

This particular ban has been found by human rights courts to enshrine
fundamental values for democratic societies in particular. In addition, it
has become well understood that there are no exceptions to this basic prohibition, since there can be no derogation from this protection "even
having regard to the imperatives of a public emergency threatening the
life of the nation or to any suspicion, however well-founded, that a person
may be involved in terrorist or other criminal activities" (ECtHR, *Aydin* v.
Turkey, §81). What this means in lay terms is that there is no emergency
situation that is considered so dire that this prohibition on torture can be
set aside, even momentarily, to protect the nation.

Thus, as will be seen with the issue of detention without judicial review
in Chapter 3, but to an even greater extent on the issue of torture, there is
a very important coincidence between humanitarian and human rights law
on the issue of torture and ill-treatment. This is significant because when
assessing the issue of legitimacy we need to be addressing an exercise of
power, and prohibitions thereof, that are uncomplicated and easily
grasped by citizens. That the prohibitions are common to the different
bodies of law, and thus applicable in both war and peace, demonstrates
their fundamental nature.

In the simplest and most categorical terms, the prohibition of torture
can be described as an absolute norm of *jus cogens.* This simply means that
the ban on torture is one of the most basic norms, and it can never be
ignored or unheeded. As described in a US Court of Appeals decision,
"the right to be free from official torture is fundamental and universal, a
right deserving of the highest status under international law, a norm of *jus
cogens*" (*Siderman de Blake* v. *Republic of Argentina* [1992]).

In addition to the above-cited humanitarian and human rights treaties,
the UN General Assembly adopted the Convention Against Torture in
December 1984. As a result of there being a specific treaty dealing with
the issue, the ban on torture can be placed into a particular category of
legal exclusion beyond the status of other human rights.

From 1979 until 1984, a working group of the Commission on Human
Rights developed the draft of the convention, and one of its most significant features is to provide a legal definition of the term "torture" (Rodley

with Pollard 2009: 48). This definition, which is now considered to be customary, includes four main points necessary for the liability of torture:

1   Treatment must rise to the level of *severe* physical or mental suffering.
2   It must be intentionally inflicted.
3   There must be a purpose for the inflicted pain.
4   It must occur with the consent or acquiescence of a public official.

It should be noted that there are two slight differences between humanitarian and human rights law on this question. The first is that, naturally, humanitarian law requires the existence of an armed conflict. Second, through the jurisprudence of the ICTY, it has been established that in the context of war it is not a necessary requirement to have the presence or consent of a public official.

Additionally, there are at least two more significant elements clarified by this treaty. The first is that the Committee Against Torture established by the treaty has interpreted Article 2(1), which affirms that there is an obligation to take "effective legislative, administrative, judicial or other measures to prevent acts of torture in any territory under its jurisdiction" to mean that the scope of application is not to be limited by simple territorial control. The Committee has stated that the treaty "refers to prohibited acts committed not only on board a ship or aircraft registered by a State party, but also during military occupation or peacekeeping operations and in such places as embassies, military bases, detention facilities, or other areas over which a State exercises factual or effective control" (2007, para. 16). In fact, the Committee made this very point to the US when it came to Geneva in 2006 to submit its scheduled report. In its conclusions and recommendations, the Committee stated that the US should recognize that the provisions of the treaty "apply to, and are fully enjoyed, by all persons under the effective control of its authorities, of whichever type, wherever located in the world" (2006: para. 15).

We also find that the treaty explicitly spells out the absolute nature of the prohibition in Article 2(2), where it provides that torture cannot be justified by invoking any exceptional circumstances "whatsoever, whether a state of war or a threat or war, internal political instability or any other public emergency." Nor is it possible to legally excuse torture because it came in the form of "an order from a superior officer or a public authority," as found in Article 2(3).

Article 4 of the CAT treaty requires that "[e]ach State Party shall ensure that all acts of torture are offences under its criminal law" and that such legislation "shall make these offences punishable by appropriate penalties which take into account their grave nature" (Articles 4(1) and (2) respectively). As a result, the US was under a binding legal duty to codify in its own domestic law the illegality of torture as a crime carrying grave sanction. The infamous "Bybee memo" indeed made it clear that the US legislature passed specific legislation on torture to meet its legal responsibility [18 USC §§2340–2340A]. The memo read: "Congress criminalized this conduct to fulfill US obligations under the [CAT]" (2002b: 182). Therefore, the national legal order of the US had been directly altered by international law in the case of torture, which is not a negligible point in our context.

Another important element for understanding this treaty specifically, and the international law on ill-treatment generally, is that there has come to be a legal difference between two categories: (1) torture and (2) other ill-treatment. Torture has come to be interpreted as being a *severe* form of cruel, inhuman, or degrading treatment. It was not the intention of the drafters of the Universal Declaration of Human Rights to draw this distinction. The separation of the terms grew out of a distinction over obligations and consequences to be incurred by the two different types of ill-treatment; this approach was included in the widely ratified CAT treaty. We find the definition of torture at the beginning of the treaty and later find Article 16, which deems as also illegal the other forms of ill-treatment (cruel, inhuman, and degrading) that do "not amount to torture as defined."

Considering the stark legal nature explained here, it might at first seem odd that our approach is to treat the issue of torture through the lens of efficacy. However, our intention is to investigate first and foremost the issue of legitimacy as a target of terrorism; thus, it is merited look beyond the legal context.

Regardless of the tightly woven web of illegality found in international treaty obligations, all of which have been signed and ratified by the US, the administration pried through this netting with quasi-legal tools in what have become infamous as the "torture memos." It was through this distinction between the two levels of ill-treatment (torture v. cruel, inhuman, and degrading) that John Yoo of the OLC wrenched to offer cover to the administration in the first of these memos. Despite the fact that this first document was leaked to the press and brought political scandal to the Bush administration directly in the wake of the photos of detainee abuse in the Abu Ghraib prison facility of Iraq, there would be additional memos drafted by the OLC offering legal justification for abuse of detainees during interrogation. One of the most characteristic elements of this series of memos was once again their direct engagement with international law. We find that, for the administration's lawyers to attempt to twist open a legal avenue for mistreatment of detainees, it was necessary for them to do so through the international obligations that the state had taken on by treaty. So, when these memos became public, international law was once again directly before the US population.

As such, a brief and targeted legal analysis of the "torture memos" will be carried out in Chapter 5, along with a focus on the very problematic results from the abusive interrogations authorized at the highest levels on some of the central individuals in the "war on terror." In doing so, it will be possible to spotlight the overlap of legality and efficacy on the issue of interrogation. At the same time, we will also see that by illuminating the insurmountable hurdle of a torture program being performed on the arbitrary basis of unverifiable suspicion, this will simultaneously remove the possibility of the moral argument since all contention for the use of torture being for the greater good is based upon its efficacy.

IV A legitimacy deficit and causality

In a democratic country with a free press searching for the justifications of harsh policies reaching across borders today, one can surely expect that a discussion of international legal obligations would come directly into the mainstream conversation. With the growth of public and internet-age diplomacy as its conduit, this is to be all the more expected. As the administration's policies of detention, war-making, and interrogation moved into the newspapers and television news programs as a result of Supreme Court decisions, UNSC resolutions, UN human rights reports, photographs of detainee abuse in Iraq, and the leaked "torture memos," US citizens were repeatedly confronted with the international agreements that their country had signed and ratified. Being a constitutional democracy based on the consent of the governed means that these international accords were agreed to, passed by a super-majority in the Senate, and signed by the president, all in the name of the citizens of that nation.

Given that the US was a central player in the construction of the global system that includes these limitations on the exercise of government power (Sands 2005), it is all the more understandable that citizens of that country would consider these obligations binding on their own government. So, not only did international law come before the US citizenry in a steady stream in the counterterrorism "war," they were also implicitly asked to evaluate the logic and validity of such constraints on their government as they were brought forward by public diplomacy and media coverage.

However, it must be acknowledged that there are few, if any, reliable tools for scientifically measuring the legitimacy of a government. Calculating the quantity of pull toward compliance, or tacit obedience, of millions of citizens to their government is certainly beyond our scientific capacities. As we have seen Guglielmo Ferrero say of the nature of the principles of legitimacy, they are "extremely unstable. Any philosophical hack can demonstrate their absurdity; any dictator, at the head of a gang of cutthroats, can suppress them" (1942: 314–315). Hence the *will to obey* is something that is easiest to talk about when it does not exist. When it is accepted without question, a government functions smoothly and the existence of a legitimate authority is obvious. It is when it is waning or gone that we notice.

Nevertheless, there is undoubtedly a spectrum of legitimacy that exists between a completely valid political authority and a comprehensive state of illegitimacy in which consent sufficient to run a government is no longer present from those who grant their obedience because there has been a decisive break in the societal order. It is within this range of legitimacy that we can find the state of affairs that came to exist in the US in the years after 9/11.

What will be described in this section was a less than optimal, or strained, pull toward compliance with authority identified as leaning toward the lower end of this spectrum. In line with what has been put forward by political theorist David Beetham (1991: 205–242) we shall use the terms "legitimacy deficit" and "delegitimation" to describe what followed the implementation of the policies of the "war on terror." Beetham defines the first of these terms as follows: "*legitimacy deficit* or weakness, then, is a condition of inappropriateness or inadequacy in the constitutional rules, which limits the degree of support that they, and those deriving power from them, can command" (1991: 209; my emphasis).

In this case, we will be looking at the interpretation of those rules that are found in international law due to the cross-border nature of this conflict. Beetham correlates this weakness directly to "constitutional rules" that must be followed by a person wielding authority derived from them. This is important because there is indeed an explicit connection between the US Constitution and international law since the latter is directly referred to in the former. Most specifically, international law is placed in the category of "supreme Law of the Land" in Article VI of the US Constitution, although there has long been vigorous debate over the exact meaning of this phraseology. All the same, what is certain is that international law does have a constitutional legal significance within the US system of government and citizens exercise their own will in accordance with their interpretation.[2]

The second term coming from Beetham's work—"delegitimation"—is described as

> a process whereby those whose consent is necessary to the legitimation of government act in a manner that indicates their withdrawal of consent. Mass demonstrations, strikes, acts of civil disobedience: such actions can have damaging consequences for the moral standing of a government and also its capacity to rule.
>
> (Beetham 1991: 209)

We will find that these types of events or occurrences are more extreme than what primarily occurred in the US in relation to the "war on terror." However, there have been instances in which certain actions of open dissent, particularly from the military and whistleblowers, could be described in similar terms.

One stumbling block for clearly viewing a legitimacy deficit is the fact that knowing exactly where to focus one's attention for judging a pull toward acceptance of authority can be extremely difficult. The US federal government has three separate branches, law-enforcement officers, state-department and justice-department officials, numerous additional agency workers, and the vast military forces that include the Army, Navy, Marine Corps, Air Force, and Coast Guard. At the same time, each of the fifty states has its own parallel and integrated bureaucracies of state government. Confidence in and within these many different institutions surely fluctuates from day to day for millions of different people. Thus the present work does not posit a scientific metric for measurement of this fluid, yet imperative, phenomenon. Rather, the intention here is to put forward tools for analyzing the target at which terrorism aims in order to counsel for its defense.

Consciously recognizing this difficulty, this section describes the *legitimacy deficit* that built up over a period of several years and will focus primarily on the executive who set and directed the signature policy, along with some of the legal counselors' work in advising him. Specifically, the indications of this deficit of authority will be related to former President George W. Bush. It should also be noted that this legitimacy deficit came about in the second term of President Bush's mandate. While the policies that placed the greatest stress on the three spheres of legitimacy primarily took place during the first Bush term, it was during his second mandate in office that we can most clearly discern a weakness in the pull toward compliance with his and his administration's authority. (Accordingly, Obama's second term also provides a ripe moment for similar attention.)

As a starting place, it is possible to track the polls of President Bush over his eight-year presidency (see Gallup.com 2001–2008; PollingReport.com 2001–2008). He had job-approval ratings that soared to unprecedented levels in the ninetieth percentile following the attacks of 9/11, but left office with numbers, again unprecedented, that fell into in the twentieth percentile. What this represents is an almost uninterrupted downward spiral for President Bush's time in office after his spiked numbers in the wake of 9/11. Most starkly, the CBS–*New York Times* poll scored him with a "final approval rating of 22%," which was "the lowest final rating for an outgoing president since Gallup began asking about presidential approval more than 70 years ago" (CBS News, 2009).

Of course, it must be acknowledged that there are multiple factors that contribute to the legitimacy of an executive and its policies, and the exercise of physical force is but one of them. It is a critical element, but not unique in its impact. Analysts will, and should, point to the inadequate response to Hurricane Katrina as well as the economic collapse followed by a $700-billion bank bailout with taxpayers' money. No doubt, these events also had an important impact upon President Bush's historically low poll numbers.

However, what is posited here is that the exercise of force in the trademark policy of the "war on terror" made a significant contribution to a thinning pull toward authority among the citizens of the US. Though that impact cannot be measured with precision, it was surely a significant enough difference for analysts to direct their attention in this direction so as to help explain the effects of terrorism on a society. As well, this conception can help to construct a future counterterrorism policy that does minimum damage to this target of terrorism—a policy that defends legitimacy.

The party system in a democratic government certainly makes the reading of legitimacy all the more difficult to decipher. Since the nature of party politics in a constitutional democracy is at least partially based upon the promotion of one's own party leader's authority to rule, and at the same time the invalid status of one's opponent, it is difficult to identify political dissent that represents a legitimacy deficit or weakness. Even so, although polls are blunt instruments for testing the legitimacy of an authority since they are simply snapshots in time of an ever-moving sentiment, they do serve the purpose of offering an overall impression of what is occurring. What can be thus discerned is that, from a political perspective, the President's approval rating was taking a hit as counterterrorism policies became more fully understood and discussed in the public sphere.

As a view onto this legitimacy deficit, the evidence in this section is organized into four categories, plus a final comment on causation: (1) *new diplomacy* and domestic civil society; (2) pertinent judicial judgments; (2) further declarations and actions by civil society; (4) deeds and public affirmations made by high-ranking military officers and retirees; and (5) the question of causality.

a New diplomacy and domestic civil society

As one clear example of how *new diplomacy* shaped the conversation over legitimate counterterrorism measures one can look to May 2006 when the US came before the UN Committee against Torture to explain and defend its practices in the face of growing reports of contravention of the Treaty. The US sent an oversized twenty-five-member legal team to Geneva to submit its report, and the session was held at full capacity in one of the largest conference rooms. In attendance there were numerous journalists covering (and television cameras filming) the diplomatic proceedings in an overcrowded room that was casually described by a senior official of the UN Office at Geneva as one of the "highlights of the year at the Palais des Nations" (see Figure 2.1).[3]

The legality of ill-treatment and the US defense of its actions in the "war on terror" became an issue of high-profile scrutiny in which diplomats defended the policies in a public forum. In its response to the US report, the Committee against Torture outlined twenty-four points of principal concern, including that the Guantánamo Bay facility should be

Figure 2.1 The United States before the Committee Against Torture at the United Nations Offices at Geneva, May 8, 2006.

closed and that the "State party should ensure that no one is detained in any secret detention facility under its de facto effective control. Detaining persons in such conditions constitutes, per se, a violation of the Convention" (Committee Against Torture 2006: para. 17). This latter concern was confirmed by the fact that fourteen high-value detainees were transferred to the Guantánamo facility later that year, offering dispositive proof that they had indeed been ill-treated, and the Treaty violated, by previously holding them in a secret location.

Here it is important to stress one particular aspect of this session for our purposes; although the US diplomatic mission was directed at an international audience, such a separation from domestic viewers is purely theoretical in today's information age. Public diplomacy is generally directed toward foreign nationals (Nye 2008), yet the focus of our attention here is on the way in which such public diplomacy frames the debate for citizens back home. In this book we focus attention on domestic observers and the manner in which *new diplomacy* affects more than an outside targeted audience. Considering that the US was a key advocate for the diplomatic processes that generated the international instruments of the UN Charter, the Geneva Conventions, and human rights law, it is natural that domestic citizens would frame the debate with these diplomatic and legal tools. This is to say, the public event framed by international law boomeranged back to the general public in the US via television, print, and online coverage, demonstrating just such a dynamic.

The work of one Georgetown law professor is also acutely relevant on this point. In 2012, David Cole wrote an article looking back at the extension of presidential power in the wake of the attacks of 2001 and the internal reaction to this. He points out that although there were very few reasons to believe there would be any real constraints on the president in office, the executive branch of the most powerful nation in the world was somehow compelled to adapt its response. What is most interesting is the argument he constructs and defends to explain this result. While much attention is often on the separate powers of government checking and balancing each other in a constitutional democracy, Cole posits that there was a "civil society constitutionalism" at play in which nongovernmental organizations advocated, both inside and outside of judicial formats, for an adherence to the rule of law. Along with the more traditional pressure applied in courts (explored here in Chapter 3), Cole also identifies a coordination "with foreign governments and international nongovernmental organizations to bring diplomatic pressure to bear on the United States to conform its actions to constitutional and international law" (2012: 1205). Thus we find that some scholars indeed find and present empirical evidence for a manner in which the *new diplomacy* penetrates into domestic society to affect policy and legitimacy.

b Pertinent judicial decisions

As we will see in detail in Chapter 3, there were a series of relevant rulings by the US Supreme Court which can be understood as a reflection of sentiment emanating from the general public or even a delegitimizing force on the executive branch of the government and its policies of the "war on terror." These decisions dealt directly with the legality of the president's authority, and methodically and repeatedly struck down assertions of broad powers outside of US territory in times of armed conflict. Most significantly, this was proposed by the administration to be possible without any interference from the judiciary. Just as some commentators have suggested that rulings of the highest courts of a nation can be seen as a legitimizing force for an executive and its policies, it is suggested here that the inverse is also true. When the Supreme Court explicitly rules against the executive and its assertion of powers in high-profile cases, the result can be that it is a delegitimizing force on the policies. As an important contributing force to legitimacy, citizens who are asking the question of whether a government is exercising its power legally, there is little that can be more dispositive than a judgment from the highest court in the land. When this happens in succession, and on the same primary question of an overreach of executive power, the result is all the more impactful upon the pull toward compliance.

It should be noted that the Supreme Court was extremely cautious and measured in this series of decisions which would question the authority of the president during a time of armed conflict. Since there has been a traditional deference to the political branches in times of conflict, the methodical approach of the Court is all the more noteworthy. In fact, it was the first time in the Court's history that it ruled against the President and Congress acting together in a time of armed conflict (Cole 2008). Considering this, it would be peculiar to suggest that the Court aimed to undermine the legitimacy of the government. Nonetheless, it is an exaggeration to argue that this series of decisions had zero impact upon citizens judging legitimacy.

c Further civil dissent

There were a number of occurrences emanating from civil society that demonstrated a palpable discontent and restlessness. For example, there were debates in the mainstream press over whether President Bush was the worst president in US history (Neuharth 2007; Wilentz 2006). The highest grossing political documentary of all time, bringing in an unprecedented $119 million inside the US (outperforming the second-place film by nearly three times), was the Michael Moore film *Fahrenheit 9/11* (Box Office Mojo 2013). In addition, there were raucous public protests (Dwyer 2007; Hummel 2007; Zhou 2007), calls for resignations when officials from the administration appeared at public events (Almond 2006), and open calls for impeachment.

In 2005, Representative John Conyers argued for setting up "a select committee to investigate the Administration's intent to go to war before congressional authorization, manipulation of pre-war intelligence, encouraging and countenancing torture, retaliating against critics, and to make recommendations regarding grounds for possible impeachment" (cited in Lapham 2006; see also Carlson 2006). This call for impeachment endured and grew, and in early 2008 human rights lawyer Scott Horton wrote,

> Polling now shows that a large majority of Americans believe that President Bush and Vice President Cheney have committed serious transgressions against the Constitution which would merit consideration of the impeachment process. Impeaching President Bush and Vice President Cheney for their attempts to hijack the Constitution would make a clear statement about abuse of power.
>
> (Horton 2008)

The most significant action in pursuit of this course was the introduction of thirty-five articles of impeachment in the House of Representatives by Dennis Kucinich and co-sponsor Robert Wexler, which was eventually signed by ten other Representatives. These are surely paltry numbers demonstrating an uphill political battle, but nonetheless they demonstrate a weakening of legitimacy. Even so, it is important to recognize that there have been a total of twelve presidents out of forty-four who have had articles of impeachment introduced against them.

Next, although the evangelical community was a critical base of support for President Bush, in March 2007 the Board of Directors of the National Association of Evangelicals, representing some 30 million US citizens in about 45,000 churches, endorsed a landmark document: "An Evangelical

Declaration against Torture: Protecting Human Rights in an Age of Terror" (Evangelicals for Human Rights 2007). The document is an interesting mélange of ideas with discussions of both the Christian commitment to the sanctity of human life through specific references to the Bible and detailed citations of pertinent international law on torture. Cited in the flow of news reports that emerged after its release, the declaration boldly states that "[t]he boundaries of what is legally and morally permissible in war have been crossed in the current 'war on terror'" (2007: para. 6.10). While the document was said to be a moral and theological statement, the fact that the scholars also chose to reach for international law in addition to the Bible to bolster their arguments is certainly noteworthy in the context of this work.

d Military dissent

There was also dissent and resistance within the military. Those entrusted with the security of the nation and beholden to the command structure also found reason to oppose elements of the "war on terror." There were even actions that could fall into the category of disobedience, which would point beyond a legitimacy deficit and toward delegitimation. However, due to the top-down nature and structure of the military, dissent is difficult to recognize. Therefore, it was often retired military officers who began to voice to the public wider institutional concerns about the missions the military was carrying out. One expression of this military opposition can be found in a public radio address by retired General William Odom, calling the president absent without leave, or "AWOL," and condemning his handling of the war in Iraq because it is "squandering its [US] influence, money, and blood, and facilitating the gains of our enemies" (Odom 2007).

Additionally, there was a television ad campaign launched by VoteVets. org, an act of defiance not seen in decades. One of the most pointed commercials featured retired Major General John Batiste, a former commanding general in Iraq. The military officer bluntly stated, in response to a clip of President Bush claiming that he will always listen to his generals on the ground,

> Mr. President, you did not listen. You continue to pursue a failed strategy that is breaking our great Army and Marine Corps. I left the Army in protest in order to speak out. Mr. President, you have placed our nation in peril.
>
> (Tapper 2007)

A military officer openly and publicly expressing his view that the Commander in Chief has placed "our nation in peril" is extremely strong language from a convincing source.

In that same spring of 2007, the *Washington Post* published an opinion piece in its editorial pages by Charles C. Krulak, a commandant of the Marine Corps from 1995 to 1999, and Joseph P. Hoar of US Central Command from 1991 to 1994. This op-ed, "It's Our Cage Too: Torture Betrays Us and Breeds New Enemies," spoke to the dangers for US armed forces when the civilian commanders authorize the use of ill-treatment for interrogation purposes. The authors of the piece clearly acknowledged that their experience in combat taught them that fear can indeed wreak havoc if left unchecked, and they insisted that the politicians had an obligation "to lead the country away from the grip of fear, not into its grasp" (Krulak and Hoar 2007).

Also, they made specific reference to a policy that was seeping into the consciousness of citizens: a "secret CIA interrogation program in which torture techniques euphemistically called 'waterboarding,' 'sensory deprivation,' 'sleep deprivation,' and 'stress positions'—conduct we used to call war crimes—were used" (Krulak and Hoar 2007). Coming from retired military, this certainly gave credibility to the spreading accusations of a practice that citizens were hesitant to accept as having been carried out on behalf of their own security. This is not to mention the fact that these former military officers explicitly argued against the efficacy of employing ill-treatment for intelligence-gathering.

One published newspaper article traces a bit of the history of military dissent in the US in wartime and what was happening in 2007 and called it "The Revolt of the Generals." The journalist wrote,

> In op-ed pieces, interviews and TV ads, more than 20 retired US generals have broken ranks with the culture of salute and keep it in the family. Instead, they are criticizing the commander in chief and other top civilian leaders who led the nation into what the generals believe is a misbegotten and tragic war.
>
> (Sauer 2007)

The piece went on to explain that it is rare for members of the military to speak out at all, and that retired military officer Andrew Bacevich has said that some of the officers during the Vietnam war regret not having spoken up at that time. Bacevich also suggested that this was perhaps part of the reason why there were more US military officers willing to step up when they believed grave mistakes were being made. Nevertheless, regardless of the historical precedents and contemporary reasoning, it was surely significant to the legitimacy of the authority in the US that members of the armed forces stood up and publicly criticized the administration.

In 2008, there was an official report released by the nongovernmental organization Physicians for Human Rights entitled *Broken Laws, Broken Lives: Medical Evidence of Torture by US Personnel and Its Impact*. Of consequence here is the fact that the preface to the report was written by retired Major General Antonio Taguba, who had particularly intimate knowledge of US interrogation policies and their impact because he had led the US Army's official investigation into the Abu Ghraib prisoner-abuse scandal and testified before Congress with his findings in May 2004. This military officer introduces the report by saying that it is to detail the largely untold human story of what happens "when the Commander-in-Chief and those under him authorized a systematic regime of torture" (Taguba 2008). He went on to explain that,

> In order for these individuals to suffer the wanton cruelty to which they were subjected, a government policy was promulgated to the field whereby the Geneva Conventions and the Uniform Code of Military Justice were disregarded. The UN Convention Against Torture was indiscriminately ignored. And the healing professions, including physicians and psychologists, became complicit in the willful infliction of harm against those the Hippocratic Oath demands they protect.
>
> After years of disclosures by government investigations, media accounts, and reports from human rights organizations, there is no longer any doubt as to whether the current administration has committed war crimes. The only question that remains to be answered is whether those who ordered the use of torture will be held to account.
>
> (Taguba 2008)

Such a bold and unwavering accusation, with direct links to the international laws that were defied, reflected Major General Taguba's own loss of confidence in his former commander in chief. This harsh, public accusation of criminal conduct from a man who had been called upon to personally investigate the evidence of such war crimes surely also caused those who read the one-page statement or heard reports on it to reflect upon and question the legitimacy of the authority in charge.

Although it is enormously difficult to definitively prove an act of disobedience taking place within the military chain of command since direct orders are not usually public knowledge, perhaps one of the most intriguing examples of such conduct are the statements by Major General Peter Pace, the Joint Chiefs of Staff in early 2007. On February 11 of that year a briefing was given by anonymous US military officials in Baghdad, alleging that the highest level of the Iranian government had directed the use of weapons that had killed US troops in Iraq, and the White House spokesman confirmed this to be the administration's accusation (Associated Press 2007). The following day, on the other side of the world from Washington, DC, in press conferences in Australia and Indonesia, General Pace "demurred" and said that he had no information to indicate that Iran's government was directing the supply of lethal weapons to Shiite insurgent groups in Iraq (Deyoung 2007). It would seem unlikely that these statements, which directly contradict an earlier military briefing to the press, were authorized by civilian leadership above him. Only months later, in a "surprise decision," General Pace was replaced without retiring (Fox News 2007).

e Causality

Throughout the next three chapters, it will be shown that not only did the US government cross lines of international law, but that the portions of these legal lines that were transgressed also held significance in the realms of morality and efficacy. Consequently, our thesis is that there was indeed a cost at the domestic level, even if there was no clear sanction by the international community. The violated norms were so fundamental that a significant portion of the US population had doubts about their tacit compliance with the government carrying out such policies, and thus a legitimacy deficit was suffered that made it more difficult for the governing system to operate smoothly.

This would appear to be one of the more interesting consequences of the grand proliferation of international law since the end of World War II. The explicit commitment by a government to adhere to certain constraints, and the wide dissemination of them to the common citizens of states who are a party to the pertinent treaties, has meant that Weber's *"legitimate use of physical force"* would appear to be extending beyond borders.

The presentation of our work in this manner raises questions that lead to some of the most difficult problems of causality. Even if this author were competent enough to resolve such complex questions, this work is not the place to do so. As such, it should be recognized that this is not a work of teleology, if only partially because it is not believed that final causes always exist or are provable in human relations. Thus the intention is not to provide dispositive proof of how international law has penetrated the minds of sufficient numbers of US citizens for it to have had an effect upon its judgments of legitimacy. This is a work of political philosophy and international law that will instead focus on two other primary goals. The first has been to present the concept of legitimacy and its three primary components of *legality*, *morality*, and *efficacy* as a target of terrorism.

Next is the application of this analytical tool. The intention is to present how the three issues of detention, war-making, and interrogation, as carried out in the "war on terror," flesh out using these three lenses. There is little doubt that the detail in which this will be done is beyond the understanding of ordinary citizens' comprehension of international law. However, the detail used here does not negate the fundamental nature of the prohibitions.

Another issue that arises when speaking to the question of causality is whether this work is meant to address the way things actually are or the way things should be. This is, of course, an important question which can be traced back at least as far as the eighteenth century, to philosopher

David Hume, who wrote about the significant and often overlooked "is vs. ought" problem in *A Treatise of Human Nature* (2006: Book III, Part I, Section I, 257). Although our work does not deal solely with the issue of morality, it is necessary to treat the question of whether this text is meant to be descriptive or normative.

This work is based on rigorous research and it is presented as accurately as possible. This is attested to by the citations of and referencing to all measure of documents ranging from court decisions to government and nongovernment reports, treaties, newspapers, television, radio, online reports, and a great number of academic articles and books. Therefore, the starting point of this work is indeed descriptive.

At the same time, this next irresolvable question of definitive causality in human relations makes it problematic to assert that this work is solely descriptive. In other words, the hypothesis that it is the overlapping spheres of *legality, morality,* and *efficacy* that construct the legitimacy of an authority, and that it is being targeted by terrorists, runs into the inevitable problem that no scientific testing exists to examine this question. The problem produced by the complexity of human relations is well delineated by Guglielmo Ferrero in his work on legitimacy:

> In a universe which is governed by the law of causality, the human mind is alone distinguished by its freedom [...]. One man will react quite differently from another to the same circumstances; the same man will not necessarily react tomorrow as he reacts today.
>
> (1942: 309)

Of all the more consequence is the fact that in this book we are speaking of a great abundance of individuals interacting with each other, each one with his own free will, so collective reactions will seem all the more capricious and difficult to anticipate with absolute certainty. As Ferrero keenly continued,

> This is why no science of the mind and of history analogous to the science of matter and nature has been formulated; one is even forced to consider whether the word "science" can be applied in the same sense to the physical and intellectual life of men, to the chemistry and history of societies.
>
> (1942: 309)

Due to the inherent, insurmountable hurdle of confirming causality in the ebb and flow of legitimacy, this part of the work is best understood as normative. Simply stated, we will investigate the *legality, morality,* and *efficacy* of the most controversial counterterrorism policies instituted in the "war on terror" using the hypothesis that these three components have a direct impact upon the legitimacy of the government. To establish their relationship to legitimacy, we ground our argument in reasoning and logic, following the tradition of political and legal philosophy, rather than turning to the less suitable scientific and statistical tools of political science.

Even if it is not possible to measure with precision the number of people using *legality, morality,* and *efficacy* as measurement tools of legitimacy, there is strong evidence that significant numbers of citizens, ever increasing, indeed do. Therefore, while there can be justified squabbling over how great of an impact this has upon a society, the existence of the rational testing of legitimacy by members of society is less of a question if we accept Habermasian theory. This brings us back to the query of whether this is better understood as a descriptive or normative work; the direct response is that the treatment of the existence of a rational testing of legitimacy is descriptive, while its quantitative importance is normative.

V Conclusion

Recent military doctrine has posited *legitimacy* as the central front in insurgency. Unfortunately, these military principles are largely centered on how legitimacy should be constructed in the theaters where invasions have been launched, and they do not discuss the protection of the legitimacy of the government at home. Since the military is subordinate to the political branches, and this conflict is in essence a political struggle, it is not surprising that the officers of the armed services do not provide answers for defending the legitimacy of US authority in the eyes of its citizens.

Nonetheless, Army Field Manual 3–24 did provide a historical example of how *legality* and *morality* (and, as we will see in Chapter 5, *efficacy*) can strike at the heart of legitimacy. The manual provided a vignette on the battle of Algiers which dovetails perfectly with our own theory:

> **Lose Moral Legitimacy, Lose the War**
> During the Algerian war of independence between 1954 and 1962, French leaders decided to permit torture against suspected insurgents. Though they were aware that it was against the law and morality of war, they argued that—
>
> - This was a new form of war and these rules did not apply.
> - The threat the enemy represented, communism, was a great evil that justified extraordinary means.
> - The application of torture against insurgents was measured and nongratuitous.
>
> (US Army 2006: 7–9)

This official condoning of torture on the part of French Army leadership had several negative consequences. It empowered the moral legitimacy of the opposition, undermined the French moral legitimacy, and caused internal fragmentation among serving officers that led to an unsuccessful coup attempt in 1962. In the end, failure to comply with moral and legal restrictions against torture severely undermined French efforts and contributed to their ultimate loss, despite significant military victories. Illegal and immoral activities made the counterinsurgents extremely vulnerable to enemy propaganda inside Algeria among the Muslim population, as well as in the UN and the French media. These actions also degraded the ethical climate throughout the French Army. France eventually recognized Algerian independence in July 1963.

If we contemplate the use of public and political violence by non-state actors directed at noncombatants to provoke an overreaction as targeting legitimacy, this reading of the history of the Algerian war begins to make sense; every authority is obligated to abide by certain rules and norms to maintain the obedience of its subordinates. In the following three chapters we will successively apply the lenses of legitimacy as an analytical tool to explore this question of an uncoerced pull towards compliance.

Notes

1 UN General Assembly Resolutions 48/122 (1993); 49/185 (1994); 50/186 (1995); 52/133 (1997); 56/160 (2001); 58/174 (2003); Vienna Declaration (1993); and UN Office of the High Commission of Human Rights Resolutions 2001/37, 2003/37 and 2004/44.
2 It should be noted that there is surely a portion of the population who does not subscribe to this type of legitimacy testing in the least. This portion of the population is described by Walter Russell Mead in his article "The Jacksonian Tradition" (1999/2000). However, the recognition of this portion of the population as he describes them does not negate the existence of those who do test legitimacy as described here.
3 Account and photography comes from the author's personal attendance of the session.

3 Through the lens of legality

Detention without judicial review[1]

Legality

As judgments in different countries increasingly build on each other, mutual respect and dialogue are fostered among appellate courts. Judges around the world look to each other for persuasive authority, rather than some judges being "givers" of law while others are "receivers." Reception is turning to dialogue.

(Heureux-Dubé 1998: 17)

I Introduction

To initiate the application of our model of legitimacy we will begin with the lens of legality. To be sure, it is difficult to arrive at definitive conclusions about the illegality of a policy, even if the highest court in the land has ruled it so. It is extremely likely that there will be dissenting opinions, and thus fully extinguishing the argument for the legality of a policy is nearly impossible. Therefore, as will be the case throughout this work, we will speak to degrees of legality and not all-or-nothing conclusions. With that said, what we will find in this chapter on the issue of detention without judicial review is that in three separate cases, using different bodies of law each time, the US Supreme Court ruled that the administration and the Congress had overstepped the bounds of legality, thus affecting the legitimacy of the policy and the regime employing it. Nonetheless, we will also see that under a new president the Supreme Court has fallen silent on this question, after having boldly stepped into the fray.

Much of the original analyses put forward on the "war on terror"—whether on the use of abusive interrogation methods, a broadening of the rules governing the use of force, or the conditions of detention—concluded that this behemoth in global affairs abandoned its international legal obligations by analyzing domestic and international laws as inapplicable to their circumstances. However, it is suggested here that this characterization of the US can be understood as an oversimplification that obscures the more subtle role of the judiciary. The executive branch of the US is responsible for conducting military operations and executing the laws of the nation. As well, we know that international legal obligations are not contingent on the inner workings of a government or on internal law (*Vienna Convention on the Law of Treaties*, Article 27). Yet an analysis overlooking the interplay of all three branches of government would be incomplete. For a fuller discussion of the legitimacy of a policy it is necessary to widen our purview to delve into the work of the highest national court and how it managed the interaction with the executive and the legislature on the issue of wartime detention.

As explained in the previous chapter, the executive branch attempted to entirely exclude the judiciary from playing any role in the "war on terror" when the President signed the military order brought to him in a private lunch by the Vice President shortly after the invasion of Afghanistan. The order was intended to remove all courts (civilian, military, or international), to permit indefinite internment, and to limit all proceedings (if there were to be any at all) solely to the closed military commissions created by the President. This certainly is one of the reasons why two years after the opening of the Guantánamo detention center some notable jurists from other national jurisdictions began to publicly refer to this facility as a "legal black hole" (Lord Steyn 2004: 1). Due to the complete absence of applicable law, Guantánamo became a real diplomatic problem for the administration. If we understand "diplomacy in terms of international legal justification," it is easy to understand why (Hurd 2011: 581).

Because the administration leaned heavily on international law for framing its policies, a broader view is particularly important in the US where the internal assessments over international obligations are often seen, rightly or wrongly, through its constitutional structure (see, for example, Bianchi 2004b). This founding document divides the powers of government into three branches, and the result has many times been a passing along of the state's international legal duties with each branch maintaining a plausible lack of responsibility. More recently, a manner in which national courts have dealt with this similar difficulty is by employing a "judicial ladder of review" meant to prompt an interbranch dialogue with the court playing the role of moderator. This chapter will analyze a series of cases that came before the Supreme Court of the US (*Rasul,*

Hamdan, and *Boumediene*) relating to pertinent international norms in the "war on terror," and which can simultaneously be found in domestic and constitutional law. Because certain fundamental rules are codified across different types of law, courts have found a novel way of late to provide protections for individuals across borders and regardless of citizenship by moderating such an institutional dialogue.

Through this investigation, we will see that the US Supreme Court indeed prompted an interbranch colloquy with the executive and legislature in an attempt to affect the final legal policies of the nation. While the other branches of government implemented policies and passed legislation that poorly interpreted the applicable law, the highest national court methodically employed this novel judicial tool and took the historic step of eschewing the traditional deference shown by courts in times of armed conflict. In so doing, the Supreme Court was measured, patient, and resolute in its push back against the effective removal of judicial review for those held in detention at Guantánamo in the "war on terror." Ultimately, this series of formal legal rulings from the highest court in the land reflected a diminished, and perhaps even played a role in further eroding, legitimacy for the policy and the authority that employed it.

By exploring the series of Supreme Court decisions between 2004 and 2008 together, rather than individually, a much fuller picture will be provided of how rights found in various categories of law, including international norms, played a role in the dialogue between the various branches of government. It was not too long ago that legal analysts pointed to a reticence of national courts to apply international law in the domestic setting so as to avoid any clash with the executive and thus to afford latitude in foreign affairs (see Benvenisti 1993). However, more recently national courts have shown a growing propensity for a cross-fertilization of sources and jurisprudence, face-to-face meetings of judges in seminars, and increased citation of international law in their judgments.

Of course, this judicial globalization of sorts has not been a strongly identifiable vein in the US Supreme Court's work. Nevertheless, one can see its influence in a passionate debate on the subject of the recourse to foreign and international law in another recent decision discussed below. Through an analysis of a series of more recent Supreme Court decisions dealing with the "war on terror" it will become clear that there has been a discernable tack in the direction of this global judicial trend. This is certainly not to say that the court has warmly embraced a global judicial community and has taken up a place at this table. Rather, it is to demonstrate that a fundamental international norm in play during counterterrorism efforts has indeed been consistently interpreted to be applicable through the use of various judicial tools, thus shining a light on the US Supreme Court's current views of, and struggles over, international law.

Traditionally, there has been great deference granted to the executive branch by national courts in times of conflict (see Benvenisti 2004:

309–315; Scobbie 2008).[2] Yet, in the current conflict, something different occurred when cases relating to the administration's legal reasoning over detention and judicial review came before the US Supreme Court. Starting in 2004, the court began to push back against the Bush administration by asserting its own institutional competence in the *Rasul* v. *Bush* decision, on domestic statutory grounds, to hear habeas corpus challenges to the detention of foreign nationals captured abroad in connection with hostilities. In this same term, eight out of nine justices held in *Hamdi* v. *Rumsfeld* that the executive branch did not have the authority to indefinitely hold a US citizen on national territory without affording the rights of due process enforceable through habeas corpus, though no single opinion commanded a majority. Under quite different reasoning by the justices, the court roundly rejected the administration's contention that it possessed a wide authority to detain persons under its constitutional commander-in-chief powers.

Looking at the positioning of the Supreme Court after the term ended in 2004, it would certainly be difficult to conclude that it was acting as any type of protectorate of human rights or international humanitarian law. While the decisions indeed treated norms that exist in international law, but explicitly using domestic statutory law, they were limited and left a wide margin of flexibility to the other two branches of government to alter its course without insuring an adherence to international obligations by the state. The court had simply examined and ruled on whether the executive had been given, either through the Constitution or through statute, the institutional competence to act as it had in the specific circumstances.

However, if we take into account the continued trajectory of case law before the Supreme Court dealing with detention in the "war on terror," it is possible to discern what has been called an "emerging judicial theory" in a conceivably globally coordinated move. International jurist Eyal Benvenisti has theorized a "judicial ladder of review" (2008b) which can be distinguished and charted in the recent rulings of national courts in various jurisdictions. The author briefly sketches initial steps of the Guantánamo decisions in the US concerning detention and judicial review and put forward his theory before the *Boumediene* case was decided in June 2008. This framework of a five-step ladder is enormously useful for explaining the progression of cases dealing with counterterrorism that have come before the US Supreme Court. As we will see, the cases are best understood by discussing them together as a series of jurisprudence rather than as isolated cases. Therefore, this theoretical structure will frame our analysis so as to delve deeper into the ascension of review that the judiciary climbed in its moderating of a dialogue with the other branches of government.

At this point it is useful to provide an outline of Benvenisti's "judicial ladder of review" and to exhibit how it allows the court the ability to moderate an interbranch dialogue. This framework is based on the proposition that the judiciary prefers to affect final policy with a low profile and with as little intrusion as possible. To do so, it aims to engage the legislature as a potential ally in the task of containing the exercise of authority by the executive. Yet, if it is unable to manifest a partner to share the burden, the court holds the option of ascending the ladder alone. The intent is for the judicial branch to encroach upon the executive's authority as little as possible during a time of conflict, and thus it tailors its responses to the political circumstances and opts for a more deliberative process involving all three branches. However, it should not be overlooked that it is the judiciary that holds the tools to manage this process and thus chooses how and when to ratchet up or down the ladder according to its own assessment.

The five rungs of the "judicial ladder of review" are constructed as follows:

1   The least controversial technique is for the judiciary to refer an action back to the executive for reconsideration.
2   The next rung of the ladder is to address domestic statutes so as to call for legislative clarification of the executive's authority to act.
3   Subsequently, the judiciary may refer to substantive limitations found in international treaty obligations (one of the more interesting facets of this ladder, because it was not that long ago that courts shied away from its reference) thus constraining executive and legislative discretion.
4   If the bench is still not satisfied with the outcome, it may invoke constitutional restrictions on specific parts of a legislation but allow for re-legislation.
5   Finally, and ultimately, the court may well ascend to the height of this ladder and rule a measure utterly infringing upon constitutional safeguards and thus beyond the scope of authority of either branch.

As this chapter is to be a view of legitimacy through the lens of legality, we will analyze the progression of engagement by the US Supreme Court with the other branches of government over executive detention without judicial review. Section II of this chapter will put the US Supreme Court's current international engagement into a brief historical context and will then lay out the many different questions of international legality, from the perspective of both humanitarian and human rights law, raised by holding persons without access to any sort of judicial review. Section III investigates the *Rasul* decision and looks at the manner in which a unique familiarity with previous case law gave one Supreme Court justice an intimate knowledge of the controlling jurisprudence that ultimately had an important impact upon the judgment. Next, Section IV will investigate the court's direct use of humanitarian law in the *Hamdan* decision and its distinctive interpretation of Common

Article 3 to rule on the applicability of a portion of the Geneva Conventions to the "war on terror." Section V will assess the *Boumediene* decision and discuss it as a human rights' advancement in substance, even if the decision was based on constitutional law. At the same time, it will address the lamentable missed opportunity for creating a more harmonious concert between constitutional and human rights law. Section VI will then look into how the various branches have dealt with the question of legitimate detention during the Obama administration's first term in office while the Supreme Court has opted to remain on the sidelines. Lastly, Section VII will conclude with the relevance of detention under a new strategy and what diplomatic implications this portends. As a result, we will arrive at a sharpened view of the issues of legality, with the policy of detention repeatedly declared outside of the law, and thus having a direct impact upon legitimacy.

II The US and international law

In this section, we will illuminate the competing judicial philosophies within the Supreme Court on the status of international and foreign law in the US. Courts have long taken the view that their interpretation of international obligations found in treaties must be seen through the Constitution. What this has often meant is that it has been possible to pass the responsibility for upholding international obligations between the branches of government because of their divided functions, or in this case out of the hands of the judiciary. Next we will present an overview of the applicable international law at stake when holding individuals without judicial review at a US military facility in Guantánamo Bay, Cuba.

a Transnational judicial dialogue and the US Supreme Court

Recently, there has been increased scholarship and attention to the growing phenomenon of national courts engaging in what has been likened to a judicial globalization (see, for example, Benvenisti 2008a; Jackson 2004; McCrudden 2000; Slaughter 2003, 2004: 65–103). That is to say, judges from different national jurisdictions are speaking with one another and exchanging judicial views, participating in seminars and judicial organizations together, and citing each other's work in their own opinions. This growing tendency is not limited to transnational discourse; it also includes deepening interactions with regional and international counterparts. Constitutional courts the world over have also taken to citing ECtHR decisions, regardless of whether they are themselves a part of its jurisdiction. As another example, the International Criminal Court (ICC) and the NAFTA treaty are built on the premise that there will be a direct relation between national and international tribunals. A very interesting and useful way of conceptualizing this transnational judicial dialogue has been put forward by Anne-Marie Slaughter. She suggests that we can best understand these connections spanning national borders and oceans as a something similar to the globe hoisted by Atlas at Rockefeller Center, or a web of intersecting and expanding networks. The image of solid and real, yet not total, connections between all parts of the globe provides an effective visual for grasping nascent international—and, in this case, judicial—connections that demonstrate some current attempts at solving problems which cannot be resolved by individual and entirely autonomous nations (Slaughter 2004: 1–35).

Expanding on what is expressed in the epigraph to this chapter, over a decade and a half ago former Justice of the Supreme Court of Canada, Claire L'Heureux-Dubé, wrote about her view of the "globalization of the judicial world" and addressed the manner in which the highest court in the US fit into this mushrooming phenomenon. The observation from her advantaged perspective was that, "[m]ore and more courts [...] are looking to the judgments of other jurisdictions, particularly when making decisions on human rights issues" (Heureux-Dubé 1998: 16). While there have historically been particular courts that served as hubs, particularly during the colonial era, this hierarchy has now shifted into a different form. Justice Heureux-Dubé wrote "as courts look *all* over the world for sources of authority, the process of international influence has changed from *reception* to *dialogue*" (1998: 17; original emphasis). Acknowledging the difficulty of a scientific assessment, she believed that the US Supreme Court was having a declining impact upon this international dialogue between jurisdictions.

The possible benefits of comparing constitutional and statutory protection, along with how international legal obligations play a role in individual jurisdictions, through such judicial dialogue are numerous. It offers forthright discussion of the hurdles to safeguarding shared concepts that exist in many constitutions of the world (in somewhat varied circumstances), such as dignity, freedom, and equality. Through such evaluation with foreign counterparts, judges can gain a sharpened insight into their own systems or provisions as to why they might already work reasonably well in certain areas or need improvement in others. Comparative study can also make up for the long experience of constitutionalism that only some countries possess. On the matter of potential benefits, we can also look to the words of an unexpected source: former Chief Justice Rehnquist of the US Supreme Court. He explained that "the real value of [these] reciprocal visits is in establishing face-to-face contact with judges in another country who, despite the differences between our judicial systems, face many of the same problems faced by federal judges in the United States" (2002).

Additionally, it should be pointed out that such dialogue does not portend a homogenous result. Thus, another benefit from such structured and unstructured interaction is also that of "informed divergence" (Slaughter 2004: 181–183) in which judges consciously choose a different route than their colleagues. This can be due to the particular circumstances of their jurisdiction or to the case directly before them. Thus, as a result of such dialogue, they may choose to put forward their reasoned choice of departure.

While the US Supreme Court has been identified as one court that in some ways operates outside this burgeoning network, partially due to a sense of obligation to democratic autonomy, it cannot be said that the entire court persists upon such a path. Some commentators have described the opinion of the court on this issue as being split between two philosophical branches of thought. The appointments to the court of Chief Justice Roberts and Justice Alito have been characterized as solidifying an inward-looking alliance on constitutional interpretation with Justice Thomas and Justice Scalia. Meanwhile, Justice Kennedy now finds himself to be a swing vote on certain issues and has shown willingness to consider judgments from other jurisdictions as persuasive. Typifying the inclination of those opposed to consultation with outside sources for interpretation of the US Constitution are the words of Justice Thomas in a concurrence denying certiorari in 2002 of the *Foster* v. *Florida* case: "this court's [...] jurisprudence should not impose foreign moods, fads or fashions on Americans" (p. 990).

However, the court does indeed participate in formal exchanges with its counterpart across the Atlantic, the European Court of Justice, and has visited its equivalents in Mexico, Germany, France, England, and India. Additionally, there are statements that can be pointed out by members of the court, from the other side of the philosophical divide, which indicate a conviction that examining foreign sources of law, along with international law, will serve to benefit the depth of their own decision-making and opinions.

In 2003, Justice Breyer addressed the American Society of International Law and spoke to the historical views of justices of the Supreme Court. He said that many on the court hold "a view that now extends beyond public international law to embrace foreign law and legal institutions as well" (Breyer 2003). Justice Ginsburg, even more recently, expounded her view that,

> if US experience and decisions can be instructive to systems that have more recently instituted or invigorated judicial review for constitutionality, so we can learn from others including Canada, South Africa, and most recently the UK – now engaged in measuring ordinary laws and executive actions against charters securing basic rights.
>
> (Ginsburg 2006)

One case in which we can see very clearly these separate factions in direct duel is in the 2005 opinions of *Roper* v. *Simmons*. The case dealt with a defendant who had committed murder when he was seventeen years old and was then sentenced to death after he had turned eighteen. The Court held, on various grounds, that the Eighth and Fourteenth Amendments forbade the imposition of death on offenders who were under the age of eighteen at the time the crime was committed. After laying out a broad reasoning, Justice Kennedy in his majority opinion states that this decision

> finds confirmation in the stark reality that the United States is the only country in the world that continues to give official sanction to the juvenile death penalty. This reality does not become controlling, for the task of interpreting the Eighth Amendment remains our responsibility.
>
> (p. 575)

In what has been called the "most ambitious use of international sources to date" (Waters 2007: 633), Justice Kennedy went on to cite the International Convention on Civil and Political Rights (ICCPR), along with other regional human rights treaties, to lend persuasive authority to his opinion.

In dissent, Justice Scalia disparaged the majority opinion with his well-known sharp pen and directed some of his most caustic criticism at the use of international sources. To raise doubts over said international consensus, he writes, "the Court is quite willing to believe that every foreign nation—of whatever tyrannical political makeup and with however subservient or incompetent a court system—in fact *adheres* to a rule of no death penalty for offenders under 18" (p. 623; original emphasis). Finally, Justice Scalia's attack on the use of what he calls "foreign sources" concludes on a familiar questioning of what reasoning or authority is to be regarded as the most true to the US Constitution. Taking issue with the genuineness of the argument supporting human rights found in the majority opinion, Justice Scalia claims that

> the Court's statement flatly misdescribes what is going on here. Foreign sources are cited today, *not* to underscore our "fidelity" to the Constitution, our "pride in its origins," and "our own [American] heritage." To the contrary, they are cited *to set aside* the centuries-old American practice ... of letting a jury of 12 citizens decide whether ... youth should be the basis for withholding the death penalty.
>
> (p. 628; original emphasis)

In this last citation demonstrating some of the current internal debate, we find what has become central to the framework in the US for viewing international law: the US Constitution. If there is one line of reasoning that can be followed over the years it is that of using the US constitutional structure to interpret international legal obligations by the national courts. Whether it is the separation-of-powers doctrine, federalism, or deference to the democratically elected political branches, the manner in which treaty responsibilities are interpreted by US courts is largely shaped by this founding document. This again holds true for the current debates over what role international law and the law from other jurisdictions should play in constitutional interpretation.

This is the context in which the US Supreme Court found itself as the series of counterterrorism cases relating to detention and judicial review in the "war on terror" came before it between 2004 and 2008.

b International norms: a framework for dialogue

On January 16, 2002, detainees captured in Afghanistan began to arrive at the US military facility in Guantánamo Bay on the island of Cuba. The territory had been acquired through the Platt Amendment in 1903 while US forces were still occupying the island after the Spanish–American War, and this bilateral agreement gave the US complete jurisdiction while sovereignty remained in the hands of Cuba (Maris 1967: 261). This particular facility appears to have been chosen because neither US domestic jurisdiction nor pertinent international laws were thought by administration lawyers to fully apply to noncitizens detained on foreign land. Indeed, this stance was taken by government lawyers before the Supreme Court, and internal documents have been published asserting this legal position even prior to the decision to open the detention facility (see Philbin and Yoo 2001).

The stark and extreme legal position of the Deputy Assistant Attorney General John Yoo on the US Constitution and international law was outlined in the previous chapter of this work. It was only two weeks after the terrorist attacks that Yoo wrote his first legal memo relating to the "war on terror," stating that Congress cannot pass legislation to limit the president's power in wartime. What is more noteworthy in our discussion here, however, was the executive's vision of the role of the judiciary in this war. Just two months after the attacks, the President signed the military order "Detention, Treatment, and Trial of Certain Non-Citizens in the War against Terrorism." In it, the bold assertions of the executive's unitary control over its conduct of the "war on terror" were plain, in particular when it came to any type of judicial review. The document read,

> the individual shall not be privileged to seek any remedy or maintain any proceeding, directly or indirectly, or to have any such remedy or proceeding sought on the individual's behalf, in (i) any court of the United States, or any State thereof (ii) any court of any foreign nation, or (iii) any international tribunal.

> (Bush 2001a: 28)

It was with this legal stance of a complete exclusion of the judiciary that the Bush administration launched its "war on terror" and began detaining prisoners at Guantánamo. Yet there are a host of legal questions that need to be answered in order to assess the administration's compliance with the applicable humanitarian law in the four Geneva Conventions: Is the armed conflict international, or noninternational?[3] Are the detainees in Guantánamo entitled to "POW" status?[4] Were there any legal protections to be found at all in the Geneva Conventions that applied to members of the Taliban and Al-Qaeda?[5] Does there exist an "unlawful combatant" status that puts a prisoner outside of the framework of the Third and Fourth Geneva Conventions?[6] What happens if doubt should arise as to the status of a detainee (GC-III, Article 5)?[7] These are complex legal questions, and each is critical for resolving the issue of whether the Bush administration was exercising its power legally under the laws of war.

The manner in which the executive branch meant to settle these issues is found in a two-page document signed by President Bush (2002a) on February 7, 2002, and the uncomplicated reasoning is fleshed out in the above endnotes (3–7). Ultimately, this memo asserted the presidential finding that neither members of the Taliban nor of Al-Qaeda would be covered by any laws at all.

However, neither can it be overlooked that there are also human rights laws that remain applicable in armed conflict, even if the administration claimed otherwise. The clauses for derogation give human rights conventions the ability, not to mention the authority, to flex and bend with circumstances. This even includes threats as grave as those to the life of a nation. This is an important reason why these two branches of law have been persistently and explicitly depicted as complementary and mutually reinforcing.[8] As well, this explains the various efforts that have been made to establish the manner in which the rules from both branches converge on a minimum common standard that is applicable at all times.[9]

Of direct pertinence here is the human rights standard prohibiting "arbitrary" arrest or detention, which can be found in nearly all the major human rights conventions.[10] Yet this is a relative right. This means that whether the detention of a suspected terrorist is "arbitrary" or not must be assessed in context—that is, the detainee's right to liberty is weighed against the security of society and the interests of a government in preserving law and order. To perform this balancing, human rights law requires that a person who has been deprived of his or her liberty has the possibility of judicial review. As Article 9(4) of the ICCPR affirms,

> [a]nyone who is deprived of his liberty by arrest or detention shall be entitled to take proceedings before a court, in order that court may decide without delay on the lawfulness of his detention and order release if the detention is not lawful.

Principle 9 of the *UN Body of Principles for the Protection of All Persons under Any Form of Detention or Imprisonment* also outlines that anyone kept under detention must be held by an authority who "exercise[s] only the powers granted to him under the law and the exercise of these powers shall be subject to recourse to a judicial or other authority." Additionally, the prohibition of "prolonged arbitrary detention" is recognized by the US as a customary international law in the authoritative *Restatement (Third) of the Foreign Relations Law of the United States*, and that a state is responsible for the "denial of justice" for the loss of liberty to foreign nationals (American Law Institute 1987: §702(e) and §711 respectively).

It should also be noted that the right to judicial review is implied to be a derogable right within the text of the ICCPR. In other words, in exceptional circumstances a state is allowed to temporarily adjust its obligations under the treaty. However, there are stringent constraints upon the conditions under which derogation may take place. Not only must it be a public emergency that "threatens the life of the nation" which has been "officially proclaimed," but the denial of a judicial review must be "strictly required by the exigencies of the situation" (Article 4[1]). Nonetheless, the Human Rights Committee (HRC), created by the Covenant itself, has spoken expressly on the specific issue before us and has stated that freedom from arbitrary detention is a peremptory norm. Thus, "the right to take proceedings before a court to enable the court to decide without delay on the lawfulness of detention, must not be diminished by a State party's decision to derogate from the Covenant" (General Comment 29, para. 16).

This is just a glimpse of the mountain of international legal constraints that faced the executive branch as it plowed forward with its interpretations of the applicable law in this cross-border conflict. However, as we will see, the Supreme Court did not primarily deal with these questions through the prism of international law, other than in the *Hamdan* decision of 2006 which read the incorporation of the laws of war into domestic law. Instead, the court found the fundamental principle of applicable law affording basic judicial protection, or a judicial review of detention, to be present on both domestic and constitutional grounds allowing it to chart its own route based on the responses of the other branches of government.

III The *Rasul* decision: stimulating the dialogue

Shortly after the opening of the Guantánamo facility, the Center for Constitutional Rights filed cases within the US national court system in an attempt to provide a judicial review to the detained foreigners in Cuba through habeas corpus petitions. The detainees held there were not informed of the reason for their detention and had no right to trial; nor were they provided with any legal counsel. In the Supreme Court term of

2003–2004, two cases had worked their way up through the system to come before the highest court and were consolidated under the name *Rasul* v. *Bush*. In these cases, the petitioners claimed that they had never been combatants against the US, nor had they engaged in any terrorist acts. The lower courts found that they did not possess jurisdiction to hear the habeas petitions and dismissed the cases. Thus, as aliens outside of US sovereign territory, they could not invoke the right to habeas corpus. Additionally, handed down on the same day as *Rasul*, there was a ruling on a case concerning a US citizen accused of fighting against the coalition forces in Afghanistan. *Hamdi* v. *Rumsfeld* was also an assertion of the court's jurisdiction to review executive action regarding detention, and thus both cases represented its initial ascension of the "judicial ladder of review."

This was the first chance that the US Supreme Court had to consider any of the counterterrorism policies instituted in the wake of 9/11. Congress passed the omnibus legislation known as the US PATRIOT Act within six weeks of the attacks, and the President launched wars into Afghanistan and Iraq well before the Supreme Court was asked to weigh in on whether judicial review is legally afforded to those detained in this "global war." So, if we think about the differing controlling mandates of the powers in a modern democracy, we begin to perceive a wedge being fashioned here between the separate branches of government.

a A realignment of precedent

The majority opinion in *Rasul* v. *Bush* was written by Justice John Paul Stevens, and he opens his judgment by presenting a brief account of the terrorist attacks on the US that led to the congressional authorization to use force in Afghanistan. These hostilities against the Taliban and Al-Qaeda generated detainees, including the petitioners, who were then moved to the Guantánamo facility. Pertinent to the decision was the legal circumstance of the naval base on the island. The court observed that the lease that was signed in the aftermath of the Spanish–American war left ultimate sovereignty with Cuba but granted that the US would exercise complete jurisdiction and control. As such, the question before the court was to determine whether there was legal reason to extend habeas protection to noncitizens confined in an area where the country exercised plenary and exclusive jurisdiction but not ultimate sovereignty.

The lower courts had relied entirely upon the 1950 *Johnson* v. *Eisentrager* decision of the Supreme Court, and even the briefs put forward by the petitioners and respondent primarily focused upon this particular case law in an assumption that it was the controlling case. The *Eisentrager* case concerned twenty-one Germans who were captured in China at the end of World War II, convicted of war crimes by the US military for continuing to fight after the surrender of their country, and then repatriated to serve out their sentences under American authority on a US military facility.

They then petitioned for habeas corpus before the US courts claiming that the circumstances of their detention had violated the US Constitution. The Supreme Court held that the District Court for the District of Columbia lacked jurisdiction to hear the petition because, among other things, "[n]othing in the text of the Constitution extends such a right," and

> [w]e are cited to no instance where a court, in this or any other country where the writ is known, has issued it on behalf of an alien enemy who, at no relevant time and in no stage of his captivity, has been within its territorial jurisdiction.
>
> (p. 768)

Plainly, there was good reason to believe that this would be the controlling jurisprudence. Like the cases before the court, *Eisentrager* dealt with foreign citizens held on a US military base seeking judicial review. This certainly seemed a high hurdle to clear for the petitioners.

In a notable twist, the position taken by the court in this significant decision of 2004 was, at least in part, due to the fact that one of its members had an intimate knowledge of, and noteworthy role in, a judgment that was handed down over a half-century earlier (Thai 2006). The conventional understanding of the relevant precedents was that for the court to rule in favor of the petitioners, it would need to overrule or somehow distinguish the *Eisentrager* decision from the cases upon which the court was now deciding. A similar case of wartime jurisprudence had certainly not come before the court in the previous half-century. However, the majority opinion held in *Rasul* that, in fact, the statutory understanding implied in *Eisentrager* had already been overruled. To do so, the decision relied upon a relatively obscure dissent in a 1948 case that had been classified as dealing with venue, rather than jurisdiction. The case upon which the *Rasul* decision would pivot was *Ahrens* v. *Clark*, for which critical parts of the dissenting opinion had been drafted by a young law clerk named John Paul Stevens.

The *Ahrens* case arrived at the high court in 1947 and dealt with the detention of over 100 Germans at Ellis Island who were determined to be a danger to the US due to the war in progress with their country. They were scheduled to be deported, yet the petitioners claim on the merits of their case was principally based on the fact that this order was actually made after the conclusion of hostilities had occurred.

However, the portion of the case that concerns us here relates to the fact that the petitioners had brought the case before the District Court for the District of Columbia (that of the Attorney General) rather than the court found in the jurisdiction of their confinement (the Southern District of New York). Ultimately, the majority opinion ruled that the District Court did not have jurisdiction and affirmed the lower court's dismissal because "[i]t is not sufficient, in our view, that the jailer or custodian alone be found in the jurisdiction" (*Ahrens* [1948], p. 190). In a footnote, it also set aside the human rights question of "what process, if any, a person confined in an area not subject to the jurisdiction of any district court may employ to assert federal rights" (*Ahrens* [1948], p. 193, note 4).

It was Stevens, as a law clerk, who was asked by Justice Rutledge to prepare a first draft for the dissent in the *Ahrens* case, and, as such, he came to have an intimate knowledge of the issues at stake in the case. In his draft dissent, Stevens looked at the two issues of proper respondent and territorial jurisdiction of the prisoner to explain that the Congress did not seem to have in mind the irregular circumstance in which the two were not found in the same jurisdiction (Thai 2006: 507–510). Also in this text by the law clerk was a reading that the majority's opinion ended up deciding future cases in which a detainee was not in the specific territorial jurisdiction of any court. This reading also made it into the final dissenting opinion written by Justice Rutledge, and disagreement within the court over this question (directly relating to the human right of a judicial review available for any detainee regardless of the imprisonment location) was addressed as "[j]urisdictionally speaking, it is, or should be, enough that the respondent named has the power or ability to produce the body when so directed by the court" (*Ahrens* [1948], p. 199). Yet this was, indeed, only a dissenting opinion without the force of law. Thus, Stevens had a hand in tilting the reasoning for the dissent in this particular direction and left his own mark on a case that he would pick up over a half-century later in *Rasul*.

It is possible to quickly discern the impact that a familiarity with this particular jurisprudence allowed Justice Stevens. In the majority opinion penned by Justice Stevens himself, it was pointed out that the petitioners in *Eisentrager* filed their suit only two months after the *Ahrens* decision was handed down. Thus, the reasoning put forward was that *Eisentrager* was decided in a legal context in which *Ahrens* was well understood to be in place. Due to this legal environment, Justice Stevens argued that *Eisentrager* was in fact based on the question of a detainee's *constitutional* right to habeas corpus rather than a *statutory* right to habeas review, so as to distinguish it from *Ahrens* (*Rasul* v. *Bush* [2004], pp. 476–479). By reading *Eisentrager* in this way, it no longer became the controlling jurisprudence since the *Rasul* case was looking only at the statutory right to habeas corpus. Therefore, the Supreme Court's decision in *Eisentrager* was found to be an overruling of the constitutional right (previously found in the Court of Appeals) and not related to the statutory interpretation under discussion.

To link this novel interpretation of *Eisentrager* with the case before the court, the majority opinion turned to the case of *Braden* v. *30th Judicial Circuit Court of Kentucky* (which in fact made specific mention of the dissent in *Ahrens* by Justice Rutledge). Relying upon this particular case allowed Justice Stevens to demonstrate that in 1973 the statutory understanding of habeas had already been reformulated so that "[t]he writ of habeas corpus does not act upon the prisoner who seeks relief, but upon the person who holds him in what is alleged to be unlawful custody" (*Braden* [1973], pp. 494–495). The *Rasul* opinion was careful to point out the reasoning with which *Braden* arrived at its conclusion of overruling the *Ahrens* decision. That is to say, the proceeding developments in the congressional and judicial treatment of the habeas statute, after *Ahrens*, were of central importance to the court in *Braden*. This led to the finding that the court, on statutory grounds, could "no longer view that decision [*Ahrens*] as establishing an inflexible jurisdictional rule" (*Braden* [1973], pp. 499–500). As such, Justice Stevens was able to deftly realign the precedents so that *Eisentrager* was no longer the controlling jurisprudence because *Braden* became understood as the precedent that had already overruled the majority opinion referring to the domestic statute. Instead, largely due to an intimate familiarity with the court's jurisprudence on this particular point, the dissenting opinion in *Ahrens* became the controlling precedent.

It should be noted that the petitioners did make reference to the jurisprudence of *Ahrens* and *Braden*, but the argumentation was incomplete in that it did not present an understanding of *Eisentrager* as referring only to a constitutional right to habeas corpus and therefore not controlling (Petitioners' Brief on the Merits [2004]). What points most clearly to the unique reading of the precedents by Justice Stevens is the fact that during the oral arguments he attempted to prompt the counsel for the petitioners into the interpretation that would finally be found in the majority opinion, yet he was met only with a flustered and argumentative response by the petitioners' counsel. In a statement that can be heard in the audio recording, but which did not make it into the official transcript, Justice Stevens closes his line of questioning to the petitioners' counsel by saying "I'm trying to help you."[11]

Having prepared an initial draft for this dissent, Justice Stevens was well placed to comprehend its direct significance in the *Rasul* decision. Reading the series of cases together (*Ahrens*, *Eisentrager*, and *Braden*), it is certainly possible to reconstruct the reasoning used to arrive at the conclusion put forward in *Rasul*: the habeas statute in fact gave the noncitizens detained outside of any court's jurisdiction the right to a judicial review by US courts. However, the fact that no one had previously advanced such a formulation of the relevant case law in the lower courts or seemed to follow Justice Stevens in his prompting during oral arguments indicates just "how unlikely Justice Stevens' reading of the cases was" (Thai 2006: 528).

b Human rights norms and the Ahrens dissent

Most relevant from a human rights perspective is the fact that the only specific portion of this dissent in *Ahrens* that Justice Stevens chose to cite in his *Rasul* opinion was the questioning of what the absence of habeas juris-diction would mean for petitioners not confined within the territory of any district court. When Justice Stevens was a law clerk, he had honed in on the fact that the majority opinion in *Ahrens* would leave a wide gap of jurisdic-tion through which persons in need of protection could vanish. In a foot-note in *Rasul*, attention was drawn to the significance of this precarious breach to be found in the majority opinion in *Ahrens*. Justice Stevens cited,

> Justice Rutledge wrote: "[I]f absence of the body detained from the territorial jurisdiction of the court having jurisdiction of the jailer creates a total and irremediable void in the court's capacity to act, [...] then it is hard to see how that gap can be filled by such extrane-ous considerations as whether there is no other court in the place of detention from which remedy might be had [...]."
>
> (*Rasul* [2004], p. 477, note 7; internal citations omitted)

Additionally, Justice Stevens might well have chosen to cite the section of the dissent that discussed what some would specifically accuse the adminis-tration of having done in these particular circumstances and, as we have seen, actually discussed in internal memos: that is, deciding on a location of detention specifically for its placement outside the territorial jurisdic-tion of the courts. The Rutledge dissent asks, "may the jailers stand in defi-ance of federal judicial power, and plead either the accident of the locus of detention outside the court's territorial limitations, or their own astute-ness in so selecting the place, to nullify judicial competence?" (*Ahrens* [1948], p. 195). The dissent in *Ahrens* answered in the negative to this human rights question, and, in turn, so did the majority a half-century later in *Rasul*, by shifting the controlling question away from the petitioner because instead "[t]he whole force of the writ is spent upon the respond-ent" (*Ahrens* [1948], p. 197; internal citations omitted).

What is also interesting to note is the timing of the *Ahrens* decision in relation to the development of human rights law. When the case was handed down by the Supreme Court in June 1948, there were no legally binding human rights instruments in existence. It was not until December of that year that the non-binding Universal Declaration of Human Rights was adopted by the General Assembly of the UN. Therefore, an assertion of some form of the rights found in the ICCPR (which only entered into force in 1976) by a minority of judges in the US Supreme Court decades earlier perhaps demonstrates a rising consciousness of the issue as it is now understood by human rights lawyers. Regardless of whether this fili-ation of legal philosophy can in fact be drawn, the reality is that Justice Stevens, as a law clerk and then on the Supreme Court, asserted and then reasserted that "federal courts have jurisdiction to determine the legality of the Executive's potentially indefinite detention of individuals who claim to be wholly innocent of wrongdoing" (*Rasul* [2004], p. 485).

Indeed, this conclusion in *Rasul* only dealt with the court's jurisdiction and did not venture into what rights might be asserted in the habeas reviews the decision affords. For example, it did not explore whether the Geneva Conventions or any human rights treaties are in fact self-executing or contain any judicially enforceable rights. Even if they were, how they would be applicable in these precise circumstances was also entirely avoided or was set aside for later adjudication. However, there is a human rights victory to be found in this narrow jurisdictional and statutory decision. By reading precedent to align with the *Ahrens* dissent, jurisdiction of the court for the habeas statute would now depend on a prisoner's guardian. Justice Stevens concluded:

> No party questions the District Court's jurisdiction over petitioners' custodians [...]. Section 2241 [the habeas statute], by its terms, requires nothing more. We therefore hold that §2241 confers on the District Court jurisdiction to hear petitioners' habeas corpus challenges to the legality of their detention at the Guantanamo Bay Naval Base.
>
> (*Rasul* [2004], pp. 483–484)

Consequently, what we find in the first decisions dealing with the "war on terror" is that the court did not choose an abrupt or brusque pushback against the executive's conduct in the war, but only asserted its own institutional competence. The court investigated the authority under which the executive was acting and ruled on statutory grounds that would allow for legislative participation in the dialogue. As seen in the *Rasul* opinion, comprehensive familiarity with the pertinent interpretation by the court of the habeas statute over a half-century period permitted a creative realignment of the precedents. In turn, this allowed a reading of the statute that would grant jurisdiction to those detained outside of the traditional territorial jurisdiction of the national courts. The decision stayed within the confines of a statutory reading which afforded the courts jurisdiction to act. As such, the *Rasul* decision can be understood as an ascent of a jurisdictional rung of the "judicial ladder of review" (in this instance, the court chose to initiate the dialogue on the second rung outlined in the introduction). However, this first engagement by the judiciary was much less of a directive than it was an attempt at discussion with the executive and legislative branches. Clearly, the plain assertion of statutory jurisdiction left a wide margin of operation for the political branches. Yet courts prefer to affect outcomes in the least intrusive manner available and in fact show a stark wariness of doing so at all in certain jurisdictions.

Benvenisti describes the constraint that some courts face (which certainly applies to the US circumstance) as follows:

> [c]ourts that operate in a legal and political environment that views judicial intervention with suspicion will tend to avoid as much as

possible making a determination of illegal executive action based on second-tier [substantive] considerations. They will, rather, rule on the question of institutional authority to act, a question that is no doubt the domain of the courts and, in so doing, will prefer to leave room for the legislature to weigh-in on the matter. Their hope would be that the legislature will cooperate by imposing effective constraints on the executive.

(Benvenisti 2008b: 256)

IV The onset of dialogue and the *Hamdan* decision

This first venture by the judiciary into the policies of the "war on terror" motivated a reply from both the executive and the legislature. Each responded in its own way, but neither response could be characterized as entirely cordial to the judiciary on this matter of institutional dialogue. Within ten days of the release of the Supreme Court decisions of *Rasul* and *Hamdi*, the administration ordered the establishment of Combatant Status Review Tribunals (CSRT). The order issued was said to fulfill the requirements set out by the court and was not to preclude them from seeking additional review in federal court. In the *Hamdi* plurality opinion, the Supreme Court had made specific mention of Army Regulation 190–198 when suggesting that "[t]here remains the possibility that the standards we have articulated could be met by an appropriately authorized and properly constituted military tribunal" (*Hamdi* [2004], p. 538). Thus, the executive seized on this remark to justify the process developed in the order. Under the CSRT, each detainee would be notified of certain limited aspects of his or her detention and would be assigned a personal representative (but not a lawyer) to assist before the tribunal of three commissioned military officers.

In November 2006, Professor Mark P. Denbeaux of Seton Hall Law School released a report on the CSRT developed by the administration, and found that "the results of this review are startling" (2006: 4). The report examines the records released for the CSRT hearings of 393 of the then 558 detainees at Guantánamo and found problems with representation for the detainees, evidence withheld from the detainee or denied from being introduced, and the brevity of the process. Perhaps most disturbing, there were three reviewed instances in which the detainee was found to be not or no longer an enemy combatant, and in each case the Department of Defense ordered a new tribunal convened, in which the detainee was then found to be an enemy combatant; in one case, it even took a third tribunal being convened to finally arrive at declaring the detainee an enemy combatant.

Finally, it should also be pointed out that the CSRT are not fulfilling the obligations under Article 5 of Geneva Convention III for determining status because they "do not have the discretion to determine that a detainee should be classified as a prisoner of war – only whether the detainee satisfies the definition of 'enemy combatant'" (Declaration of Commander James R. Crisfield Jr. in *Mozzam Begg* v. *Bush* [2004]).

As for the reaction to the legislature, Congress responded by trying to strip the courts of jurisdiction to hear the habeas corpus petitions of detainees held at Guantánamo. This provision was tied to a statute aimed at prohibiting the cruel, inhumane, and degrading treatment of prisoners known as the Detainee Treatment Act (DTA) of 2005. In one sense, the Graham–Levin amendment (as the jurisdiction-stripping portion was initially known) finally brought the legislature into the fray on the issue of judicial review for the detainees at the Guantánamo facility. For example, this amendment created a mechanism for Congress to at long last become involved by mandating that reports be given to specific congressional committees and to adopt certain safeguards in the CSRT procedure. Yet a primary provision of this legislation aimed to ensure that "no court, justice, or judge shall have jurisdiction to hear or consider … an application for a writ of habeas corpus filed by or on behalf of an alien detained by the Department of Defense at Guantanamo Bay, Cuba" (DTA, §1005[e] [1]). Additionally, it provided that the US Court of Appeals for the District of Columbia Circuit would have the exclusive jurisdiction to hear appeals on the CSRT determinations or decisions of military commissions, with a remarkable limitation upon the scope of review to only those judgments already handed down and the rules that had created them.

However, there was an important question as to whether this exclusive jurisdiction and limited scope of review applied to pending cases or only to those filed from that date forward. The Supreme Court had postponed a judgment on the motion by the government to dismiss the case until it had been argued on the merits, and, as such, this was the first question with which the landmark judgment of *Hamdan* v. *Rumsfeld* dealt. (Salim Ahmed Hamdan was captured in Afghanistan, and, as a driver for Osama bin Laden, he was charged with conspiracy and providing material support for terrorism.)

On June 29, 2006, the decision was rendered, with Justice Stevens again writing the plurality opinion, while there were additionally two concurrences and three dissents. This was an involved and contentious case dealing with delicate issues related to the nation's security, not to mention that, to differing extents, every branch of government had now become involved.

When it came to the question of the applicable scope of the DTA legislation, of specific significance for the court was the fact that Congress considered the temporal reaches of a different construction of the statute and rejected one particular form because it would have circumscribed the temporal scope of the statute too far. That is to say, there was a noteworthy episode which is found within the legislative history that indicates that Congress made an overt elimination of one construction of the text *specifically because* it would throw pending cases out of court. As the court put it, "Congress' rejection of the very language that would have achieved the result the Government urges here weighs heavily against the Government's interpretation" (*Hamdan* [2006], pp. 579–580).

a The Geneva Conventions as part of the UCMJ

One of the central questions that the court was forced to confront at the outset of this case was that of self-execution or judicial enforceability of an international treaty. The reason that these particular questions are of such importance to this judgment is because in its next move up the "judicial ladder of review," the Supreme Court indeed reached for international law to help bolster its further ascension. As mentioned before, this is a particularly intriguing development due to the historical resistance of national courts to applying international norms, especially when doing so is thought to constrain the activities of the executive. Additionally, national courts

> who uphold the human rights of the individual members of those targeted groups [in the war] often find themselves without widespread support due to limited popular demand for governmental accountability in situations of high security [...] and must confront criticism for exposing the population to excessive risks.
>
> (Benvenisti 2004: 308)

In the context of such history, along with the circumstance of national anxiety manifest in the "war on terror," the decision of the Supreme Court to look toward, and apply a portion of, the Geneva Conventions was certainly a bold one.

As well, these questions of self-execution and judicial enforceability are of significance in the *Hamdan* case because they had been answered in alternating ways by courts along the case's trajectory to its arrival in the US Supreme Court. As to whether these two terms in fact have the same meaning, at least in this particular instance, the answer is largely affirmative. In the US, the judicial nature of a treaty is something that becomes resolved as the rights outlined within it are claimed in a case before a court, and *Hamdan* was indeed asserting rights found within the Geneva Conventions. While the initial District Court opinion made numerous references to the term "self-executing" in arriving at its conclusion that the court did indeed have the authority to apply the Geneva Conventions because the treaty was of this nature, the phrase was not used again in the Court of Appeals nor in the Supreme Court decisions. In a reverse decision by the Court of Appeals, a volte-face of terminology also applied in that the phrase "judicially enforceable" (rather than "self-executing") was used in the determination that the Geneva Conventions were not of such character. In the end, the Supreme Court avoided invoking either term, which we may well interpret as an agile avoidance of speaking to the nature of the treaty within US law.

Initially, Judge Robertson of the District Court ruled that the Geneva Conventions were self-executing. The controlling case "established the proposition that a 'treaty is a law of the land as an act of congress is, whenever its provisions prescribe a rule by which the rights of the private citizen or subject may be determined' "; in turn, it was held that "[t]he Geneva Conventions, of course, are all about prescribing rules by which the rights of individuals may be determined" (*Hamdan* [2004], p. 164).

The Court of Appeals then concluded that the US has "traditionally negotiated treaties with the understanding that they do not create judicially enforceable individual rights" (*Hamdan* [2005], p. 38) and that a footnote found in the *Eisentrager* decision determines that the "1949 Geneva Conventions does not confer upon Hamdan a right to enforce its provisions in court" (*Hamdan* [2005], p. 40). Even if it were applicable, Hamdan was participating in a conflict that fell outside of the scope of the treaty. The Court of Appeals came to this conclusion because Al-Qaeda was not a "High Contracting Party" (referring to Common Article 2 of the Geneva Conventions) and that the phrase "not of an international character" (referring to Common Article 3) was equally inapplicable because clashes did indeed take place outside of the US.

To deal with these divergent holdings, the Supreme Court began by concluding that the *Eisentrager* decision and its accompanying footnote (which referred to the enforcement of treaty rights only through political and military authorities) did not control the case before the court. Instead, the court ruled that Hamdan's rights were a part of the laws of war, and the Government did not dispute this. In what might be called a sleight of hand, Justice Stevens put forward for the majority that "compliance with the law of war is the condition upon which the authority set forth in Article 21 is granted" (*Hamdan* [2006], p. 628). It is this phrase that encapsulates the manner in which the Supreme Court avoided treating the whole question of whether the Geneva Conventions are "self-executing" or "judicially enforceable." The court instead concluded that because the Uniform Code of Military Justice (UCMJ) requires compliance with the laws of war, of which the Geneva Conventions are clearly a part, the court can apply its provisions.

As a result of this nimble maneuver to avoid deciding on the exact status of these international laws, the Supreme Court discussed its interpretation of the application of the Geneva Conventions to the *Hamdan* case without dealing with the applicability of general treaty law. It should be noted that such a reading falls short of the general interpretation under international law that treaties indeed have judicial force. While this is lamentable from the perspective of international law, it is at the same time a bold step forward for US courts. Internally, this means that precedent was set for the Geneva Conventions to be judicially applicable to cases dealing with military justice within the US national court system, as long as there is not a relevant change within the articles of the UCMJ.

b The application of Common Article 3

One of the most significant and contentious issues at stake in the controversy over detainees and judicial review was whether there was indeed any law applicable to those held in Guantánamo. While the Bush administration had determined that Taliban fighters were covered by the Geneva Conventions, and the Al-Qaeda detainees were not, in an internal document of February 2002 it was clarified that the executive considered that neither category of prisoner was entitled to POW status or the protections of Common Article 3 (Bush 2002a). The determination made by the administration was that the detainees at Guantánamo were "unlawful enemy combatants" who could be held indefinitely without trial, even if they were to be acquitted by a military tribunal. Therefore, the executive held that its own interpretation of international law led to the conclusion that there was no applicable binding law at all for the detainees at Guantánamo.

This judgment was particularly worrisome in light of the commentary on Article 4 of the Fourth Geneva Convention, which elaborates specifically upon this point. It reads,

> a general principle [...] is embodied in all four Geneva Conventions of 1949. Every person in enemy hands must have some status under international law: he is either a POW and, as such, covered by the Third Convention, a civilian covered by the Fourth Convention, or again, a member of the medical personnel of the armed forces who is covered by the First Convention. *There is no* intermediate status; nobody in enemy hands can be outside the law. We feel that that is a satisfactory solution – not only satisfying to the mind, but also, and above all, satisfactory from the humanitarian point of view.
>
> (Pictet 1960, Vol. IV: 51)

Additionally, jurisprudence from the Trial Chamber of the ICTY also speaks directly to this point of whether there exists any fissure between the Geneva Conventions through which a detainee in the hands of the enemy may slip unprotected. It was held that

> there is no gap between the Third and the Fourth Geneva Conventions. If an individual is not entitled to the protections of the Third Convention as a prisoner of war (or of the First or Second Conventions) he or she necessarily falls within the ambit of Convention IV.
>
> (*Prosecutor* v. *Zejnil Delalić Zdravko Mucić* [1998], para. 271)

To be sure, the Supreme Court faced the difficult question of qualifying the conflict in Afghanistan, where there appeared to be two different armed conflicts under way that would be determinative in assessing the applicable law: one with the Taliban regime that controlled the territorial state, and another outside the territory of the US with the non-state group Al-Qaeda (of which Hamdan was allegedly a part). While the government argued that the character of the latter conflict would place Hamdan outside the protection of the Geneva Conventions, the Supreme Court resolved that it "need not decide the merits of this argument because there is at least one provision of the Geneva Conventions that applies here even if the relevant conflict is not one between signatories" (*Hamdan* [2006], p. 629).

With a noteworthy interpretation, the court found that Common Article 3 of the Geneva Conventions did indeed apply to the conflict with Al-Qaeda because the phrase "not of an international character" found therein is applied "in *contradistinction* to a conflict between nations" (*Hamdan* [2006], para. 630; my emphasis). The use of the term "contradistinction" by the Supreme Court is quite intriguing because with this one simple expression the conservative US court made a move beyond the surface language of this common article of the conventions that was originally meant to apply to victims of civil wars and internal conflicts. With the tension explicitly laid out in the majority opinion between the traditional understanding of the surface language of the article and the humanitarian hopes for its application, the Supreme Court found applicable law for protection of all persons caught in this armed conflict.

However, it cannot be said that this particular approach by the Supreme Court was out of line with the international understanding of treaty obligations. For example, in the judgment of *Nicaragua v. United States of America*, the ICJ discussed Common Article 3 as universally applicable customary international law because it is a baseline for the least amount of protection, or "minimum yardstick," afforded to those found *hors de combat* in an international conflict (para. 218). The ICTY Appeals Chamber also held that Common Article 3 provisions "are so fundamental that they are regarded as governing both internal and international conflicts" and as rules which "may thus be considered as the 'quintessence' of the humanitarian rules found in the Geneva Conventions as a whole" (*Prosecutor v. Zejnil Delalić Zdravko Mucić* [2001], para. 143). Finally, in the case of *Kadic v. Karadzic* before a US Court of Appeals under the Alien Tort Act (which creates federal-court jurisdiction for suits alleging torts committed abroad against aliens in violation of the law of nations), it was held that "the most fundamental norms of the law of war [are] embodied in common article 3" ([1995], p. 10).

Thus, for the Supreme Court to have singled out Common Article 3 as applicable to the conflict with Al-Qaeda is certainly not eccentric. Perhaps the only surprising element is the fact that the court chose not to discuss its applicability as customary international law, but to instead interpret its surface language as granting application through "contradistinction."

c Common Article 3 and the military commissions

Having established that the law applicable to the US armed conflict with Al-Qaeda was found in Common Article 3, the Supreme Court next moved on to determine whether the judicial rights afforded to Hamdan (as an alleged combatant in this conflict) were indeed protected by his trial before a military commission created by the President. As the language in this article is somewhat imprecise due to its basic nature, ascertaining the exact meaning required further investigation by the court. The specific language of the provision that was pertinent to Hamdan in this case was Common Article 3(I)(d), which states that "[t]he passing of sentences and the carrying out of executions without previous judgment pronounced by a regularly constituted court affording all the judicial guarantees which are recognized as indispensable by civilized peoples."

To begin to assess whether Hamdan's rights under this provision were protected, the plurality looked to the commentary of the Geneva Conventions to find a meaning for the phrase "regularly constituted court." While nothing which gives further shape to its meaning is found in the article itself nor in its accompanying commentary, Article 66 of Geneva Convention IV deals with the type of competent courts that are to be used to try civilians in breach of penal provisions in occupied territories. Although this was certainly not the circumstance before the court, the commentary reveals the same phraseology of "regularly constituted" court and that "[t] his wording definitely excludes all special tribunals" (*Hamdan* [2006], p. 632; citing Pictet 1960: Vol. IV, 340). Additionally, the court turned to the Red Cross publication *Customary International Humanitarian Law*, where they found this phrase in Common Article 3 to mean "established and organized in accordance with the laws and procedures already in force in a country" (*Hamdan* [2006], p. 632; citing Henckaerts and Doswald-Beck 2005: 355). This specific reference was taken from the petitioner's brief submitted to the court, where it is also found, and thus taken to be persuasive. Additionally, the brief cites this same text on the way in which a "regularly constituted court" should be able to operate in relation to other branches of government in that it "must be able to perform its functions independently of any other branch of the government, especially the executive" (Petitioner's Brief [2006], p. 48). On this point, the petitioner's brief elaborates,

> the commission is an ad hoc tribunal fatally compromised by command influence, lack of independence and impartiality, and lack of competence to adjudicate the complex issues of domestic and international law. The rules for trial change arbitrarily—and even changed

after the Petition for Certiorari was filed. It is not regularly constituted; its defects cannot be cured without a complete structural over-
haul and fixed rules.

> (Petitioner's Brief (2006): 48; internal citations omitted)

The majority does not go as far in its opinion and instead relies on the
reasoning put forward by Justice Kennedy in his concurring opinion that

> [a]t a minimum a military commission like the one at issue—a com-
> mission specially convened by the President to try specific persons
> without express congressional authorization—can be "regularly consti-
> tuted" by the standards of our military justice system only if some prac-
> tical need explains deviations from court-martial practice.
>
> (*Hamdan* [2006], p. 645)

A practical need for the commissions was not found to be demonstrated
by the government. We also see that the court indicated a manner in
which the political branches may resolve one of the deficiencies of the
military commissions: congressional authorization. However, this was not
without a caveat.

In the *Hamdan* case, the US Supreme Court did not show traditional
wartime deference and again chose to moderate the dialogue over the
conduct of the administration, and now the legislative branch, in the "war
on terror." This time, the court reached for the provisions of international
humanitarian law to find applicable law and judicial guarantees available
to noncitizens detained in Guantánamo. In so doing, the court gave
further credence to international law as a valid set of norms that could
constrain the government even in times of armed conflict. To be sure,
there were both creative and questionable interpretations of humanitarian
law and its applicability, yet it cannot be denied that these interpretations
of applicability are now stamped as precedent into the domestic law of the
US. Perhaps most importantly, the finding that Common Article 3 is
indeed applicable law to the "war on terror" became legally established,
with far-reaching implications.

By utilizing international law to buttress its decision, the court also
further ascended the "judicial ladder of review" and in turn set a higher
hurdle for legislative authorization should the legislature choose to further
engage in this institutional colloquy. However, it must not be overlooked
that Justice Kennedy, in his concurring opinion, put forward a cautionary
caveat indicating how further moderation of the dialogue might take
place: "[s]*ubject to constitutional limitations*, Congress has the power and
responsibility to determine the necessity for military courts, and to provide
the jurisdiction and procedures applicable to them" (*Hamdan* [2006],
p. 645; internal citations omitted, my emphasis).

V The continuation of dialogue and the *Boumediene* decision

After the *Hamdan* decision, the executive branch found itself in a precarious position regarding the status of detainees at the Guantánamo facility since the Supreme Court had found the military commissions it had established to be illegal under the applicable law, in particular without congressional approval. In reaction, on September 6, 2006, the administration announced the transfer of fourteen high-value detainees, including the alleged mastermind of 9/11, from undisclosed "black sites" to the Guantánamo Bay Naval Base. The public statement and transfer were made in an effort to urge Congress to authorize new military commissions so that these and other terror suspects could be put on trial under new rules. President Bush urged Congress to act quickly to authorize the military commissions he proposed, evoking the deaths of 3,000 Americans and explaining that this was the way to bring those who had orchestrated 9/11 to justice. The President put the legislation before Congress to deal with the worst of the Al-Qaeda leaders, now brought into open detention at Guantánamo, just weeks before the midterm elections.

a The Military Commissions Act of 2006

In less than one month, with truly remarkable speed, the Military Commissions Act (MCA) of 2006 was drafted and passed by the Congress, bringing the legislative branch fully into the debate on detention without judicial review in the "war on terror." Two days after this Bill was signed into law, John Yoo, who had now returned to academia after serving in the Bush Department of Justice, published a sharp editorial article for the *Wall Street Journal*, providing his assessment of the new law and how it should be understood with regard to the broad dialogue that had been opened between the three branches of government. He wrote,

> The new law is, above all, a stinging rebuke to the Supreme Court. It strips the courts of jurisdiction to hear any habeas corpus claim filed by any alien enemy combatant anywhere in the world. It was passed in response to the effort by a five-justice majority in *Hamdan* v. *Rumsfeld* to take control over terrorism policy.
>
> (Yoo 2006)

While a remand to the legislature in the *Hamdan* decision hoped for a deliberative and careful look at the matter of military commissions and detention now that the Supreme Court had clarified some of the law and issues at stake, the result was less than optimal. From a political point of view, the announcement was a part of a series of speeches the President gave in the lead-up to the fifth anniversary of 9/11 and carried potential political benefits for a president intent on maintaining the Republican control of Congress. The presumed political advantage was due to the fact that the midterm congressional elections were to be held just two months later, and the speed with which the legislature was enacted can be at least partially attributed to the political and electoral urgency forced by the executive's transfer of high-value detainees.

As a likely result of this haste, along with overt intention, a series of criticisms have been leveled against specific provisions of the MCA. As an example, one part of the Act that meant to circumvent dialogue, and that directly raises serious concerns over international legal obligations, was Sections 3 and 5 which stipulated that "[n]o person may invoke the Geneva Conventions or any protocols thereto in any habeas corpus or other civil action or proceeding" as a source of rights. (It should be noted that this particular provision has been improved in the MCA of 2009. While the original provision professed to bar any invocation of the Geneva Conventions, under the new terms they can be used offensively in habeas proceedings or defensively in penal proceedings. But they still do not give rise to any independent action.) It is not within the scope of this study to flesh out all of the critiques relating to this statute. Instead, attention will only be drawn to the provision that dealt directly with the interbranch colloquy charted in this chapter since it attempted to strip jurisdiction from the federal courts.

Section 7 of the MCA concerned access to judicial review in the national courts. In what can be described as a direct retort to *Hamdan*, the provision read,

> [n]o court, justice, or judge shall have jurisdiction to hear or consider an application for a writ of habeas corpus [...] or consider any other action against the United States or its agents relating to any aspect of the detention, transfer, treatment, trial, or conditions of confinement of an alien who is or was detained by the United States and has been determined by the United States to have been properly detained as an enemy combatant or is awaiting such determination.
>
> (MCA 2006: §7)

Under this language, even a claim that a detainee was being subjected to continued torture and ill-treatment while in detention could not be heard before a federal court of the US. Thus, this provision raises serious doubts as to its conformity with the numerous obligations under human rights and humanitarian law since it would effectively neuter the court system from dealing with any claims against the government in its "war on terror." Further action was also taken in the MCA to clarify, and remove all doubt, as to its temporal effect upon the federal courts' jurisdiction. Section 7(b) read that the legislation,

> shall take effect on the date of the enactment of this Act, and shall apply to all cases, *without exception,* pending on or after the date of the

enactment of this Act which relate to any aspect of the detention, transfer, treatment, trial, or conditions of detention of an alien detained by the United States since September 11, 2001.

(MCA 2006; my emphasis)

This rejoinder from the legislature, at the behest of the executive, was plainly a boisterous statement in the ongoing dialogue. The Supreme Court first needed to place its attention here in order to determine if Congress had properly exercised its legal authority in stripping the courts of jurisdiction in such circumstances.

Although the case was initially denied certiorari six months after passage of the MCA, with decisive votes against it by Justices Stevens and Kennedy, the very next term brought about a reversal of position by these two key justices. A hearing was granted for *Boumediene* v. *Bush*, and the court rendered its decision on June 12. The petitioners in this case were all foreign nationals, with only some of them captured on the battlefield in Afghanistan, but none of them were citizens of a nation at war with the US. More importantly, each individual denied that they were a member of the Al-Qaeda terrorist network or the Taliban regime that had offered the group sanctuary.

With these facts established, Justice Kennedy began his analysis for the majority by clarifying that the phraseology of the MCA statute was clear. Section 7 of the law did indeed deny jurisdiction to federal courts and thus the cases must be dismissed, *if* the provision was determined to be constitutionally valid. Additionally, Justice Kennedy explicitly acknowledged that the language found in the MCA must be understood as a part of ongoing interbranch colloquy over judicial review for the detainees at Guantánamo. As he explained it, "[i]f this ongoing dialogue between and among the branches of Government is to be respected, we cannot ignore that the MCA was a direct response to *Hamdan*'s holding that the DTA's jurisdiction-stripping provision had no application to pending cases" (*Boumediene* v. *Bush* [2008], p. 738). The court thus turned to analyzing the constitutionality of §7 of the MCA.

b The constitutional right to habeas corpus

If unsatisfied with the direction of the interbranch dialogue, the next rung in the "judicial ladder of review" would be for the court to examine actions taken by the political branches to determine whether they were in line with all constitutional constraints. In his concurring opinion in *Hamdan* Justice Kennedy had indeed suggested that the requirement of constitutionality would be how any further legislation by the Congress would be assessed by the Supreme Court should further litigation come before it. Therefore, it is not a surprise that the court reached for, grasped, and boldly ascended to the next rung of the "judicial ladder of review"—that of constitutionality—to buttress its opinion of the illegality of the government action. In this manner, and for the first time in the court's history, it ruled against the President and Congress acting together in a time of armed conflict.

To establish whether the congressional stripping of habeas corpus rights from the detainees at Guantánamo was constitutional, the Supreme Court briefly examined the history and origins of the "Great Writ" of habeas corpus as particularly understood by the Framers of the US Constitution. Through this investigation, the court found that the Suspension Clause in the Constitution was one that should be understood as central to its construction and must inform a proper interpretation of a document that initially lacked a Bill of Rights. This fundamental writ was included directly into the Constitution's original text to guard against abuse by the other two branches so as to maintain the delicate balance of governance that the Framers intended. Justice Kennedy's majority opinion reveals a deep concern for the separation of powers in reference to the importance of habeas corpus and explains that "[t]he Framers' inherent distrust of governmental power was the driving force behind the constitutional plan that allocated powers among three independent branches. This design serves not only to make Government accountable but also to secure individual liberty" (*Boumediene* [2008], p. 742).

For this reason, he contended that this structure of government also affords that it is not only citizens who are granted the substantive guarantees found in the Constitution and Bill of Rights. He deduced this from the fact that the court had previously found that "foreign nationals who have the privilege of litigating in our courts can seek to enforce separation-of-powers principles" (*Boumediene* [2008], p. 743). This is particularly significant because the separation of branches of government in the US has often allowed for a certain amount of buck-passing, or responsibility avoidance, when it comes to international law. Thus, in this case, it is important that the Supreme Court explicitly indicated that it is this very same constitutional principle that in fact allows for noncitizens to have a voice in the national courts. Of course, this privilege ultimately turns on standing and on the ability to litigate "in our courts." Therefore, the challenge continued to be centered on the geographic reach of constitutional protections to these foreign nationals.

The most powerful citation put forward in the opinion would certainly be that of Alexander Hamilton, which can be found in the *Federalist Papers*. Importantly, this series of essays, published in a New York newspaper with the intent of informing voters and advocating for the Constitution's ratification, serves as a primary source for its interpretation. In *Federalist No. 84*, Hamilton wrote, and the court cited,

> [T]he practice of arbitrary imprisonments, have been, in all ages, the favorite and most formidable instruments of tyranny. The observations

of the judicious Blackstone ... are well worthy of recital: "To bereave a man of life ... or by violence to confiscate his estate, without accusation or trial, would be so gross and notorious an act of despotism as must at once convey the alarm of tyranny throughout the whole nation; but confinement of the person, by secretly hurrying him to jail, where his sufferings are unknown or forgotten, is a less public, a less striking, and therefore a *more dangerous engine* of arbitrary government." And as a remedy for this fatal evil he is everywhere peculiarly emphatical in his encomiums on the *habeas corpus* act, which in one place he calls "the BULWARK of the British Constitution."

(cited in *Boumediene* [2008], p. 744; original emphasis)

With these incisive words and perspective on the historical moment, one quickly grasps the reasoning for including a means for a judicial review of detention directly into the text of the Constitution. Additionally, we clearly glean its direct relevance to legitimacy.

In large measure, what can be found in Justice Kennedy's majority opinion is the intent to lay out the contours of a constitutional principle rather than a formal rule based on a reading of the common law in the essentially arbitrary year of 1789. However, in his dissenting opinion Justice Scalia took great issue with what he interpreted as an usurpation of power by the court and maintained that "[i]t is nonsensical to interpret those provisions themselves in light of some general 'separation-of-powers principles' dreamed up by the Court" (*Boumediene* [2008], p. 833). Instead, he asserted the originalist interpretation, for which he is widely known, to insist that "[t]he writ as preserved in the Constitution could not possibly extend farther than the common law provided when that Clause was written" (*Boumediene* [2008], p. 832). Thus, one place in which a line can be drawn between the two camps of the court on the *Boumediene* decision is over a formal historical test for the reach of the writ, and the majority who preferred a more flexible functional test.

There were two primary ways in which the majority overcame the argument of a strictly formal test for the right to habeas corpus: (1) by breaking down the *Eisentrager* decision as one not based on this formalism, and (2) by looking at the court's finding in the so-called "Insular Cases" in which the application of the Constitution to incorporated and unincorporated territories was based upon practical constraints.

On the first point, Justice Kennedy indicated that in the government's principle brief for the *Eisentrager* case in 1949 it indeed advocated a "bright-line" test, much like the government did in this case, for determining the scope of habeas corpus application. However, "the Court mentioned the concept of territorial sovereignty only twice in its opinion" and instead "devoted a significant portion [...] to a discussion of practical barriers to the running of the writ" (*Boumediene* [2008], p. 763). For the majority, this suggested that the court was not only focused upon the formal legal status of the prison where the detainees in *Eisentrager* were being held, but also upon the practical degree of control that the US exercised over the facility. Ultimately, Justice Kennedy concluded, "[n]othing in *Eisentrager* says that *de jure* sovereignty is or has ever been the only relevant consideration in determining the geographic reach of the Constitution or of habeas corpus" (*Boumediene* [2008], p. 763).

At the beginning of the twentieth century, the Supreme Court decided a series of legal actions over newly acquired lands, known as the "Insular Cases," in which it addressed whether the Constitution was applicable in territory that is not a state in the Union. Justice Kennedy found the court's reasoning in these cases instructive to the issue at hand and pointed out that the force of the Constitution is independent in these territories and not contingent upon legislative grace. This being the case, a doctrine was devised by the court for determining the reach of the Constitution based on practicable necessities and in particular whether judicial enforcement would be "impracticable and anomalous" (*Boumediene* [2008], p. 770).

With these readings of pertinent jurisprudence, the court discerned a common thread between them and found that these questions of extraterritoriality actually turn on objective factors and practical concerns and not on formalism. A real concern was expressed by the majority over the idea of strict adherence to such formalism in an issue concerning the application of the Constitution because it would allow the political branches the possibility of constructing circumstances to fit a desired legal outcome. The terms of the lease with Cuba concerning "ultimate sovereignty" and "exclusive jurisdiction" were negotiated, drafted, and signed by the political branches, but this certainly did not afford them the "power to switch the Constitution on or off" (*Boumediene* [2008], p. 765). To do so, as affirmed in Justice Kennedy's opinion, would grant Congress and the president the principal authority exercised by the Supreme Court, and delineated in the landmark judgment of *Marbury* v. *Madison*, to determine "what the law is." Therefore, reliance on such formalism must be rejected because of the opening it allows for grave distortions to the US system of government. As was warned,

> [t]hese concerns have particular bearing upon the Suspension Clause question in the cases now before us, for the writ of habeas corpus is itself an indispensable mechanism for monitoring the separation of powers. The test for determining the scope of this provision must not be subject to manipulation by those whose power it is designed to restrain.
>
> (*Boumediene* [2008], p. 766)

Thus, upon the strength of this reasoning, so as to avoid devolution of the tripartite system of government, a majority on the Supreme Court again found that the detainees in the "war on terror," this time constitutionally, had a right to a judicial review. In the majority's words,

[w]e hold that Art. I, §9, cl. 2, of the Constitution has full effect at Guantanamo Bay. If the privilege of habeas corpus is to be denied to the detainees now before us, Congress must act in accordance with the requirements of the Suspension Clause. [...] The MCA does not purport to be a formal suspension of the writ; and the Government, in its submissions to us, has not argued that it is. Petitioners, therefore, are entitled to the privilege of habeas corpus to challenge the legality of their detention.

(*Boumediene* [2008], p. 771)

While the reasoning in this *Boumediene* decision is clearly based upon constitutional interpretations, there is good reason to trumpet this finding as a partial human rights victory. Holding that constitutional protections extend to noncitizens outside of US territory indeed belies its standard contention that the protections of the ICCPR are extended only to individuals who are both "within its territory *and* subject to its jurisdiction" (Article 2[1]; my emphasis). As such, this advancement in the US legal position should be recognized. Yet, there is no doubt that the practical constraints placed on this extension of rights by the court in the *Boumediene* decision are difficult to reconcile with the concept of "effective control" held by the HRC to be the proper mechanism for determining applicability. It is indeed lamentable that an opportunity was missed to present a full-throated human rights-law argument to the court in *Boumediene* so as to help inform the content of constitutional norms and develop a more harmonious concert between constitutional standards and human rights law (see De Londras 2008).

Additionally, it should be noted that the court's constitutionally based decision was modest in two important regards. The first is that the Suspension Clause expressly permits Congress to suspend habeas rights in "cases of rebellion or invasion," and therefore this step could be taken without surmounting the enormous hurdle of a constitutional amendment. While this is surely not an action to be taken without due consideration, it does speak to the modesty of the decision. Second, the judgment was very fact-specific and not a broad categorical rule, which should therefore be understood as quite narrow. Nevertheless, using the "judicial ladder of review" as our guide for understanding this interbranch colloquy, we can also appreciate the calculation of using such a reading of the habeas rights found in the Constitution, rather than a categorical interpretation of human rights law as a constraint on the other branches of government in times of armed conflict.

c *Deficiencies of the DTA and the unconstitutionality of MCA, §7*

Even though under ordinary circumstances the Supreme Court would remand the issue of whether an adequate substitute has been made available to the detainees at Guantánamo to the Court of Appeals (because that court did not rule on this issue), it instead determined that "[t]he gravity of the separation-of-powers issues raised by these cases and the fact that these detainees have been denied meaningful access to a judicial forum for a period of years render these cases exceptional" (*Boumediene* [2008], p. 772).

To begin its analysis of the procedures afforded by the Congress, the court highlighted that both the DTA and the MCA must be understood as legislation meant to "circumscribe" and "dilute" the ordinary habeas protections. As Justice Kennedy cited from the Congressional Record, Senator Jon Kyl had emphasized that "the limited judicial review authorized [is] not habeas corpus review. It is a limited judicial review of its own nature" (*Boumediene* [2008], p. 778). The Supreme Court did not attempt to put forward the requisites for an adequate substitution of habeas corpus at this point. It did, however, stress that there is no controversy over the fact that the privilege of habeas corpus must offer a prisoner a meaningful opportunity to make evident that he or she is not being detained within the requirements of the relevant law. Additionally, the court points out that habeas proceedings have traditionally been most critical and extensive at the initial phase of detention and most pressing when the confinement has been carried out by executive order.

The court assessed the CSRT process and the appeal afforded by the DTA to find four primary shortcomings: (1) the lack of the ability to contest the CSRT's finding of fact; (2) the need for a legal avenue for supplementing the CSRT findings with exculpatory evidence; (3) the absence of provisions allowing detainees to challenge the President's authority under the AUMF to hold them indefinitely; and (4) the denial of judicial power to order release.

The first failing found by the court was that the circumscribed procedure did not allow a detainee to properly rebut the factual basis for the government's claim that this individual was an enemy combatant. This inadequacy included, but was not limited to, the fact that the detainee did not have the assistance of legal counsel; that the means to gather and present evidence was extremely limited; that the most critical allegations might not be presented to the detainee; and the limitless admission of hearsay evidence. Thus, the majority determined that there was considerable risk of error in the CSRT's findings of fact, and that the writ, or its substitute, must encompass the means to correct such possible errors.

The DTA, however, granted exclusive jurisdiction to a Court of Appeals only to review whether the CSRT complied with the standards and procedures set out by the Secretary of Defense and not to inquire into the legality of detention. While the government advocated at oral argument a reading of the DTA that would remedy these infirmities, if it would allow the jurisdictional-stripping provision (§7) of the MCA to remain intact, the court saw no way to construe the statute so as to provide the constitutionally required opportunity for such a detainee to present newly discovered exculpatory evidence.

There was additionally no forum in which these individuals would have the opportunity to have their primary claim adjudicated: "that the President has no authority under the AUMF to detain them indefinitely" (*Boumediene* [2008], p. 788).

Finally, it was held that an essential element of judicial power in habeas, or habeas-like, proceedings must also include the authority to issue an order directing the prisoner's release if necessary.

The majority thus held that the process of judicial review under the DTA could not serve as a replacement for the constitutionally derived right of habeas corpus because its cumulative deficiencies were too great. To buttress this push back in the interbranch colloquy followed in this chapter, the Supreme Court grasped the constitutional rung on the "judicial ladder of review" and once again ascended. Or, as Justice Kennedy explained,

> [o]ur decision today holds only that the petitioners before us are entitled to seek the writ; that the DTA review procedures are an inadequate substitute for habeas corpus; and that the petitioners in these cases need not exhaust the review procedures in the Court of Appeals before proceeding with their habeas actions in the District Court. The only law we identify as unconstitutional is MCA §7, 28 USCA §2241(e).
>
> (*Boumediene* [2008], p. 795)

VI Further exchange on detention under Obama, but without moderated dialogue

The Supreme Court laid out some specific legal constraints during its moderating of the dialogue and ascension of the "judicial ladder" that would have a direct effect upon subsequent administrations. To begin, the legal interpretations put forward while on the first rung in *Rasul* have little further bearing on this particular conflict because Congress reacted with the DTA and MCA legislation that have readjusted the statutory requirements of habeas corpus to those detained in Guantánamo, in Afghanistan, and in this armed conflict. As well, the court's decision that statutory habeas rights extended to the detainees in Guantánamo was at least partially based on the finer points of the lease with Cuba creating a distinctive division of sovereignty and jurisdiction. However, what is certainly worthy of note from a human rights perspective is that this decision explicitly realigned precedent of jurisdictional questions to focus on a prisoners' guardians rather than on the detainees themselves.

There are also undeniable implications to come out of the Supreme Court's next statement in the interbranch colloquy concerning international law in *Hamdan.* The first is that, barring any radical changes in the UCMJ, the Geneva Conventions do not now need to be determined by a court to be self-executing in cases involving the military justice system. To be sure, this advancement (albeit limited and open to congressional revision) is one worthy of acknowledgment, and certainly has repercussions beyond the current conflict. Second, the finding in *Hamdan* that Common Article 3 is applicable to the "war on terror" will surely help shape future administrations' policies. This ruling will additionally further ingrain Common Article 3 as a baseline of protections afforded to all individuals in any type of armed conflict, as well as to offer further form to the provision which reads "judicial guarantees [...] recognized as indispensable by civilized peoples." Moreover, it was the specific use of international law in this decision that offered the Supreme Court a palpable buttress to push back against the political branches and to mount the ladder further. Considering the judiciary's infrequent use of international law as legitimate norms to constrain the domestic political process, particularly in times of armed conflict, this is undoubtedly noteworthy.

Finally, the remark in this institutional discussion found in *Boumediene* is perhaps most unclear when viewed in light of international law. On the one hand, there is little doubt that the finding of a constitutionally afforded right of habeas corpus to noncitizens held outside the territory of the US is an extension of human rights by the Supreme Court; on the other, it is an open question as to whether this ruling will serve to better protect prisoners held in Afghanistan, in an Abu Ghraib-type prison in Iraq, or even in undisclosed "black sites." This is one key reason why a decision including, or plainly based upon, human rights jurisprudence would have been preferable so as to protect all detainees held under the effective control of the US, regardless of geography or land-lease agreements.

As will be seen below, there continue to be a great number of unresolved questions for legal and legitimate detention in counterterrorism, but the Supreme Court has yet to weigh in again to moderate the dialogue. The explanation for this is not clear. Nonetheless, the fact that the US Supreme Court found a way to take the historic step of eschewing the traditional and seemingly routine deference to the political branches in times of armed conflict, and in so doing to extend rights across borders and nationalities, should not go unnoticed.

To view the question of legality for detention under Obama, there are several directions where attention can be placed to appreciate what has transpired concerning counterterrorism detention since the last pronouncement of the Supreme Court in 2008. The first is related to the applicability of habeas corpus to detainees held by the US beyond the facility at Guantánamo. Another concerns the actual habeas procedure afforded to those held at the US detention center on the island of Cuba. Next, there is the National Defense Authorization Act for the Fiscal Year

2012 (NDAA, 2012) which is meant to codify, if not expand, the authority to detain persons in this conflict. Finally, one can discuss the intention to close the Guantánamo facility. Each offers a view on how the different branches of government have been dealing with the question of detention, but it should be noted that a shift in policy under a new administration has changed the relevance of the matter.

a Detention without judicial review beyond Guantánamo

With regard to the applicability of judicial review for detention beyond Guantánamo, one must flag a case dealing with whether these constitutional habeas rights are applicable to noncitizens held in detention in Afghanistan. A preliminary reading of the *Boumediene* decision of 2008 would certainly suggest that from that day forward, with ever-increasing advances in travel and technology, it would be correspondingly more difficult to argue that a habeas review is "impracticable and anomalous."

Following this line of interpretation, in 2009 a District Court granted habeas corpus to petitioners held in a military facility in that country, stating that "[a]lthough the site of detention at Bagram is not identical to that at Guantanamo Bay, the 'objective degree of control' asserted by the United States there is not appreciably different than at Guantanamo" (*Al Maqaleh et al.* v. *Gates* [2009], p. 229). While it was recognized that Afghanistan was still an active theater of war, the judge found that this hurdle was not insurmountable. Most importantly, it was found that "for these petitioners, such practical barriers are largely of the Executive's choosing— they were all apprehended elsewhere and then brought (i.e., rendered) to Bagram for detention now exceeding six years" (*Al Maqaleh* [2009], p. 229).

Therefore, although the Justice Department under the direction of a new president argued that there continued to be a facility in which detainees in the "war on terror" could be held without access to a court to challenge their detention, the judge followed the Supreme Court's reasoning by highlighting the centrality of habeas corpus as an instrument meant to achieve the delicate balance between three separate branches of government. The opinion cites the *Boumediene* decision, explaining that "[w]ithin the Constitution's separation-of-powers structure, few exercises of judicial power are as legitimate or as necessary as the responsibility to hear challenges to the authority of the Executive to imprison a person" (*Al Maqaleh* [2009], p. 228).

This case continued through the court system where, in May 2010, the DC Court of Appeals reversed the lower court's ruling. Interestingly, in this overruling there was next to no mention of the principles of habeas corpus and the separation of powers as found in *Boumediene*. Instead it focused on the burdens created by the continuing state of war in the country of Afghanistan and the nature of the bilateral agreement creating the detention facility itself. In what was described as a victory for the Obama administration, the Court of Appeals applied a three-part test derived from *Boumediene* very strictly and did not venture into any of the philosophical reasoning for constraining the power of the executive that had been carried out by Justice Kennedy in that decision.

From a human rights perspective, the most troubling part of this decision from the Court of Appeals is that the opinion explicitly rejected the idea that anyone subject to detention in a US military facility has an automatic right to challenge her detention. The court claimed that some sort of limiting principle must be asserted by the petitioners held in Bagram, otherwise their argument "would seem to create the potential for the extraterritorial extension of the Suspension Clause to noncitizens held in any United States military facility in the world" (*Al Maqaleh et al.* v. *Gates* [2010], p. 19). Here we see the shortcoming of the *Boumediene* decision: the narrow reading of the constitutional application (inherent to "judicial ladder of review") left a wide margin for the interpretation of circumstances other than Guantánamo. It should be remembered that, in direct contrast, the UN Human Rights Committee interprets that "a State party must respect and ensure the rights laid down in the Covenant to anyone within the power or *effective control* of that State Party, even if not situated within the territory of the State Party" (UN HRC 2004, General Comment No. 31: para. 10; my emphasis). Under this view, effective control over the person is decisive and territorial jurisdiction is immaterial.

This leads us to incongruence in the Obama policy when seen in practice. During his presidential campaign, Obama asserted that he would defend judicial review for terrorism suspects and gave a firm speech on the Senate floor supporting a habeas corpus amendment to the Military Commissions Act of 2006. Senator Obama avowed,

> it is understandable that mistakes will be made and identities will be confused. I don't blame the Government for that. This is an extraordinarily difficult war we are prosecuting against terrorists. There are going to be situations in which we cast too wide a net and capture the wrong person.
>
> But what is avoidable is refusing to ever allow our legal system to correct these mistakes. By giving suspects a chance—even one chance—to challenge the terms of their detention in court, to have a judge confirm that the Government has detained the right person for the right suspicions, we could solve this problem without harming our efforts in the war on terror one bit.
>
> (Obama 2006)

Yet Obama's Department of Justice argued against this principle before a district court and immediately appealed the ruling when it lost. Because the detainees were captured abroad and then transferred to Afghanistan, this detention is indeed at a site "of the Executive's choosing."[12] Of course, this means that the Obama administration has always held the option of relocating the detainees; this includes Guantánamo, where they would enjoy habeas rights as per the *Boumediene* decision.[13]

b "Meaningful review"

The next prong of this partition is the precise judicial procedure that the detainees held at Guantánamo have received following the *Boumediene* decision, as this question was left up to the lower courts to settle case by case. The central issue before the district courts was whether the government had shown by a "preponderance of evidence" that a detainee was a "part of" Al-Qaeda or the Taliban since such detention had been authorized by the AUMF. This is basically a factual inquiry reviewing the evidence of hostile acts, a stay at an Al-Qaeda-sponsored guesthouse, attendance at a training camp, or a specific travel route. Between 2008 and mid-2010, the process began by yielding disparate results. There were thirty-four rulings, with fifteen decided in favor of the government and continued detention, while nineteen detainees won their habeas petitions.

However, in July 2010, the DC Circuit Court of Appeals reversed a grant of habeas relief in *Al-Adahi* v. *Obama,* and a new standard was established. The independent fact-finding powers of the district courts were tightly constrained on appeal, and the Supreme Court chose to remain silent on the issue by denying appeal in early 2011. As a result, a more lenient standard for government evidence was implemented, triggering an about-face by the district courts, with eleven out of the next twelve petitions being denied. Based on scrutiny of the evidence presented in the cases both before and after this pivotal decision, one leading source tracking the legal questions at Guantánamo found that judicial deference to government factual allegations had become the norm. Looking at this legal landscape, his conclusion of May 2012 is difficult to deny: "such review has been rendered essentially meaningless" because "almost no detainees will prevail at the district court level, and if any do, the D.C. Circuit will likely reverse the decision to grant them relief" (Denbeaux 2012: 2).

The one habeas relief granted during this time was again overturned by the DC Court of Appeals. Because this court had not cleared the way for one single detainee to leave Guantánamo via a judicial ruling (prisoners have left, but not through this route), many hopes were hung on this *Latif* v. *Obama* case being accepted for review by the Supreme Court. Beyond the obvious fact that the new standards being implemented post-*Adahi* had resulted in only this one case winning a grant of habeas relief, there were several other reasons why *Latif* was considered significant. First, this decision established an even more deferential standard for the "presumption of regularity" and accuracy for government intelligence reports, putting a novel burden on detainees' lawyers to disprove that evidence. Next, the main opinion included a scathing denunciation of the Supreme Court's instruction to grant habeas review to the detainees at Guantánamo, insisting that it fundamentally changes the parameters of war: "*Boumediene's* logic is compelling: take no prisoners" (*Latif* [2011], p. 764). Finally, the decision provoked a rare vigorous dissenting opinion:

> I fear that in practice it "comes perilously close to suggesting that whatever the government says must be treated as true." In that world, it is hard to see what is left of the Supreme Court's command in *Boumediene* that habeas review be "meaningful."
>
> (*Latif* [2011], p. 779; internal citations omitted)

Nonetheless, in June 2012, the Supreme Court denied this appeal, and six others, leaving the distinct impression that it was satisfied with the results. Many commentators believe that if this case did not provide an opening for the court to intervene, then it had no intention of doing so to further moderate the dialogue.

Throughout this chapter we have seen that the Supreme Court stepped directly into the fray time and again when it felt the political branches of government were acting outside of their authority; thus this silence begs many questions. Perhaps the court has determined that any judicial review during times of armed conflict, no matter how cursory, is sufficient? Or maybe the departure of Justice John Paul Stevens reveals just how instrumental he was in guiding the court up this judicial ladder?

Unfortunately, it does not appear possible at this point to fully explain the court's silence over these five years, and it must therefore be left aside for now. However, since the question of detention in counterterrorism operations is yet to be settled, it is worthwhile to watch the Supreme Court, since, as we have seen, it has the distinct authority and ability to moderate dialogue on these matters of legality.

c NDAA 2012

At the end of 2011, President Obama signed into law the National Defense Authorization Act for Fiscal Year 2012. This Act provided for the first time a statutory definition of the covered persons whose detention is pursuant to the AUMF. Besides the evident approval of military funding and other provisions, this legislation authorized the detention of certain categories of individuals and requires military detention of a subgroup of them, governs the status determinations for those held within the AUMF regardless of location, regulates and requires review proceedings for the continued detention of those at Guantánamo, and prolongs the funding restrictions that relate to the transfer of detainees to foreign countries. Additionally, even though it does not directly bar criminal trials for terrorism suspects, it negates the use of military funds for the transfer of detainees from Guantánamo into the US. At passage, there was a good deal of controversy over whether it simply codified the authority already granted in the AUMF or if, in fact, it expanded it. That dispute continues unsettled at the time of this writing and is likely to remain so for some time.

Due to the numerous disagreements over the scope and meaning of this legislation as it relates to counterterrorism, it is necessary to focus attention here on only one particular point that also relates to the drone program discussed in the conclusion to this book. The NDAA 2012 expressly states that it is not intended to limit or expand the authority of the president or the scope of the AUMF, yet this is not particularly helpful since it is the interpretation of that existing authority that causes much of the controversy. For that reason, it is most useful to explore the Obama administration's definition of its detention authority; notably, it does not deviate greatly from that embraced by its predecessor.

In a court brief of March 2009, the Obama administration framed its detention authority as pertaining not only to those responsible for the attacks of 9/11, but that the president "also has the authority to detain persons who were part of, or substantially supported, Taliban or al-Qaida forces or *associated forces*" (Respondents' Memorandum [2009]: 2; my emphasis). While the "substantial support" prong of this definition can raise similar concerns, we direct particular attention to the inclusion of "associated forces." Of course, membership in al-Qaeda or the Taliban plainly falls within the authority granted by Congress, but the insertion of "associated forces" is a category of indeterminate breath thus raising real difficulties.

As an indication of the problem, one can look to the *Hedges* v. *Obama* litigation which spurred a district court judge to issue a permanent injunction enjoining enforcement of the provision containing this language. The NDAA 2012 means to delineate the covered persons for indefinite detention, and, in a linguistic formulation almost precisely following what is found in the administration brief discussed above, the relevant provision of the statue moves beyond those directly responsible for the original attacks. It reads:

> A person who was a part of or substantially supported al-Qaeda, the Taliban, or *associated forces* that are engaged in hostilities against the United States or its coalition partners, including any person who has committed a belligerent act or has directly supported such hostilities in aid of such enemy forces.
>
> (NDAA 2012, §1021(b)(2); my emphasis)

The presiding judge rejected the government's argument that the statute simply affirmed the AUMF because of the difference in language between the two. Namely, the statute no longer requires a link to 9/11, and so something novel is indeed being introduced in this legislation.

More pertinent to our point here, it is the vagueness of the terms used to define detention authority that occupies an important portion of this opinion. It is pointed out that "'associated forces' is an undefined, moving target, subject to change and subjective judgment" (*Hedges* [2012], p. 107). Additionally, in a footnote, the judge dissects one of the pre-trial government memoranda, concluding that the "argument is carefully crafted and does not exclude the concept of associated forces constituting groups the executive branch 'believes' may be tied to al-Qaeda or the Taliban" (*Hedges* [2012], pp. 105–106).

This subjective margin of maneuver seems to be something the Obama administration is intent on maintaining. Indeed, it had argued in the original 2009 brief that

> [i]t is neither possible nor advisable, however, to attempt to identify, in the abstract, the precise nature and degree of "substantial support," or the precise characteristics of "associated forces," that are or would be sufficient to bring persons and organizations within the foregoing framework.
>
> (Respondents' Memorandum [2009]: 2)

Thus we find, as will be seen throughout this book and regardless of party, an attempt to base the authority for exercising the force of government on terms or parameters that cannot be objectively fenced in. When it comes to judging the legitimate exercise of authority, this is a problem.

Finally, there is another reason why the inclusion of the term "associated forces" into the administration's definition of the scope of its authority is significant. Although the drone program will be more fully explored in the conclusion of this book, it is worthwhile to point out here that in the letter to Congress from Attorney General Eric Holder in May 2013 it was clarified that targeting decisions for the use of lethal force will be based (even after a constriction of the drone program) on whether a person is "a senior operational leader of al Qa'ida or its *associated forces*."[14] Hence, this broad term takes on an added significance, and its subjectivity for targeting decisions is undoubtedly problematic for legitimacy.

d *The closing of Guantánamo?*

President Obama issued an executive order on his second full day in office, calling for the closure of the Guantánamo Bay detention camp within one year, and he directed a full review of the legal status of the 242 individuals detained in the facility (Obama 2009b). More than four years later, that facility is still open with 166 detainees remaining and a majority of them on a hunger strike at the time of this writing. At the start of Obama's second term, this widely recognized failure was a blight on his record for all of the reasons discussed throughout this chapter.

Conscious of this failing, in May 2013 the President gave his second speech devoted to national security since he took office (the first taking place exactly four years earlier). He again insisted that the fight against Al-Qaeda must be fought within a framework of the rule of law and consistent with the Constitution and international law (Obama 2013). He once more asserted that Guantánamo does more harm than good and that failing to adhere to our highest principles had played into the enemy's hands and undermined our safety. The President also defended the use of force and detention as appropriate tools in a continuing armed conflict. However, in contrast to President Bush, he insisted that such means must conform to legal limits.

There was one key element of this speech that should be highlighted here. Just before turning to the closing of Guantánamo, restating it as a top priority for the administration, President Obama opened the door to an intriguing avenue. Echoing an idea suggested in the previous months by his former Legal Adviser to the State Department and his former General Counsel of the Department of Defense (see Koh 2013 and Johnson 2012), the President stated that he intended to engage Congress about the existing AUMF in order "to determine how we can continue to fight terrorists without keeping America on a perpetual war-time footing" (Obama 2013). He suggested that this authorization needed to be reassessed and ultimately repealed.

Of course, such a shift would have important implications for the applicable law in this conflict. It would largely transfer the questions of legality into a law-enforcement model and eliminate indefinite detention without trial, since this would mark an end of hostilities and require a release and repatriation of those not convicted of war crimes. Although he dodged the extremely difficult question of what to do with those detainees who cannot be tried due to the fact that the evidence against them has been tainted by the use of ill-treatment in interrogation, the proposition of repealing the authorization for war is certainly thought-provoking in the context of legitimacy.

VII Conclusion: detention and diplomatic implications

While all of these developments are important for establishing the question of legality in counterterrorism detention under a new administration, one point should not be overlooked. There has been a shift in tactics under the Obama administration. The Bush administration's policy focused on the detention and interrogation of terrorist suspects, and they received a good amount of scrutiny by the citizenry, diplomats, and the courts. Presumably as a result of this negative attention, there has been a marked increase in unmanned drone attacks under President Obama. As confinement and questioning became strongly criticized activities both at home and abroad, killing became more appealing because it evades the need for either. Since the Obama administration has taken a negligible number of suspects into custody during his first term as a result (Becker and Shane 2012), the relevance of the detention regime has primarily been diminished to dealing with those captured under Bush (remaining an open wound visible to domestic and international audiences, but less festering with silence from the Supreme Court).

What this also means is that much of the *new diplomacy* has shifted from Guantánamo to the drone program. The attention of public and internet-age diplomacy, rebounding to the US citizenry, has primarily shifted to the use of lethal force by these unmanned aerial vehicles. This can be evidenced by President Obama's counterterrorism speech of May 2013 in which, for the first time after four years of relative silence, he began to tackle head-on the difficult questions of this secret program. Consequently, an analysis through the three lenses of legitimacy is broached in the conclusion to this book.

The use of the lens of legality in this chapter has sharpened our view of the detention policy in the "war on terror." As we have also seen, the issue of applicable law and judicial protections for those held in this conflict has yet to be settled, with sparring by the executive, the legislature, and the lower courts while the Supreme Court remains muted in the dialogue. To the extent that diplomatic practice turns on international legal obligations, then the lack of meaningful judicial review for those held at the Guantánamo facility and the denial of such a procedure for those within the effective control of US forces clearly have continued implications for diplomacy.

However, coherent philosophical principles grounded the majority opinions in the Supreme Court cases analyzed here, and it is thus logical that this translated into understanding by those who exercise their *will to obey*. In other words, grasping that individuals held in prison have the right to challenge the grounds for their perpetual detention, regardless of location and nationality, is not arcane or overly complicated. Most importantly for legitimacy through the lens of legality, the Supreme Court ruled three times in four years that the detention policy of the administration was operating outside the law.

Notes

1 This chapter is an updated, revised, and expanded version of my chapter "Judicially Moderated Dialogue and the 'War on Terror'" in *Balancing Liberty and Security: The Human Rights Pendulum*, L. Hennebel and H. Tigroudja (eds) (Nijmegen, Holland: Wolf Legal Pub., 2012).

2 Notably, the issue was also famously treated in Justice Jackson's opinion in *Korematsu* v. *US*, 65 S. Ct. 193, at 245 [1944]:

military decisions are not susceptible of intelligent judicial appraisal. They do not pretend to rest on evidence, but are made on information that often would not be admissible and on assumptions that could not be proved [...] Hence courts can never have real alternative to accepting the mere declaration of the authorities that issued the order that it was reasonably necessary from a military viewpoint.

3 To resolve this question one must begin with Common Article 2 and determine whether the conflict is "between two or more of the High Contracting Parties." It was as a result of the interpretation of this provision that al-Qaeda detainees were found to have no legal protection:

I accept the legal conclusion of the Department of Justice and determine that none of the provisions of Geneva apply to our conflict with al Qaeda in Afghanistan or elsewhere throughout the world because, among other reasons, al Qaeda is not a High Contracting Party to Geneva.

(Bush 2002a: 134)

4 To determine prisoner of war status one must turn to Article 4(A) of GC-III and ascertain if an individual who has fallen into the power of the coalition forces in Afghanistan fits into one of the categories fleshed out in the Article. It is through the interpretation of this provision (specifically 4(A)(2)) that the Taliban detainees were found not to fit into any of these categories, and thus afforded no legal protection: "I determine that the provisions of Geneva will apply to our present conflict with the Taliban"; yet, "I determine that the Taliban detainees are unlawful combatants and, therefore, do not qualify as prisoners of war under Article 4 of Geneva." There was also no prisoner of war protection for al-Qaeda: "I note that, because Geneva does not apply to our conflict with al Qaeda, al Qaeda detainees also do not qualify as prisoners of war" (Bush 2002a: 135).

5 For the application of this Article as a baseline for all detainees in any conflict, see the discussion of the *Hamdan* ruling in Section IV. Yet the administration's assessment of this legal question was:

I also accept the legal conclusion of the Department of Justice and determine that common Article 3 of Geneva does not apply to either al Qaeda or Taliban detainees, because, among other reasons, the relevant conflicts are international in scope and common Article 3 applies only to "armed conflict not of an international character."

(Bush 2002a: 134–135)

6 As evidenced in the previous three notes above, the US administration interpreted there to indeed be a gap in the Conventions through which detainees could (and did) slip without any legal protection. This possibility has certainly been considered elsewhere, only the conclusions have largely been the reverse.

7 Article 5 of GC-III provides that

[s]hould any doubt arise as to whether persons, having committed a belligerent act and having fallen into the hands of the enemy, belong to any of the categories enumerated in Article 4, such persons shall enjoy the protection of the present Convention until such time as their status has been determined by a competent tribunal.

As such, there is indeed a process foreseen. This requirement could create a heavy case load; however, a leading case will largely be able to determine a group's status, and only some individual cases will merit a full hearing.

9 Turku Declaration of Minimum Humanitarian Standards; the Paris Minimum Standards of Human Rights Norms in a State of Emergency; and the UN Commission on Human Rights, The Siracusa Principles on the Limitation and Derogation Provisions in the International Covenant on Civil and Political Rights.

10 See, for example, International Covenant of Civil and Political Rights, Article 9(1); the American Convention on Human Rights, Article 7(3); the European Convention for the Protection of Human Rights and Fundamental Freedoms, Article 5(1); the African Charter on Human and People's Rights, Article 6; and the Universal Declaration of Human Rights, Articles 3 and 9.

11 To read and listen to the oral arguments visit *Rasul* v. *Bush,* The Oyez Project at IIT Chicago-Kent College of Law, www.oyez.org/cases/2000–2009/2003/2003_03_334 (accessed June 2013).

12 Relying on a statement in the Court of Appeals ruling that its analysis might be different if evidence were presented that the executive chose a theater of war to evade judicial review, the petitioners argued just that to a district court in 2012. The attempt failed, and the government's motion to dismiss was granted.

13 An agreement was signed March 9, 2012, to transfer control of detainees from the US to Afghanistan, and a passing of authority took place on September 10, 2012. Yet dozens of foreign detainees will remain under US military control for the indefinite future (Savage and Bowley 2012).

14 Holder, E. (2013) Letter to Chairman of the Judiciary Committee, US Senate, May 22.

4 Through the lens of morality

Just war and public diplomacy

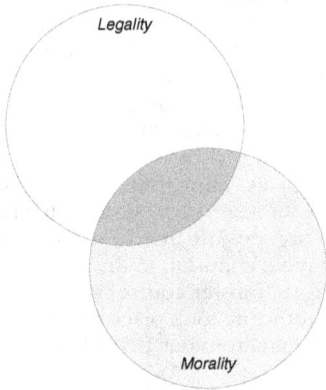

[W]herein two things are to be proved, the one that a just feare (without an actuall invasion or offence) is a sufficient ground of Warre, and in the nature of a true defensive; the other that we have towards Spaine cause of just feare, [...] not out of umbrages, light jealousness, apprehensions a farre off, but out of a clear foresight of imminent danger.

Sir Francis Bacon, 1624

War in defence of life is permissible only when the danger is immediate and certain, not when it is merely assumed. I admit, to be sure, that if the assailant seizes weapons in such a way that his intent to kill is manifest the crime can be forestalled; [...] But those who accept fear of any sort as justifying anticipatory slaying are themselves greatly deceived, and deceive others.

Hugo Grotius, 1625

I Introduction

Moral debate over war has been with us for centuries, and its historical filiations in the Western world are best traced through the familiar just war doctrine. Its protracted existence and constantly developing recurrence in Western thought speaks to the depth to which the moral dimensions of war run within the populations from which it sprang. Even though there has been a history of formulating a reasoning for casting aside any ethical and legal considerations in war-making, classical, modern, and contemporary forms of moral (at times mixing clearly with legal) analysis are a testament to the durability and relevance of such an approach. However, it should be remembered that limits on warfare have come together over scores of years from an amalgamation of sources. These include Christian theologians who developed a moral doctrine inside the church, international lawyers who enunciated principles that guided and set in motion the first texts of this discipline, and military professionals who focused on considerations of fair play rooted in chivalry (Turner Johnson 1981). Therefore, as the just war theory will serve as the overarching vehicle that will drive this axiological analysis, it should be understood as a relatively imprecise term that rightfully reflects the intersection of the vital concepts of law, morals, and prudence. As such, it is certainly a fitting tradition to be used in this work treating the equally interdisciplinary subject of legitimacy.

In Chapter 1, we discussed the concept of overlap and shone a light on a coincidence that exists between legality and morality. In particular, we spoke to the prohibition of free violence that must exist in any and all legal or moral codes. This exclusion directly relates to the work of this chapter as we will be exploring the rules that have been laid down over the centuries for reducing or eliminating unconstrained military attacks. As this will not be an exhaustive study of just war theory, we will focus on the primary aspects of the tradition that are directly pertinent to the justifications put forward for the invasion of Iraq in 2003. The classic doctrine of just war had three basic requirements—right authority, just cause, and right intention—and these conditions provided the fundamental shape for how the theory would further develop over time. Nevertheless, these basic criteria also held within them concepts that have become more explicit, including that war must only be defensive in nature, that it is to be used only as a last resort, that there be a reasonable chance of success, and that armed hostilities are proportional to the harm that was suffered. In this chapter, we will explore the three particular concepts of "anticipatory attacks" for self-defense, "last resort," and "right authority" since they are most directly relevant to our question here.

While all of these criteria from the just war theory correlate to the attempt to exclude wanton bloodshed from international society, our attention in the first half of this chapter will be focused on the distinction

between "preemptive" and "preventive" war. The divergence found
between these two terms and concepts helps explain the disquiet that grew
over what has become known as the "Bush Doctrine." As will be seen,
there was an important bifurcation in the just war tradition during the late
sixteenth and early seventeenth centuries, and a part of the cleavage was
based on this very issue of anticipatory attack (a point masterfully illuminated by Turner Johnson 1975 cf. O'Driscoll 2008: 27–50). While some
advocated that a "just feare" was a reasonable standard for triggering war
(an argument that resulted in no progeny), others insisted that the criteria for launching an attack must be more objective and verifiable (argumentation that helped found international law).

Although it is often forgotten, there was a call within the US (if only by
poll) for a sanctioned justification by the UNSC before the invasion of
Iraq (Kull *et al.* 2003/2004: 569, note 1), lending validity to the idea that
in a notable number of people's minds this body indeed holds the
mandate found within its charter. What this meant was that the debate
over an invasion of Iraq manifested itself in two primary ways that directly
affected public diplomacy: first, there was a worldwide movement of
people who descended into their streets to protest this anticipatory attack,
making it clear that there was a "moment for deliberation"; second, this
display of objection coincided with one of the most high-profile diplomatic debates of contemporary times at the UNSC over the question of
whether an invasion on the grounds presented would be legal and moral.
All of this demonstrated a growing belief that Article 39 of the UN Charter
indeed vests the UNSC with the "right authority" to "determine the existence of any threat to the peace, breach of the peace, or act of aggression."
Thus, the second half of this chapter will treat the significance and the
details of this diplomacy taking place on a public stage.

To once again clarify the overlap that exists between legality and morality, we return to *The Concept of Law*, where H. L. A. Hart put forward a list
of five essential causal connections between natural conditions and systems
of rules. There are two which primarily concern us in the discussion of a
restriction on unprovoked violence: *human vulnerability* and *approximate
equality* (Hart 1994: 194–195). The first of these connections deals with the
exposure that every human confronts when interacting with others. Each
of us is vulnerable to bodily attack that could shorten or end our existence, and, as such, we enter into a societal contract (either implicitly or
explicitly) which requires mutual forbearance by all members. Hart
described the basic starting point for all rule-governing interaction by
stating that "[o]f these the most important for social life are those [prohi-
bitions] that restrict the use of violence in killing or inflicting bodily
harm" (1994: 194). So vital is this protection to our human vulnerability
that without it there would be no reason to have rules of any other kind.

The second causal connection dealing with equity in treatment springs
from only slight differences in strength, dexterity, speed, and intellectual

capacity that exist between all persons. Yet, no one is so superior that they possess the capacity to single-handedly subdue or dominate others for more than a short time. Even the strongest or shrewdest among us must drop their guard for repose and sleep at some point. As such, this natural condition of negligible inequality, because it is only transitory by nature, leads to the need for a system of rules that balances out these slight inherent differences and places all persons on a level playing field. As Hart explains,

> [t]his fact of approximate equality, more than any other, makes obvious the necessity for a system of mutual forbearances and compromise which is the base of both legal and moral obligation. Social life with its rules requiring such forbearances is irksome at times; but it is at any rate less nasty, less brutish, and less short than unrestrained aggression for beings thus approximately equal.
>
> (Hart 1994: 195)

Thus we will proceed on the assumption that there is indeed a very important overlap between morality and law at the precise point which concerns us in this chapter. Survival, or self-preservation, is a shared value among all humans, and this mutual interest stretches across borders, cultures, or tribes.

Hart himself argued in 1961 that the inequality of states renders the requirement of a prohibition against free violence as unsuitable to the international realm. However, there is good reason to doubt that this reasoning remains applicable. For example, the fact that governments now regularly invoke self-defense in protecting themselves against non-state actors suggests that this disparity is irrelevant because even individuals can cause significant harm with today's weaponry. Additionally, the fear that weapons of mass destruction could end up in the hands of violent persons again changes this calculus of great inequality in the international sphere. It is thus argued that the difference in strength is no longer wholly relevant.

There are certainly some who argue that such analogies are inappropriately applied because international relations should be understood as *realpolitik*, and every state preserves its own *raison d'état*, thus invalidating moral and legal perspectives. In other words, politics between nations must be understood through a nation's material considerations and national interest rather than through abstract ideals. However, in the circumstance before us, we are analyzing the legitimacy of a regime or policy, and, therefore, the perception of individuals, and public opinion at large, are directly consequential. Even though there was indeed an historical moment in which states unblushingly argued that recourse to war was their own prerogative to exercise at will and that any appeals to international laws were meaningless, this was an idea that "never seized the public imagination"

(Walzer 1977: 63). Thus, since legitimacy most certainly turns on the perceptions of people and their individual *will to obey* the government, the domestic analogy loaded with concepts of right and wrong, good and bad, along with morality and immorality, is directly pertinent here for our analysis of the use of force in the "war on terror." It would seem absurd to assume that a public is readily and easily going to extract itself from calculations of war, particularly when all are asked to support it, and members of the society are asked to kill and be killed. As Michael Walzer points out, "[u]ntil wars are really fought with pawns, inanimate objects and not human beings, warfare cannot be isolated from moral life" (1977: 64).

Of course, this *jus ad bellum* discussion of the invasion of Iraq that is to follow raises at least two other questions: how does the question of legality relate to Operation Enduring Freedom which committed a coalition of armed forces into Afghanistan? And what *jus in bello* questions are relevant for evaluating morality and the "war on terror"?

Due in large part to the unanimously approved UNSC Resolutions 1368 and 1373, offering an authoritative interpretation of the character and legal meaning of the 9/11 attacks, the invasion of Afghanistan in 2001 in reaction to the attacks on US soil rested on very different legal grounds than that of the mobilization of troops into Iraq. The specific use of language in both resolutions—"the inherent right of individual or collective self-defence"—has largely been taken by international lawyers to mean that the UNSC determined that 9/11 had indeed triggered a right to respond with force. Additionally, in letters submitted to the UNSC, both the US and the UK justified the military operation in Afghanistan as individual and collective self-defense (Permanent Rep of US to UN 2001; Permanent Mission of UK 2001).

As to the second question raised, specific examinations of *jus in bello* regarding the "war on terror" will be primarily limited to the issues of detention without judicial review and torture and ill-treatment during interrogations that are to be found in the previous and following chapters. There is no doubt that the means by which a war is waged factors directly into the calculations of its moral character, which can be plainly surmised through its later inclusion into the doctrine of just war. For this reason, two complete chapters of this work are dedicated to analyzing particular aspects of humanitarian and human rights law in war, although through somewhat different lenses of analysis. To be sure, the war in Iraq raised other *jus in bello* questions, such as the use of white phosphorous against insurgents and civilians during the assaults on Falluja, the use of cluster bombs, and whether feasible precautionary methods in targeting were properly implemented. However, the scope of this work will not include the armed-conflict operations in Iraq after invasion and will instead concentrate on the *jus ad bellum* question of law and morality.

This chapter is organized around an application of the most pertinent portions of the tradition that has served as the baseline of moral analysis in Western civilization for at least some 1,500 years when it comes to armed conflict. We will begin by tracing the historical filiations of the just war tradition on the question of anticipatory military action in Section II. It will be demonstrated that the distinction between preemptive and preventive war is one that has long existed and forms a critical understanding within the tradition that armed hostilities must be launched in response to a verifiable injury. In Section III we will deal with what has become known as the "Bush Doctrine." This was presented to the public as a "preemptive" policy, although it is more properly termed "preventive war." Yet, in the end this rhetorical sleight of hand could not hide the war in Iraq's moral failings as the claims of future dangers showed themselves to be nothing more than erroneous suspicions.

In the second half of this chapter, beginning in Section IV, there will be a treatment of whether military confrontation was employed as the "last resort." It will entail a discussion of the manner in which morality inevitably enters into such debate when there is clear evidence of a choice through a public "moment for deliberation." In Section V there will be a discussion of "right authority" in the context of the United Nations as the world's public forum for diplomacy. Here it will be argued that the "right authority" of the UNSC was bypassed through expedient interpretations which transferred a questionable authority into the hands of governments to unilaterally sanction the opening of hostilities themselves.

Finally, Section VI will provide conclusions while pointing out that the Obama administration has also honed in on the precise question of "imminence" as the standard for anticipatory lethal force across international borders in its unmanned drone program rendering the historical research of this chapter acutely pertinent once again.

II Anticipatory attacks and the just war doctrine

In this section, we will provide an historical analysis of one specific aspect of the just war doctrine to analyze an important part of the argument put forward by the Bush administration for a war against Iraq—often popularly termed the "Bush Doctrine." Although this did not become the official reasoning for the invasion, this doctrine did enter directly into the popular debate over war policy. The intention here is to trace some of the history of discussion over the difference between preemptive and preventive war to show that there is indeed a significant chasm that exists between these two standards of anticipatory self-defense. This gulf will be shown to be one that has long existed within the just war tradition, and thus it can be understood as an identifiable stark moral and legal line. One primary reason for a self-imposed prohibition of this nature would simply be for exercising the use of force only in a manner that is likely to be deemed legitimate by citizens. When this line is crossed, one leaves the solid ground of what is knowable or known, for the shaky and unverifiable position of war based upon conjecture of our enemy's future intentions.

Of course, as discussed in Chapter 2, self-defense as a legal doctrine did not emerge until after there was an explicit codified prohibition of the use of force; the two concepts clearly go hand in hand since you must have a prohibition before there is an exception. As we will see in our investigation of the just war doctrine, there has long been discussion over the justness of different types of defensive anticipatory action. It was only during the nineteenth and early twentieth centuries that it was argued that every state had an uninhibited right to wage war completely at its own discretion. During that period states could generally "resort to war for a good reason, a bad reason or no reason at all" (Briggs 1952: 976, cited in Dinstein 2001: 71). Regardless of this historical gap, it is useful to first plot out the different forms of defense that have been contemplated and to place them on a timeline. In this way, we will provide a coherent shape to our discussion of the moral and legal delineations of anticipatory war in the just war doctrine and contemporary international law.

The most useful breakdown of the different modes of anticipatory action is in terms of four temporal moments: *reactive self-defense, interceptive self-defense, preemptive attack,* and *preventive war.* (While some terms have been adjusted slightly, the outline comes from Kolb 2004: 122–125).

Reactive Self-Defense: This action is the one most obviously contemplated within the text of Article 51 of the UN Charter. The language of the provision clearly allows for the use of force "if an armed attack occurs," but there is also the explicit requirement that the state exercising self-defense bring the situation immediately before the UNSC so that it can take steps to restore peace and security. This is surely the most uncontroversial type of action, even if some doubt remains about what intensity of assault rises to the level of an "armed attack."

Interceptive Self-Defense: This action can be described as that undertaken by a state to interrupt an attack that has already been launched but that has not yet struck its target. Examples would include the disruption of a launched missile, aircraft or sailing naval fleet. Some have likened this action to a hypothetical attack by the US on the Japanese naval fleet before it reached Pearl Harbor. Of course, the validity of such an action depends upon the accuracy of intelligence information analyzing threats and coming assaults. However, few would question the justifiability of intercepting an onslaught already underway.

Preemptive Attack: This act raises the eyebrows of some jurists who believe that it crosses the line of legality because verifiability in retrospect is extremely difficult, if not impossible. This is in addition to the fact that, once again, one becomes wholly reliant upon excellent or perfect security intelligence. However, the critical element that solidifies this particular action in our time axis is that of immediacy. In international law, the term that the majority of jurists focus on as paramount for defining this type of deed is that it is triggered by a strike that is *imminent* in time. Troop movements to an international border, visible military preparations for an attack, or even a declaration that an act of violence will soon be under way are some of the observable circumstances that would demonstrate this imminence. The example that is often put forward for this form of self-defense is the case of Israel's attack on Egypt in 1967 in response to a troop buildup in the Sinai Peninsula and escalating belligerent rhetoric between the states (Walzer 1977: 80–85; cf. Popp 2006).

Preventive War: This final variety of action is purported to be a defensive use of force against an adversary that is not now preparing for immediate military confrontation but the risks involved in waiting for a timing of the enemy's choosing are too great to warrant restraint. This act is surely the most questionable when it comes to international law because of the palpable lack of immediacy. This is not to mention the fact that it is impossible to apply proportionality and necessity, which are also a part of the customary law relating to self-defense. Most significant from a moral perspective is that any effort launched on the basis of such an idea or doctrine, while regularly justified through a loud rhetoric of fear and security, is based solely upon speculation and conjecture. In the just war doctrine, this particular type of action can be most often found under the descriptions of offensive war and that of attacking the growing power of a neighbor.

The intention of this section of our work is to focus a spotlight on the moral and legal difference between a *preemptive attack* and that of a *preventive war*. This disparity was glossed over in the presentation of the Bush Doctrine by the administration. Throughout the development of the just war doctrine, this distinction has been essential, and its filiation can be traced. This is not to say that no one has ever attempted to argue that preventive war based on fear and speculation of the unpredictable future should be deemed justifiable; rather, the point is that when this case has been made it falls in a distinctly different category not founded on moral and legal arguments. Thus the space separating *preemptive attack* from *preventive war* is best described as a chasm, or even a precipice.

a The classic doctrine

The fact that nearly all groups who resort to mass violence seem virtually incapable of doing so without formulating a logic for its need certainly points to the fact that such reasoning is inherently human. This is regardless of whether the employment of war is used as tool for self-defense, punishment, peacemaking, politics, or otherwise. However, the filiations of the first recognized formulations of the justifiability of war-making, known as the just war doctrine, are traced back to St. Augustine of Hippo. Rather than pretending to trace the entire thread of thought on this vast subject, this survey will focus on some of the better known figures who have weighed in on limits in war, particularly on the subject of the difference between offensive and defensive wars. In doing so, it will be seen that there has long been debate over where exactly a line should be drawn between legitimate defense and unjust war.

As a starting point, it should be recognized that Augustine of Hippo left an ambiguous legacy for his successors. Part of this, no doubt, is due to the fact that in attempting to formulate a doctrine on the justness of the participation in war by Christians, Augustine had few "shoulders of giants" to stand upon so as to construct his own intellectual edifice. That is to say, Augustine was largely trying to cobble together political and legal thought that was not initially suited to or meant for application to a kind of rules or guidelines in international affairs. For example, Roman law did not contain much useful discussion of the structure of how relations with other independent political bodies should take place, other than to distinguish the immortal *civitas* from the mortal citizen. Cicero's defense of the just empire "seems to have turned principally on a denial of the parallel between an individual and the *respublica*" (Tuck 1999: 22). This distinction was found to be morally unsatisfactory not only because of how it led to an unleashing of those in power from restraint, but also, more importantly, for what it meant for Christians asked to participate in unconstrained war-making.

As a result, one essential characteristic of this moral doctrine at its nascent stage (particularly important because of how directly it relates to our own discussion) was that of creating a very tight connection between human law and the conduct of warfare. In contrast to Roman law, Augustine made a direct correlation between the individual analogy in law to the interaction of political bodies. It should be recognized that it is this same moral parallel that common citizens are likely to employ when judging the legitimacy of the use of force. This fusion of justifiable legal rules and equitable treatment among humans to the international sphere typifies the classic just war doctrine. This is surely why we see it develop into the beginnings of international law. One eminent scholar has pointed to the very existence of "canon law" as evidence of this connection and asserted that this "linkage between the theologians and the lawyers, in this area, persisted throughout the Middle Ages, and is the most distinctive feature of the theology of war throughout the period" (Tuck 1999: 57).

The underlying assumption of the just war doctrine today is that there are indeed times when it is morally acceptable to engage in war, along with the supposition that, once begun, there continue to be ethical constraints on those conducting it. However, the earliest theorists did not necessarily begin their work with such assumptions and instead reasoned through the different possibilities to arrive at these now assumed conclusions. It was the firm establishment, by the likes of Augustine and then Gratian, that there were indeed circumstances in which Christians could participate in war that paved the way for what is now known as the just war doctrine.

One can find only a nascent and rudimentary form of *jus in bello* in the writings of Thomas Aquinas in the thirteenth century through his treatment of the "right intention" standard drawn directly from Augustine (Turner Johnson 1975: 40–43). In general, the classic just war doctrine is a reversal of what is found today—that is to say, although the *jus ad bellum* principle dominated the classic doctrine, it is much less prevalent and less developed in international law today. In contrast, the *jus in bello* constraints found in the Geneva Conventions and Hague Regulations are far more elaborate than anything found in the classic doctrine.

Of particular importance for our discussion here is the powerful moral principle of "double effect" devised by Thomas Aquinas. This idea is central to understanding whether there could ever be a moral justification for killing. Thomas shrewdly drew an important distinction between carrying out a violent action with the intent to kill and taking a life while using violence to defend one's own person. Not only was there an important moral distinction between the two acts, but this conceptualization of "double effect" also provided, and should continue to provide, an extremely useful guideline for determining under what circumstances self-defense can be plausibly invoked. In other words, "[t]he use of force had to be directed against the attack, not the attacker" (Fletcher and Ohlin 2008: 27).

Therefore, we must also arrive at the important conclusion that there must be an attack (perhaps imminent); otherwise there is nothing to repel. Thomas eloquently explained this significant concept, and it is well worth reproducing his words here:

> Nothing hinders one act from having two effects, only one of which is intended, while the other is beside the intention. Now moral acts take their species according to what is intended, and not according to what is beside the intention, since this is accidental. [...] Accordingly the act of self-defense may have two effects, one is the saving of one's life, the other is the slaying of the aggressor. Therefore this act, since one's intention is to save one's own life, is not unlawful, seeing that it is natural to everything to keep itself in "being," as far as possible.
> (Thomas Aquinas (1265–1274) *Summa Theologiæ*, II-II: Q. 64, Art. 7;
> internal citations omitted)

Thomas formulated a fundamental distinction in the thirteenth century that even today sheds light on our understanding of the use of force or violence directed onto another. Killing or harm must come only as a side effect of our own needed and proportional self-preservation.

On the question pertinent to our analysis on immediacy, one can indeed find that the first documented thinkers on *jus ad bellum* did discernibly sketch out a basic requirement concerning an anticipatory attack—that is, just war must be in response to a specific wrongful act that has taken place. While there were three primary requirements for a just war in the classic doctrine—right authority, just cause, and right intention—implied throughout is the stipulation that "just war be of a defensive or retributive nature only; offensive wars and wars of preemptive retribution are not permitted" (Turner Johnson 1975: 46). And it was this distinction that was critical throughout the tradition: offensive war vs. defensive war. Not only was it a difference that mattered from the inception of the doctrine, but it is one that can be followed up to contemporary times.

This is certainly not to say that the first use of force was entirely ruled out by these early theologians. Thomas, for example, certainly did not do so, either implicitly or explicitly. But there was the fundamental requirement that some fault must have been committed, and thus there was an injustice that needed to be corrected. In other words, the idea of dealing with a sinful act that has not yet occurred through war was implicitly excluded throughout the classical writings. As one scholar of the tradition put it,

> [a]ctual wrong must have been done, moreover; it is not enough for evil *intentions* to have existed. Preemptive redress of wrongs or punishment of sin (which to the medieval mind was an instance of redress of wrongs) is ruled out.
>
> (Turner Johnson 1975: 38; original emphasis)

Therefore, we find that within the just war doctrine, those who first contemplated the moral limits that should constrain even those who were charged with the defense of large populations must still base the launching of war on veritable actions, and not on assumed future intentions. Thus, the space between preemptive and preventive war was a gap that has been thought to be critical for centuries.

b Transition to the modern era: a telling bifurcation over "just feare"

Sixteenth-century Europe was awash in blood spilled in the religious wars of the Protestant Reformation that lasted until the Peace of Westphalia in 1648 over 130 years later. At the very same time, Europeans were confronting the moral and legal ramifications of the 1492 "discovery" of a New World inhabited by a people previously unknown to them in lands formerly untouched by the peoples of their continent. The carnage and bloodshed that this confrontation of peoples unleashed in a struggle for dominance and riches has been well documented. In the crucible of these violent clashes there was a proliferation of serious thought on the justness of war and conflict, some of it novel and progressive and some of it self-absorbed and expedient.

This no doubt spawned a pivotal development in the just war doctrine. It was during this time period in Europe that the classic doctrine of just war was secularized and became what is now recognized as the discernible roots of contemporary international law, with direct implications for when anticipatory war could be legally employed. Moreover, we will see that during this era of violent conflict some devout religious thinkers morphed the traditional just war doctrine into a justification of war on spiritual grounds, with contrary conclusions on anticipatory defense. As such, thought surrounding armed conflict during this time period has been presented and classified as a division between humanist and scholastic traditions and simultaneously described as a bifurcation of the just war doctrine. Regardless of which school of thought one adheres to, there is an illuminating division over what constitutes a justifiable trigger for the launching of war.

i The humanist tradition and holy war

Some political philosophers have suggested that the most useful way to understand how the original strands of thought progressed on issues of war and peace through the sixteenth century is with the designations of "humanist" and "scholastic" traditions (see, for example, Tuck 1999: 16–77). The distinction between the two might be best described as the rhetorical versus the philosophical. The humanist tradition largely reflected a perspective taken by rhetoricians defending their population's interests before its own political bodies entrusted with the welfare of those very people. Thus it can be understood as representing a relatively narrow self-interest. The scholastics took a wider philosophical view beyond just one community to formulate a precept that could be acceptable to all populations and governments concerned with the justifications of war. The first drew extensively on the texts and rhetorical writings of the Romans, who were openly skeptical of philosophy; and the second tradition was constructed from earlier Christian literature, along with the writings of the Greek philosophers.

Scholars of the humanist tradition often looked to the Roman orator and jurist Cicero to help formulate their own stance on issues of war and peace. One primary reason for this was that the idea of warfare fought in the interests of one's own *res publica*, as often eloquently argued by one of the most versatile minds of Ancient Rome, resonated strongly within the humanist tradition. Although Cicero did indeed argue for anticipatory action against internal enemies such as Marcus Antonius, he also thought that there was a dramatic moral difference between the peoples of Christian civilization and all others. Thus, Cicero maintained that all strikes executed in advance of any proper harm were justifiable if the republic was threatened in some way. This significant Roman orator for the humanist point of view "repeatedly implied that the violence of enemies did not actually have to be manifested in order to be legitimately opposed by violence" (Tuck 1999: 19).

In the well-known speech *Pro Milone*, Cicero defended this idea on behalf of a friend who was on trial for the killing of a fellow Roman standing for the office of *praetor*. The argument was that a justification for self-defense extended to fear of a future hostility. In recognizable terms, which reflect a filiation that can be traced back to Thucydides and forward to Hobbes's translated phrase "necessity of nature," Cicero spoke of conflict under arms as being governed by "law not of the statute-book, but of nature" (1931: 17). Further emphasizing the inherent quality of what he considered to be defensive measures, Cicero went on to explain that it was "a law which we possess not by instruction, tradition, or reading, but which we have caught, imbibed, and sucked in at Nature's own breast" (1931: 17). Also in this speech we find Cicero articulating what has largely become a conventional wisdom expressed in the proverb *silent enim leges inter arma*. As he explained,

> that should our lives have fallen into any snare, into the violence and the weapons of robbers or foes, every method of winning a way to safety would be morally justifiable. *When arms speak, the laws are silent,* they bid none to await their word.
>
> (1931: 17; my emphasis)

In the end, the defense of Milo was unsuccessful. Such a claim was found to be at the very periphery of decency, if not beyond it, in the domestic law. Overall, even in Roman law, one finds that "the only 'fear' which could be pleaded in extenuation of an individual's act was an immediate and obvious one" (Tuck 1999: 21).

What is most noteworthy about these citations from one of the humanists' favorite sources is the explicit evacuation of both laws and morals from any reasoning concerning an application of the use of force. This was particularly the contention for a circumstance that can be construed as self-defense only if the future were already written and a known entity. Offering final clarification that he indeed thought permissible defense reached beyond what is described in this chapter as a breach, by allowing for attack on those assumed or thought to be preparing a future ambush, Cicero explicitly argued that "the slaying of a *conspirator* may be a justifiable act" (1931: 19; my emphasis). In other words, the belief that there is the planning of future injury is enough to unleash deadly punishment.

Another variety of the humanist tradition in this era, or of those who applauded warfare in the interests of their own community, can be found in the works of some Protestant thinkers who advocated the launching of hostilities against those who were not of the same religious persuasion because brutal conflict was ever-present and constituted a implacable threat during that era. The time period of the Reformation was marked by bloodshed over a deep and severe division between Catholics and Protestants within the Christian church. As a result, there were some who picked up the banner of the just war doctrine and used its terminology and framework to advocate the cause of "holy war" against religious enemies (Turner Johnson 1975: 81–149).[1]

This sixteenth- and seventeenth-century trend of employing religious grounds to justify war-making has also been identified as one branch of a bifurcation of the just war doctrine, leading to holy war in this case and the beginnings of a secularized international law in the other. It is important to recognize that argument in favor of warfare grounded in justifications based on difference in religious ideology was relatively limited in duration and has no direct progeny of which to speak. In other words, the philosophy that professed that it was indeed *moral* to attack a perceived enemy before any injury had been suffered was a relatively short-lived and limited historical phenomenon.

The country in which the translating of the just war doctrine into an advocacy for holy war was most identifiable was England. However, this is not to say that this position did not exist in other parts of the continent. Rather, our attention is drawn to the English idea of holy war because it was brought into particularly sharp relief in the light of a palpable rivalry with the staunch Catholicism and maritime dominance of Spain during this time period. One specific characteristic of this doctrine of holy war found at the time was a shift in emphasis away from the traditional just war concept of a *limitation* on the Christian's right to make war, and instead a focus on the *permission* to go to war.

One of the commonalities found in these figures who advocated for the use of religion as a *casus belli* and conceptualized a reformulation in the classic doctrine of just war was indeed specifically on the point of anticipatory war. That is to say, those who promoted the idea of holy war also found it justifiable to forestall the evil *intentions* of another by initiating war rather than waiting for a first strike. One of the earliest calls for just such hostilities against Catholic Spain came from Stephen Gosson in his 1598 sermon at Paul's Cross Church in a parish where many high-ranking government officials worshipped. *The Trumpet of Warre* oration gained a popularity that led to its later publication. Because there was no ongoing armed conflict with Spain at that time, "this sermon must be understood as a call to preemptive [or preventive by our terms] defensive war" (Turner Johnson 1975: 102). What this means specifically is that Gosson endorsed and encouraged the protecting of his religious sect and country by launching war on the Spanish, whom he identified as propagating offensive religious wars on the Continent. Most importantly, his contention was that such a campaign would simply be an exercise in self-defense because Spain's assumed malevolent future intentions were considered enough to be a trigger to action.

This sermon anticipated the position of a more well-known English dignitary in the early seventeenth century: Sir Francis Bacon. While not a religious zealot, one of Bacon's writings in particular dealt directly with the subject at hand: *Considerations Touching a Warre with Spaine* (1629). In this piece we see that Bacon wrote judiciously, and his position at the court of Queen Elizabeth and then at that of King James gave him the experience necessary to prudently craft his argument. However, he was unmistakably favorable to holy war in this study document, which was prepared for the King while he was serving as a special royal adviser in 1624. We see here that holding the position that religious causes could indeed give rise to justifiable hostilities once again led to the result that armed struggle could be waged in anticipation of a wrong, and could be based solely on perceived malicious intentions.

To Bacon's mind, the defense of his religion was grounds enough to initiate a battle against the nation that had professed itself generally to be the protectors of the Catholic world. Most importantly, he saw this as self-defense. The memorable expression upon which he based this reasoning, and the leading thrust of the article under discussion here, was that of a "just feare." If it could be discerned that another country, which proclaimed a different faith, was prepared for battle (regardless of whether this preparation was intended for its own defense or aimed specifically at one's own country), then the initiation of armed conflict was in fact a *response* based upon justifiable reasoning. As Bacon explained it for the specific circumstance facing England,

> [t]o proceed therefore to the second ground of a warre with Spaine; we have set it downe to be a just feare of subversion of our civill estate: [...] wherein two things are to be proved, the one that a just feare (without an actuall invasion or offence) is a sufficient ground of Warre, and in the nature of a true defensive; the other that we have towards Spaine cause of just feare, [...] not out of umbrages, light jealousness, apprehensions a farre off, but out of clear foresight of imminent danger.
>
> (Bacon 1629: 8)

We see in this citation that Bacon certainly believed there to a justifiable reason to fear Spain, and that this was enough to trigger a war to be initiated (defensively) by England.

It is also interesting to note the cunning rhetorical flourish employed at the citation's closing. By invoking the language of an "imminent danger" there certainly would be an understandable and perhaps unsuspicious draw to the logic applied by Bacon. However, it should not go unstated that the word "foresight," no matter how clear, directly contradicts the imminence of which he speaks; it is unreasonable for something to be just about to happen at any moment, yet at some unspecific point in the future. Hence, the phrase "clear foresight of imminent danger" should be understood as a contradiction in and of itself. In other words, knowledge of the future has never been shown to be within our human capabilities, and therefore this is better understood as a linguistic embellishment meant to obscure, rather than a reasonable argument.

To be sure, there were (and continue to be) very practical reasons for the exercise of military power to be seen as just, and Francis Bacon also spoke to this necessity. In other words, a war deemed just would have a direct effect on its efficacy. Bacon identified both funding and troop morale to be vital to a military exercise and at once based upon the perception of the justice of the war-making. As such, we must take Bacon's arguments and reasoning seriously since he recognized that the perceived justness of war would be an important element in rallying the necessary support at home and abroad. As he put it,

> [t]here must bee a care had that the motives of Warre bee just and honorable: for that begets an alacrity, as wel in the Souldiers that fight, as in the people that affoord pay: it draws on and procures aids, and brings manie other comodities besides.
>
> (Bacon, cited in Piirmäe 2002: 500)

However, venturing into the unstable moral territory that lies beyond our human capabilities must certainly shake the grounds of "the motives of Warre bee just and honorable," giving rise to real doubt about Bacon's reasoning for a successful anticipatory war.

ii The scholastic tradition and a secular doctrine

There was indeed another side to this philosophical bifurcation that characterized the transition into the modern era: the scholastic tradition. During this same critical time period when the Christian church was splintering into warring factions and Europeans were trying discern their obligations to other peoples they were confronting in the New World, there was a particularly significant historical development. That is, at this fateful moment of violent confrontation on multiple continents, there was the secularized advancement of the just war doctrine into what is recognized today as the origins of international law (Scott 1934 and Hamilton 1963).

Since one of the most pressing concerns of the time was to expand the law of discovery and occupation to a breadth never before contemplated, it is perhaps not surprising that the most prominent scholars to advance a natural law just war doctrine were found in the Iberian peninsula: the Spanish Dominicans. Among some of the most well-known were the religious philosophers of the sixteenth century, Francisco de Vitoria and Luis de Molina, who generally wrote out their thoughts on war in the characteristic scholastic repertory of commentary on Thomas Aquinas and other Christian and medieval philosophers. In distinction to the humanists, the scholastics' primary concern was not simply the preservation of the commonwealth. The attempt was rather to determine the universal rights of states relating to what could be termed a just war from differing perspectives. We will also see that the branch of the bifurcation in the direction of more secularized thought on armed conflict contained ideas on anticipatory war quite similar to their predecessors, with one important advancement.

This is certainly not to say that Spain was the only location in which such ideas were to become developed and propagated. The geographical juxtaposition presented here might give the impression that the English busied themselves with justifications for religious war and that the Spanish were contemplating foundations for an international order. This was certainly not the case, and such a conclusion should not be drawn on an enormously complex historical development. Just as England simply provided an unique crucible in which to find some of the most fervent and clear citations of supporters of preventive holy war, Spain will similarly serve to highlight the moral and legal philosophers who secularized the just war doctrine and took it in the direction of an international law. As perhaps the most definitive proof that such simplified geographical conclusions would be erroneous is the simple fact that these Spanish origins were a mode of thought that produced an eminent progeny all over the continent. This philosophy was ripe and continued to mature within the whole of the European mainland over the following centuries.

Perhaps the clearest statement from the Spanish Dominicans on the question of the justness of military action came from the first of these major figures, Francisco de Vitoria. With a terminology and reasoning that sharply reflected the just war tradition he inherited, Vitoria wrote that there is but "a single and only just cause for commencing a war, namely, a wrong received" (Scott 1934: 208–209). While demonstrating an adherence to their heritage on the limitations of war by focusing justness on a wrong received, there was also a vital distinction made by this group of Spanish philosophers that explains a great deal of the subject at hand.

In complete contrast to the branch of holy war, Vitoria explicitly ruled out faith as grounds for hostilities, saying that "[d]ifference of religion is not a cause of just war" (Scott 1934: 208). The reason that this element of the bifurcation is particularly significant here is that there was a realization that such an allowance could result in both sides in a war owning a valid claim to a justness of defensive war, and thus the imperative distinction between offensive and defensive war would be lost.

On this point, Molina explained that a circumstance in which both the attacker and the attacked were fighting justly "would be a contradiction in terms: each party to the war would be blameless and so from the nature of the situation they could not kill each other. This goes against any conception of justice" (de Molina, cited in Hamilton 1963: 142). As such, in the secularizing of the just war doctrine, the interpretation of the traditional claim of harm became more focused on *material* injury. Very importantly, this clarification also set in motion movement toward a *legal* concept of defense in international law, with a standard for self-preservation moving toward verifiable evidence.

In illumination of this point on anticipatory action, Vitoria espoused a position that falls in line with the standard of imminence that largely characterizes the view of most international lawyers today. He asserted that "defense can only be resorted to at the very moment of the danger, or, as the jurists say, *in continenti*, and so when the necessity of defense has passed there is an end to the lawfulness of war" (cited in Scott 1934: 203–204). Meanwhile, Molina's stance has been described as "[w]ars in pursuit of glory, or pre-emptive strikes, were utterly forbidden" (Tuck 1999: 52). Thus, we can indeed see a more clarified moral and legal position starting to emerge on anticipatory action in the sixteenth century.

c The dawn of international law

While the case has been made that the origin of international law can be traced to the Spanish philosophers just discussed, the analysis of this study does not turn on such a clear designation of a particular parentage to this legal tradition. The development of the just war doctrine into what is now recognized and labeled with Jeremy Bentham's term of "international law" concerns us here for its moral analysis of anticipatory strikes. Although the just war thought is clearly present in the works of Hugo Grotius, Samuel Pufendorf, and Emmerich de Vattel, it is developed without the same theological base that we have seen in their predecessors. However, it should not be presumed that this difference somehow meant that these legal philosophers had a dearth of moral intensity or adulterated the tradition of just war.

As a starting point, we will look to Dutch legal philosopher Hugo Grotius and his celebrated work *De jure belli ac pacis*, which attempted to flesh out the natural law that Grotius believed governed nations going to and engaging in war due to its divine origin exposed through human reason. The methodology that he employs reveals an important element of his work which concerns us here because there is a palpable attention to what can be measured with verifiable externals. This purveyor of international law shifted the tradition by replacing "right authority" with sovereignty, he only scantily treated the most subjective criteria of "right intention" in connection with other topics, and "just causes" were regulated by those that can be discerned by an objective observer (Turner Johnson 1975: 213–214). The line between preemptive and preventive war pivots on this very distinction of objectivity and subjectivity, and thus his stance on the issue can be partially foretold by his tack.

Grotius is certainly an ambiguous figure whose work has properly provoked much scholarly investigation, and there continues to be a lack of consensus on exactly how to classify his contribution to law, theory, and thought. He has been classified within the humanist tradition since he was brought up within it and did put forward some of the most far-reaching sets of rights at that time for a state to make war. In particular, Grotius offered a robust form of the international right of a state to punish, which certainly opened a wide passageway to justifications for war. As well, he put forward a legal validation for occupying territory uncultivated by its inhabitants, which was in fact a rationalization used for the European incursions into the New World during this era. Yet, when we look at the question of preventive war, Grotius certainly did not fit into the conventional conception of the humanists.

First, Grotius believed that there were only very limited conditions in which a state might strike an adversary before harm had been done. Most importantly, in his work on the rights of war and peace, he outlined the necessity of an impending peril being both "immediate" and "certain" for a nation to take up its arms. He wrote,

> V. *War in defence of life is permissible only when the danger is immediate and certain, not when it is merely assumed*
> The danger, again, must be immediate and imminent in point of time. I admit, to be sure, that if the assailant seizes weapons in such a way that his intent to kill is manifest the crime can be forestalled; for in morals as in material things a point is not to be found which does not have a certain breadth. But those who accept fear of any sort as justifying anticipatory slaying are themselves greatly deceived, and deceive others.
>
> (Grotius 1925: Book II, chpt. 1, sec. V, at 173)

This explicit formulation surely coincides quite well with a contemporary understanding of the limits of anticipatory military action in that it focuses attention on the certitude that a coming attack is just about to befall a nation.

Grotius then entered into a discourse over the concept of "fear," offering numerous citations in support of his view that this emotionally charged concept should be understood as an insufficient trigger for action. This point, published in 1625, is perhaps most interesting because it appears as an almost direct rebuttal of the ideas put forward by Francis Bacon, which used "just feare" to give reason for an English attack against Spain just one year earlier in 1624. Thus, one can clearly discern the bifurcation under discussion within the just war tradition when Grotius and Bacon are viewed side by side, as has been exhibited in the epigraphs to this chapter.

In his own discussion of fear as a just cause, Grotius cited both Greek and Roman authors who can be found to support his formulations excluding preventive strikes from a legal framework of the laws of war and peace, except in the most certain of circumstances. Grotius first framed this discussion by using a citation from the Roman Consul Gellius, which explained that the normal human circumstance must not be understood as equal to those who find themselves forced into violent armed combat. Gellius was cited as follows:

> When a gladiator is equipped for fighting, the alternatives offered by combat are these, either to kill, if he shall have made the first decisive stroke, or to fall, if he shall have failed. But the life of men generally is not hedged about by a necessity so unfair and so relentless that you are obliged to strike the first blow, and may suffer if you shall have failed to be first to strike.
>
> (cited in Grotius 1925: 174)

Interestingly, Cicero was put forward as querying

> [w]ho has ever established this principle, or to whom without the gravest danger to all men can it be granted, that he shall have the right to kill a man by whom he says he fears that he himself later may be killed?
>
> (cited in Grotius 1925: 174)

Finally, Grotius went on to cite Thucydides, declaring that "[t]he future is still uncertain, and no one, influenced by that thought, should arouse enmities which are not future, but certain" (1925: 174).

There is little doubt that these quotations used by Grotius support his conclusion that anticipatory defense must only be used when a threat is immediate and not supposed. Yet we can perhaps deduce that Grotius, as versed as he was in the humanist tradition, was engaging in selective citation since Cicero has been identified as a central author in constructing the intellectual roots of the humanist tradition. At the same time, Thucydides was one of the Greek historians preferred by this same group of Roman thinkers, at least in part owing to the form of arguments that he presented in *The Peloponnesian War*. As one example, when discussing the case of the Mytilenaeans in the face of growing Athenian power, Thucydides gave further validity to the line of argument supporting preventive war by putting forward "seeing it is in their hands to invade at pleasure, it ought to be in ours to anticipate" (Thucydides 1989: 163).

Taking a more scholastic position in his seminal legal work, Grotius closed this part of his discussion on anticipatory self-defense by drawing attention to the fact that if an attack has not yet been launched there are indeed other means of protecting oneself. That is to say, if a state is not dealing with an "imminent" and "certain" strike then it must look to other methods of defense, since it cannot be deemed moral and lawful to resort to war when the future remains unwritten and will surely offer other unforeseen means for resolution. Grotius proclaimed,

> Further, if a man is not planning an immediate attack, but it has been ascertained that he has formed a plot, or is preparing an ambuscade,

or that he is putting poison in our way, or that he is making ready a false accusation and false evidence, and is corrupting the judicial procedure, I maintain that he cannot lawfully be killed, either if the danger can in any other way be avoided, or if it is not altogether certain that the danger cannot be otherwise avoided. Generally, in fact, the delay that will intervene affords opportunity to apply many remedies, to take advantage of many accidental occurrences; as the proverb runs, "There's many a slip 'twixt cup and lip."

(Grotius 1925: 174–175)

Additionally, Grotius treats a second element of the preventive strike when he speaks of the rising military power of another country that has been classified as an enemy. This situation deals with a threat that is all the more distant than those discussed above since it is not even based on a plan or preparation that is under way, but rather on a danger that seems to be in the process of growing. Here again, Grotius breaks with the humanist tradition and proclaims that a country may not lawfully engage in such warfare simply because it risks being in a disadvantageous position in the future:

XVII. *A public war is not admitted to be defensive which has as its only purpose to weaken the power of a neighbour*
Quite untenable is the position, which has been maintained by some, that according to the law of nations it is right to take up arms in order to weaken a growing power which, if it become too great, may be a source of danger.
That this consideration does enter into deliberations regarding war, I admit, but only on grounds of expediency, not of justice.

(Grotius 1925: Book II, chpt. 1, sec. XVII, at 184)

We see that on this point of discussion, where subjectivity fully reigns, Grotius is all the more strident in his position. In part, this is surely because Grotius is expounding on one of the bases upon which much liberal thought lies. That is, there are in fact important trade-offs for entering into a liberal society and the security it is supposed to offer. When one chooses to step out of a lawless freedom where force can be wielded at the sole discretion of each and every member, there will indeed be uncertain fears. Thus, trust and faith must step to the fore in exchange for the promise of further security. However, to complete this transaction there is one essential element that must be present: the equality of all members must prevail. As Grotius puts it,

that the possibility of being attacked confers the right to attack is abhorrent to every principle of equity. Human life exists under such conditions that complete security is never guaranteed to us. For protection against uncertain fears we must rely on Divine Providence, and on a wariness free from reproach, not on force.

(Grotius 1925: Book II, chpt. 1, sec. XVII, at 184)

While Grotius does make a distinction between using force to stop an attack on the brink of discharge and the attempt to prevent a future risk from becoming too great through war, his conclusion is similar. Lawfulness is granted only in the most "certain" and "immediate" of circumstances.

d Following the lineage: Pufendorf, Vattel, and Kant

We know where this story leads. On the one side of the bifurcation, the idea of a "just feare" as a trigger for war did not take root and thus ran aground philosophically. On the other side, international law has become the diplomatic language used between states, and we see it placed on the public stage of the UNSC in the lead-up to the invasion of Iraq. Therefore, it is worthwhile to present an overview of some of the further clarifications on the question of anticipatory defense, its contours, and the resilience of a belief in constraint on the use of force to establish the continuation of this filiation. To be precise, other jurists and philosophers who followed Hugo Grotius built upon this lineage and drew lines of distinction and interpretations that were quite similar.

For the seventeenth-century German philosopher Samuel von Pufendorf, the language he chose for such an action to be deemed acceptable was that of "moral certainty." Pufendorf takes up this issue and speaks of temporal constraint, explicitly excluding suspicion or fear as a just cause for a legal and moral military action. As a general precept he asserted,

[t]o render the Defence of our selves entirely Innocent, it is commonly thought a necessary Condition, that as to the time, the Danger be just upon us, or as it were in the very point of seizing us: And that no Suspicion or Fear, whilst yet uncertain is sufficient to justifie our assaulting another [...] yet before I can actually assault another under colour of my own Defence, I must have tokens and Arguments amounting to a Moral Certainty, that he entertains a Grudge against me, and hath a full design of doing me a Mischief, so that unless I prevent him, I shall immediately feel his Stroke.

(Pufendorf 1703: Book II, chpt. V, sec. 6, at 145)

There is a particular potency in the language employed by Pufendorf at the end of this excerpt. Pufendorf's phrase "unless I prevent him, I shall immediately feel his Stroke" conjures up a vivid image in the reader's mind and offers a rhetorical force that can be easily committed to memory. Most importantly for our purposes, what we find from Pufendorf is an effort to rule out preventive war.

In the same tradition of natural law, eighteenth-century Swiss legal philosopher and diplomat Emerich de Vattel also provided a pertinent view on the legal and moral use of force. However, an investigation of his thought on preventive war reveals more ambiguous results. Although at face value they can be construed as being to some extent similar, there is little doubt that Vattel pushed the temporal limits for anticipatory attack further than his predecessors analyzed here. There are times when he seems to be arguing both sides, at once laying down strict boundaries followed by unclear exceptions. As a hypothesis for this perplexing presentation by Vattel it is suggested that one must blame the subject matter. As Vattel moves onto the ground of unverifiable facts for his exemptions, combined with explicit prohibitions, the result is a bit muddled, demonstrating the shaky ground he attempts to traverse.

When speaking to the question of anticipatory war, Vattel framed the issue using the right to defense rather than the prohibition of unlawful force:

> [i]t is safest to prevent the evil when it can be prevented. A nation has a right to resist an injurious attempt, and to make use of force and every honorable expedient against whosoever is actually engaged in opposition to her, and even to anticipate his machinations, observing, however, not to attack him upon vague and uncertain suspicions, lest she should incur the imputation of becoming herself an unjust aggressor.
>
> (Vattel 1758: Book II, chpt. 4, §50 at 169)

By approaching the subject from a positive right one can discern the difference in tone, and even breadth, for anticipatory action. However, we do find that Vattel went out of his way to explicitly underline that there was indeed a boundary that must not be crossed: that of becoming "an unjust aggressor."

Finally, it is informative to highlight the work of Immanuel Kant in the eighteenth century. As a starting place, it should be understood that Kant did not deal explicitly with the concept of preventive strikes and their relation to a peace among nations in as clear a manner as we have seen in the other authors analyzed here. However, one can discern Kant's position on this important issue through work treating his vision of relations among states, along with law and morality in general (Tuck 1999: 219).

To find perhaps the most convincing argument that what Kant intended was a full exclusion of preventive war in all its forms on moral grounds, one should turn to his familiar moral precept of a "categorical imperative." Kant put forward the most coherent formulation of this principle in *Fundamental Principles of the Metaphysic of Morals*. He attempts to present a clear and precise development of moral principle so that it can be discussed and more frequently put into operation without the normal distractions that tend to divert our attention.

Most importantly, in this text Kant provides his basic and coherent formulation of how to assess and understand morality:

> [i]n forming our moral judgement of actions, it is better to proceed always on the strict method and start from the general formula of the categorical imperative: Act according to a maxim which can at the same time make itself a universal law.
>
> (2010: 251)

In the simplest terms, fundamental moral principle must be abstracted from individual circumstances, and every action must be defensible as within a rule that can be envisioned as applicable to all.

As a way to grasp the fundamental nature of an interconnectivity and compassion for the other that provide for a foundation of morality, Kant explains that

> although, no doubt, common men do not conceive it in such an abstract and universal form, yet they always have it really before their eyes and use it as the standard of their decision. Here it would be easy to show how, with this compass in hand, men are well able to distinguish, in every case that occurs, what is good, what bad, conformably to duty or inconsistent with it, if, without in the least teaching them anything new, we only, like Socrates, direct their attention to the principle they themselves employ; and that, therefore, we do not need science and philosophy to know what we should do to be honest and good, yea, even wise and virtuous.
>
> (Kant 2010: 219–220)

On Kant's account, there are basic forms of morality that are in fact accessible to all.

To conclude this section, three points will be made. Building on Kant's logic of a "categorical imperative" we will look at: (1) the instability created by interpreting rules to allow for future intentions to trigger armed conflict; (2) how this opens the door to fear acting as this trigger; and (3) the unpredictability that ensues because such a law in inapplicable in an equal form. As a result, we will be able to see why for centuries there has been a draw toward verifiability for the justifications applied to the use of force.

First, on Kant's reasoning, there is a fundamental moral failure in authorizing preventive war because it is, by nature, based upon pure speculation of intent and, at times, capabilities. While the latter can theoretically be proven empirically (if one has perfect intelligence), the former is impossible to discern with any certainty because there is no such thing as a window into another's mind. The intention to attack may have not even yet materialized in the enemy's mind or planning. Once we have removed the verifiable certitude that accompanies the concept of a harm incurred or an attack launched, one begins to deal with worst case scenarios and decisions driven by Hobbesian diffidence.

Second, next to no one asserts that fear brings clarity in decision-making, and trepidation is thus rightfully eschewed from drafting legal and moral standards. This is something we have seen clearly exposed in Grotius's discussion on fear, in which he cited both Greek and Roman authors from the humanist tradition on this point. The central distinction that exists between preventive war in advance and a reactive response to an attack on the cusp of its launching is based on this essential divergence between concern for what might happen and substantive knowledge. As such, Kant's logic would also clearly rule out fear as a standard for a universal law.

Finally, it can be construed as absurd to contend that preventive war is the standard for any multilateral or bilateral treaty since it is, by its definition, based on unsubstantiated and unverifiable claims. It is important to remember that this unverifiable status of an assertion remains true both before and after an attack. Under such circumstances, each country would expose itself to an attack based on the subjective assessments of another. In essence, a system allowing for preventive war does nothing to enhance anyone's security because it would simply codify a state of nature in which all must continue to fear all. To suggest that such a rule could in fact be considered any kind of prohibition at all, or a step out of the state of nature, is empty of logic.

As we have seen throughout our tracing of the just war doctrine on this issue, there has been significant agreement on this subject. Whether we look at the classical doctrine or its secularized form found in the beginnings of international law, moralists and jurists have congregated around the need for an injury to have been suffered, or at least that its occurrence is immediate and certain, to trigger a just war.

When it comes to interpreting the justifiable use of self-defense allowed in Article 51 of the UN Charter, Kant would suggest that it must not be understood in a way that "would make peace among nations impossible and [that] would lead to a perpetual state of nature" (1991a: 170). The prohibition of the use of force found in the Charter must create a real constraint on states. To do so in a self-administered system without an enforcement mechanism requires verifiability. Thus, interpretations of the Charter absent of this verifiability should be considered as absurd, and contrary to its "object and purpose." (*Vienna Convention on the Law of Treaties*, Art. 31(1)).

III The Bush Doctrine: preemptive or preventive war?

Now that a brief survey of the historical treatment of anticipatory military attack has been put forward, offering a clearer understanding of how the moral lines have been drawn within the just war tradition, it is necessary to clarify how exactly the policy of the Bush administration should be classified. As a starting point, it is useful to turn to the dictionary created by the US Department of Defense (DOD). Unsurprisingly, in the dictionary through October 2009, we will see that there is an understanding that parallels our own since there is a notable distinction between the terms "preemptive attack" and "preventive war."

> **preemptive attack**—An attack initiated on the basis of *incontrovertible* evidence that an enemy attack is *imminent.*
>
> (DOD 2001: 424; my emphasis)

> **preventive war**—A war initiated in the *belief* that military conflict, while not imminent, is inevitable, and that to delay would involve greater *risk.*
>
> (DOD 2001: 428; my emphasis)

So, we see that a distinction between the two terms is indeed made by the DOD. By our analysis, this makes perfect sense since there is a real moral and legal chasm between the two.

Of particular interest here is the fact that, under the Obama administration, the DOD dictionary has now been revised. The latest online version (DOD 2010) no longer includes the term "preventive war." This change, which could be described as a "scrubbing" of pertinent materials, is surely to be lamented since this is a pivotal point of grave importance. Because this is the precise point which the administration has used to justify targeting in its drone program, one must ask if this was deliberate? Yet, removing the distinction from the DOD dictionary will not eliminate the long running historical conversations over this point found in this chapter. Neither will it erase the moral reasoning underpinning the need for using the verifiable standard of "imminence" that is meant to avert a slide into the subjective measure of "just feare."

Nevertheless, the opening salvo for the executive to express its position on where to draw this line in the post-9/11 world was launched on June 1, 2002, in a graduation speech at West Point military college by President George W. Bush. The US had recently toppled the Taliban regime in Afghanistan (originally thought to be sufficient to achieve military victory), and a tension from the terrorist attacks still gripped the nation. This is the first place that the Bush White House rolled out the term "preemptive action" and began to put forward their understanding of its meaning. However, if we look at the manner in which the President was suggesting to exercise military action, we will see that what was being described was in fact a preventive war and not preemption at all. He asserted,

> [i]n the world we have entered, the only path to safety is the path of action. And this nation will act [...]. And our security will require all

Americans to be forward-looking and resolute, to be ready for *preemptive action* when necessary to defend our liberty and to defend our lives.

(Bush 2002c; my emphasis)

The assertion that the "only path to safety is the path of action," is based on the simple binary notion that there are only two options available at a given time: military action or insecurity. Concerning the problematic use of fear in decision-making, Grotius cited the Roman historian Titus Livy on this same subject: "[i]n the effort to guard against fear, men cause themselves to be feared, and we inflict upon others the injury which has been warded off from ourselves, as if it were necessary either to do or to suffer wrong" (Grotius 1925: 174).

It is certainly problematic to suggest that at any given time there are no more than two alternatives, yet in political debates over security this is certainly not uncommon. More importantly, however, the notion that the unknown should move us to military action is no longer premised on incontrovertible evidence of an impending attack. It is based on the "belief that military conflict, while not imminent, is inevitable," or preventive war as defined by the DOD.

In the speech, Bush continued to make the case that the unknown, or "just feare" that we have seen argued by Francis Bacon was enough to trigger military action. As he put it,

We cannot defend America and our friends by *hoping* for the best. We cannot put our *faith* in the word of tyrants, who solemnly sign non-proliferation treaties, and then systemically break them. If we wait for threats to fully materialize, we will have waited too long. [...] Yet the war on terror will not be won on the defensive. We must take the battle to the enemy, disrupt his plans, and confront the worst threats before they emerge.

(Bush 2002c; my emphasis)

Looking closely at this excerpt, we see that the language employed certainly does not advocate using irrefutable evidence of danger to justify action. Instead, the argument here rests on the severity of the threat and the imprudence of hesitation. The line of reasoning is that the potential for sizeable casualties would be so great if weapons of mass destruction fell into the hands of those who employ terrorism that not launching military action in advance of such a scenario no longer made sense. This framing of the issue argues for the need for foreign policy to be based on worst case scenarios since such scenarios cannot be ruled out.

Perhaps the most revealing and problematic assertion found in this speech is that this struggle against terrorism "will not be won on the defensive." The reason why this declaration is so worrisome is because it raises serious concerns, and may even provide definitive evidence, that the conception of the "Bush Doctrine" is in fact in direct violation of the UN Charter and the development of customary law it has been traced. Lest we forget, the Charter provides only one unilateral exception to the prohibition of the use of force found in Article 2(4), and that is the "inherent right of individual or collective self-*defence*" found in Article 51. If the counterterrorism project that is envisioned "will not be won on the defensive," how exactly can this be squared with self-*defence*? And how can this be in line with the prohibition of offensive war that runs all the way back through to the classic doctrine of just war?

To further investigate the exact contours of the policy advocated by the Bush administration, we will turn to the NSS of September 2002, which was penned and distributed by the White House. This document, which is prepared for Congress periodically by the executive, was the first text of its kind to be released after 9/11 and President Bush decided to use it to outline his overall strategy for combating terrorism. This is the first formal document detailing the framework for the vision of what is referred to as "preemption." It reads,

> Legal scholars and international jurists often conditioned the legitimacy of preemption on the existence of an *imminent* danger—most often a visible mobilization of armies, navies, and air forces preparing to attack.
>
> We must *adapt* the concept of imminent threat to the capabilities and objectives of today's adversaries. [...]
>
> The United States has long maintained the option of preemptive actions to counter a sufficient threat to our national security. The greater the threat, the greater the *risk* of inaction—and the more compelling the case for taking anticipatory action to defend ourselves, even if *uncertainty remains* as to the time and place of the enemy's attack. To forestall or prevent such hostile acts by our adversaries, the United States will, if necessary, act pre-emptively.
>
> (White House 2002; my emphasis)

What should first be noted here is that there is an explicit recognition of the fact that preemption is defined by anticipating an *imminent* attack, which, of course, falls in line with the historical analysis that has been put forward here, and with the definition found in the DOD dictionary. However, this traditional understanding is rejected, and an argument is made for adapting by enlarging what actions are covered by the term "preemption." The problem, of course, is that a term already exists for this concept of anticipation: "preventive war." Since once we leave the temporal constraint of imminence there are no longer any objective standards to be applied, one must inevitably cross the chasm between the two and arrive at the purely subjective term.

The line of reasoning is that the destructive power of today's weapons warrants an immediate response, lest we suffer a terrible fate at the hands of weapons the world has not previously known. However, it should be remembered that every preceding generation, as is always the case with all discussions in the present tense, has not known the destructive power of today's weaponry. Due to humanity's proclivity for creating ever more devastating armaments, the course of history has continually introduced death and destruction on a level that has never been seen before. We are always at the apex of our potential for destruction, therefore to assert that we are living in a new world describes the circumstances with which every human generation has had to struggle.

It is also useful to take note of the fact that the means for evaluating threats to the US operates with billions of dollars in its annual budget, and the accuracy of the intelligence-services conclusions was brought into question in several serious circumstances during this same time period. The intelligence community was under serious scrutiny after the failure to find weapons of mass destruction in Iraq (Iraq Survey Group 2004), the discovery of an elaborate black-market nuclear weapons proliferation program in Pakistan (Broad *et al.* 2004), the 2007 conclusion that Iran had halted its nuclear weapons program back in 2003 (which had been previously unknown) (National Intelligence Council 2007), and, perhaps most gravely, the inability to foresee or forestall 9/11. Highlighting these failures is not to disparage the intelligence services; rather, it is to draw attention to the fact that these revelations raise serious doubts about the capacity for reliable and accurate conjecture. Both anticipatory military actions of preemption and preventive war presuppose a capability to produce correct assessments of imminent and looming dangers. Thus, to base military action solely on the imprecise human activity of assessing the capacities and intentions of enemies who are attempting to hide their plans runs the risk of launching a war in wrongful circumstances and closely aligns with the "just feare" standard put forward by Francis Bacon.

IV Last resort and a moment for deliberation

The phrase "a moment for deliberation" is borrowed from Secretary of State Daniel Webster's well-known statement regarding the *Caroline* incident in the nineteenth century, which is frequently invoked in discussions of anticipatory self-defense. While the circumstances surrounding the incident make the particular case ill-suited for application to many discussions of self-defense in international law, there is, however, an important usefulness in the language that was wielded. Webster states that the "necessity of that self-defence is instant, overwhelming, and leaving no choice of means, and no moment for deliberation" (Webster 1906: 412). There is a powerful force behind the words used because they capture a sentiment of great consequence in the discussion over anticipatory self-defense. The rhetorical force of the words used by Webster, and not its legal applicability as a case, is the reasoning for borrowing a portion of the famous phrase for our heading here—that is, the expression a "moment of deliberation" puts a spotlight on *choice* and *free will* that inevitably draws the element of morality into discussions of war.

Michael Walzer, in one of the best known contemporary moral analyses of war, opened his work *Just and Unjust Wars* by exploring the familiar Melian dialogue of Thucydides' ancient text *The Peloponnesian War* (1977: 5–13). His intention was to directly confront the classical realist view on international politics in an attempt to dissolve at least one form of the argument that rises from it: that of *necessity*. This realist view would challenge the idea that there is any room for moral or legal perspectives in matters as serious and absolute as war and suggests that the only real security available lies in the expansion of power. Thus, there is at times a conclusion drawn by some that there is a necessity for action or, more specifically, the use of military force.

In illustration of this frame of mind, Thucydides recounts the exchange between the Athenian generals and the magistrates of Melos concerning their subjugation to the growing empire. The Athenians argue that while they do not really wish to expand their control over the inhabitants of Melos, they are beholden to the laws of power which dictate that any backpedaling from the expansion of their domain would result in a show of weakness which would inevitably be exploited. Because from the Athenian perspective the difference in strength stipulates that justice is no longer applicable, or "right, as the world goes, is only in question between equals in power," the only relevant factors in their debate are what is required by necessity (Thucydides 1998: 352). The Athenians make clear in the discussion that their intention to subjugate the Melians is not based on their own choosing but is, rather, fated and required by the circumstances of our human condition:

> [o]f the gods we believe, and of men we know, that by a necessary law of their nature they rule wherever they can. And it is not as if we were the first to make this law, or to act upon it when made: we found it existing before us, and we shall leave it to exist forever after us; all we do is to make use of it, knowing that you and everybody else, having the same power as we have, would do the same as we do.
>
> (Thucydides 1998: 354)

Hobbes translated this same segment describing the idea of an inherent requirement to dominate wherever possible as a "necessity of nature" (Thucydides 1989: 368) and would later make this phrase his own because it dovetailed so nicely with his own philosophy. However, there is an important piece of history missing from the Melian debate which colors our understanding of the Athenian argument. At the point of contact with the magistrates of Melos, another debate had already occurred, and a decision had previously been made. The Athenian generals described their course of action as inevitable, yet there certainly was a deliberation over this decision in Athens, even though it is not described in Thucydides' account. It is at this point of discussion, within the Athenian senate, that the notions of necessity and inevitability dissolve. There was indeed a moment of political deliberation over whether war was or was not a worthy *choice*. As Walzer so evocatively put it, "[s]tand in imagination in the Athenian assembly, and one can still feel a sense of freedom" (1977: 10).

From this point of view, at this moment of decision, the Hobbesian "necessity of nature" is simply an argument for a particular course of action. This argument can be, and has been for centuries, disputed. The moment of deliberation is the definitive evidence that morality is a factor in the use of force. Choice and free will inexorably mean alternatives are available, morality is involved, and *necessity* does not command all that is to come.

This was surely the case for the US, as there was indeed a moment in time when decision, the freedom of choice, was available on whether or not to invade Iraq. Even if it was a short-lived debate, sometimes described as manipulated and truncated, there was a time period in which the ideas of necessity and immediacy were only argument.

Additionally, the choice of verbiage in the heading is meant to reference Ian Johnstone's germane work, *The Power of Deliberation*. This investigation explores the discursive interaction among states and non-state actors (the language of international law and forums for diplomacy looming large) and how this shapes their behavior and the international order. Thus, in a similar manner, we also present and examine "legal discourse as a distinctly powerful form of argumentation" (Johnstone 2011: 3), along with how this form of disputation manifested itself within the public sphere (see also Brunnée and Toope 2010: 1–19).

Thus our focus in this section will be on how the diplomatic debate at the UNSC and public protest forced the US administration to put forward a legal argument for war. However, this does not mean that true deliberation occurred within the corridors of power since there are indications that a decision was made much earlier (furthering doubts about necessity). Nevertheless, one can say that this official debate over the invasion of Iraq, although there were certainly other examples of its occurrence in the public sphere beforehand, began in earnest with President Bush's general address at the UN on September 12, 2002.

While this speech at the UN marked an important turn in the administration's internal struggle over whether there was a need to make the case for invasion before the world community and seek a UNSC authorization, it also signaled the launch of a national—indeed, a global—debate over the use of force in Iraq. In the speech, President Bush presented, and commingled, the three arguments that the administration would use as justification for the invasion of Iraq: (1) the interpreted violations of UNSC resolutions; (2) the human rights abuses committed against the Iraqi people by its government; and (3) the allegation of the continued development of weapons of mass destruction which posed a threat to the US and its allies either directly or through terrorist connections. In conclusion, President Bush clearly and bluntly stated his government's position: "[t]he purposes of the United States should not be doubted. The Security Council resolutions will be enforced—the just demands of peace and security will be met—or action will be unavoidable" (Bush 2002d).

However, the most grave claims and imagery invoked while putting forward the argument for the necessity of immediate action (primarily meant for domestic consumption) tended to come from other members of the administration and fellow Republicans. For example, Vice President Dick Cheney gave a public speech to the Veterans of Foreign Wars in which he asserted that "[s]imply stated, there is no doubt that Saddam Hussein now has weapons of mass destruction. There is no doubt he is amassing them to use against our friends, against our allies, and against us" (2002).

Additionally, National Security Adviser Condoleezza Rice alluded to the most serious claim by evoking visions of a nuclear explosion. While this same imagery would later be again invoked by the President, it was on the mainstream media outlet CNN that Secretary Rice famously claimed

> [w]e do know that he is actively pursuing a nuclear weapon. [...] The problem here is that there will always be some uncertainty about how quickly he can acquire nuclear weapons. But we don't want the smoking gun to be a mushroom cloud.
>
> (CNN 2002)

Interestingly, the National Security Adviser here clearly ties the idea of uncertainty to urgency—that is to say, she argues that a lack of information forces action and creates necessity.

While there is certainly justifiable criticism that the responses from the political opposition to the grave and foreboding claims by the executive branch of the US government were muted at best, there were still some discernible voices that publicly spoke out in opposition. Soon after the President's speech at the UN, an authorization from Congress for the use of military force against Iraq was sought by the White House. Even this legislation, introduced in both Houses of Congress and passed in less than two weeks, begins to demonstrate that a *moment for deliberation* indeed existed. The primary reason that opposition to this act was so muffled surely stems from the fact that midterm elections for Congress were fast approaching in the following month, and Democrats did not want to depart for the break before the voting with a fresh cudgel of "soft on security" in the hands of campaigning Republicans only one year after the attacks of 9/11.

Nonetheless, Democratic Senator Edward Kennedy from Massachusetts rose to the floor in Congress to clearly point out that a public decision had not been taken by the President on whether force was in fact necessary; hence, Congress was being asked to delegate its constitutional war-making powers. Additionally, Kennedy drew attention to the exact point under discussion here: "you want to be sure that you're using force and expending American blood and lives and treasure as the ultimate *last resort*" (Kennedy 2002; my emphasis). In the end, the brisk congressional debate resulted in passage of the legislation.

However, the debate was not confined to the consideration in Congress over delegating its war-making authority. At the same time that the first version of this joint resolution was announced there was an anti-war rally in the Federal Plaza of Chicago, organized by Chicagoans Against War in Iraq. People were there to demonstrate and to voice their opposition to an invasion of the sovereign country of Iraq, and it represented what was the first high-profile public disapproval in Chicago. The reason why this particular rally draws more attention today than some of the others at that time is because at the very moment that an authorization for war became a real legislative possibility, the future president of the US stepped out onto a public stage to voice his opposition. Barack Obama, a State Senator of Illinois at that time, attended the protest and delivered a short speech demonstrating the manner in which he was in alignment with the crowd. He explicitly stated that he was not opposed to all wars but that he was against "a dumb war ... a rash war" (Obama 2002).

The necessity described by those advocating war was not so great as to forestall the mobilization of what would eventually become massive numbers of protesters worldwide. As Obama put it at this very early stage of the debate that day, more than five months before the eventual invasion:

> I also know that Saddam poses *no imminent and direct threat* to the United States or to his neighbors, that the Iraqi economy is in shambles, that the Iraqi military a fraction of its former strength, and that in concert with the international community he can be contained until, in the way of all petty dictators, he falls away into the dustbin of history.
>
> (Obama 2002; my emphasis)

It should be kept in mind that although Barack Obama was involved in this demonstration against a war in Iraq at the beginning of October 2002, there is no record, nor any claim, that he was involved with what has been described as an unprecedented global outpouring of anti-war sentiment (Simonson 2003). Most consider the protests that took place in

Washington, DC, and San Francisco on October 26, 2002, with approximations of 100,000 and 50,000 attendees respectively, as the starting point of this global movement dedicated to questioning the necessity for war. No doubt the intention of the millions of protesters worldwide certainly had something—if not everything—to do with stopping an impending war. However, while this hope was not fulfilled, the millions of people who took part in thousands of protests did indeed succeed in demonstrating that argument and debate were most definitely an essential element of the circumstances surrounding the run-up to the invasion of Iraq. Thus, these protesters clarified that there was indeed a *moment for deliberation.*

While there were large protests organized on January 18, 2003 (see, for example, Simonson 2003: 13), in conjunction with celebrations for the birthday of Dr. Martin Luther King Jr. (due to his sometimes overlooked vocal opposition to the Vietnam War), the culmination of these manifestations was certainly those which were globally coordinated for February 15, 2003. This day was chosen to coincide with, and counter-balance, the case for an immediate war that was being put forward in the UNSC.

Of course, the debate and discussions taking place in the UNSC over weapons inspections and the need for war also provide further evidence of the existence of time for consideration of the options. This forum became the public stage for worldwide debate during this deliberation. Common citizens across the globe became riveted by this moment in time when argument over war was rendered entirely public by Article 39 of the UN Charter vesting the UNSC with the "right authority" to decide on this question of a "threat to the peace." With the debate framed by the legal and diplomatic language of UN Charter provisions, the Internet provided a novel tool for communication and organizing in a clear example of *new diplomacy.* As a result, the author of this book was able to follow and attend the major public displays of argumentation and deliberation from Denver, to Washington, DC, to London.

Previously the norm for anti-war demonstrations had been localized protests only after war had begun; however, the eruption of a global public outcry in this case represented a sharp historical difference both in quantity and quality. The number of participants on February 15, 2003, outstretched previous public demonstrations in some of the nearly 600 participating cities worldwide. If this event is counted as one global entity of some six to ten million people, the numbers are historic. Estimates of attendance at the London protest are between one and two million people, which would make it "one of the biggest days of public protest ever seen in the UK" (BBC News 2003). That same day there were estimates of three million in Rome, 1.3 million in Barcelona and 500,000 in Melbourne, all protesting against an invasion of Iraq (Simonson 2003: 30–33).

The fact that the protests took place before a shot had been fired also qualified this phenomenon as something new in human history. The worldwide events of that day had enough of an effect for one journalist in the *New York Times* to claim that there could very well be another super-power in the world along with the US: that of "world public opinion." The journalist went on to assert,

> In his campaign to disarm Iraq, by war if necessary, President Bush appears to be eyeball to eyeball with a tenacious new adversary: millions of people who flooded the streets of New York and dozens of other world cities to say they are against war based on the evidence at hand.
>
> (Tyler 2003)

Assessing the effectiveness of these copious and persistent demonstrations might be left to sociologists to analyze were it not for their direct relevance to questions of morality, its relationship to legitimacy, and the diplomatic implications. Clearly, the organizing of millions of people in the streets did not achieve the intended prevention of an invasion of Iraq. However, the discussion over and passage of an authorization by Congress, the debate in the UNSC, weapons inspections, and the actions of ordinary citizens stepping into the streets of cities across the US and the world leave no doubt that *necessity* was only an argument. There was, indeed, a *moment for deliberation* between the president's speech at the UN on September 12, 2002, and the commencement of "shock and awe" operations in Iraq on March 19, 2003. This space of six months, and very public debate, are clear indications that a moral choice had entered into the discussion. Whether the administration actually used this moment for true considera-tion of the options is another question; however, these events clearly dem-onstrated that the opportunity to do so in fact existed.

In a speech delivered on the Senate floor the day bombs began to fall in Baghdad, Senator Robert Byrd captured our point quite succinctly. At the cusp of war, the Senator from West Virginia exclaimed "[w]e cannot convince the world of the necessity of this war for one simple reason. This is a war of choice" (2003).

Of significance for morality and legitimacy, the phrase "war of choice" is one that slowly seeped into the public discourse and crystallized the final assessment for many. It did so to such an extent that three years after the invasion one poll found that a majority of US citizens, by a stark two-to-one margin, classified the war in Iraq in these very terms of a *"war of choice"* (Lobe 2006, citing a poll by the University of Maryland).

V Right authority and the UNSC

Even though it is possible to trace the just war tradition back further, its formal coalescence as doctrine developed in later medieval times, particu-larly on the question of "right authority." A difficulty that was raised by earlier theorists of just war, Augustine and Gratian specifically, was how to determine who exactly had the authority to settle disputes with force. In response to the legacy bequeathed to them and social conditions spawned by the congealing feudal structure of the time, canon lawyers in the thirteenth century focused quite intently on this specific question. It was felt to be important to circumscribe such a powerful license, otherwise there would be nearly no limits emanating from the doctrine and thus no reduction in the incidence of warfare. In order to delineate the important difference between private and public violence, it was first necessary to define the proper locus of sovereign power within a political community and even to contemplate the nature of political authority itself. Thus, much of the canon law of this time focused on defining who possessed the "right authority" to pronounce and launch a just war. This determination was surely not easy. Even though the pyramidal structure of the feudal system had become quite universal in Europe, "lines of fealty could become hopelessly tangled, and responsibilities could contradict each other" (Turner Johnson 1981: 150–165). Despite this difficulty, two primary lines were drawn, one vertical and one horizontal. First, the vertical line established that, generally, all religious leaders were separated out as not possessing the right authority to conduct war. Second, a horizontal line was drawn so that only secular leaders who had no earthly superior had such a mandate. In the end, what the canonists of this medieval period put together was largely formalistic and useful for their time, but because their solution was so narrowly temporal what they provided is of little later relevance.

In contemporary times, the nature of war and global society is quite different. As international law has developed to become the normative framework of a state-structured system, it is the codified treaty that has become its principal expression and the accepted form for states to communicate their will and consent to legally binding obligations (an example of how public diplomacy has transformed over the past century). We have just recounted how the public, both domestically and worldwide, involved themselves to make their voice heard in this moment of deliberation. We will now turn to see the interplay of this phenomenon with one of the highest profile expressions of public diplomacy in modern times. That is, the UN Charter has created a forum for debate over the use of force in the halls of the Security Council, and a portion of the general public made clear that it was watching how the facts would be squared with the law.

It is acknowledged that the specific norm investing the UNSC with this power is controversial, and no position holds absolute unanimity among legal scholars (Farer 2008: 375–378). Nonetheless, the public attention on the UNSC debate, not to mention the Bush administration's decision to make its case before this body (Brunnée and Toope: 271–349), point to the need to assess this public diplomacy in the context of legitimacy.

The UN Charter has been ratified by virtually all countries in the world, and member states agree to a principle of the non-use of force and the peaceful settlement of disputes. As discussed, the Charter provides for two exceptions to the prohibition of force between states: (1) in self-defense of an armed attack; or (2) when a military is deployed across borders because it has been authorized by the UNSC under Chapter VII. While the implications of the first case were discussed in the section covering anticipatory defense, what concerns us here is the second exclusion. Under Chapter VII, Article 39 of the UN Charter reads,

> [t]he Security Council shall determine the existence of any threat to the peace, breach of the peace, or act of aggression and shall make recommendations, or decide what measures shall be taken in accordance with Articles 41 and 42, to maintain or restore international peace and security.

While Article 41 addresses means to be employed that do not include force, Article 42 gives the UNSC the power to deem those measures inadequate and to authorize the use of armed force. This authority is tremendously significant when we consider that the ultimate purpose of this international organization is enshrined in Article 1(1), explicating that it is has been founded "[t]o maintain international peace and security, and to that end: to take effective collective measures for the prevention and removal of threats to the peace, and for the suppression of acts of aggression or other breaches of the peace." Hence, it is safe to say that under the Charter framework, excluding cases of self-defense, it is the UNSC that is meant to be the "right authority" in international society.

It should also be pointed out that the inevitably public nature of the use of force is in part related to the growth of codified international law and public diplomacy. This is due to the fact that any case for war today becomes largely couched and argued within its framework because of the forum of the UN where the Security Council, 193 states, and the general public sit with an unobscured view of the case for war, sometimes described as "jurying" (Franck 2002: 186). In other words, the existence of a specific treaty dealing with international legal obligations concerning the use of force, or threats of force, provides a structure within which arguments for war must be formulated so as to justify a military action because it is called for by other states, domestic forces, and the imperatives of diplomacy. The duties found in the UN Charter brought into plain view the case for an invasion of Iraq, even if war was not averted.

Within international institutions, the language of treaty obligations has become the common idiom of diplomacy, and, as such, the primary form of communication is through law. Of course, there are some who see standing in the international community as simply distracting from what is vital: power politics and the national interest. Regardless of whether this is true or not, the US did indeed go before the UNSC to debate their case for a war on Iraq, and did so using the common language of that body. Therefore, the public aspect of a decision (be it already concluded in secret, or still to be made at a later date) in the end required that the US speak overtly in the language of codified international law and diplomacy.

The case put forward by the US is encapsulated in the presentation delivered to the UN Security Council on February 5, 2003, by the US Secretary of State Colin Powell, since it was at this point that the US was trying to secure an explicit authorization for an invasion. Enormous energy and attention was indeed exerted by the Bush administration to make this public case for war before the body of diplomats, and its consideration of that case captivated the world.

The case differed slightly when presented to the domestic news media versus what was put before an international institution charged with overseeing treaty obligations. At the UNSC it focused on the material breach of UNSC Resolution 687 and then on Resolution 1441 requiring disarmament, and thus on the weapons of mass destruction presumed to be possessed and hidden by that country. Conversely, the case put before the domestic audience, while still focusing on weapons of mass destruction, was mainly attentive to their destructive power and the direct threat they posed to the nation. Therefore, one might say that there was a legal argument (compliance with UNSC resolutions) put forward at the UN, and a moral one (the need for preventive war, though described as preemptive) presented to the people of the US; though each was based upon the presence of weapons of mass destruction. Essentially, however, both arguments possessed a moral as well as a legal dimension because free violence, as has been shown, transgresses a line that exists for both codes.

a Chapter VII and Iraq

In response to Iraq's invasion of Kuwait in August 1990 the UNSC passed Resolution 678 four months later, explicitly stating that it was acting under Chapter VII of the Charter. This resolution authorized states to use "all necessary means" to uphold previous resolutions and "to restore international peace and security in the area." This was the first time since the Korean conflict in 1950 that the UNSC had exercised its authority for the use of force against an aggressor, which can be largely attributed to the logjam in the UNSC created by the Cold War. It is generally accepted that the formulation of "all necessary means" was meant to include the use of force, thus this resolution served as the authorization for the first Persian Gulf War in 1990–1991 and later became the basis of legal reasoning by which the US and the UK launched their invasion of Iraq in 2003. The reliance upon UN resolutions has been called "the strongest part of the legal case for military action against Iraq" (Roberts 2003: para. 7). Nonetheless, our intention is to demonstrate that even though this legal reasoning was the least flawed of those put forward, it still had its own moral failures under the concept of "right authority."

At the close of the Gulf War in 1991, the Security Council passed Resolution 687 establishing the terms of the cease-fire agreement, which would require Iraq to surrender all weapons of mass destruction, and setting up the UN Special Commission (UNSCOM) on Iraq to monitor its compliance. By the authority created in the UN Charter, Iraq was required to disclose the locations of all chemical and biological weapons and ballistic missiles with a range of over 150 kilometers, and to submit to inspections. Specifically, this meant that UNSCOM would "carry out immediate on-site inspection of Iraq's biological, chemical and missile capabilities, based on Iraq's declarations and the designation of any additional locations by the Special Commission itself" (UNSC Resolution 687 [1991], para. 9). Additionally, Iraq was obliged to fully refrain from acquiring or developing nuclear weapons, weapons-grade nuclear material, or anything related to furthering these ends. In other words, the UNSC required Iraq to fully disarm and to submit to international verification of this disarmament, so as to bring an end to the use of force authorized in Resolution 678.

After a series of confrontations between the Iraqi government and UNSCOM in 1997 and 1998, the US unilaterally threatened a reinitiation of the use of force against Iraq, accompanied by a buildup of US troops in the region, to coerce its compliance with the inspections regime. At that time, various scholars put forward competing positions as to whether the US was entitled under international law to make this threat of force. In a debate that would foreshadow the final legal position taken by the US and the UK for the invasion of Iraq in 2003, there is much to be gleaned.

In 1998, Ruth Wedgwood wrote an article arguing that "compliance by Iraq with its disarmament obligations is central to restoring peace and security in the area, and that serious interference with inspections constitutes a material breach of the cease-fire" (1998: 727). Wedgwood's legal opinion was that the US possessed the authority to threaten or use force at its own discretion by the authority granted to it by the combination of UNSC Resolutions 678 and 687.

Shortly afterwards, putting forward an argument that would presciently warn of troubles to come in 2002–2003, Jules Lobel and Michael Ratner published an article in the same journal arguing that "the tendency to bypass the requirement for explicit Security Council authorization, in favor of more ambiguous sources of international authority, will probably escalate in coming years" (1999: 125). Furthermore, the title of this article captures our point: "Bypassing the Security Council."

While Wedgwood makes several important points concerning the lack of compliance by the Iraqi state to its obligations under the cease-fire agreement of Resolution 687, she ultimately does not deal with some of the most pressing questions that arise from her position. She rightly points out that there were real concerns expressed by the UNSC itself regarding the Iraqi compliance. The unequivocal determination of how to characterize the specific circumstances of Iraq's actions as a "flagrant violation" in 1997 is indeed useful for capturing the UNSC's assessment; however, it does not provide any insight into an agreement for how to deal with such noncompliance. As Wedgwood herself explains, "Iraq's calculated defiance of these cease-fire terms in the 1997–1998 confrontation allowed the United States to deem the cease-fire in suspension and to resume military operations to enforce its conditions, *subject to the requirements of necessity and proportionality*" (1998: 726; my emphasis).

These customary international law requirements of "necessity" and "proportionality," emanating from the just war doctrine, are exactly the critical elements upon which the UNSC did not agree in 1997 and 1998, not to mention in 2003. And these are the precise questions which Wedgwood deftly dodges. Is there a necessity to use armed force in these circumstances? How much force would be proportional to noncompliance with the terms of the cease-fire? Wedgwood suggests that these questions can be answered without quandary by member states themselves and that attributing such power to them would not infringe upon the UNSC's mandate as the "right authority."

Lobel and Ratner point out that the basis for any future authorization to use force without explicit sanction by the UNSC ultimately went back to UNSC Resolution 678 of 1990, which had only been suspended by the cease-fire agreement of Resolution 687. That is to say, the interpretation being put forward held that the original resolution of 1990 does not in fact ever extinguish itself because no temporal time limit was included in the text, and thus it can be resurrected by any failure to meet the obligations of the cease-fire. The ultimate question, however, is who has the authority to enact this resurrection? It was this legal interpretation that was found to be so dangerous by Lobel and Ratner because it ultimately must be understood as "a loaded weapon in the hands of any member nation to use whenever it determined Iraq to be in material breach of the cease-fire" (1999: 125).

It was against the backdrop of this bleak forewarning of potentially dangerous interpretations of the authority to use force against Iraq that the UNSC was called upon to assess the need for further action in the tense international environment that followed 9/11.

In the final months of 2002, the US returned to the UNSC to discuss this issue and was able to secure Resolution 1441, which clearly stated that "Iraq has been and remains in material breach" and "warned Iraq that it will face serious consequences as a result of its continued violations of its obligations" (paras. 1 and 13 respectively). This action succeeded in getting weapons inspectors back into Iraq at the end of that year in order to verify its destruction of weapons of mass destruction so as to comply with the cease-fire agreement of 1991. Nonetheless, the US soon began to make a case that Iraq was still in material breach and was once again thwarting the efforts of UNSCOM, culminating with Secretary of State Colin Powell's high-profile presentation of February 5, 2003. In the end, the US and the UK were unable to secure a "second resolution" from the UNSC clarifying the position of its members after the reentry of weapons inspectors and perhaps again explicitly authorizing force (although this actually would have been the eighteenth resolution regarding the use of force and the disarmament of Iraq).

The difficulty of getting a majority of the UNSC to agree on authorizing the use of force against one of the organization's members cannot be denied. Yet, considering that weapons of mass destruction were not found in Iraq after the invasion, it can also be said that the actual case for authorizing a war was weak and unconvincing because the allegation of Iraq possessing these weapons was simply untrue. In fact, UN weapons inspectors remained in the country until they were notified of the imminent invasion of troops primarily from the US and UK on March 19, 2003.

One eminent British scholar elaborated on this concept of "continuing authority" in a memorandum submitted to the UK House of Commons shortly after the invasion of 2003. He pointed out that it is an understanding that has not been widely accepted, even if it was the strongest legal reasoning for the use of force. In the specific case of 2003, he pointed to the "right authority" to determine penalties,

> [p]roblems that have emerged have included the question of what consequences flowed from the Iraq breaches: in particular, even if the US and partners have continuing authority to use force, it remained a question whether that entitles them to launch a full-scale attack to achieve regime change.
>
> (Roberts 2003, para. 21)

With these fundamental flaws in the interpretation of the resolutions, it is extremely difficult to conclude that the concept of "right authority" had been contemplated and respected. This is particularly problematic to assert when each of the resolutions in question explicitly reference the UNSC's intention to continue to deal with the issue of Iraq. The most unambiguous declaration comes in the cease-fire resolution, Resolution 687, which affirms that the Security Council "[d]ecides to remain seized of the matter and to take such further steps as may be required for the implementation of the present resolution and to secure peace and security in the area" (para. 34).

This argument for the legality of Operation Iraqi Freedom is explicitly set out by UK Attorney General Lord Goldsmith in a late statement made just days before the launching of the war, though a similar assertion was never domestically required in the US. The statement was remarkably simple and consisted of only nine paragraphs. The proclamation of legality by the Attorney General rested largely on the previous assessments made by the UNSC (clearly recognizing its authority) that Iraq had been in material breach of its obligations, but then shifted to assuming the authority of member states to make the final determinations and consequences. The most pertinent paragraphs read:

> 7   *It is plain* that Iraq has failed to comply and therefore Iraq was at the time of Resolution 1441 and continues to be in material breach.
>
> 8   Thus, the authority to use force under Resolution 678 has revived and so continues today.
>
> > (Lord Goldsmith 2003: 811; my emphasis)

The remarkable consequence of this memo is that just three little words—"it is plain"—are considered enough to cover the determination of just cause, necessity, proportionality, and "right authority."

Such an interpretation sidelined the UNSC as the "right authority" once it granted its initial authorization for the use of force over a decade earlier. While this may have seemed expedient at the time, it is hardly a reading that embodies the object and purpose of the charter system. Nor does it fall completely in line with the moral standard of limiting the use of violence in the international realm. The question must be asked: what is to stop any other nation (e.g. Iran, as one possibility) from declaring that Iraq is in material breach of the cease-fire agreement and thus asserting that it can militarily enforce a regime change? If Chapter VII is meant to make the UNSC the "right authority" on determining threats to the peace and sanctioning the use of force, then this must remain the case even after an initial authorization. Just because the authority to use force has been delegated through Article 42, this does not mean that it then delegates the authority of Article 39 to determine when a threat exists. Otherwise, the concept of "right authority" as understood in the Charter has very little meaning.

b Humanitarian intervention in Iraq

During the 1990s, there was a noticeable adjustment in the general understanding of the principle of sovereignty in response to the debates over the legality and validity of humanitarian intervention. This shift is best encapsulated in the international report entitled *The Responsibility to Protect* (2001). The essence of this "emerging norm" is based on the meaning of sovereignty itself. The principle of sovereign equality is clearly enshrined in Article 2(1) of the UN Charter, while Article 2(7) lays out that there shall be no intervention "in matters which are essentially within the domestic jurisdiction of any state." What was identified by the international commission in its report was a possible tension between two different conceptions of sovereignty: one vested in the state, the other in its peoples.

Former Secretary-General Kofi Annan was a strong advocate for the understanding that the UN Charter belongs to the peoples of the world and not the states who are their representatives. He made this clear in a 1998 speech: "[t]he Charter protects the sovereignty of peoples. It was never meant as a license for governments to trample on human rights and human dignity. Sovereignty implies responsibility, not just power" (cited in Wheeler 2003: 195). However, this should not be understood as a challenge to the traditional notion of sovereignty, but rather an attempt to infuse it with additional meaning. That further meaning is captured in the phrase "sovereignty as responsibility." Those who claim the rights of sovereignty must also take responsibility for the protection of their citizens. If they do not, then the international community has a responsibility to provide this protection itself.

One year after 9/11, the Policy Planning Director from the US State Department, Richard N. Haass, took this changing conception of sovereignty as his point of departure for putting forward one of the justifications that would arise for an invasion of Iraq. In a speech to the International Institute for Strategic Studies in London, Haass spoke of the "limits of sovereignty." His contention was that "sovereignty should only provide immunity from intervention if the government upholds basic, minimum standards of domestic conduct and human rights" (2002). The NATO intervention in Kosovo was cited as evidence that the international community had come to support such humanitarian intervention despite the fact that it went unendorsed by the UNSC. A few months earlier, Haass had made a very similar statement in an interview:

> [w]hat you're seeing from this Administration is the emergence of a new principle or body of ideas—I'm not sure it constitutes a doctrine—about what you might call the limits of sovereignty. Sovereignty entails obligations. One is not to massacre your own people. Another is not to support terrorism in any way. If a government fails to meet these obligations, then it forfeits some of the normal advantages of sovereignty, including the right to be left alone inside your own territory. Other governments, including the US, gain the right to intervene.
>
> (Cited in Lemann 2002)

However, what was never explicitly addressed by Haass was who exactly was meant to hold this awesome power of determining whose sovereignty had been forfeited and when. While it is reasonable to depict the changing international consensus on the concept of sovereignty in the way that this member of the US State Department has here, there is an enormous problem in simply ignoring the question of "right authority." If the question is left undetermined, then there is no limitation on the use of humanitarian grounds as a justification for military action.

The example of the Kosovo intervention, as put forward by Haass, can be instructive on this point. Although there was no UNSC resolution supporting "Operation Allied Force" in Kosovo, the wider membership of the Council rejected a resolution put forward by Russia condemning the action afterwards (with only the support of China and India) showing an understanding of the moral context in which NATO had been forced to take its action. It is important to recognize that the authorization of the use of force in this case was blocked by the veto of permanent members. This forced the operation to instead be carried out by a regional international organization, which still demonstrated a broad support for the moral necessity of intervention. In this case, a "jurying" process over intervention indeed took place in the UNSC, and it can even be said that something similar took place within NATO. The international organization's diplomatic processes certainly went a long way toward bolstering the conclusion from the Independent International Commission in *The Kosovo Report* that "Operation Allied Force" was "illegal but legitimate" (2000: 142). Thus, it is inaccurate to assert that the absence of an authorization passed by the UNSC in this case means that it played no part in determining the validity of humanitarian action. Even if the UNSC can at times be dysfunctional as the "right authority" in cases of humanitarian intervention, this certainly does not give automatic license to each and every state to usurp this role for itself.

Consequently, we see that in the case of the invasion of Iraq the US administration directly confronted this issue of "right authority" now found in the UN Charter. Much like in its original form in the just war doctrine, the determining of who possesses the "right authority" to launch armed hostilities is meant as a means for limiting the use of force in international society. It is recognized that the norm which would invest an unmitigated authority in the Security Council is one that continues to be controversial, and there is not one view that is accepted by all legal scholars on this question. Yet it is surely excessive to entirely and overtly discount the authority vested in the UNSC, especially when we are analyzing how citizens analyze their government's exercise of "*legitimate use of physical force.*"

VI Conclusion: diplomatic implications and the Obama Doctrine

The Bush Doctrine launched in reaction to 9/11 suggested that in a world believed to be changed by that event, armed hostilities could be triggered by the suspicions of what other countries might do in the future. It is this standard that has been shown to leave no legal or moral constraints in place, thus opening real problems for the legitimacy of a government that would promote such an anarchic norm as its own.

Using the just war doctrine as our moral guide through this chapter, we have seen that when it comes to the idea of anticipating future events and aiming to evade perceived dangers by using war, the prohibition of such usage runs deep within the just war theory. Throughout the classic doctrine it was understood that there must remain a distinction between defensive and offensive war. Thus, hostilities must be launched in response to an actual wrong received, and it was not enough for evil intentions to have existed. Most pertinent is the conspicuous bifurcation over this very question while Europe was steeped in bloody religious conflict. These pervasive clashes throughout the continent helped give rise to two distinct views on the valid trigger for war. One was a concept of holy war that allowed for "just feare" to be a sufficient *casus belli*, which sowed no progeny and dried up as a defensible justification. At the very same historical moment, legal philosophers and theologians aimed to focus the just war doctrine on more objective factors, which helped provide the naissance of international law. This division, and the subsequent linage (or lack thereof) of each, are particularly revealing of the moral foundations of "anticipatory attacks."

Considering the important point of overlap between legality and morality on a prohibition of the free use of violence, it is quite comprehensible that the citizens of the US would have doubts about the exercise of force by their own government. This is particularly true in the light of the very public diplomatic debate at the UNSC and the suspicions of weapons of mass destruction possessed by the Iraqi regime being shown as patently false through evidence produced by the invasion itself. In the end, the moral and legal grounds asserted by the Bush Doctrine undermined the legitimacy of the "war on terror" because it blatantly flaunted the concept of any sort of equal treatment within the international community. As this doctrine was aptly described, "[t]his revolutionary response to the threat from global terrorism establishes the United States as the sovereign that decides when the sovereignty of others can be infringed" (Wheeler, 2003: 185).

Of course, such an expedient and unconstraining interpretation of international rules is hard to swallow for any diplomat. This is of particular note as we broach a continued analysis of the legitimacy of counterterrorism policy carried out by the US. The Obama administration has once again honed in on this very same question of "imminence" and anticipatory attack, again raising real diplomatic questions in a system that is meant to be based upon "sovereign equality" in Article 2(1) and "refrain ... from the threat or use of force" in Article 2(4) of the UN Charter. It has done so in its expansion of the use of unmanned aerial vehicles, commonly referred to as drones, to target and kill suspected terrorists across new international borders, and its legal justification could be dubbed the Obama Doctrine.

While many of the details of the program remained concealed throughout the first mandate of the Obama administration, and much of it continues to be shrouded in secrecy, there has been a new openness to the discussion of this program. The administration began more detailed public discussion in September 2011, just before it successfully targeted and killed (without admission at the time) a US citizen in Yemen with an unmanned drone. After that there were a series of speeches divulging more details, leaks to the media (including an OLC White Paper providing outlines of the legal justifications), and ultimately a speech by President Obama in May 2013 admitting to and defending the drone program. As is often the case, these incomplete disclosures have both answered certain questions and raised important new ones. With direct relevance to the investigations of this chapter, it has now become clear that the current administration has chosen to put pressure on this precise same point of law concerning anticipatory defense.

As noted earlier in this chapter, in the 2010 revision of the DOD dictionary there was the removal of the term describing a war initiated in the belief that military conflict, while not imminent, is inevitable: "preventive war." Thus it appears as though the thinking on this precise question of "just feare" as a standard did not change under a new administration.

For further evidence of the seamless transition on this point, we can compare public statements. After 9/11 the Bush administration insisted that the US "must adapt the concept of imminent threat to the capabilities and objectives of today's adversaries" (White House NSS 2002). Then, in a speech at Harvard Law School in September 2011 revealing the first outlines of the unmanned drone program, the Assistant to the President for Homeland Security and Counterterrorism used language that was acutely reminiscent. John O. Brennan acknowledged that the Obama administration also believed that the central issue of self-defense "turns principally on how you define 'imminence.'" He then continued: "the traditional conception of what constitutes an 'imminent' attack should be broadened in light of the modern-day capabilities, techniques, and technological innovations of terrorist organizations" (2011).

With these two citations side by side, it is possible to see that the explorations carried out in this chapter tracing the historical filiations of thought on anticipatory defense remain entirely as "just feare" remains the trigger for the use of lethal force across international borders. Accordingly, a fuller discussion of how this same interpretation of anticipatory attack and imminence translates into Obama's drone program, creating a real diplomatic problem in the UN security system, can be found in the conclusion to this book.

Note

1 Although President George W. Bush made a public statement using the word "crusade" days after 9/11, it is not within the scope of this work to investigate any underlying religious impetus that might or might not have existed within the administration.

5 Through the lens of efficacy

Torture on suspicion

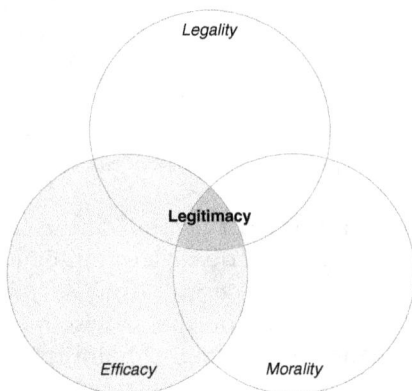

Some locutions begin as bland bureaucratic euphemisms to conceal great crimes. As their meanings become clear, these collocations gain an aura of horror. In the past century, final solution and ethnic cleansing were phrases that sent a chill through our lexicon. In this young century, the word in the news—though not yet in most dictionaries—that causes much wincing during debate is the verbal noun *waterboarding*.

If the word torture, rooted in the Latin for "twist," means anything (and it means "the deliberate infliction of excruciating physical or mental pain to punish or coerce"), then waterboarding is a means of torture.

(Safire 2008)

I Introduction

In this final chapter we shall gaze through the lens of efficacy to analyze torture as an intelligence-gathering tool, and this examination will reveal that the issue shares a manifest overlap with our other two lenses of legality and morality. As discussed, the prohibition of torture in international law has reached the special status of an absolute norm of *jus cogens*, putting it on par with the crimes of slavery and piracy. Put another way, the international law on torture has a clarity and comprehensiveness—no torture, by any authority, against any individual, in any circumstances, anywhere in the world—that places it in a very select category of illegality. For international courts interpreting the laws against torture, its stark status of illegality is not affected by notions of efficacy, and thus the approach of this chapter is legally unorthodox.

However, there is valid reasoning for this unconventional approach. Some national courts have entered into evaluations of efficacy that have traditionally been reserved for the political branches; there have been important decisions dealing with counterterrorism policies by national courts from Israel to Germany that utilized the aspect of efficacy to render their judgment. Yet what must remain front and center is that this work focuses on the legitimacy of the "monopoly of physical force" exercised by the government, and therefore valid policy must aim at defending this core of society that is being targeted. When we speak about state-sanctioned torture, we are looking at the exercising of the government's most coercive and violent dominance over a defenseless individual. Because of the perceived immediacy and necessity that is coupled with the use of torture for intelligence-gathering, any systematized controls that might exist are often discarded as too cumbersome, and torture becomes an unchecked exercise of the government's power. Employing profoundly forceful authority in a capricious manner cannot bode well for defending legitimacy.

To begin, it is necessary to define what is meant by *efficacy* in the specific context of a program of counterterrorism interrogation. As has been discussed, effectiveness can appear deceptively simple when in fact it is enormously complex. Therefore, it is necessary to put forward the precise manner in which the testing of empirical validity will be carried out when discussing interrogation for counterterrorism. Building on the Oxford English Dictionary definition of *efficacious* ("that [which] produces, or is certain to produce, the intended or appropriate effect"), and the definition of torture found in Article 1 of the CAT treaty, *efficacy* in our context will mean: *the purposeful infliction of severe pain or suffering on detained suspects, be it physical or mental, producing, or certain to produce, timely and reliable intelligence information for stopping attacks against noncombatants.* In this context it is necessary for the elements of *timeliness* and *reliability* to be a part of this definition of efficacy because these are indeed a part of the "intended or appropriate effect." Otherwise there will be the possibility that noncoercive methods would have provided the very same results. It is insufficient to claim that the acquisition of information that turns out to be true or useful at some later point in time is enough to demonstrate the efficacy of torture. For torture to be considered efficacious, it must be shown to be a superior technique.

Most critically, our definition also includes the necessity that it must be calculable in advance that a method of coercive interrogation produces the desired result. No doubt there are terms dealing with effectiveness that suggest no need for this high standard. For example, the term "effectual" is defined in the Oxford English Dictionary as "that [which] produces its intended effect, or adequately answers its purpose." The idea that a technique brings about a desired result without a demonstrable reason for causality ahead of time, or that it is "adequate," simply will not do in this context. Torture is far too grave an intrusion into human dignity to use a pliable standard. And it is always possible that an action *happens* to work in a specific instance in retrospect. A single shot fired, even randomly, into a crowd has the capacity for immobilizing a suicide bomber. But without the calculability of how many shots must be fired, and how to ascertain who the correct target is, its true efficacy as a method simply cannot be judged. This brings us to the crux of our argument.

Can torture of innocent or ill-informed individuals ever be considered to be effective? This essential question clarifies the inquiry of this chapter and helps explain the manifest international movement toward the comprehensive illegality of torture. Because the inherent nature of ill-treatment for intelligence-gathering obligates the use of unverifiable suspicions as a trigger for abuse, such a program will always include the innocent and ill-informed among its victims. It is impossible to know in advance (or afterwards) what is inside the head of a detainee, and therefore those who do not have the information we seek will inevitably be brought into the program. The result is that their torture leads to completely unpredictable outcomes coupled with the guaranteed abuse of human beings.

Because terrorism targets legitimacy, counterterrorism policies must be consciously designed with the knowledge that terrorist acts are meant to provoke a government into overreaching with an exercise of force deemed to be illegitimate. Violent force wielded on unchecked suspicion, ensuring that the innocent and ill-informed will be pulled into the program, is a surefire way to jeopardize legitimacy.

Also, we must distinguish between punishment for past crimes and the intention to prevent future ones. When we speak of the efficacy of torture in this chapter, it has nothing to do with the former and everything to do with the latter. Demonstrating agreement, former Vice President Dick Cheney gave a speech in 2009 discussing the security measures implemented when he was in office, and spoke to the intention behind using "enhanced interrogation techniques" (EITs). In the speech he made clear that the administration's use of coercion was solely for intelligence-gathering purposes. While claiming that the tactic worked (without offering any evidence to back up the claim), Cheney propounded,

> We know the difference in this country between justice and vengeance. Intelligence officers were not trying to get terrorists to confess

to past killings; they were trying to prevent future killings. From the beginning of the program, there was only one focused and all-important purpose. We sought, and we in fact obtained, specific information on terrorist plans.

(Cheney 2009)

The defense of the institutionalization of a program of ill-treatment here was because information was gained "on terrorist plans." The standard that is asked to be applied to the counterterrorist campaign was not that of imminent or timely plans, but just plans. This negligible hurdle does nothing to explain why torture should be chosen over other methods.

That torture could be *known* to be necessary to avert serious injury and death presents an onerous burden of proof that must lie on the shoulders of those who wish to subvert or change the comprehensive international and domestic ban on torture and ill-treatment. Because it is impossible to know that the information being sought to prevent harm actually exists within the mind of a proposed victim, or that coercion will actually extract it if it does exist therein, there is never any way of *knowing* that the use of ill-treatment will further that cause. If it were possible to know what is in the mind of a specific detainee, torture would in fact be unnecessary. The absurd claim is that we can know the mind of the proposed victim, but not in its entirety. This is an insurmountable hurdle simply created by the constraints of our humanity. One scholar on torture suggested, when speaking to the possibility of technological advancements providing a means to overcome such human limitations: "if such technology existed, it would surely be just as widespread as electricity" (see Rejali 2007: 453).

This chapter will be an investigation into the empirical validity of treatment during interrogation, and the intelligence gained thereof, by laying out the facts concerning six high-profile detainees. A host of government documents and official statements available in the public sphere will be analyzed which catalogue the suspicions, treatment, and level of cooperation of individuals who have been touted as important figures within the al-Qaeda organization. While these assumptions still held true, their capture and interrogation were lauded as advancements in the "war on terror." However, we will see that the original assumptions frequently turned out to be erroneous, thus drastically recasting the efficacy of the program. The cases of the six detainees that will be presented here are those of (1) Ibn al-Shaykh al-Libi, (2) Abu Zubaydah, (3) José Padilla, (4) Binyam Mohamed, (5) Mohammed al Qahtani, and (6) Khalid Shaykh Mohammed.

Former President George W. Bush still stands behind the value of the program of ill-treatment he authorized and even claims that he would do it again (Bush 2010: 168–171). Most importantly for our purposes, what will be clearly seen through the tracing of the known facts relating to these cases is that even when it came to dealing with the detainees

considered to be the most valuable, the program still pulled in the innocent and ill-informed with a vetting process we must assume to be at its
most rigorous.

Nonetheless, when it comes to discussing the ill-treatment of detainees
in US military or intelligence-agency custody since 9/11, there are regret-
tably numerous cases that can be explored. Today it is possible to find a
host of government and nongovernment reports providing extensive
empirical data:

- report from the US Senate Armed Services Committee (2008);
- internal military reports such as the *Taguba Report* (Taguba 2008), the
  Church Report (Church 2005); and the *Schmidt-Furlow Report* (Schmidt
  and Furlow 2005);
- Inspector General reports from the CIA (2004) and the FBI (2008);
- leaked confidential reports from the ICRC (2004, 2007);
- nongovernmental reports from the Open Society Justice Initiative
  (2013); The Constitution Project (2013);
- accounts from interrogators at the scene (Soufan 2009, 2011); or
- investigative manuscripts from major book publishers (Mayer 2008).

All of these works detail prisoner abuse, and sometimes death, in both
Afghanistan and Iraq, along with the ill-treatment and torture of a
detainee in Guantánamo. The most recent (and, at 600 pages, most
extensive) is the bipartisan Constitution Project, which broadcast its conclusion that it is "indisputable that the United States engaged in the
practice of torture" (2013: 3). Of note, this investigation also dove into
the question of efficacy and asserts a truism that also guides this study:
"to say torture is ineffective does not require a belief that it never works;
a person subjected to torture might well divulge useful information"
(2013: 11).

There is also one government document treating this specific question
of efficacy that has not yet come to light. The US Senate Intelligence Committee completed a 6,000-page report in 2012 that conducted a methodical assessment of whether EITs led to more intelligence breakthroughs or
to false leads. While both of these reports are welcome and surely add to
the empirical data on the subject, this chapter approaches the question
from a different angle.

It was the broadcasting of graphic photographs exhibiting prisoner
abuse in the Iraqi detention facility of Abu Ghraib that brought this issue
to the fore of citizens' minds (see Leung 2004). This began to demonstrate the extensive nature of the ill-treatment being meted out in the "war
on terror." However, this chapter will not attempt to detail the widespread
abuse that infected many parts of the US detention system, but rather will
focus on just one particular aspect—that is, torture must be carried out on
suspicion, not on certain knowledge.

The idea that using forceful coercion can be useful in gathering vital intelligence to save lives is not new. Versions of this argument have been used by philosophers for some time now, lately in the form of the "ticking-bomb scenario." This was popularized in the US as the public learned about the use of abuse in interrogation. The problems, presented as assumptions, that we find repeated in such a "ticking-bomb scenario" are that we are *certain* the detained individual has the knowledge needed to diffuse the bomb, therefore we hold the correct *target* for torture; that time is of the essence so there is *immediacy*; and that severe *coercion* will grant access to the required information (Statman 1997). These are all immensely complicated questions to resolve in an isolated situation, but settling these difficulties to institute a *program* of ill-treatment is truly insurmountable.

It is often accepted that in a single circumstance it is possible for the ticking bomb scenario to pose a daunting moral question for an individual. However, this is not the situation we will be dealing with here. It was an intelligence-gathering *program* based on suspicion and ungoverned by law that was initiated, and therefore the already grave problems of the certainty, targeting, immediacy, and effectiveness of coercive techniques were all multiplied exponentially.

Crucially, there is an angle on this ticking bomb scenario that is less often stressed; the application of torture for gaining intelligence will inevitably be based on *suspicion*. The scenario is often presented in a manner that conceals the importance or centrality of this point, and it is worthwhile to review some of them since they reveal this very point (Ginbar 2008: 379–386). In the nineteenth century, in a precursor of this scenario (but devoid of bombs), Jeremy Bentham put forward the philosophical question with a formulation that properly identifies the root of suspicion in this question. Bentham wrote:

> Suppose an occasion, to arise, in which a *suspicion* is entertained, as strong as that which would be received as a sufficient ground for arrest and commitment as for felony—a *suspicion* that at this very time a considerable number of individuals are actually suffering, by illegal violence inflictions equal in intensity to those which if inflicted by the hand of justice, would universally be spoken of under the name of torture. [...] To say nothing of wisdom, could any pretence be made so much as to the praise of blind and vulgar humanity, by the man who to save one criminal, should determine to abandon a 100 innocent persons to the same fate?
>
> (Bentham 1804, cited in Ginbar 2008: 357; my emphasis)

In this scenario we find that there is an explicit recognition that the intentional application of severe physical or mental pain or suffering would be inflicted on the grounds of *suspicion*. While Bentham acknowledges this would be a high level of suspicion by which a court would find it sufficient to convict the detainee, the element of speculation which is inherent to all such scenarios is often glossed over. Additionally, it should be remembered that the level of evidence that would satisfy a court is quite diverse in different jurisdictions, and can even be said to differ with each judge and jury. Nevertheless, because we are speaking about what might or might not be found inside someone's mind, we are without question discussing an unverifiable suspicion.

As such, in this chapter we shall delve into the facts that are known to address the sphere of empirical validity. Social science provides the most useful tools for ascertaining what techniques have or have not been effective in the past, but this discipline has been largely prevented from applying them to torture because governments have not allowed access to the raw data necessary for a full and objective assessment. It is also the case that historians have not been able to locate any reports produced on the effectiveness of torture for any government. As one thorough scholar on the subject has put it, "[t]hose who believe in torture's effectiveness seem to need no proof and prefer to leave no reports" (Rejali 2007: 522). Due to the dearth of information on the subject, this chapter will analyze the empirical data that has become available on the use of brutal interrogation methods as implemented on six particular suspected terrorists in the "war on terror."

The fact that proving torture to be superior has never been achieved, even after centuries of its use, is extremely telling. If there were conclusive empirical data showing its effectiveness, there would most likely not be such an unmistakable international movement toward torture's prohibition without exception.

II Legality: the torture memos

It is the legal interpretation employed by the lawyers of the OLC, an office that assists the US Attorney General in his function as legal adviser to the President and all the executive branch agencies, that provides evidence of the efforts by the Bush administration to legally justify harsh interrogation techniques. Thus, a series of memoranda authored inside this office concerning the question of limitations on coercive interrogations became known as the "torture memos." Those that fall under this name are primarily from the OLC, which provides interpretations of law that are legally binding on the executive branch, and have been claimed to effectively "immunize officials from prosecutions for wrongdoing" (Goldsmith 2007: 150).

While a comprehensive analysis of all of these legal documents is not within the scope of this study, there is a vital significance that can indeed be discerned for our questions of legitimacy and international law. Even a cursory reading of these memos reveals the extent to which any discussion of torture demanded a reference to international legal norms. Importantly, the Bush administration saw itself as obliged to analyze its own policies through international legality, since the CAT treaty required that this prohibition become a part of domestic law. It is therefore reasonable to conclude that average citizens were also going to be concerned that counterterrorism policies align with this applicable law. Thus, these torture memos show how international law has become intricately intertwined with the rule of law and the constraints on the legitimate use of force.

The most infamous document in this series is entitled "Re: Standards of Conduct for Interrogation under 18 USC §§2340–2340A," known as the Bybee memo, though it was largely drafted by John Yoo and only signed by Jay Bybee. It was public reaction to photos of detainee abuse in the Iraq detention facility of Abu Ghraib that prompted the leak of this particular memo in June 2004. After the appalling images of widespread prisoner abuse by US soldiers and contractors hit the airwaves and newsstands, citizens of the United States began to piece together what had been reported in the nation's leading newspapers since late 2002, and at times on their front pages. That is, a realization started to dawn that a different type of interrogation regime had been instituted and now governed the questioning of detainees in the global "war on terror." With this national wince towards prisoner abuse in the face of incontrovertible photographic evidence, someone inside the government leaked the Bybee memo to the press, which sent out a signal that the coincidence between the treatment of detainees in Iraq and other reports from the "war on terror" had a common thread.

The reaction from commentators, law professors, and others in the legal community was highly critically of the level of professional work found in the Bybee memo. The Dean of the Yale Law School, Harold Koh, a member of the OLC during the Reagan administration and subsequently the Legal Adviser of the Department of State in the Obama administration, said on record before the Senate, "in my professional opinion as a law professor and a law dean, the Bybee memorandum is perhaps the most clearly legally erroneous opinion I have ever read" (cited in Dean 2005). A law professor at the University of Chicago said "It's egregiously bad. It's very low level, it's very weak, embarrassingly weak, just short of reckless" (Liptak 2004).

While not all of the criticism was as harsh, the overall reaction of the legal community was negative. Best capturing this mood was a letter signed by nearly 130 lawyers, retired judges, law school professors, and a former director of the FBI, condemning the released memoranda and calling for an investigation into possible connections between the OLC opinions and the detainee abuse at the Abu Ghraib prison facility (Higham 2004: A04). Within a week of the appearance of the Bybee memo on the *Washington Post* website, the now unclassified memo was publicly vacated of its legal status (Goldsmith 2007: 156–165).

a The Bradbury memos

The Bybee memo largely captures where the interpretation of the legal obligations under the CAT stood as of August 2002, and it was under this legal regime that the most severe consequences from abusive interrogations began. What next happened behind closed doors was disturbing because neither the interim cosmetic memo, nor those that were to follow, did anything to pull back from the conclusions of allowable interrogation methods found in the August 2002 memos. Around the edges, the analysis became more scholarly, with additional attention on pertinent precedent, acknowledgment of contrary arguments, and an abandonment of the doctrine that allowed the President to bypass congressional legislation in wartime.

In May 2005, the lawyer who would later assume the permanent position as the head of the OLC, Steven Bradbury, issued three memos that reached even broader, more sweeping conclusions than before. This time, all of the authorized abusive techniques which were previously not believed to be torture were now found not to be so much as cruel, inhuman, or degrading treatment. This conclusion, again meant to be kept secret, even included controlled drowning evoking death, also known as waterboarding.

The Bradbury memos (released by the Obama administration in 2009) arrive at that finding on the basis of two primary facts. The first is that US personnel subjected to many of the same techniques in the counter-torture training program Survival, Evasion, Resistance and Escape (SERE) have reportedly not experienced severe pain or suffering or prolonged mental harm (US Senate Armed Services Committee 2008: xii). Second, the fact that doctors would be present at the interrogations would permit them to stop the application of particular techniques if it were deemed that the threshold into prohibited treatment was going to be crossed.

Whether the previous application of certain techniques in an explicitly finite and voluntary environment or the presence of medical personnel charged with monitoring inherently subjective pain are enough to avoid legal liability for treaty violation will not be assessed here. Suffice it to say that reciprocity had no place in this analysis because the SERE program had already been explicitly built on preparing "American personnel to withstand interrogation techniques considered illegal under the Geneva Conventions" (US Senate Armed Services Committee 2008: xiii). Next, the idea that the US Government would accept such treatment of its own soldiers because of the presence of medically trained persons in a controlled environment appears dubious at best.

The Bradbury memo identified as the most egregious and problematic is entitled "Re: Application of United States Obligations under Article 16 of the Convention against Torture to Certain Techniques that May Be Used in Interrogation of High Value al Qaeda Detainees (*Article 16 Memo*)" (Bradbury 2005b). As Article 16 of the CAT treaty speaks specifically of ill-treatment that does not rise to the level of torture, this memo rightfully drew critical attention.

The most noteworthy criticism came from a former member of the Bush administration who had been engaged behind the scenes in push-back against the legal analysis found in these memos. Philip Zelikow worked on intelligence and terrorism issues for Secretary of State Condoleezza Rice and gained access to the OLC opinions after they were issued in May 2005. Just after the Obama administration made a public release of related memos, Zelikow published an article (2009) detailing some of his own actions in response to an analysis that he found to be deeply flawed.

Because Zelikow was directly involved in working through the internal legal minutia on the interrogation program, his dissenting opinion (demonstrating a "legitimacy deficit") is particularly useful here. The first point he makes is that the focus on waterboarding, used as an expedient to extract information in dire circumstances, distracted the public from the fact that what had developed was a *program* of interrogation intended to "disorient, abuse, dehumanize, and torment individuals over time" (Zelikow 2009). The detainee would be stripped naked, dowsed regularly with cold water, slapped around, thrown into hollowed walls, forced into cramped boxes, and shackled to the ceiling to force the prisoner into a standing position to be deprived of sleep for extended periods, before ever getting to the controlled drowning.

While Zelikow wrote that all of the memos "have grave weaknesses" (2009), he reserved his most severe condemnation for the Article 16 memo because it downgraded all of the previously authorized techniques (since they did not constitute "torture") to being considered even less than cruel, inhuman, or degrading treatment. This memo was deemed to be the "weakest of all" because of the specific legal knowledge Zelikow gained from working for many years on the jurisprudence of the US constitutional standard of "shocks the conscience:" the US constitutional standard prohibiting ill-treatment.

The US attached a reservation of understanding to the CAT treaty when it was ratified in 1994, saying that it would interpret Article 16 dealing with the lower forms of ill-treatment to mean the legal precedent found in constitutional law. This is of central importance to the Zelikow denunciation because this legal question became directly and completely intertwined with domestic constitutional law. This is why Zelikow took steps at that time, outside of his normal duties, to explicitly refute this Article 16 memo, which he believed presented a "distorted rendering of relevant US law" (Zelikow 2009). So, we again see that the ratification of an international treaty has been bolstered by the domestic jurisprudence giving the CAT further shape and meaning on the matter of ill-treatment.

As Zelikow understood the legal interpretation of the "shocks the conscience" standard, there was no way that these techniques could be deemed legal. He pointed out that the memo endorsed the absurd legal conclusion that "the methods and the conditions of confinement in the CIA program could constitutionally be inflicted on American citizens in a county jail" (Zelikow 2009). One must, in effect, argue that federal courts have ruled in the past, and could be reasonably expected to rule in the future, that US citizens can be stripped naked, slapped, handcuffed to the ceiling, and even subjected to controlled drowning. Zelikow, according to his study of the pertinent case law, did not believe this was in any way a reasonable argument.

b Pushback from the legislature and the judiciary

What must be understood about this series of secret memos is that, while their conclusions pushed even farther than before, the other branches of government were placing further clarified legal and public limits on inter-rogations. As discussed in Chapter 3, in 2005 the US Congress passed spe-cific legislation concerning interrogation: the Detainee Treatment Act (DTA), 2005. This legislation contains provisions that require Department of Defense personnel to employ the US Army Field Manual guidelines while interrogating detainees, and it specifically prohibited the use of cruel, inhuman, and degrading treatment or punishment. It is commonly known as the "McCain Amendment" since these provisions were added to the defense spending Bill via amendments introduced by Senator John McCain, who was tortured in detention during the Vietnam War. The overwhelming bipartisan support for the Bill when it passed in the Senate by a vote of ninety to nine suggested a new independence among Republi-cans to challenge the White House on counterterrorism policy.

There was also the landmark decision of *Hamdan* v. *Rumsfeld* which estab-lished, among other things, that Common Article 3 of the Geneva Conven-tions with its prohibition of ill-treatment was fully applicable to the "war on terror." Thus, we find both the legislative and the judicial branches palpably pushing back against the executive on the issue of interrogation.

Also of importance is what happened when the legislation containing the McCain Amendment came across the desk of President George W. Bush. The Bill was indeed signed into law; however, attached to it was a "signing statement," (an official document in which the President explains his interpretation of the new legislation), that brought into question the intention of the executive branch to enforce this new provision. In this signing statement, President Bush expressed that he would understand this new law "in a manner consistent with the constitutional authority of the President to supervise the unitary executive branch and as Com-mander in Chief and consistent with the constitutional limitations on the judicial power" (Bush 2006a).

While this statement may seem innocuous at first blush, particular attention should be focused on the terms "constitutional authority," "unitary executive," and "Commander in Chief." The OLC had interpreted the President's constitutional power in wartime as the commander in chief to be unassailable by the other branches of government. So, when we read that the President will interpret this new law in the context of a "unitary executive," we must understand that he is saying that he will act in a manner that will leave the President's action unfettered by this law which is meant to curtail and constrain his authority on interrogation techniques. While the concept of a "unitary executive" was once a relatively obscure theory of expanding and protecting presidential power, it gained significant ground during the George W. Bush presidency.

President Bush attached a host of signing statements (not a new invention by his office) to the legislation he signed over his years in office, but it was this instance that began to draw attention to this practice. In an act that can be described as real concern and dissent from civil society, the American Bar Association (ABA) appointed a task force to investigate the signing statements as a challenge to the constitutional structure of the US democracy. The conclusions were stark and grave, finding that the practice had become "contrary to the rule of law and our constitutional system of separation of powers" (ABA 2006: 1).

The reason why the rise of this issue of "signing statements" and the "unitary executive" within the public sphere is pertinent here is because the question of an abuse of power directly addresses the issue of legitimacy. In assessing the torture memos and the response to their public disclosure through the lens of legality, we see that serious troubles were exposed. The deep flaws in the Bybee memo were evidenced by its immediate retraction just after the public gained knowledge of it and began its outcry. This was followed by actions in Congress to pass legislation to place explicit constraints upon other forms of ill-treatment in Department of Defense interrogations. Additionally, the Supreme Court found Common Article 3 of the Geneva Conventions to be applicable law in the "war on terror," furthering the legal constraint on interrogation. Despite these explicit moves by the other branches to curb what was considered to be an overreach, the administration proceeded in secret to provide legal cover for its actions. Yet, through the issue of signing statements, the sense of an illegitimate use of force or abuse of power was taking root in a growingly uneasy public.

c A flawed attempt at efficacy for legality

While it is clear that administration lawyers needed to push against international legality for extending coercive interrogation limits, the issue of efficacy also came to the fore. One purported relationship between legality and efficacy can be observed by the fact that the effectiveness of the applied coercive interrogations is treated quite extensively within this series of OLC memos themselves, in the legal analysis of the Office of

Professional Responsibility (OPR) (US Department of Justice 2009: 96, 146–147, 158, 243–251, 259) and in the 2004 CIA Inspector General report (2004: 82–91). However, that this issue of efficacy has been widely analyzed in these documents does not mean there is a legal link between the concepts in the way it has been described in the memos. The CAT treaty and international courts have explicitly dismissed the use of balancing such competing interests. Rather, what we find in these documents represents a flawed analysis of a connection between legality and efficacy made particularly gross by the use of erroneous empirical data.

Both the OPR and the Inspector General reports identify the same three difficulties in arriving at an objective assessment of the applicable value of coercive interrogations. Using the exact same wording, they each assert that,

> Measuring the overall effectiveness of EITs is challenging for a number of reasons including: (1) the Agency cannot determine with any certainty the totality of the intelligence the detainee actually possesses: (2) each detainee has different fears of and tolerance for EITs; (3) the application of the same EITs by different interrogators may have different results [redacted].
> (CIA Inspector General 2004: 89; US Department of Justice 2009: 96)

In assessing the efficacy of ill-treatment during interrogation, we will continually return to the first element put forward here as it is a hurdle that cannot be surmounted under the conditions of humanity as understood today: we cannot know what is known.

It is the Article 16 memo authored by Stephen Bradbury that treats the issue of effectiveness most fully for the OLC, if only because he was forced to meet this argument as it was raised in the hyper-critical CIA Inspector General report. In this memo, Bradbury admits that "it is difficult to quantify with confidence and precision the effectiveness of the program" (2005b: 10). He refers to the report and the complexity of parsing the direct successes of the techniques employed but stresses the increased general knowledge gained on how al-Qaeda and its affiliates operate. Bradbury asserts that there has been "specific actionable intelligence" gained and additionally cites the CIA as having produced over 6,000 intelligence reports as a result of the authorized coercive techniques (2005b: 11).

However, one thing that must be noted in this memo by Bradbury is that, as he makes the best case he can for efficacy, there is absolutely no reference to any imminent threat being averted nor any other timely action of necessity. Although many who argue for the use of it point to coercion as the most time-efficient means in moments of a crisis, this lacuna in the government's assessment of the interrogation program leaves open the possibility that the intelligence gained could have been obtained through other means.

To evaluate whether the coercive interrogation techniques would transgress the standard of cruel, inhuman, or degrading treatment, Bradbury leaned heavily on the information provided to him by the same agency that wanted to have legal authorization to employ this type of pressure. He was informed by the CIA that the EITs would only be used on a "high-value detainee." The agency defined this as

> a detainee who, until time of capture, we have *reason to believe* (1) is a senior member of al-Qai'da or an al-Qai'da associated terrorist group [...]; (2) has knowledge of imminent terrorist threats against the USA, its military forces, its citizens and organizations, or its allies; or that has/had direct involvement in planning and preparing terrorist actions against the USA or its allies, or assisting the al-Qai'da leadership in planning and preparing such terrorist actions; and (3) if released, constitutes a clear and continuing threat to the USA or its allies.
>
> (Bradbury 2005b: 5; my emphasis)

Most important to note about this definition is the fact that the CIA uses the phrase "reason to believe" to qualify who will be considered a high-value detainee. This classification is not based on a verified, proven, or confirmed association or specific action.

However, for the use of the most extreme enhanced technique, waterboarding, even further criteria would need to be met. Among the authorized techniques, waterboarding drew the focus of the public's attention for both legal and historical reasons. The technique has been legally considered as torture by the US throughout the twentieth century. This can be evidenced by the US experience in the Philippines at the turn of the century (where it was employed by soldiers, leading to courts martial), the Tokyo War Crimes trials that followed World War II, and the *United States* v. *Lee* case before the domestic courts in 1984 (Wallach 2007: 477). Yet this interrogation technique was placed in the CIA's arsenal for the first time in the nation's history in 2002, and Bradbury legally authorized it again.

The use of this controlled drowning necessitated a series of further conditions be met before it could be employed. The only circumstances under which it could be introduced align very closely with what is often thought to be the ticking bomb scenario:

> credible intelligence that a terrorist attack is imminent; substantial and credible indicators that the subject has actionable intelligence that can prevent, disrupt or delay this attack; and other interrogation methods have failed to elicit the information [or] CIA has clear indications that other ... methods are unlikely to elicit this information *within the perceived time limit for preventing the attack.*
>
> (Bradbury 2005b: 5; original emphasis)

However, there is no discussion of how the host of qualifiers are to be determined. Who determines what is "credible," and how is it measured? What is the time frame used for "imminent"? For how long are other methods tried before they are determined to have "failed"? What are considered to be "clear indications" that other methods will not work in time? How is the "perceived time limit for the attack" measured? Are there any checks on these determinations? Are there any consequences if these many qualifiers are misconstrued from the outset or found to be patently incorrect? None of these questions are addressed by Bradbury in the memo, and all of them clearly indicate the ultimate reliance upon suspicion.

Most important, however, is that this document is from August 2004, after the EITs had already been employed and two months after the public disclosure of the Bybee memo. There is no indication that these qualifiers existed for restraining the use of the waterboard before this. Therefore, the use of controlled drowning was in fact employed without the above standards in place.

Also of importance, Bradbury relied on CIA documents, including a still undisclosed document from March 2005 entitled "Re: Effectiveness of the CIA Counterterrorist Interrogation Techniques" (effectiveness memo; cited in Bradbury 2005a: 8). Based primarily on this memo, Bradbury concluded in his analysis that the program had indeed been effective in producing important information including actionable intelligence. The Article 16 memo arrived at the conclusion that, due to the reservation attached to the CAT treaty by the US, the restriction on cruel, inhuman, and degrading treatment would be punishment prohibited by the Fifth Amendment, since it was the part of the Bill of Rights which was applicable in this particular context.

Thus, the relevant standard was treatment that "shocks the conscience." Bradbury interpreted this to mean that an action must not be "arbitrary in a constitutional sense," or, more precisely, that an act must have "reasonable justification in the service of a legitimate governmental objective" according to his own reading of precedent (Bradbury 2005b: 2–3). To fulfill this legal requirement manufactured by Bradbury, enhanced interrogation techniques needed to be effective. To discern whether the action of waterboarding was constitutionally arbitrary, Bradbury relied on the effectiveness memo to establish that it furthered a government's legitimate objective. He determined that preventing future terrorists attacks by al-Qaeda surely fulfilled the concept of a legitimate objective, and, since the technique was said to have worked in the CIA memo, the standard of furthering said objective was met.

However, not only was Bradbury's legal analysis flawed, his uncritical reliance upon the effectiveness memo in order to conclude that EITs were successful was unjustified to boot. The most blatant problem was that there was patently false information found within the document that could easily have been crosschecked. This memo claimed that the techniques had directly led to the capture of an al-Qaeda suspect in May 2003. Considering that enhanced coercive questioning procedures were first authorized by the Bybee memo of August 2002, this was feasible. However, the suspect in question was actually apprehended with much public fanfare as the "dirty bomb" suspect, and an official announcement was made by Attorney General John Ashcroft from Moscow, where he was meeting with his counterpart officials. The suspect was taken into custody in May, and the pronouncement took place in **2002** (one year earlier). Therefore, it would be impossible, as the effectiveness memo claimed, for this capture to have resulted from intelligence gained from the EITs, as they had not yet been authorized (US Department of Justice 2009: 246–247). Such a gross error could easily have been caught by any of the memo's original drafters, the attorney who relied on this claim, or any of the policy-makers touting it as a victory resulting from expanded tactics in interrogation. What is abundantly clear, however, is that the capture of this suspect was not the fruit of any authorized enhanced techniques.

Additionally, treated in another memo of the same month, the application of the specific technique of waterboarding is said to have often, if not always, "exceeded the limitations, conditions, and understandings recited in the Classified Bybee Memo and the Bradbury Memos" (US Department of Justice 2009: 247). In other words, the application of the waterboard did not stay inside its authorized limits. This is particularly troublesome because it is enormously problematic to claim to know the efficacy of a technique that was never applied in the manner specifically described and authorized. Bradbury was aware of these systematic excesses as he wrote his memos in the wake of the most devastating internal report on the CIA program of interrogation to that date. For this reason, Bradbury was forced to acknowledge this excess and address it head on in his legal analysis, if only in a footnote. He wrote:

> The *IG Report* noted that in many cases the waterboard was used with far greater frequency, than initially indicated, and also that it was used in a different manner ("[t]he waterboard technique was different ... from the technique described in the DoJ opinion and in the SERE training. The difference was in the manner in which the detainee's breathing was obstructed. At the SERE school and in the DoJ opinion, the subject's air flow is disrupted by the firm application of a damp cloth over the air passages; the interrogator applies a small amount of water to the cloth in a controlled manner. By contrast, the Agency interrogator ... applied large volumes of water to a cloth that covered detainee's mouth and nose. One of the psychologists/interrogators acknowledged that the Agency's use of the technique is different from that used in the SERE training because it's for real and is more poignant and convincing.")
>
> (Bradbury 2005a: 41, note 51; internal citations omitted)

Bradbury uses a citation from one of the psychologists who engineered the transfer of the SERE torture-resistance training to the CIA interrogation program, and somehow this is meant to bolster reasoning for the stark difference in application. However, this argument is clearly flawed. Serious weight was given to the claim that the techniques could not be construed as ill-treatment because they had been applied regularly to US personnel in the SERE program. If they were significantly different in their application to high-value detainees, regardless of the reason, this argumentation falls apart. The techniques cannot be acceptable because they have been applied to US personnel and at the same time warrant a different usage in real interrogations. The fact that the waterboard in this circumstance is "for real and is more poignant and convincing" means that it must be legally assessed as such.

Nonetheless, the CIA Inspector General report raised much graver issues which are certainly not dealt with by this psychologist/interrogator's statement. The report spoke of serious concerns introduced by medical personnel which were fully available to Bradbury. In fact, this trouble was cited and treated by Bradbury in the same footnote. In the original report it reads:

> OMS [CIA's Office of Medical Services] contends that the reported sophistication of the preliminary EIT review was exaggerated, at least as it related to the waterboard, and that the power of this EIT was appreciably overstated in the report. Furthermore, OMS contends that the expertise of the SERE psychologist/interrogators on the waterboard was probably misrepresented at the time, as the SERE waterboard experience is so different from the subsequent Agency usage as to make it almost irrelevant.
>
> (CIA Inspector General 2004: 21–22, note 26)

And of direct consequence to the issue of efficacy, the CIA report went on to state that "Consequently, according to OMS, there was no *a priori* reason to believe that applying the waterboard with the frequency and intensity with which it was used by the psychologist/interrogators was either efficacious or medically safe" (2004: 21–22, note 26).

To deal with the genuine disquiet with the drastic difference in the application of the waterboard, Bradbury worked with both the OMS concerns through personnel in that office and with a full copy of the internal CIA report. His conclusion was that careful consideration had "resulted in a number of changes in the application of the waterboard, including limits on the frequency and cumulative use of the technique" (Bradbury 2005a: 41, note 51; internal citations omitted). However, there continues to be a huge problem. While it certainly is more humane to reduce the frequency and intensity of the use of the waterboard, it does not in any way address the efficacy upon which Bradbury's analysis relies. If the program produced results in the past (yet serious doubts have already been raised as to the veracity of this claim), it did so under different conditions. Bradbury cannot rely on the effectiveness memo and its conclusions for his legal analysis while at the same time instituting meaningful changes to the application of the waterboard. If the modifications are consequential, and he states them to be just that, then any evidence of previous efficacy is inapplicable.

The intriguing aspect of what we have found here in our analysis is the attempted integration or overlap of legality and efficacy. Even though the CAT treaty explicitly rules out exceptions, Bradbury saw fit to include it into his legal analysis. While this must be characterized as legally flawed, it also speaks to the profound draw that many feel toward wishing to calculate what could be the lesser evil. For Bradbury's legal analysis, the facet of effectiveness was essential to his finding that a specific act did not "shock the conscience" and thus was not "constitutionally arbitrary." What is most disturbing to find, however, is that Bradbury's complete reliance upon the information he was provided with by the CIA had such palpable empirical weaknesses regarding the claims of the program's efficacy. Thus, this dearth of valid evidence proving the program's efficacy raises even further questions about his conclusions concerning the legality of the program, undermining a legal analysis that was flawed at its outset.

III Efficacy: six high-profile suspects

Social scientists have never been given access to the raw empirical data on the use of torture employed by a government, nor have historians uncovered documents that reveal a methodical tracking. Therefore, when exposing empirical validity we are left with what is to be found in this chapter: a fair-minded assessment of the public data. This means that we will delve into the documents on six high-profile detainees whose captures have been touted as individual victories in the "war on terror." First, however, to establish that the analysis data in this chapter will not expose a distorted picture of what can be expected when a government authorizes a program of torture and ill-treatment, we will take a brief look at compiled empirical data from other campaigns employing torture.

The US has its own historical experience with the use of physical and psychological coercion for interrogation purposes, so it is pertinent to begin here. There are two CIA interrogation manuals that describe the use of coercive techniques for intelligence-gathering that now appear online: the *Kubark: Counterintelligence Interrogation* of 1963 and the *Human Resources Exploitation Training Manual* of 1983. Yet neither offers instruction in applying torture techniques nor suggests how to choose subjects for interrogation. In the mid-1960s, the CIA did run what was called the Phoenix Program during the Vietnam War, with the purpose of capturing, interrogating, and killing Vietcong operatives (Rejali 2007: 470–472).

The managers of the Phoenix Program left behind a unique database that documented their assessment of the reliability of the intelligence gathered, and the conclusions are revealing. The standard for confirming a target was simply three independent pieces of intelligence. Nevertheless, one important statistic that emerges is that 94 percent of those who were actually confirmed by this process to be Vietcong were able to elude capture or death. At the same time, 20 percent of those who never reached the level of being fully confirmed by three separate sources had been terminated by the action squads. This statistic alone—of the less suspicious being more likely to suffer than the highly suspicious—begins to illuminate the gross problems with authorizing such a program. Additionally, there were "at least" thirty-eight innocents for every actual Vietcong agent victimized, with the most conservative estimate being that 4.7 innocent individuals were killed for every member of the Vietcong successfully exterminated (Rejali 2007: 471).

It is also instructive to look at another historical case where a good deal of empirical data has been collected and analyzed concerning the application of torture: the battle of Algiers. French General Jacques Massu reestablished colonial authority in the capital city of Algeria in just seven short months after being given *carte blanche* to clear out the Front de Libération Nationale (FLN) group that was employing terrorist tactics in an insurgency against the foreign power (Duquesne 2001: 69–78; see also Horne 1977: 183–207). While there are some who cite this case to silence critics of torture due to this simple fact, the archives on the war in Algeria are now partially open, and interrogators have written their biographies, revealing a more complete view of what happened in that armed conflict. A wider purview exposes a general failure to produce reliable information through torture.

It is important to note that this ostensibly successful military campaign did not apply a selective process to filter out the innocent. A wide net was cast in the center of Algiers. In the end, nearly 30 percent of the population of the Casbah (24,000 of 80,000 people) were taken into custody, with a great majority of them subjected to torture (80 percent of the men and 66 percent of the women) (Rejali 2007: 482). One historian of the conflict has claimed that 1,400 operators of the FLN had actually been assembled in Algiers (Horne 1977: 184). This means that, even if every member had been detained, there were still around 22,600 individuals who suffered from wrongful detention, with a great many of them also being tortured. When the figures are calculated, the French military was torturing nearly fifteen individuals in order to stumble upon one actual member of the insurgency. Looking at such astounding figures and analyzing the efficacy of torture, one historian wrote "From a purely intelligence point of view, experience teaches that more often than not the collating services are overwhelmed by a mountain of false information extorted from the victims desperate to save themselves from further agony" (Horne 1977: 205).

Also of significance to our work, even though torture was instituted as an official military tactic and widely applied in the Casbah of Algiers, there is not one soldier who ever claimed to have secured timely information and prevented a ticking bomb from exploding (Rejali 2007: 481, 489). Of course, simply looking at what happened in Algiers in 1957 narrows our purview to only one battle in a war that lasted from 1954 to 1962. The former French Secretary-General at the Algiers prefecture, Paul Teitgen, concisely explained this problem: "Massu won the Battle of Algiers; but that meant losing the war" (Horne 1977: 207).

Thus, it is fair to suggest that an examination of the empirical data on a selection of six high-profile suspects detained in the "war on terror" in which a good number were of questionable intelligence value does not present a distorted picture of a torture program. In fact, the results here are even more generous to the administration's use of suspicion than what has been found in these similar cases.

IV Ibn al-Shaykh al-Libi: *casus belli*

On December 19, 2001, Ibn al-Shaykh al-Libi was captured by Pakistani officials blocking the chaotic escape through the mountains of those fleeing the war and disorder caused by the invasion of Afghanistan by US armed forces. Considered to be the first big al-Qaeda prize in the "war on terror," and alleged to have trained hundreds, if not thousands, of jihadis at a camp in Afghanistan, al-Libi was quickly handed over to the US. He was first interrogated by an FBI team who had been advised to run the interrogation strictly by the book with the criminal-justice model in mind so as to secure his testimony as a future witness in a domestic court. They were able to build a rapport with al-Libi that paid off with "specific action-able intelligence" (Mayer 2008: 105). Without coercion, he provided information on a terrorist bomb plot in its final stages to strike the US embassy in Yemen, which was later corroborated; this averted what would likely have been a deadly attack. Nearly as importantly, al-Libi was pressed hard on ties between al-Qaeda and the Saddam Hussein regime in Iraq, and he told his interrogators that he did not know of any.

What is known about what happened next casts a bright light on torture and the efficacy of abusive interrogation for gathering accurate intelli-gence. After several days of interrogation by the FBI team building trust with the detainee, CIA officers entered the room, strapped al-Libi to a stretcher and loaded him into a pickup truck that drove directly into the cargo hold of a waiting airplane.

In 2006, the US Senate Select Committee on Intelligence released a report on the use of intelligence by Bush administration officials in the run-up to the invasion of Iraq. This account reveals valuable evidence regarding the inefficacy of torture since it provides a record of exactly how abusive interrogation, in the specific instance of al-Libi, lent false support for the invasion of a sovereign country. Most importantly for the purely self-interested lens of efficacy, dependence upon the intelligence gathered through coercion helped provide a *casus belli* to invade Iraq at the estimated cost of $1 to $3 trillion dollars (Bilmes and Stiglitz 2008), the lives of nearly 5,000 US troops, more than 30,000 soldiers wounded in action, and immeasurable damage to the international stature and credibility of the US.

Following the unusual internal transfer between US agencies, al-Libi was then moved to a third country under a program of rendition that was originally aimed at the handover of criminal suspects to find justice before a court. After 9/11, the program was transfigured into what has now been generally labeled "extraordinary rendition," meant to abduct terror suspects, not to bring them before a court of justice but instead to conceal the detainee from the legal system by transferring them to a third country for immobilization and interrogation. Under questioning in this third country (reported to be Egypt), al-Libi stated that there was a link between al-Qaeda and the Saddam Hussein regime in Iraq. Al-Libi told his captors that training for the use of weapons of mass destruction had been made available to two al-Qaeda operatives, and the CIA relied heavily upon this intelligence information (US Senate Select Committee on Intelligence 2006).

Yet how exactly this information was gathered is of critical importance to the question before us in this chapter. This was the first time that al-Libi had claimed that there was an official relationship between Iraq and al-Qaeda, and it was presented only after the use of abuse and ill-treatment. When al-Libi was questioned on this subject he had a very tough time since he had already decided to fabricate information so as to avoid mistreatment, but he knew nothing on the subject, so even inventing a story proved difficult. His interrogators were displeased with his initial lack of response to the line of questioning and forced him into a tiny box where he was left for some seventeen hours. After being let out of the box, he was again questioned on the link between Iraq and al-Qaeda and then pushed to the floor and beaten for fifteen minutes when he did not satisfy his interrogator. In reaction to this treatment, al-Libi began to concoct the story of an operational link using names of al-Qaeda members he knew, after which his treatment slowly began to improve (US Senate Select Committee on Intelligence 2006: 80–2).

This "intelligence" information made it all the way to the nation's top diplomat. It was included in the Secretary of State's speech before the UN Security Council in February 2003, seen as particularly important in the case for a war against Iraq because Colin Powell was considered by many as the figure with the most credibility within the Bush administration. Powell spent a good deal of time at the CIA headquarters combing through the available intelligence in preparation for this high-profile speech so as to put forward the most reliable arguments for the invasion of a country that had not attacked the US.

During the preparation for this speech, Powell became so frustrated with the thin evidence that he nearly threw out all of the information relating to a connection with terrorism. But it was this key nugget of information from al-Libi that swayed Powell in a dramatic moment to "put his name and reputation behind the most fateful speech of his life" (Mayer 2008: 137). This corrupted intelligence made it into his final speech before the Security Council:

> I can trace the story of a senior terrorist operative telling how Iraq provided training in these weapons to al-Qaida [...]. When we confront a regime that harbors ambitions for regional domination, hides weapons of mass destruction and provides haven and active support for terrorists, we are not confronting the past, we are confronting the present. And unless we act, we are confronting an even more frightening future.
>
> (Powell 2003)

Almost one year to the day, al-Libi recanted the statements of collusion between Iraq and terrorists that he had made under duress. In 2004, he was back in CIA custody in Afghanistan, and a cable was sent back to headquarters at Langley that al-Libi's story of a connection was no longer reliable. This cable seems to have sat idle for some time back in the US, until it was picked up and given political life by the Senate Committee in its report of 2006. All signs are that al-Libi concocted "information in response to physical abuse and threats of torture," since we now know that "[t]he Intelligence Community has found no postwar information to indicate that Iraq provided CBW [Chemical and Biological Weapons] training to al-Qa'ida" (US Senate Select Committee on Intelligence 2006: 108).

As such, we can conclude that the interrogation of Ibn al-Shaykh al-Libi was ineffective in the sense that his ill-treatment led directly to the providing of false intelligence that helped bolster a *casus belli* at enormous costs in blood and treasure. It is still not clear what sort of relationship al-Libi had with Al-Qaeda, but there is little doubt that the suspicions of what information he might possess were incorrect, and extremely costly to the US.

V Abu Zubaydah: the pivotal moment in torture policy

In the early morning of March 28, 2002, local law-enforcement officers in Faisalabad, Pakistan, joined by personnel from the CIA and the FBI, raided ten different suspected safe-houses and captured a thirty-year-old Saudi Arabian by birth (although he refers to himself as a Palestinian because he migrated there as a youth) who had been familiar to US terrorism analysts for years. In a bloody firefight they apprehended Zayn al Abidin Muhammad Hussein, or, as he is most widely known, Abu Zubaydah. It was strongly believed that Zubaydah had timely, and potentially life-saving, actionable intelligence, so for an administration that felt itself under intense pressure to demonstrate positive advancements in its response to the 9/11 terrorist attacks, Zubaydah provided one of the first testing grounds for its theories on intelligence-gathering.

In 2006, when the administration first divulged information about Zubaydah in a speech before families of the victims of 9/11, President Bush explained the importance of this particular detainee when he said "We believed that Zubaydah was a senior terrorist leader and a trusted associate of Osama bin Laden" (Bush 2006b). The use of the term "believed" is important to note since it indicates the centrality of the concept of suspicion in interrogation. Nonetheless, a thorough interrogation of this detainee was at the forefront of the administration's agenda because of this belief of who he was, yet the CIA agency put in the lead by the administration had zero experience in detention and no trained interrogators (Mayer 2008: 139–181).

Unlike Ibn al-Shaykh al-Libi, the US decided that Zubaydah would be classified as a high-value detainee and kept in US custody. As he was nearly fatally wounded during apprehension, the first step was to fly over a top trauma surgeon from Johns Hopkins Hospital to save his life. Yet Zubaydah has testified that he still suffered medical complications resulting from bullet wounds to his head and thigh, continued to endure seizures and speech problems, and was left with only one testicle. (Zubaydah 2007: 25).

a The clash between the FBI and the CIA

To best understand what unfolded next, the most illuminating information comes from Ali Soufan, a highly experienced FBI agent practiced in interrogation through the questioning of numerous al-Qaeda terrorists. Soufan grew up in Lebanon, which allowed him to achieve the rare capability to fluently conduct questioning in both English and Arabic. He was a key investigator of the USS *Cole* bombings in 2000, has been described as "one of the most impressive intelligence agents from any agency," and "could quote Qur'anic passages to radical jihadist prisoners, challenging them about the meaning of the prophet's words and ultimately gaining trust to engage them in extended conversations about their lives" (Isikoff 2009).

Soufan was one of the first to question Zubaydah at a secret location (black site) in Thailand where he was installed for detention and interrogation. Soufan and his fellow FBI agent were very familiar with Zubaydah and were able to gain important actionable intelligence from the severely wounded prisoner within the first four hours of interrogation (see Soufan 2009). Using a knowledge-based approach, the FBI team was able to secure that the mysterious "Mukhtar," to whom many of the transmissions relating to 9/11 referred, was Khalid Shaykh Mohammed. The speed at which all of the fresh information was gained, much of it still classified, was deemed so important that the Director of the CIA wanted to extend official congratulations to the team on behalf of the agency, until he learned that they were in fact from the FBI. Instead, he immediately ordered a CIA counterterrorism team to the site in Thailand. This new intelligence was gathered using what Soufan calls the "Informed Interrogation Approach," wholly free of any physical or mental coercion.

Within days, the CIA team arrived at the site with a contractor, a psychologist who claimed to be a specialist in human behavior resulting from his experience working with the SERE program (teaching resistance techniques to US personnel). It was under the instruction of this contractor, James Mitchell (see Eban 2007), that the FBI team was removed and Zubaydah was promptly stripped naked and subjected to low-level sleep deprivation. After a few days of getting no information with the application of these tactics, Soufan and his colleague were called back in. Soufan asserts that this time the rapport-building led to the gathering of further intelligence. Yet the contractor again stepped back in to take over the interrogation and had the CIA apply further coercion, including loud noise and temperature manipulation. This back-and-forth between competing interrogation approaches continued as far as introducing a confinement box, and one CIA psychologist left the location because he objected to what was being done to the detainee (Soufan 2011: 373–435).

A direct confrontation eventually erupted between the FBI agent and the CIA contractor, with the latter insisting "Science is science. This is a behavioral issue" (Isikoff 2009). The contention that it has been scientifically proven somewhere that it is possible to coerce away an individual's will, and that the most efficient and effective method for doing so is through brutal physical and psychological treatment, must have been particularly galling for an experienced interrogator. The contracted psychologist brought in to assist an agency that had little previous experience in interrogation was himself applying an "untested theory" and conducting an "experiment" (Soufan 2009).

Mitchell's experience came from training personnel to deal with enemies who did not follow the law, and he had never sat across the table (or across a confinement box, for that matter) from a suspected terrorist. He had no background in the Middle East, no intelligence experience, was unversed in the Muslim religion, and spoke no Arabic (Mayer 2008: 156). Of particular note is that it has been stressed by some familiar with the development of the interrogation program that those who brought to the CIA the theory of reducing a detainee to complete helplessness and dependence "had no proof of their tactics' effectiveness" (Eban 2007).

In May 2009, Ali Soufan testified on this pivotal episode before the US Senate Judiciary Committee, from behind a screen in order to protect his identity. In this testimony, Soufan laid out some of the most powerful arguments in support of the Informed Interrogation Approach, and the condemning reasoning against the introduction of harsh techniques for gathering intelligence from suspected terrorists (Soufan 2009). He directly correlates the knowledge-based approach with what is laid out in the Army Field Manual, and it leverages everything that is known personally, culturally, and ideologically about the detainee to focus on the primary points of influence. Soufan explains that this approach combines interpersonal, emotional, and cognitive strategies, and "If done correctly it's an approach that works quickly and effectively because it outwits the detainee using a method that they are not trained for or able to resist" (2009).

On the other hand, the thinking behind the use of harsh techniques ignores the knowledge we have on the mindset, history, vulnerabilities, and culture of those to be interrogated and instead focuses on what is believed to be a "science" of how to remove the volition from any human, regardless of background. This theory can be described as operating on a "force continuum" that gradually applies rougher and rougher techniques in an attempt to "subjugate the detainee into submission through humiliation and cruelty" (Soufan 2009). Most interesting is that Soufan only addressed efficacy (not morality or legality).

The first problem Soufan identifies is that coercion is tactically ineffective. Al-Qaeda terrorists are trained to resist much worse techniques than those employed by a democracy because their operatives often have direct experience with dictatorships. He points out that looking at the facts that have been acknowledged about the interrogation of high-value detainees demonstrates that this force continuum was predictably mounted to its highest point of waterboarding. The only option was to apply it repeatedly for a total of 266 times between two detainees because a ceiling had been reached since the interrogator's bluff had been called. Also, since al-Qaeda operatives are expecting harsh treatment and because applying it simply plays into their expectations, this gives them a sense of predictability and strengthens the will to resist.

The second problem is that there is no way to know whether the detainee is being truthful, and thus unreliable and incorrect information will inevitably be introduced into the intelligence-gathering. An interrogator who focuses on the application of pain as the means for extracting information has not taken the time to become an expert on the detainee or on the subject matter. As such, this interrogator is even less able to know whether the information being squeezed out is within the realm of believability. As an example of the disastrous consequences that can result from pursuing this approach, Soufan points to the false information that was barked out by Ibn al-Sheik al-Libi of weapons training given to al-Qaeda members by the Iraqi regime (Soufan 2011: 424).

The next major problem listed by Soufan is that the method is slow. The public argument for incorporating harsh treatment into interrogation has often been that there is not time for a patient and methodical application of the informed approach because it might be the case that information needs to be acquired as quickly as possible in order to save lives that are in imminent danger. However, the EITs were part of a progressively harsher program detailed in the torture memos. This was to take place over a long period of time, with sleep deprivation being the most obviously time-consuming. In one memo, the CIA was authorized to deprive Zubaydah of sleep for up to eleven days; this clearly has nothing to do with averting an imminent threat.

Additionally, for decades, guerrilla groups have made "torture contracts" with their members, affirming that if one is captured they must try to keep the interrogators busy for twenty-four to forty-eight hours while codes, passwords, and locations are changed (Rejali 2007: 475). Thus, competent terrorist organizations would surely be equally agile enough to change plans that are known by the captured. As clear evidence of this understanding, the handbook uncovered in the raid of an al-Qaeda cell, known as the *Manchester Manual*, explicitly lays out a forty-eight hour window for changing plans as an obligation to its members (Soufan 2011: 425).

Finally, Soufan powerfully points out that this approach ignores the endgame. Because these brutal methods certainly do not intend to take the life of the detainee, what is to happen to the detainee next is a critical question. As terrorist operatives have transgressed the laws of war by targeting civilians, a trial condemning them for this violation is the logical next step. However, there are rules of evidence in the due process afforded to defendants before US courts, which are exactly where FBI agents anticipate bringing the criminal detainees they interrogate. When abuse is introduced into the system, all evidence runs the severe risk of becoming tainted, even evidence obtained through other means. A sharp example of the way in which this ill-treatment has rendered one specific detainee "disposable," and of direct consequence to bringing those responsible for the attacks of 9/11 to justice, will be discussed below with the case of al Qahtani.

What Soufan saw at the black site in Thailand was only the beginnings of a program of ill-treatment that would become much more extensive and cruel. He witnessed Zubaydah stripped naked, subjected to low-level sleep deprivation, blaring noise, temperature manipulation, and the presence of (and the request to use) a wooden confinement box. While this treatment is clearly short of the worst treatment listed in the torture memo responding to the request for the application of further techniques, Soufan characterized what he already saw as "borderline torture" (2009; and FBI Inspector General 2008: 68). In fact, he was so aghast at what he saw being perpetrated that he exclaimed to his headquarters "I'm going to arrest these guys!" (Isikoff 2009).

As a result of this second volatile confrontation between FBI and CIA agents in the field, there was palpable fallout in the form of a decision by the FBI Director to no longer participate "in interviews in which aggressive interrogation techniques were being used" (FBI Inspector General 2008: 71). Soufan immediately left the secret facility, later followed by his partner. Thus, the CIA interrogators were deprived of the presence of the agency with an expertise in counterterrorism interrogation, and they lost the language capability and knowledge of the specific detainee's culture and religion possessed by Soufan.

On these grounds, the entire FBI agency consciously and conspicuously bowed out of taking any part in any of the harsh interrogations that were to follow. And, as evidenced by the FBI Inspector General report detailing the meeting at which this crucial decision was made, looming large was the argument that it was not believed that the coercive tactics to be employed would work to gather accurate intelligence or serve the strategic goals of the nation in its conflict with Islamic extremists: i.e. efficacy (FBI Inspector General 2008: 71–73).

b Authorizing further ill-treatment and torture on suspicion

After the FBI withdrew its agents from the scene at the black site in Thailand, the next significant step that is publicly known was the submission of the infamous OLC Bybee memo. However, an additional memo was submitted the same day (August 1, 2002), but this one remained classified until President Obama authorized its release in 2009. This memo was less theoretical and dealt directly with the specific techniques requested by the CIA to be employed against Zubaydah. Soufan suggests that the fact that Zubaydah again shut down and the team being consulted by the contractor drove further up the force continuum again indicates the inefficacy of this theory. On the other hand, the proponents of this model based on force would suggest that this simply denoted that Zubaydah was not sharing the intelligence information he knew and so something more had to be done. The fact that the exact same behavior can be interpreted in divergent ways reveals one of the essential, insurmountable problems with torture: the interrogator cannot know what the subject knows or is hiding. Torture and ill-treatment must be based on suspicion.

That the CIA request to use harsher interrogation techniques was based on belief, not on knowledge or fact, is borne out in the legal document authorizing the specific techniques. The OLC lawyers wrote in the first paragraph "As we understand it, Zubaydah is one of the highest ranking members of the al Qaeda terrorist organization" (Bybee 2002c: 1). Of course, the phrase "as we understand it" can only refer to the OLC's understanding and not that of the government as a whole, or the understanding of the CIA together with the OLC. However, this critical contention of who exactly Zubaydah was and what role he played in the al-Qaeda organization would be later called directly into contention.

The next assertion is interesting because it mixes the idea of conviction with information that directly contradicts this certitude:

The interrogation team is *certain* that he has additional information that he refuses to divulge. Specifically, he is withholding information regarding terrorist networks in the United States *or* in Saudi Arabia and information regarding plans to conduct attacks within the United States *or* against our interests overseas.

(Bybee 2002c: 1; my emphasis)

Although the team has asserted that it is "certain" and claims knowledge of a specific piece of intelligence that the detainee has, the use of the word "or" belies such certainty. If the interrogation team does not know whether the possessed information relates to the US or Saudi Arabia, then it does not *know* at all. It suspects. As well, the claim that Zubaydah has information on plans for attacks within the country, or anywhere else in the world ("or against our interests overseas") is again immensely imprecise. At least the final sentence of this paragraph uses the proper language to describe what is being requested: "In light of the information you *believe* Zubaydah has and the high level of threat you *believe* now exists, you wish to move the interrogations into what you have described as an 'increased pressure phase'" (Bybee 2002c: 1; my emphasis).

We must also bear in mind that by the time the OLC authorized the most brutal techniques to be used, Zubaydah had been in US custody for *four months*. If we accept that the al-Qaeda organization is at all skilled in applying its insurgent tactics and is able to move as nimbly and flexibly as any mildly competent insurgent group must to follow its own instructions in the *Manchester Manual*, it is near impossible to believe that during the 126 days that Zubaydah was in confinement the plans he would have been privy to had not been changed.

As additional evidence of the extent to which suspicion was used as a basis for this particular case, one can look at the section describing his background and experience so as to render traditional interrogation methods insufficient and thus harsher techniques imperative. The classified Bybee memo reads,

Your psychological assessment indicates that it is *believed* Zubaydah wrote a Qaeda manual on resistance techniques. You also *believe* that his experiences in al Qaeda make him well-acquainted with and well-versed in such techniques. As part of his role in al Qaeda, Zubaydah visited individuals in prison and helped them upon their release. Through this contact and activities with other al Qaeda mujahedin, you *believe* that he knows many stories of capture, interrogation, and resistance to such interrogation. Additionally, he has spoken with Ayman al-Zawahiri, and you *believe it is likely* that the two discussed Zawahiri's experiences as a prisoner of the Russians and the Egyptians.

(Bybee 2002c: 7; my emphasis)

None of this information concerning Zubaydah's personal history was verified, so the CIA was not sure who it had in custody. There were obviously some worrisome suspicions about his role and identity, but this paragraph reveals that the CIA only had clues, not knowledge.

c The apex of the waterboard and its eighty-third application

As predicted by Soufan, the CIA found it necessary to mount the entire authorized force continuum and quickly arrived at its apex: waterboarding. It turns out that once the interrogators did reach this tortuous height, they subjected Zubaydah to the technique of controlled drowning simulating death eighty-three times (Bradbury 2005b: 37). The consistent historical illegality of waterboarding in US law has been pointed out, but the use of suffocation by water as a torture technique should briefly be further explored in the context of Zubaydah, since he was the first detainee in the "war on terror" to be subjected to this treatment.

The classified Bybee memo that authorizes this technique contends that the waterboard "inflicts no pain or actual harm whatsoever" (Bybee 2002c: 11). While this was the safe and mild view of waterboarding held by the OLC attorneys without any field experience, there are others with first-hand knowledge who took serious umbrage when they learned of its application by US agents.

One former Master Instructor and Chief of Training at the SERE School, Malcolm Nance, wrote a powerful article in 2007 in reaction to the public disclosure that waterboarding had been reverse-engineered from the controlled training setting he knew intimately to the live interrogation of suspected terrorists. Nance had undergone the process himself, along with leading, supervising, and witnessing hundreds of individuals being subjected to the same treatment for training purposes. He entitled his piece "Waterboarding Is Torture … Period" and claimed that the media got it wrong when it reported that waterboarding is "simulated drowning" (Nance 2007). Nance insisted that it is best described as "controlled drowning" because the lungs are actually filling with water, pointing out that there is no way to simulate "the agonizing feeling of the water overpowering your gag reflex, and then [to] feel your throat open and allow pint after pint of water to involuntarily fill your lungs" (2007). He explains that waterboarding is

> slow motion suffocation with enough time to contemplate the inevitability of black out and expiration—usually the person goes into hysterics on the board. For the uninitiated, it is horrifying to watch and if it goes wrong, it can lead straight to terminal hypoxia. When done right it is controlled death. Its lack of physical scarring allows the victim to recover and be threaten [*sic*] with its use again and again.
>
> (Nance 2007)

Nance also speaks about the enhanced interrogation techniques approved in the classified Bybee memo of 2002 and warns that their discussion in the media often became a form of "doublespeak" that concealed their true nature and purpose. His position was that, while the interrogation techniques might be applied in a training setting for short periods of time without endangering those subjected to them,

> when performed with even moderate intensity over an extended time on an unsuspecting prisoner—it is torture, without doubt. Couple that with waterboarding and the entire medley not only "shock the conscience" as the statute forbids—it would terrify you.
>
> (Nance 2007)

Nance's judgment in this discussion is worthwhile when he says that "Anyone strapped down will say anything, absolutely anything to get the torture to stop. Torture. Does. Not. Work." (2007).

It has been reported that Zubaydah confessed to terrorist plots to blow up supermarkets, malls, banks, bridges, statues, and nuclear power plants (Mayer 2008: 178–179). As a result, law-enforcement agents were deployed to chase down every lead that Zubaydah offered. As one investigative journalist put it, "the United States would torture a mentally disturbed man and then leap, screaming, at every word he uttered" (Suskind 2006: 111). One former FBI agent stated that there is "nothing in the way of intelligence that I've seen from the program" (Mayer 2008: 179, attributed to former FBI agent Daniel Coleman).

One of the most grave warnings that came from Zubaydah, although it certainly did not come from waterboarding because of the timing, is that of the plot to detonate radioactive material with conventional explosives, or a "dirty bomb." The known details of the two detainees implicated in this accusation will be discussed below since their individual cases also illuminate the insidious nature of torture on suspicion. Of pertinence here is that the application of the most severe technique of controlled drowning paralleled the increase in information given to interrogators.

So, at first blush one might be tempted to take the increased information flow as evidence of torture's efficacy in intelligence-gathering. However, this is premised on the idea that it is possible to *know* Zubaydah's role in the al-Qaeda organization and to distinguish accurate from misleading information (be it intentional or simply to stop the anguish). Otherwise, the intelligence provided may or may not be reliable for preventing imminent terrorist attacks. Of at least equal importance, such certainty about the knowledge of a detainee would also allow the interrogators to know when it is no longer necessary to twist and squeeze the detainee for further intelligence.

It is upon this question of knowing how and when to stop torture that we see one of the clearest acknowledgments in the torture memos that the employing torture is based on suspicion, not on knowledge. In Bradbury's Article 16 memo, we find a vital admission in a footnote: that torture indeed occurred, at least at one particular point, with no demonstrable purpose for furthering a legitimate end. Bradbury discussed the manner in which the waterboarding of Zubaydah came to a close, and it is here that a grave, but clarifying, set of circumstances came together:

> This is not to say that the interrogation program has worked perfectly. According to the IG Report, the CIA, *at least initially*, could not always distinguish detainees who had information but were successfully resisting interrogation from those who did not actually have the information. On at least one occasion, this may have resulted in what might be determined in retrospect to have been the unnecessary use of enhanced techniques. On that occasion, although the on-scene interrogation team judged Zubaydah to be compliant, elements within CIA Headquarters still *believed* he was withholding information. [redacted] At the direction of CIA Headquarters interrogators therefore used the waterboard one more time on Zubaydah. [redacted]
>
> This example, however, does not show CIA "conduct [that is] intended to injure in some way unjustifiable by any government interest," or to the possibility of such unjustifiable injury. As long as the CIA *reasonably believed* that Zubaydah continued to withhold sufficiently important information, use of the waterboard was supported by the Government's interest in protecting the Nation from subsequent terrorist attacks.
>
> (Bradbury 2005b: 31, note 28; internal citations omitted, my emphasis)

So, Bradbury admits that the CIA enhanced interrogation program had problems in its implementation. While he states that there was a difficulty in distinguishing those who had information from those who did not, with the phrase "at least initially" he hints that this obstacle was somehow later overcome. This gives the impression that being able to know what is known by a detainee is no longer an issue because this problem has somehow been solved. Furthermore, he goes into a brief explanation of "reasonable, good faith, belief" as the proper standard:

> *The existence of a reasonable, good faith, belief is not negated because the factual predicates for that belief are subsequently determined to be false.* Moreover, in the Zubaydah example, CIA Headquarters dispatched officials to observe the last waterboard session. These officials reported that enhanced techniques were no longer needed. Thus the CIA did not simply rely on what appeared to be credible intelligence but rather ceased using enhanced techniques despite this intelligence.
>
> (Bradbury 2005b: 31, note 28; my emphasis)

However, this is not actually an explanation, but rather an unsupported assertion. There are no cases cited, no legal authorities quoted, no dictionaries referenced, nor even full justification as to why this particular standard of suspicion is enough to subject a detainee to controlled drowning even if "the factual predicates for that *belief* are subsequently determined to be false." This is precisely the essence of the problem: a government program of torture must be based on belief or suspicion, thus the need for an *ex post facto* legal justification.

This is especially problematic considering that, in this same memo, Bradbury cited the effectiveness memo from the CIA (found to have had blatant factual flaws) and reasoned that it was necessary for an action to meet the standard of not being arbitrary in a constitutional sense. In other words, the act must be "in the service of a legitimate governmental objective" (Bradbury 2005b: 2–3), not a *belief* that it might further a legitimate government aim. If we suddenly adjoin a "reasonable belief" that this furtherance of a government objective will occur, then there would be no reason for Bradbury himself to speak of efficacy. He claims that waterboarding is legal because it has been shown to work, as evidenced by the effectiveness memo. Yet in this footnote he contradictorily claims that it is only necessary to have a "reasonable belief" that the detainee has the desired information. This is surely a failing that undermines a legal analysis that was flawed at its inception.

The final point about this quote from the Article 16 memo is the manner in which the use of controlled drowning came to a close for Zubaydah. As critically explained, "When a detainee did not respond to a question posed to him, the assumption at Headquarters was that the detainee was holding back and knew more; consequently Headquarters recommended resumption of EITs" (CIA Inspector General 2004: 83).

This is exactly what we see at the end of the quote from the footnote in Bradbury's Article 16 memo. Even though the onsite interrogators thought that all intelligence had been extracted from Zubaydah, this was not believed to be the case by the higher-ups back in the US. Amazingly, Bradbury concludes by writing that the CIA "ceased using enhanced techniques despite this intelligence." However, this is contradictory to what he himself explains. The interrogators were forced to subject Zubaydah to the eighty-third session of controlled drowning in front of their superiors in order to personally satisfy them that the intelligence they were relying upon was incorrect. Only after senior officers saw this brutal technique practiced on the detainee with their own eyes did they come to believe Zubaydah rather than an intelligence report. If this does not palpably demonstrate that torture is based upon suspicion, and that this suspicion can be markedly different depending on perspective, it is hard to know what else could prove this point.

d Erroneous suspicions

Of course, suspicions can be wrong. What has come to light, years after his torment, is that Zubaydah was not who he was believed to be. Following a multitude of unauthorized disclosures and leaks from agents and career officers from inside the government who had moral and legal concerns with the enhanced interrogation program, a more coherent and complete story can be pieced together. Seven years after his capture, subsequent to a review by the CIA, who had difficulty refusing authorization for publication because of the quantity of leaks rising from a legitimacy deficit, an editorial article was published by Zubaydah's lawyer (Mickum 2009). As to be expected, this article painted a very different picture of the detainee.

To begin, reference was made to a remarkable article published in the *Washington Post* the previous day entitled "Detainee's Harsh Treatment Foiled No Plots" (Finn and Warrick 2009). This article revealed that there were a good number of government officials who believed that nothing had been gained in the way of intelligence after the CIA began the use of controlled drowning. One former intelligence official asserted "We spent millions of dollars chasing false alarms" (Finn and Warrick 2009). Providing an answer to the critical question of efficacy, the article concluded,

> In the end, though, not a single significant plot was foiled as a result of Abu Zubaida's tortured confessions, according to former senior government officials who closely followed the interrogations. Nearly all of the leads attained through the harsh measures quickly evaporated, while most of the useful information from Abu Zubaida—chiefly names of Al-Qaeda members and associates—was obtained before waterboarding was introduced, they said.
>
> (Finn and Warrick 2009)

Of great significance to Zubaydah's lawyer was the question of why this information led nowhere. For an answer to this question, it is necessary to understand Zubaydah's role in the jihadi movement. It is uncontested that he worked and organized for extremist Muslim groups training to fight their enemies. He began to become involved with these groups when he came to Afghanistan to join the mujahideen fighting Afghan Communists in 1991, a conflict during which he suffered a severe head injury that continues to compromise his memory. However, to assume that there is just one monolithic extremist Muslim force with uniform plots and plans which are being widely implemented by all those involved in armed struggle is an oversimplification, and incorrect according to his lawyer. Zubaydah was a committed jihadist who did move men in and out of Afghanistan and through military training camps, some of whom were members of al-Qaeda. He became widely known as a type of travel agent for those seeking such training, which is why his name resurfaced again and again in terrorism intelligence traffic (Mayer 2008: 140).

Because of these many figurative fingerprints that had been found linking him to jihadi military training, Zubaydah was assumed to be a major figure in the al-Qaeda organization. In fact, it was because he was the above-ground support that his name kept cropping up in intelligence data, and also why he did not possess the timely and actionable intelligence. His role was much more like that of a front-desk clerk, which is not someone who would be in the loop on upcoming major attacks and plots.

As Zubaydah's lawyer pointed out, "[t]hese facts really are no longer contested: Zayn was not, and never had been, a member of either the Taliban or al-Qaida. The CIA determined this after torturing him extensively" (Mickum 2009). Due to this mistaken identity issue, Zubaydah's attorney argued for an open process in which he could present exculpatory evidence of his client's innocence. Yet there is little doubt that what Zubaydah would know, and would be able to reveal under interrogation, would be limited.

Zubaydah's habeas corpus proceedings in US domestic court are of significant value. The contention that he could be held without any legal rights led to the undisclosed detention of Zubaydah from March 2002 until September 2006, when he was transferred to Guantánamo. It was not until the *Boumediene* v. *Bush* decision in June 2008 that the right of habeas corpus was extended to the prisoners in that facility in Cuba. As his detention became governed by law, admissible evidence and provable theories beyond mere suspicion became necessary.

This higher standard of evidence brought about a significant change in the government's position. Previously, in order to authorize his ill-treatment, it was asserted that Zubaydah was "one of the highest ranking members of the al Qaeda terrorist organization" (Bybee 2002c: 1). Additionally, this legal memo assessing the urgency and necessity of extracting all intelligence information out of Zubaydah went on to describe in great detail what was thought to be his authority within the organization and his involvement in other plots and attacks. The detailed presumptions of his status were that he

1 "rose quickly from very low level mujahedin to third or fourth man in al Qaeda. He has served as Usama Bin Laden's senior lieutenant";
2 "has been involved in every major terrorist operation carried out by al Qaeda";
3 "was one of the planners of the September 11 attacks";
4 "Prior to his capture ... was engaged in planning future terrorist attacks against US interests."

(Bybee 2002c: 7)

No doubt, the detail and extent of Zubaydah's presumed role was worrisome, to say the least. However, the position of the government holding him was to change significantly in 2009.

In a court document submitted to the District Court of Washington, DC, in September 2009, the Justice Department's retreat from these grave accusations became clear. In response to 213 discovery requests, the government denied the necessity for many of them because the charges for which Zubaydah was being held no longer needed such substantiation. Documents proving what had been the position of the government when it authorized Zubaydah's harsh treatment in the classified Bybee memo did not now need to be disclosed to him because "the Government has not contended in this proceeding that Petitioner was a member of al-Qaida or otherwise formally identified with al-Qaida. Instead, the Government's detention of Petitioner is based on Petitioner's actions as an affiliate of al-Qaida" (Respondent to *Zayn al Abidin Muhammad Husayn* v. *Gates*: 35–36). This is a far cry from what was suspected of Zubaydah when there was no court overseeing the admissibility of evidence.

It is also worth pointing out that the government additionally backed away from perhaps the most emotionally volatile, not to mention vital, charge when analyzing what pertinent and timely information might be known by Zubaydah. The government "has not contended in this proceeding that Petitioner had any direct role in or advance knowledge of the terrorist attacks of September 11, 2001" (Respondent to *Zayn al Abidin Muhammad Husayn* v. *Gates*: 9). This withdrawal is in direct contradiction to the emotional claim that he was "one of the planners of the September 11 attacks" found in the authorization for his controlled drowning, and it raises serious questions about what knowledge he possessed when he was tortured and ill-treated four months after his capture.

Lastly, it should be pointed out that much of this information turned on a misinterpretation of the relationship between al-Qaeda and other military training camps in Afghanistan. Zubaydah's acknowledged role was linked to the Khalden training camp established in Afghanistan during the Soviet occupation. (This also happens to be the same camp to which Ibn al-Shaykh al-Libi was linked.) However, it now is clear that there had been confusion over exactly how the Khalden camp was tied to al-Qaeda. Most importantly, the government came to agree with Zubaydah's contention that this camp was "organizationally and operationally independent" from al-Qaeda camps (Respondent to *Zayn al Abidin Muhammad Husayn* v. *Gates*: 23), which is in line with how Zubaydah had described the Khalden camp back in his CSRT hearing of 2007. Importantly for his defense, Zubaydah describes the camp as being dedicated to "defensive jihad," which he depicts as fighting against an aggressor on Muslim lands (Zubaydah 2007: 9). As examples of this type of aggression, Zubaydah pointed to the Soviets in Afghanistan, the Serbians in Bosnia, the Russians in Chechnya, and the Israelis in Palestine. At the same time, he drew a distinction between what he was involved in with the Khalden camp and the "offensive jihad" advocated by Osama bin Laden. He claimed that "defensive jihad" only targeted the military and their direct civilian support and disagreed with the idea of targeting civilians as had been done at the World Trade Center.

It is not within the scope of this work to discern the veracity of Zubaydah's claim. However, if this is truly the case, then this ignorance of the subtleties of the jihadist movement would certainly help explain how Zubaydah (and al-Libi for that matter) were swept up and ill-treated in the "war on terror." More pertinently, it would help to explain the inefficacy of torture because its basis in suspicion inevitably allows misinformation, incorrect beliefs, and wrongful identifications to become a part of the system of abusive interrogation at large.

Through this tormented tale of torture and ill-treatment there are at least two conclusions that one should take away. First, the Zubaydah case was the pivotal moment for the beginning of the application of torture and ill-treatment by US agents. This outcome was not inevitable; there were agents on the ground from the FBI pushing vigorously for noncoercive interrogation. The second is that this brutal treatment of Zubaydah was carried out on a presumption of whom he was thought to be, and what he should therefore know. In his concluding testimony, FBI Agent Soufan fittingly emphasized our question of efficacy:

> In summary, the Informed Interrogation Approach outlined in the Army Field Manual is the most effective, reliable, and speedy approach we have for interrogating terrorists. It is legal and has worked time and again.
>
> It was a mistake to abandon it in favor of harsh interrogation methods that are harmful, shameful, slower, unreliable, ineffective, and play directly into the enemy's handbook. It was a mistake to abandon an approach that was working and naively replace it with an untested method. [...]
>
> The mistake was so costly precisely because the situation was, and remains, too risky to allow someone to experiment with amateurish, Hollywood style interrogation methods that in reality taints sources, risks outcomes, ignores the end game, and diminishes our moral high ground in a battle that is impossible to win without first capturing the hearts and minds around the world. It was one of the worst and most harmful decisions made in our efforts against al Qaeda.
>
> (Soufan 2009)

VI The "dirty bombers": the insidious nature of torture

It can be very difficult to assess the exact usefulness of the techniques employed to acquire intelligence from Zubaydah for several different reasons. One is that he was interrogated by both FBI agents and CIA agents using very different methods. While some of that information can be parsed and accredited to either the noncoercive or to the coercive approach, the full details of what Zubaydah said, when, and under what circumstances have not been publicly released. The CIA Inspector General report did highlight that perhaps the most significant intelligence gained from Zubaydah related to a worrisome terrorist threat indeed: "information from Abu Zubaydah helped lead to the identification of José Padilla and Binyam Muhammed—operatives who had plans to detonate a uranium-topped dirty bomb in either Washington, DC, or New York City" (CIA Inspector General 2004: 87).

The detention of José Padilla and Binyam Mohamed was publicized for years as a major advancement in protecting the homeland from the terrifying threat of plans to blow up radioactive material with conventional explosives inside a major US city. Yet a thorough investigation of the judicial processes they finally underwent casts real doubt on whether they were victories in the "war on terror" at all and, in fact, exposes the insidious nature of using torture for intelligence-gathering.

a José Padilla

The capture of Padilla was announced with much fanfare on June 10, 2002. Subsequently, his federal court case was diligently followed by the media, at least partially due to the attention given to him as a serious terrorist threat thwarted by the administration, along with his status as a US citizen. In the end, it appears that it was his citizenship that spared him the same fate as his alleged accomplice (discussed directly below). Padilla was first apprehended at Chicago's O'Hare International Airport in May 2002 on a material witness warrant, but one month later was deemed an "enemy combatant" by President Bush and transferred to a military brig in Charleston, South Carolina. Padilla's case made its way through the US federal court system to be argued before the Supreme Court in April 2004 (*Rumsfeld v. Padilla*). To be sure, the issues at stake were strikingly similar to another case decided the same day, the *Rasul* decision, only here the swing vote of Justice Kennedy oscillated to the other side. The majority found that the court where the original habeas petition was filed lacked jurisdiction, and there was no impediment for Padilla to file his petition in the jurisdiction of his immediate custodian.

In his dissenting opinion, Justice Stevens pertinently pointed out that, in the written command by the President deeming Padilla an enemy combatant, the government claimed to have a particular interest in this detainee because "he possesses intelligence that, 'if communicated to the US, would aid US efforts to prevent attacks by al Qaeda'" (*Rumsfeld v. Padilla* [2004], pp. 456–457).[1] Thus, part of the justification for transferring Padilla out of the civilian courts system into military custody hinged on the need for gathering intelligence from the detainee. This is troubling because it indicates that the administration believed there to be a meaningful difference in interrogation standards between the two systems.

After this, Padilla's petition for habeas corpus was then refiled in the jurisdiction of his military confinement, and his case was rebooted and proceeded anew. Following a finding by the lower court that his detention had not been authorized by Congress, the Fourth Circuit Court of Appeals reversed this decision and found that the President was authorized to detain enemy combatants under the AUMF Resolution. What happened next was most problematic in the context of intelligence gleaned from Zubaydah. Just days before the government's brief in response to Padilla's petition for certiorari was due to be filed in the Supreme Court, an indictment was gained in the civilian courts of Florida for terrorism charges against Padilla. However, the charges were only that he provided material support to terrorists who were part of a cell said to have sent money and recruits overseas.

In a stinging rebuke of the government's management of the case, a justice who during the same time period was reported to be on the short-list for an appointment to the Supreme Court, Circuit Judge Luttig, wrote the opinion denying the transfer of Padilla and the withdrawal of the appellate court's earlier judgment (*Padilla* v. *Hanft* [2005]). It was said that the government's request smacked of manipulation and an attempt at the "intentional mooting" of the previous court judgments. The court made an effort to suggest that there could be legitimate reasons for the government's stark change of position in this case of significant public consequence, but at the same time it went out of its way to highlight the dangers of diminishing the government's credibility (or legitimacy) before the courts and in the mind of the public.

Of greatest importance in the context of the Zubaydah interrogation, we see that when evidence was required to back the ominous allegations that sprang from this pivotal detainee, alleged to be a top al-Qaeda operative, the government was unable to put forward enough to substantiate the threat of a "dirty bomber." Padilla was detained by the military until the Supreme Court granted his release in January 2006, with a total of five federal court hearings judging his right to habeas corpus in the intervening years. In the end, this allegation of a plot to detonate a radioactive bomb with conventional explosives simply vanished. It was, indeed, a very serious and frightening accusation. Nonetheless, it was one based upon suspicions which came from someone falsely identified and ill treated.

b Binyam Mohamed al Habashi

This brings us to José Padilla's suspected accomplice. Binyam Mohamed al Habashi, an Ethiopian national and a British resident as an asylum seeker from 1994, was arrested in the airport of Karachi, Pakistan in April 2002. He was traveling on a forged passport and, in what appears to be tremendous misfortune, attempted to do so in the same airport where Padilla was also briefly detained on a passport irregularity. Mohamed's whereabouts were concealed and unknown to the outside world until he appeared back in formal US custody in May 2004, when he was transferred to the publicly acknowledged Bagram Airfield prison in Afghanistan. Not coincidentally, it is at this official facility that Mohamed was allowed to visit with a representative of the ICRC for the first time in his two years of detention. Mohamed had been held incommunicado, off the records of any justice system, and, after almost four months of interrogations by Pakistani and FBI agents, was extraordinarily renditioned to a third country we now know to be Morocco, where he was kept for eighteen months. In September 2004, Mohamed was transferred to Guantánamo. Eventually, in February 2009, Mohamed was transferred to the UK, where he was detained for a few short hours and then released.

The details of Mohamed's detention and treatment spanning nearly seven years slowly trickled out into the public domain. Though it still remains an incomplete story, critical portions of Mohamed's ordeal have now been brought into the light, with the most complete source of information being the decision in *Farhi Saeed Bin Mohammed et al. v. Obama.* This case did not deal directly with Mohamed himself, but rather with his allegations against another detainee at Guantánamo. In an unclassified opinion released in December 2009, Judge Kessler reviewed the testimony of Mohamed which was relied upon by the US government to hold this habeas petitioner in confinement.

Judge Kessler found that although the statements that were being used did not come from coercion at Guantánamo, they were the product of earlier mistreatment. In other words, she acknowledged the veracity of Mohamed's claims that he had been tortured and abused prior to his arrival at the facility in Cuba. Of great importance is that the US neither confirmed nor denied these claims. Instead, the position taken by the government was that the allegations were not pertinent because the statements made by Mohamed at Guantánamo were admissible and relevant because they were not made under coercion at that time. However, the Judge ruled that "the Court finds that Binyam Mohamed's will was overborne by his lengthy prior torture, and therefore his confessions [redacted] do not represent reliable evidence to detain Petitioner" (*Farhi Saeed Bin Mohammed* [2009], p. 70).

This habeas case, forced into the courts by the *Boumediene* decision of 2008, was the first place in which many of the gruesome details of Mohamed's extended suffering outside of the law came to be entered into the public record. Over a third of the eighty-five-page opinion in *Farhi Saeed Bin Mohammed* was dedicated to describing the extended suffering and explaining why his later testimony was not admissible in court. Mohamed had given a statement shortly after his arrival in Guantánamo, stating that he knew the petitioner from an al-Qaeda training camp they had both attended in Afghanistan. However, after his release from Guantánamo in 2009, he signed a sworn declaration retracting this allegation and saying that he had never met the petitioner before his arrival at the island detention center. He also asserted that he was forced to make many more untrue allegations against other detainees and that they were made as a result of "'torture and coercion," that he was "fed a large amount of information" while in detention, and that "he resorted to making up some stories. The Government does not challenge Petitioner's evidence of Binyam Mohamed's abuse" (*Farhi Saeed Bin Mohammed* [2009], p. 42; internal citations omitted).

In this episode we can glimpse one of the insidious elements of torture beyond the obvious. Suspicion again ultimately leads to inefficacy within a system aimed at intelligence-gathering. When torture is introduced, it is based upon suspicion. Since torture must occur outside of the legal system because its fruits are considered too tainted for any credible system of justice, there is no filter holding back the introduction of false information into the intelligence apparatus. This false information raises more suspicions of the partially innocent and wholly innocent; incorrect claims snowball into more false information. Since interrogating the ill-informed can never be deemed helpful, one can see why such a program should be defined as inefficacious.

By the time Mohamed arrived at Bagram in May 2004, and then at Guantánamo in September of that year, it certainly appears as if the most severe abuse had come to an end. However, he had no way of knowing this since he had been in US control during his entire detention, even though it took place in a series of foreign facilities. Judge Kessler points to sworn declarations, recorded testimony, a diary, and various media interviews in which Mohamed put forward his "harrowing story" (*Farhi Saeed Bin Mohammed* [2009], pp. 48–49).

After his initial detention by Pakistani officials in Karachi, four FBI agents participated in his daily interrogations. However, according to Mohamed, all of the abuse was left to the Pakistani agents and began just weeks after his detention commenced. If the US agents were unsatisfied with his responses, they would leave the room while he was threatened, beaten with a leather strap, and subjected to a mock execution with a semi-automatic weapon in his chest. About three and a half months later, Mohamed was flown to Islamabad, where he was handed over to US authorities dressed in black and wearing masks. He was then stripped, searched, shackled, blindfolded, and made to wear earphones for his next flight to Morocco, where the most severe abuse and torture took place. Most problematic was that he was told the US wanted a story from him because he had been linked to "important figures in al-Qaida, including Khalid Shaykh Mohammed, Abu Zubaydah, Ibn Shaykh Al Libi, and José Padilla" (*Farhi Saeed Bin Mohammed* [2009], p. 50). As we have already seen, three out of four of these figures were of questionable importance to the al-Qaeda organization.

Within two weeks of Mohamed's arrival in Morocco, the threats of intense ill-treatment became real as his food was rationed, he no longer had access to a bathroom, he was repeatedly punched and kicked, and he was left on the floor where he vomited and urinated on himself. Demonstrating the extent to which this was an "intelligence-gathering" exercise, Mohamed asserts,

> While being beaten, he was fed information about himself and told to verify it. If he denied it, he was beaten; he would then confirm the information, and be ordered to provide more details about it. When he failed to provide more information, he was again beaten.
>
> (*Farhi Saeed Bin Mohammed* [2009], p. 51)

Of course, one immediately sees the patent ineffectiveness of such crude interrogation for intelligence-gathering. If Mohamed was being "fed" the information he is to confirm, nothing is gained from an intelligence perspective. And this description of his abuse was repeated persistently in his testimony: "He was told that if he simply repeated in court the information being fed to him, then the torture would cease"; "captors coached Binyam Mohamed on what to say"; "[h]e was given names of people he allegedly knew"; and the two to three interrogation sessions a month he was regularly subjected to in Morocco were "described as being 'more like trainings, training [him] what to say'" (*Farhi Saeed Bin Mohammed*, pp. 53–54). Under such conditions, the efficacy of torture surely crumbles to pieces.

The worst of Mohamed's treatment came under the direction of a man named "Marwan," and it is claimed that this interrogator made it clear that the Moroccans were working for the US. This time Mohamed was beaten by three "goons" while tied to a wall when he faltered in repeating the proper information, was left hanging by his hands after the beating, and was subjected to this same beating throughout the night. After he made the error of mocking his interrogator,

> Three men stripped him of his clothes with "some kind of doctor's scalpel." The witness claims he feared rape, electrocution, or castration. His captors cut one side of his chest with the scalpel, and then the other. One of the men then "took [Mohamed's] penis in his hand and began to make cuts" with the scalpel as Marwan looked on. They cut "all over [his] private parts" while Binyam Mohamed screamed. He estimates that they cut him 20–30 times over two hours; "[t]here was blood all over."
>
> (*Farhi Saeed Bin Mohammed* [2009], pp. 52–53;
> internal citations omitted)

Neither did the treatment under the CIA occur without coercion. Mohamed asserts that while in the "Dark Prison" in Kabul he attempted to renounce the story that he had been coached to adopt because the US interrogators looked more amiable than those he had been used to in

Morocco. However, his attempt to retract the stories he had been forced to learn was met with two weeks of being chained to the rails. They simply wanted him to repeat the tale that he had been taught for a year and a half, which included his involvement in the radioactive "dirty bomb" plot. Clearly, this was an extremely serious accusation that caused great alarm within the public who learned of it via Attorney General Ashcroft's public video announcement. Within one day, the media was reporting on Padilla's alleged accomplice.

This "dirty bomb" charge continued to be levied against Mohamed for years to come, and it even appeared in his charge sheet as late as May 2008.[2] It was only that October, over six years later, that this grave charge (along with the plan to blow up apartment buildings and to release cyanide gas in nightclubs) mysteriously disappeared from the government's accusations against Mohamed. This is just as we saw happen with the "dirty bomb" charge against José Padilla, which disappeared from his indictment once the transfer request was made to move him from military to civilian custody. Although the US government originally said it would refile other charges against him, Mohamed returned to the UK on February 23, 2009, and was released without charge within hours.

There are three main points that should be taken away from the appalling episode of Padilla and Mohamed being accused of the "dirty bomb" plot. The first is that the whole idea of this startling conspiracy was borne of the interrogation of Zubaydah, which was already described as "borderline torture" by FBI agent Ali Soufan.

Second, as it became necessary for the plot allegation to be proven before a court of law, this allegation conspicuously disappeared from the charges against both detainees. In the case of Padilla, although he was convicted of supporting terrorist activities and it was thus possible to keep him from furthering any illegal actions targeting innocent civilians, there was no effort to provide evidence linking him to said plot. In the case of Mohamed, there was never an attempt to prove such an allegation in criminal court proceedings, and no charge was put forward that merited confinement whatsoever. With Mohamed being set free when it was time to prove his culpability before a court, it is fair to say that a guiltless man was tortured on the strength of suspicions created by the foul fruit of ill-treatment.

Third, this deplorable episode demonstrates an aspect of a torture program that cannot be ignored when analyzing its efficacy. Torture will predictably lead to untrue accusations for at least four reasons:

1   It is based on suspicion at its inception.
2   One must expect purposeful misleading.
3   Harsh treatment produces both false information along with available truth, and since interrogators are pursuing unknown information they are unable to distinguish between the two.

4   This takes place outside of a system governed by law, thus there is no filter to sift through and discard falsehoods as real leads and erroneous suspicions expand.

Together, these points and these cases vividly display the snowballing effect of a torture program. Suspicion leads to torture, which leads to suspicions, which leads to torture. This less-discussed aspect of torture is surely a part of its nature and explains how a program based on its use cannot produce calculable efficacy.

VII   Mohammed al Qahtani: destroying the endgame

Mohammed Mani' Ahmad Sha'Lan al Qahtani is a Saudi national captured near Tora Bora, Afghanistan, in December 2001, and then transferred to the newly opened Guantánamo detention facility in early 2002. For months, al Qahtani's captors did not know who he was or his relationship with al-Qaeda. It was only after seven months in captivity that visiting FBI agents put together his identity through fingerprint analysis, year-old surveillance footage from Orlando airport, and phone records. It turned out that he had attempted to enter the US one month before 9/11 and had been stopped by an alert customs agent who was disquieted by his demeanor. Through conventional investigative work, the FBI pieced together that the 9/11 ringleader Mohammed Atta was caught on video waiting outside the airport in a rental car. Investigators then came to believe that al Qahtani was the missing twentieth hijacker of 9/11 who was meant to fill the fifth position on the aircraft that crashed in Pennsylvania. The government was thus extremely eager to gather all intelligence information from someone who was supposed to be a part of the largest terrorist attack carried out on US soil in its history.

Because Guantánamo was under military control, the rules meant to govern interrogation in the facility would be found in the Field Manual 34–52 (US Army 1992). Even a cursory glance at this document reveals the extent to which international humanitarian law was interwoven into the fabric of this rule-based institution. In addition to this clear attention to legality, what can also be found in this document is a focus on extracting *reliable* information. It should go without saying that the extraction of false information is counterproductive to the goal of intelligence-gathering, but the Army is not an institution that leaves the obvious unsaid. To clarify this point, the manual relies on its history of successful interrogation practices and explains that "[u]se of torture and other illegal methods is a poor technique that yields unreliable results, may damage subsequent collection efforts, and can induce the source to say what he thinks the interrogator wants to hear" (US Army 1992: 1–8). The manual also points out some of the other adverse effects of failing to live up to legal obligations: "Revelation of use of torture by US personnel will bring discredit upon the US and its armed forces while undermining domestic and international support for the war effort" (US Army 1992: 1–8).

Nonetheless, the unambiguous rules that governed the military interrogators did not have the effect of avoiding the torture and ill-treatment of al Qahtani. The first evidence of this abuse became public in June 2005 when *Time* published extracts of the interrogation log of Detainee 063 (as al Qahtani was known by his captors) (Bennett *et al.*, 2005). Then, in March 2006, the same magazine published the eighty-three-page military log in its entirety on its website.

Although the FBI resisted the implementation of coercive techniques for al Qahtani largely on the grounds of efficacy (FBI Inspector General 2008: 86–91, 113–114), the verbal authorization of Secretary of Defense Donald Rumsfeld began the aggressive interrogation on November 23, 2002. Then, on December 2, the memo that has been described as the key document that opened the door to the torture of al Qahtani was signed by Rumsfeld, and it stayed in effect until it was suspended six weeks later. This document, drafted by William J. Haynes II, the General Counsel at the Defense Department, has become infamous for at least two reasons. The first is the ill-treatment it unleashed. Second, Secretary Rumsfeld scrawled a note below his signature questioning some of the limitations: "However, I stand for 8–10 hours a day. Why is standing limited to 4 hours?" (Sands 2008: 2–6).

As a result of the multiple investigations into the al Qahtani interrogation and the memos that spawned it, a list can be compiled of some of the most egregious coercive techniques employed. The nearly two months of consecutive eighteen- to twenty-hour interrogations included: threatening the detainee with a military dog; telling him he is lower than a dog, attaching a dog leash to him, walking him around the room on the leash, and having him perform dog tricks; stress positions; forced shaving for psychological purposes; repeatedly pouring water on his head; stripping him naked in the presence of a female; holding him down while a female interrogator straddled him; manipulation of temperature; describing his mother and sister as whores; instructing him to pray to an idol shrine; a female interrogator telling him she was menstruating and showing him her finger (red with ink), then wiping it on the detainee's arm; discussing repressed homosexual tendencies attributed to him; a male interrogator dancing with him; a female interrogator massaging his neck and back over his clothes and placing women's underwear on his head and a bra over his clothing (FBI Inspector General 2008: 102–103; Schmidt and Furlow 2005).

However, no matter how coercive, even sophisticatedly so (if cruelty can be sophisticated), the interrogators were never going to extract timely information from Mohammed al Qahtani. He was captured in December 2001, but it was not until almost one year later that his aggressive interrogation began. After over eleven months of detention, it is absurd to think that he possessed any up-to-date information about al-Qaeda's planning. Any sophisticated terrorist group must be assumed to be extremely controlled with regard to such sensitive material that could quickly unravel the goals of the organization. If all of the suspicions of who al Qahtani was were correct, he possessed some useful knowledge concerning the basic structure and operational procedures even a year after his capture. But he certainly did not hold any *timely* information. It will thus be forever arguable that noncoercive methods would be more effective (not to mention legal and moral) in securing this structural, and not time-sensitive, intelligence. Therefore, there is no reason to believe that this case shows torture to be any kind of a superior method.

As for specific intelligence, under these coercive tactics al Qahtani admitted to being a member of al-Qaeda, that he was sent to the US in August 2001 to fulfill a mission, where he had obtained his entrance visa, and the names of three possible associates. What is more, the commander in charge of Guantánamo at the conclusion of the interrogation wrote that the techniques were "essential to mission success" (FBI Inspector General 2008: 118). However, the military's Memorandum for Record documents conclude otherwise. These documents looked at the methods used, the detainee's reaction to them, the information provided by the detainee, the interrogation team's analysis of that information, and an assessment of the detainee's truthfulness and level of cooperation. Al Qahtani actually became fully cooperative with interrogators in April 2003, several months after the intensive coercion. After failing a polygraph test, he began to become noticeably concerned about cutting a deal and avoiding prosecution for his crimes. As the FBI Inspector General put it,

> The next day, Al-Qahtani began to describe his knowledge of al-Qaeda in great detail, and the subsequent MFRs [Memorandum for Records] reflect that from that point on he provided a significant amount of detailed information about al-Qaeda and its pre-September 11 operations.
>
> (FBI Inspector General 2008: 119)

The military interrogators and analysts found that the major factors that influenced al Qahtani's shift in attitude were the failing of the polygraph test, a perception of betrayal by other Al-Qaeda members, lack of contact with others, and the incentive of being returned to Saudi Arabia. Of central importance to the issue of the efficacy of torture, "[t]he analysis did not cite the application of harsh interrogation techniques prior to January 15, 2003, as a factor in Al-Qahtani's changed behavior" (FBI Inspector General 2008: 119).

Nonetheless, the primary intent in addressing the al Qahtani case here is more about what torture does to justice. While some would care to focus attention on an immediate imperative, that which is left for later must eventually be addressed. The central addressed, which continues to plague the Obama administration, is "What do you do with a detainee who has been tortured?"

This was the question faced by Susan Crawford, named the convening authority for military commissions in February 2007, in charge of deciding whether to bring Guantánamo detainees to trial. Just days before the commencement of the Obama presidency, an interview with Crawford was published in the *Washington Post* in which she explicitly stated "We tortured Qahtani" (Woodward 2009). In her exhaustive review of his treatment under interrogation, along with the abundant evidence against him as the twentieth hijacker, Crawford came to the conclusion that "[h]is treatment met the legal definition of torture. And that's why I did not refer the case" (Woodward 2009). Hence, al Qahtani's treatment immunized him from prosecution in a court of law, even in a military tribunal with a wider standard of admissible evidence due to the Military Commission's Act of 2006.

What had the largest impact upon Crawford's decision was the life-threatening medical condition that al Qahtani suffered during the interrogations. On two different occasions during the fifty-four days of aggressive interrogation, he needed to be hospitalized for bradycardia, a condition in which the heart rate falls to dangerous levels (below sixty beats per minute), which, in extreme cases, can lead to heart failure and death. One of those instances was about two weeks into the intensive twenty-hour interrogations. At one point al Qahtani's heart rate dropped to just thirty-five beats per minute, and he was immediately taken to hospital for medical treatment. With medical approval, he was then hooded, shackled, and restrained to return to the interrogation booth less than forty-eight hours later for interrogations that would continue for five more weeks (US Army Personnel 2002–2003: 26–83).

So, the US government's decision to scrap the constraints of the Army Field Manual led to treatment that was legally determined to be torture. As a result, someone suspected of being involved in the most horrendous crime ever committed on US soil cannot be brought to justice. Can it be said that this interrogation, which immunized from prosecution the only living 9/11 hijacker (by his own admission) was effective in furthering the goals of the "war on terror"?

VIII Khalid Shaykh Mohammed: correct suspicions and efficacy

Of course, it is possible for suspicions to be correct. It is readily admitted that this appears to be the case with Khalid Shaykh Mohammed, alleged to be the mastermind behind 9/11. On March 1, 2003, he was captured in Rawalpindi, Pakistan by local authorities with US officials hanging back while he was handcuffed and hooded. By March 4, this high-value detainee was moved into the CIA black-site prison system, which kept him out of reach of the ICRC.

One intention behind this mandated access to the ICRC is to protect the life and dignity of all those held in detention by verifying that they are being held in accordance with relevant humanitarian law and to help ensure that they are not subjected to ill-treatment and torture. The simple fact of documenting each prisoner's exact location and health condition and allowing outside human contact helps to avoid abuse because it becomes clear that someone is watching, if only through confidential reports. This practice of holding someone in secret and outside of the law is one which is gaining an increased recognition of international illegality with the recent entry into force of the International Convention for the Protection of All Persons from Enforced Disappearance, and is thus gaining currency as a part of diplomatic language. In this instance, even though such visits in noninternational armed conflict are not legally obligated, they are a constant practice of the ICRC and are internationally recognized. Yet the ICRC was not given such access to this detainee during the three and a half years of his initial detention. Nevertheless, our primary concern in this section is that of efficacy.

Khalid Shaykh Mohammed was subjected to the series of techniques designed for and applied to Zubaydah. As a result, knowledgeable officials have stated that he was "singing like a bird" (Mayer 2008: 269), i.e. giving up valuable intelligence on the Al-Qaeda organization, other terrorist operatives, and plans for future attacks.

The overwhelming combination of harsh techniques began with Mohammed being stripped naked and forced into a prolonged stress standing position with his arms shackled to a hook in the ceiling above his head (he was left undressed for over a month and continuously shackled for nineteen months) (ICRC 2007: 16). In addition to the pain and discomfort produced from this stress position, it was meant to deprive him of sleep during the time that he was not being directly interrogated. Mohammed also explained that "a thick plastic collar would be placed around my neck so that it could then be held at the two ends by a guard who would use it to slam me repeatedly against the wall" (ICRC 2007: 12). To aggravate the distress of the extended time he was kept in complete nudity (even during waterboarding), Mohammed's cell was kept at an exceptionally cold temperature, and he was repeatedly doused with cold water (used to wake him or to rinse away the feces that had run down his legs). In addition, threats to the detainee and his family were made, along with beating and kicking, including slapping and punching to the body and face. Finally, on top of all this other ill-treatment, Mohammed was subjected to torturous controlled drowning a total of 183 times in March 2003 (Bradbury 2005b: 37; CIA Inspector General 2004: 45 and 91).

From the available reports, it does seem that the application of the intense regime of EITs provided actionable intelligence. This is the case put forward by the former President himself, since it was this circumstance that he used in his post-presidency account to justify his fateful decision to employ ill-treatment. Bush went into some detail after explaining that "Khalid Sheikh Mohammed proved difficult to break. But when he did, he gave us a lot" (Bush 2010: 170). He stands firmly behind his decision to authorize tactics of dubious morality and almost certain illegality and points to gathered intelligence as justification for them. Yet, this characterization of the effectiveness of the enhanced techniques is oversimplified. The reality is much more nuanced.

The CIA Inspector General report made a concerted effort to directly address this issue in a section entitled "Effectiveness." And to open a more complex discussion of the success of the application of the enhanced tactics, it was explained that

> [t]he detention of terrorists has prevented them from engaging in further terrorist activity, and their interrogation has provided intelligence that has enabled the identification and apprehension of other terrorists, warned of terrorists plots planned for the USA and around the world, and supported articles frequently used in the finished intelligence publications for senior policy makers and war fighters. In this regard, there is no doubt that the Program has been effective. Measuring the effectiveness of EITs, however, is a more subjective process and not without some concern.
>
> (CIA Inspector General 2004: 85)

Simply capturing those who are intent on carrying out attacks on civilians clearly prevents them from causing death and injury. But this is a benefit of the detention of all enemies who mean to inflict harm. Therefore, attention has been correctly located on information gained by the specific techniques that have led to the further capture of terrorists or "warned of terrorist plots." In this regard it was pointed out that "Many other detainees [...] have provided leads to other terrorists, but probably the most prolific has been Khalid Shaykh Muhammad" (CIA Inspector General 2004: 87). Thus, Mohammed's interrogation produced important and quantifiable results.

As to what particular technique seemed to unlock access to this actionable intelligence, the Inspector General looked to waterboarding. However, due to the severity of this particular interrogation tool, it was not simply flagged as effective. The report began by explaining that "In as much as EITs have been used only since August 2002, and they have not all been used with every high value detainee, there is limited data on which to assess their individual effectiveness" (CIA Inspector General 2004: 89). The report specifically highlighted the waterboard and asked whether the risks were justified by the results, if it was unnecessarily applied at times, and whether the fact that it was applied differently than authorized meant that the OLC memos were applicable.

However, in its specific use on the high-value detainee in question, there is a distinct mention of its medical impact. It was also discovered that there was a change in behavior in this detainee after the controlled drowning was applied. The large amount of redacted text here makes it difficult to fully analyze the conclusions concerning the application of this tool. It was concluded that what had been produced prior to its application was largely "outdated, inaccurate, or incomplete" (CIA Inspector General 2004: 91). Yet, by most accounts, this detainee did produce valuable information.

At the same time, it is important to focus our attention on two points, one of them being a fundamental and critical piece of information also found in this report. At first glance, this information would seem to point in the direction of a conclusion that applying the most severe of the EITs was successful. However, on this occasion, the suspicion of Khalid Shaykh Mohammed's position in the Al-Qaeda organization appears to be correct. As such, the physical and mental twisting of this detainee brought out intelligence that was at times accurate and useful. There is no doubt that much false intelligence was interspersed with the valid information, and, of course, it took a good amount of valuable time and effort to distinguish between the two. It is important to remember that such moments of valid information cannot be used to characterize the entire program as effective because these results are unpredictable given that suspicion undergirds the whole program. The torture of the innocent and ill-informed must remain part of the assessment of the efficacy of a program.

Second, the CIA Inspector General's report dealt with the terrorist plots of which the interrogators were warned by all of the high-value detainees. The plots that were not redacted in the report were: an attack on the US Consulate in Karachi, Pakistan; the hijacking of planes to fly into London Heathrow Airport; a loosening of track spikes in an attempt to derail a train in the US; the blowing up of several gas stations in the US to create a panic; the cutting of lines on suspension bridges in New York in an effort to make them collapse; and the hijacking of an aircraft to fly it into the tallest building on the West Coast to emulate 9/11. However, the report explicitly spelled out one critical component: "*This Review did not uncover any evidence that these plots were imminent*" (CIA Inspector General 2004: 88; my emphasis).

In other words, none of the gathered intelligence was timely information leaving no alternative means. Yet, the decision to use a mounting form of ill-treatment was determined as necessary very shortly after capture according to George W. Bush himself. The fact that it took at least one full month of constant nudity, shackling, threats, beatings, walling, dietary and temperature manipulation, stress positions, and 183 episodes of controlled drowning evoking death to acquire not one piece of timely information is particularly problematic from the point of view of efficacy. Taking into consideration that Al-Qaeda's *Manchester Manual* instructs members to change plans known by those captured within forty-eight hours surely explains the reason why. Thus, there is always the possibility that other means would have produced the same, if not better, results.

IX Torture on suspicion: clarifying the moral argument

To complete our discussion of the use of torture and ill-treatment through the lens of efficacy, focus will be placed on its overlap with morality. The morality of an act is certainly altered by its efficacy or inefficacy. For the man standing at the edge of a cliff offering feathered wings to believers who have enough faith to fly themselves to the heavens, the morality of such an act at least partially turns on whether there is any chance that this flight is humanly possible. The recognition that torture is meted out on suspicion and thus inevitably pulls innocent and ill-informed individuals into a program based on its use likewise changes the morality of the question.

The ticking bomb scenario is traditionally framed within one of moral philosophy's great ethical debates of utilitarianism (or consequentialism) versus deontology. However, for our purposes, the classification of this argument is unnecessary, since our concern is with legitimacy as a target. As well, this framing is changed when we are speaking about a government program of ill-treatment for intelligence-gathering rather than the case of the private morality of an individual. In the latter case, it is possible to contemplate a single scenario with no strategic implications for a larger campaign.

Yet when we are thinking about the public sphere and drafting a rule for regulation, this is not the same circumstance, nor is the morality exactly the same. Most important in this context is that while it is often accepted that a ticking bomb scenario could be plausible in an individual case (even if highly unlikely), calculating the so-called error costs in a program of torture and ill-treatment becomes unachievable. The already demanding questions of certainty, immediacy, targeting, and effectiveness of coercive techniques all become exponentially more complicated. This is particularly the case as the errors multiply upon themselves as false information enters the intelligence-gathering apparatus.

Additionally, the critical difference between that of private and public morality is the central thesis of this work: the latter directly affects the legitimacy of the government. It is vital that a government exercises its monopoly of the use of force in a manner that is deemed legitimate by its citizens, or the structure of the society itself can suffer. As the historian by training, and human rights scholar by vocation, Michael Ignatieff wrote,

> There is not much doubt that liberal democracy's very history and identity is tied up in an absolute prohibition of torture. [...] Liberal

democracy stands against torture because it stands against any unlimited use of public authority against human beings, and torture is the
most unlimited, the most unbridled form of power that one person
can exercise against another.

(Ignatieff 2004: 136–137)

Understanding the gravity of this prohibition sheds a bright light on how
torture has become directly tied up with the legitimacy of government
power itself.

A useful way to confront the moral question is through the work of an
academic who has become well known for his argument that torture is going
to happen whether it is outlawed or not, therefore, the best way to deal with
this reality is to allow courts to issue "torture warrants" when there is a
ticking-bomb case. Alan Dershowitz put forward this argument in his 2002
book *Why Terrorism Works* (2002: 131–163). The argument is meant to be
focused on the moral questions raised by the ticking bomb scenario since
he believes there to be room for a legal argument in domestic law.

In his chapter discussing the issue, Dershowitz has a section entitled
"The Case for Torturing the Ticking Bomb Terrorist." However, as
demonstrated in our six case studies, the main problem is basic to the constraints of our human condition. The essential idea is to pry into
someone's mind because we know the information inside can save lives.
To say that we "know" that an individual possesses the life-saving information we seek is absurd on its face. If we were able to know what is inside
this person's mind, there would be no reason to contemplate torture. Suspicion might be extremely high, but it will always remain a suspicion. As
cited above, if the technology existed to unlock someone's mind, "it would
surely be just as widespread as electricity" (Rejali 2007: 453). Resolving this
limitation would fundamentally change our human existence as we know
it and would be a piece of knowledge impossible to conceal.

Nonetheless, to make his point, Dershowitz extrapolates on a real-life
circumstance. He put forward the case of Zacarias Moussaoui, who was
captured a few weeks before 9/11 and later believed to be the missing
twentieth hijacker. Although the government did not seek a warrant to
search his computer at that moment, Dershowitz conjures up a scenario in
which this had happened and it was revealed that he was a part of the plan
for an upcoming terrorist attack on occupied buildings, but without
further details. After all legal interrogation methods and injections of
truth serums did not produce information about the approaching attack
(which then becomes believed to be imminent), an FBI agent might then
propose the use of nonlethal torture. This set of circumstances would
appear to be sufficient for Dershowitz to justify the need for torture.

While it is conceivable that Moussaoui would have had critical information that would have led to disruption of the attack, it is also possible that
he did not. In fact, what we have learned since then is that Mohammed al

Qahtani was actually meant to be the twentieth hijacker. This means that the initial suspicions about Moussaoui were incorrect. To suggest that torture could have been, in an alternative scenario, an effective tool for avoiding this major disaster is entirely misplaced. In fact, it is a vivid demonstration of how terribly suspicions can go awry if they are used to justify the most severe violations of human dignity. If torture were on the table that day, as Dershowitz suggests, and had actually been implemented, we now understand that this abuse would have been carried out on someone who was not involved in the plot of that fateful day. He was not a "ticking bomb terrorist" at all, as it had previously seemed.

It is interesting to note the timing of this argument. The book containing this ticking bomb scenario was published in September 2002, and it was that very same month that the FBI first learned that al Qahtani had intended to join the other hijackers of 9/11. Therefore, when Dershowitz wrote his chapter on torture, he could not have known that the actual twentieth hijacker was being detained in Guantánamo. At that moment, under those suspicions, it seemed a potent argument to Dershowitz. Today, now that our knowledge has changed, we know that this is an argument that would have led to torturing an ill-informed person on a false suspicion.

Finally, Dershowitz also raises a scenario which was in fact dealt with by the German Federal Constitutional Court in 2006, and which also reveals the crucial overlap of *morality*, *efficacy*, and *legality*. Dershowitz introduces the choice of evils that would be faced if a hijacked passenger plane were on a collision course with a large, populated building in a major city and the only way to avert this tragedy were to shoot down the aircraft. Dershowitz recognizes that it would be "*probable*, not certain" (2002: 154; original emphasis) that the plane was going to be used as a projectile weapon, but this does not deter his argument.

Of direct pertinence, a law was passed in Germany in 2004 granting the minister of defense the authority to shoot down an aircraft in such a circumstance. However, in 2006, the Bundesverfassungsgericht (the German Federal Constitutional Court) ruled on the constitutionality of the legislation and struck it down in a manner relevant to our argument.

Demonstrating the presence of morality in its legal decision, the Court first used Kantian logic and ethics to determine that "[h]uman dignity [...] will be violated if the state treats individuals as objects or denies them the status to be an end in themselves" (Lepsius 2006: 776). Next, it looked into questions of fact and proportionality and found that the statute must pursue a legitimate end. This meant that the law must meet the three requirements of being suitable, necessary, and appropriate or reasonably fair. It is in this argumentation that we find the application of efficacy to help determine legality. The Court found that "[t]he statute, simply, could never achieve what it pretended to pursue" because it could never be definitively determined ahead of time that a passenger aircraft was being directed as a weapon against civilians on the ground (Lepsius 2006: 774).

Along with the conspicuous overlap of the three elements under discussion in this book, the portion of this decision that is useful in illuminating our specific question on torture is where the Court broaches the drawing of definitive conclusions. Terrorists will not announce their intentions in advance, and the pilots would not sign their own death warrants by reporting such a hijacking even if they could. Therefore, the best that can be expected is to deduce what is occurring through "uncertainty," "presumption," and "conjecture" (Lepsius 2006: 775). The Court explains,

> This conjecture becomes even more problematic since there are dubious incidents in air traffic every other day. [...] If one would accept uncertain information as a sufficient base for downing decisions there would be a significant danger of fatal errors with regard to the amount of unclear situations in today's air traffic.
>
> (Lepsius 2006: 775)

It is also suggested that the aircraft would likely be monitored by a dispatched military jet sent out to accompany the suspicious passenger plane. Yet even this would not reveal enough to resolve the grave dilemma, as the Court keenly observed that it is almost impossible to see into the cockpit windows from outside.

This depiction of events is quite analogous to the circumstance we find when faced with a detainee suspected of involvement in a perceived imminent terrorist attack. While any number of suspicions can arise as to what is actually occurring inside the aircraft, or inside the mind of the prisoner, our external means do not allow us to penetrate inside. We cannot definitively ascertain what plots detainees are a party to, whether plans have changed since their capture, or to what extent they are involved with our enemies who wish us harm. In the case of torture, we do not even have the luxury of windows to peer through to glean what is happening inside. Therefore, the authorization to violate human dignity with torture, like the use of deadly force to down a suspect aircraft, "could never achieve what it pretended to pursue." A downed aircraft could, in fact, have been hijacked by terrorists, but this does not mean that the policy meets the legitimacy requirements. It is this absence of calculable efficacy that clarifies the question of morality.

Thus it is necessary to reformulate the questions that arise from the ticking bomb scenario in the case of a program. As discussed, nearly all of the traditional formulations of this scenario leave out or gloss over the pivotal clarification that all torture will be authorized on suspicion; only Jeremy Bentham explicitly included it in one of the earliest articulations. The contention here is that the element of suspicion must be allowed to play a sufficient role in the formulation of the moral dilemma for a public policy of torture and ill-treatment. In light of the cases analyzed above, the insurmountable element of suspicion could be best included into the moral questions as follows:

- If a captured person is suspected of being involved in an attack that appears to be imminent, should the government authorize torture on this person?
- Should the government authorize torture on someone knowing that he may or may not have the information necessary to halt an approaching attack?
- Should the government authorize torture on someone knowing that the plans they are knowledgeable of have possibly been changed?

X Conclusion: remedy, redress, and diplomatic implications

Indications are that the Obama administration has lived up to its commitment to halt the illegal, immoral, and ineffective techniques authorized by the President's predecessor. Yet the obligations under CAT include provisions to launch an investigation "where there are reasonable grounds to believe that an act of torture has been committed" and to provide remedy and redress when this has occurred (Articles 12–14). Throughout this chapter we have certainly seen that the "reasonable grounds" standard has been met and surpassed. And as has also been indicated, a bipartisan report has declared that its occurrence is "indisputable" (Constitution Project 2013: 3). It is in this area that the Obama administration has failed to live up to its international obligations. How exactly this might affect the legitimacy of the government's counterterrorism policies in the long term is yet to be determined. But simply ending a crime does nothing to prevent its reoccurrence. Nor does it acknowledge the sufferings of the victims of the illegal policy. There are numerous signs of this failure by the Obama administration, but here we will present just one obvious case where this has occurred.

In 2009, the Justice Department filed a far-reaching *amicus curiae* brief in the case of *José Padilla* v. *John Yoo* before the Ninth Circuit Court of Appeals. As we have discussed both of these individuals in this work, it suffices to explain that in this case one of the victims of the program of ill-treatment instituted by the Bush administration was attempting to hold one of its legal architects accountable in court. What concerns us here is the fact that the Obama administration had no legal requirement to step forward to defend John Yoo in this case. The Justice Department had initially taken on Yoo's defense, but then stepped aside so that he might bring in a high-powered lawyer for his own defense (taxpayers still covering the expenses). Yet, even though it had no obligation to do so the Department of Justice filed an *amicus* brief insisting that if the case was not dismissed there was "the risk of deterring full and frank advice regarding the military's detention and treatment of those determined to be enemies during an armed conflict" (Hertz 2009: 25). Rather than simply standing aside to let the courts decide how to proceed on this delicate issue, the Obama administration's Justice Department argued in favor of reversing the lower court's decision to let the lawsuit continue to provide an avenue for a victim of ill-treatment to receive remedy and redress from an agent of government.

Because the United States has long been attentive to its legal liability for questions of international law it would be extremely difficult for an individual from the Bush administration to be brought before a foreign or international court to answer for their own role in this program. For example, in 2002 the US announced that its signature to the Rome Statute of the International Criminal Court (ICC) was to have no legal effect and the Bush administration then pursued and signed bilateral agreements with over one hundred countries in an effort to shield US citizens from the jurisdiction of the court (Coalition for the International Criminal Court 2006). Although the Obama administration has softened its position to the ICC by sending observer delegations and taking a stance of principled engagement, it has also stated that it has no intention of ratifying the Rome Treaty.

Nonetheless, there have been noteworthy efforts reflecting the impact of *new diplomacy*. In 2009, a Spanish human rights group petitioned Spain's National Court to indict six former Bush officials for creating a legal framework that permitted torture. Even though the case came to be stalled following confidential pressure from the Obama administration on Spain, publicly disclosed by Wikileaks (Corn 2010), it does demonstrate the growing forces created by public diplomacy in the information age. Also in this vein, Bush himself cancelled a planned trip to Geneva, Switzerland after Amnesty International and the Center for Constitutional Rights human rights groups called for Swiss authorities to investigate him for potential prosecution due to a legal obligation as a party to the UN Convention against Torture (Elliott 2011). Yet, for the more traditional forms of public diplomacy, the avenues are most likely to be found again at the UN Committee Against Torture that is meant to receive periodic reports from state parties every four years.

Torture is illegal in all circumstances, and this prohibition can neither be limited nor derogated. Not only is its illegality absolute, this norm has also reached the same level of prohibition as slavery and piracy. Regardless of the flawed and feeble attempts made by the OLC in the torture memos to twist this legality, maintaining relevance only as long as they were kept from the public eye, this unambiguous legal status remains.

However, with legitimacy as the focal point of inquiry, it has been necessary to go beyond this stark illegality and to investigate the efficacy and morality of a program of torture and ill-treatment. Because it is impossible to suggest that torturing the innocent and ill-informed will further the information-gathering goals of counterterrorism, and since there is no way to ensure that a program will exclude such individuals, it also fails the test of efficacy. At the very same time, the recognition that a program of torture is based on suspicion also clarifies the moral questions at stake for public policy.

While our minds can dream up far-fetched scenarios that would seem to satisfy most people that absolute certainty has been achieved in a ticking bomb scenario, we still have not been able to find a way to predict the future nor to unlock the mind of another human being. The crude and ancient forms of ill-treatment employed in the "war on terror" demonstrate that even the richest country in the world has not made technological steps forward to surmount these human constraints.

What we also now know after our analysis of numerous government documents and official statements is that nothing like a ticking bomb scenario ever occurred, so other methods were always available. Thus, there is no way to defend this illegal and immoral policy as the only option.

This work is investigating the monopoly on the use of physical force exercised by a government and hypothesizes that terrorists aim to provoke the illegitimate use of this power. Therefore, it is useful to make an analogy to another form of state authority, and in this case it concerns capital punishment.

In March 2011, the Governor of Illinois signed legislation abolishing the death penalty in that state, and the signing statement he attached is instructive on the point made here. Specifically using the legitimacy of the state as his primary reasoning, he wrote,

> I have concluded that our system of imposing the death penalty is inherently flawed. The evidence presented to me by former prosecutors and judges with decades of experience in the criminal justice system has convinced me that it is impossible to devise a system that is consistent [. . .] and that always gets it right.
>
> As a state, we cannot tolerate the executions of innocent people because such actions strike at the very legitimacy of a government.
>
> (Quinn 2011)

In the case of capital punishment, it is possible to say that defendants have received their day in court and that there has been a veritable judicial check on the exercise of government power. This possibility will not exist for those who are to be subjected to torture and ill-treatment, and authorities will be clearly unable to exclude the innocent and ill-informed from brutal treatment. Thus, the result will inevitably be torture on suspicion which "strike[s] at the very legitimacy of a government."

Notes

1 There is a question as to the severity of treatment Padilla endured while under detention and sustained solitary confinement. For example, concerning his 3 1/2 year confinement it has been reported,

> [w]ith no clock, watch or natural light to guide him, terrorism suspect Jose Padilla was jailed at a Navy brig in timeless isolation while anonymous jailers monitored him around the clock, a brig official testified Tuesday. [...] confirmed for the first time some of the conditions of Padilla's detention. His defense attorneys contend that Padilla's sensory deprivation and treatment were tantamount to torture
>
> Williams, C. (2007) "New Light on Padilla's Treatment" *Los Angeles Times*, Feb. 28, available at http://articles.latimes.com/2007/feb/28/nation/ na-padilla28 (accessed June 2013).

However, we will not enter into the allegations of ill-treatment here.

2 Charge Sheet of BINYAM AHMED MOHAMED under the US Military Commission Act of 2006, May 28, 2008, available at: www.defense.gov/news/Mohamed% 20-%20sworn0603.pdf (accessed June 2013).

Conclusion

Jeopardizing legitimacy and drones

> It is the paramount duty of political leaders in a democracy under attack to keep the forces of order intently focused on the political requirement of maintaining *legitimacy*.
>
> (Ignatieff 2004: 143; my emphasis)

Throughout this work we have placed legitimacy at the center of our analysis of the asymmetrical tactic and strategy of terrorism. Because non-state actors do not have the weaponry to strike a government's forces head on, it is necessary to investigate this line of attack differently than conventional warfare. We have shown how and why adversaries who use public and political violence against noncombatants are in fact targeting legitimacy. They are principally engaged in a contest of psychological warfare, attempting to provoke the government into jeopardizing its own legitimacy. The Italian historian Guglielmo Ferrero has provided the most vivid and useful imagery for better understanding this vital element of society that is being targeted. He aptly explains that,

> [a]uthority comes from above: that we are agreed upon. This is one of man's necessities, expressed by a historical constant—authority comes from above, in democracies as in monarchies. But in monarchies as in democracies legitimacy comes from below. The government only becomes legitimate and is freed from fear by the active or passive, but sincere, consent of the governed. We must never forget this inverse dual movement of authority and legitimacy.
>
> (Ferrero 1942: 295)

This lucid description of society gives explanation to our directing of attention toward this bottom-up component of the social order and hypothesizing *legitimacy as a target*. If the dramatic effect of a terrorist act is what gives it its potency, it is because the people in the audience have a role to play. That role can be described as twofold, and these collide to create a veritable tension. Spectacular, violent events first ignite an outcry for security measures that will provide protection from such atrocity. What then follows, with attention fixed on the implementation of such actions, is a judging of the exercise of force that is put into practice. People want action, and, at the same time, it must continue to be legal, moral, and effective because the power being exercised has been granted to the government by its citizens. It is this tension that epitomizes the difficulties that any government under attack from the purveyors of terror must confront. However, it should be well understood that if overreach goes too far and legitimacy at home is lost, this truly is the collapse such enemies crave. Thus, sound counterterrorism strategy must begin with defense against this type of societal breakdown.

This is the reason why the reaction to 9/11 is so disconcerting. There is no doubt that Al-Qaeda was astonishingly successful, tactically, in inflicting nearly 3,000 fatalities that day. Nevertheless, from a strategic point of view, this terrorist group was even more successful in provoking a robust and fierce response with those stunning events caught on film and broadcast widely. Just as this type of non-state actor hopes, they were able to goad a massive response from their enemy. The US countered in the strongest way possible, with a declaration of a grand and wide-reaching war: the "war on terror."

As has been seen in this work, the seeds of this overreach were sown very early on by lawyers within the governing administration. Due to the growing importance given to law for steering a society and delineating boundaries, it is through these legal interpretations that we can best grasp the policy of this "war on terror." In January 2005, in near temporal coincidence with the inauguration of President Bush's second term, a voluminous tome of nearly 1,300 pages of internal documents from his first mandate, entitled *The Torture Papers*, was compiled and published (Greenberg and Dratel 2005). Although this collection of documents ultimately turned out to be an incomplete picture of the extent to which the administration had pushed the law and, as we have seen, at times clearly transgressed it, this volume provides a stark look into the legal reasoning behind the policies that had bounded their way into the public square. Most importantly for our purposes, inside these documents we have found the legal justification for circumventing the international obligations found in treaties such as the Geneva Conventions, the United Nations Charter, and the CAT.

In the very first memo we saw that John Yoo of the OLC pressed hard for no external limits on the president's authority in war. Two weeks after the attacks he reasoned that neither domestic nor international law could bind the president; the US Constitution gave the commander in chief wide authority to exercise force as he saw fit. Not only did the president have the authority to "retaliate against any person, organization, or State *suspected* of involvement," it was also concluded that he could do the very same against "foreign States *suspected* of harboring or supporting such organizations" (Yoo 2001: 3; my emphasis). At its inception, *suspicion* was put forward as the pertinent standard for this "war."

In the very last footnote of this foundational document, a more explicit explanation of this formula was to be found. It is attached to a brazen assertion that the president has the authority to launch military action against even those who "cannot be demonstrably linked to the September 11 incidents" (Yoo 2001: 24). Determining guilt is extremely difficult in the particular circumstances of confronting an organization built on secrecy and evasion, and this is explicitly leaned upon for justification in the memo. It was claimed,

> [w]e of course understand that terrorist organizations and their state sponsors operate by secrecy and concealment, and that it is correspondingly difficult to establish, by the standards of criminal law or even lower legal standards, that particular individuals or groups have been or may be implicated in attacks on United States. [...] But we do not think the difficulty or impossibility of establishing proof to a criminal law standard (or of making evidence public) bars the President from taking such military measures as, in his best judgment, he thinks necessary or appropriate to defend the United States from terrorist attacks. In the exercise of his plenary power to use military force, *the President's decisions are for him alone and are unreviewable.*
>
> (Yoo 2001: 24; my emphasis, internal citations omitted)

The only constraint presented by Yoo is that which comes solely from the president. It would seem a plausible argument that the criminal standard, or even lower standards, of evidence could at times be too high in this circumstance. However, what is incredible about this recognition is that there is zero effort to replace the criterion that is thought to be prohibitive. The fact this would prove difficult at times could certainly be accepted by many reasonable people. But to suggest that because it is difficult there is absolutely none in existence is one major reason why the "war on terror" eroded the legitimacy of the government, along with hampering counterterrorism action. Specifically, we highlight the misguided notion that "the President's decisions are for him alone and are unreviewable."

What is not generally recognized is what occurs when the suspicions of the president are manifestly incorrect and his actions do not meet Weber's adage of the "*legitimate use of physical force.*" And, let us be clear, a criterion of speculation will inevitably be imperfect. What we have seen throughout this work is that this so-called standard, absolutely unchecked by any other branch, has led to *detention on suspicion, war on suspicion,* and *torture on suspicion.* Such action erodes legitimacy because it is unavoidably flawed and always "reviewable" by the citizenry.

The revolution in information technology has drastically changed the way in which a society receives facts about the actions of its own government. As a reflection of this shift, this work has purposefully cited a number of the abundant sources found on the Internet which have poured into the public sphere, documenting illegal, immoral, and ineffective policies. This is by no means meant to replace or avoid the toil of traditional scholarship. (It is believed that this too has been accomplished in this work.) Rather, the intent has been to draw attention to the fact that the revelations that were widely disseminated via an online network had an impact upon the views of citizens about the legitimacy of government actions. Many of the reports, perhaps most vividly the leaked photos of the abuses endured by the detainees of the Abu Ghraib prison in Iraq, actually had a viral effect. That is, ghastly images of representatives of the government engaged in the abuse of prisoners spread from computer to computer and from home to home with a speed never before known. In speaking to the issue of legitimacy, it is necessary to treat and analyze such sources that have come within the public domain and that have driven its expansion, since a portion of the citizenry indeed uses them to judge the exercise of force by their government.

As presented at the opening of this book, it was back in 1989 when Cassese made the point that "[i]nternational law is no longer a tool handled exclusively by national governments; it can also be used by individuals, by private organizations and by certain categories of peoples" (1989: viii). Since that time there has been a continued development in the diffusion of international law via *new diplomacy*. Through sourcing the work of diplomats at international organizations, NGO reports, newspaper and television disclosures, government studies backed by bipartisan support, and leaked secret documents, we have seen that a striking transformation in information technology has multiplied exponentially the amount of empirical data available. And, just as we have seen in the internal US government documents, it has been international law that has framed the questions of rights and duties for this counterterrorism operation upsetting the structure of the international system. As such, in a manner very similar to the tack of Cassese, the judgments made on the *"legitimate use of physical force"* have been shifting to align with the framework of international law made increasingly available to a wired citizenry via its figurative conduit of *new diplomacy*.

Noting that the necessity to distinguish between combatants and civilians is the very first rule of customary international humanitarian law, or the Principle of Distinction (Henckaerts and Doswald-Beck 2005: 3–8), underscores the problem of using suspicion as a sufficient standard. Carrying out this task, which becomes all the more difficult and demanding in asymmetrical conflict, is essential to the conduct of legitimate warfare. This onerous requirement is indeed the essence of armed conflict involving non-state actors who attempt to disappear and blend into a larger community of noncombatants. Yet this obstacle does not release a government from its duty to distinguish legitimate targets from civilians.

This principle of distinction certainly does not mean that violence against noncombatants, no matter how grave and unwelcome, is in itself a crime of war or illegitimate. The general public and government officials alike understand that war carries risks and regrettable losses. However, it is generally believed that such violence against those who are not participants in an armed conflict must be avoided to the greatest extent possible. Applying this principle of distinction to unconstrained authority for launching and carrying out armed hostilities on suspicion is not a perfect analogy since there are numerous difficult legal questions that arise, many of which we have discussed throughout this work. However, when considering the evidence presented in this book it is difficult to conclude that common citizens and public officials alike have determined that the president can legitimately make the distinction, and impose irrevocable harm, on suspicion.

As we saw in Chapter 3, President Bush's policy of removing any role for the national courts and asserting that there was no applicable law was struck down three consecutive times by the US Supreme Court over a four-year time span. The third time that the court determined it necessary to pursue the bold tack of constraining executive action in times of armed conflict it was in fact an historic first for action in conjunction with the legislative branch during wartime. In the first years after its opening in January 2002, those being held at the Guantánamo Bay Detention Facility had absolutely no way to contest the reasoning for their confinement, nor was the administration tasked with defending its decision to detain any particular person. In other words, there was no check on the administration's efforts, or lack thereof, to distinguish between combatants and civilians; this was *detention on suspicion.*

In the same memoranda of September 2001 discussed above, John Yoo also arrived at the conclusion that "[t]he President may deploy military force preemptively against terrorist organizations or the States that harbor or support them, whether or not they can be linked to the specific terrorist incidents of September 11" (2001: 3). As we have seen in Chapter 4, the absurd interpretation of "preemptively" was meant to disconnect the initiation of war from any empirical fact or action. Under the Bush Doctrine, suspicion of future intent was a satisfactory trigger for military action. This was a reading that would run counter to one of the primary currents throughout the just war doctrine (with just one short-lived exception) and was part of the naissance of international law. In the case of Iraq, many concluded that the administration failed to properly distinguish who was actually the enemy in this "war on terror" by speculating on future intent. This can be comprehended as *war on suspicion.*

In Chapter 5, we saw that the program of ill-treatment instituted to extract timely and reliable intelligence from those believed to have such information had no external check on who was pulled into the system of brutal abuse. The result was disastrous from the point of view of efficacy in that the subjects of mistreatment were frequently suspected incorrectly, and for this very reason their treatment had absolutely no moral justification. The fallout was palpable: the case for a war against Iraq was partially rationalized on false information gained from ill-treatment; the program (which included controlled drowning evoking death) was first implemented on a man whose role within the Al-Qaeda organization was incorrectly suspected and led to false accusations and torture of other detainees; the application of such brutality made the prosecution of the missing twentieth hijacker impossible; and not one shred of timely intelligence was extracted from the detainee who was correctly suspected of a high rank within the Al-Qaeda organization. Throughout that chapter we repeatedly observed the failings of using conjecture for the program of ill-treatment to gather intelligence: i.e., *torture on suspicion.*

In May 2007, as more and more information concerning the use of torture and ill-treatment bled into the public square through the continuation of leaks (clear acts of disobedience), two former high-ranking military officers took to the op-ed pages of one of the nation's leading newspapers. In their article, the authors condemned the policy that condoned and even authorized torture. Their public and forcefull speaking out against the sitting commander in chief represents a part of the legitimacy deficit to which we speak, since the traditional culture of salute was rejected as these officers had determined that the policy was illegitimate.

These former military officers explained what their experience in combat had taught them and recognized that this campaign against those who employ the tactic of terror is very different from conventional warfare. They calculated, just as we have seen in the Army Field Manual overseen by General Petraeus, "[v]ictory in this kind of war comes when the enemy loses *legitimacy* in the society from which it seeks recruits" (Krulak and Hoar 2007; my emphasis). Because they understand the battle lines in this perspective they harshly criticized the approach that had been taken and concluded that "[t]his way lies defeat, and we are well down the road to it" (Krulak and Hoar 2007). The policy was swelling the numbers of those who are willing to take up battle against that government (multiplying the number of enemies), and at the same time it was whittling away at the uncoerced pull toward compliance that acts as the glue of any society. It is in this way that exercising force based on suspicion jeopardizes the legitimacy of a government.

In this book the primary focus has been on the "war on terror" launched by President Bush, who made this conflict his signature policy. As explained, this was due both to the completeness of documents available and for analytical clarity. Furthermore, it is important to note that the legitimacy deficit described here was suffered almost entirely during his second term, even if the most extreme policies were carried out in the first. Not only does this indicate that the administration was believed to have enough legitimacy to be reelected to office, it also suggests that attention on legitimacy should be intensified in a second mandate as more details are known about policy. Yet there was ostensibly a drastic change in the 2008 election, and campaign promises were repeatedly asserted about how this conflict was to be redirected.

On his second full day in office, President Obama issued an executive order directing the closure of the Guantánamo Bay detention camp to be carried out within one year and calling for a full review of the legal status of the 242 detainees who remained in the facility at that time (Obama 2009b). The newly inaugurated president also signed an executive order to ensure lawful interrogation. This order explicitly stated that any person held under the "effective control" of any agent of the US could only be treated with techniques authorized by the Army Field Manual and revoked all of the OLC memos dealing with interrogation methods during the Bush administration (Obama 2009a). Though these commands carried important political value at the beginning of his tenure in office, President Obama began his second term without real progress on the project of closing the Guantánamo facility. Moreover, the restrictions on interrogation methods remain an executive order that could be changed without congressional approval or judicial oversight.

While there have been some changes in the approach to counterterrorism by Bush's successor, it is unclear how the similarities that remain will affect the Obama administration and its legitimacy. The fact that this president ordered the raid that killed the leader of the organization that perpetrated the 9/11 attacks surely had a notable impact. Even though there was more hesitancy to regard it as such internationally, it appears that US citizens largely concluded that this operation was legal, moral, and effective. Additionally, President Obama took the step of rebranding the conflict as "Overseas Contingency Operations" (Wilson 2009). Even if this were to be only a cosmetic change, it had the effect of signaling that this conflict was not his signature policy and helped induce a certain amount of patience from the international diplomatic community.

Nonetheless, the authorized war powers remain in place (AUMF 2001) and continue to be exercised in a way that raises questions of legitimacy. Hence it is worthwhile to briefly examine Obama's most controversial counterterrorism policy. While the Bush administration's policy focused on detention and interrogation, there was a conspicuous rise in unmanned aerial vehicle attacks (commonly referred to as drones) under Obama. As both of the former tactics became highly scrutinized activities by the citizenry, foreign diplomats, and international lawyers, killing became more appealing because it circumvents the need for confinement or questioning. Without capture, neither is necessary. This can explain why only one person was reportedly taken into custody in President Obama's first term and why some members of Congress believe that a take-no-prisoners policy was instituted (Becker and Shane 2012).

Thus, to conclude, we will present a brief glance through the lenses of legitimacy to view the Obama drone program, which has come to epitomize his approach to countering terrorism for the general public. As convincingly explained by a veteran of the Israel Defense Forces as a Judge Advocate General involved in targeted killing decisions, and whose approach parallels our use of three lenses, "[t]he state's decision to kill a human being, in the context of operational counterterrorism, must be predicated on an objective determination that the 'target' is, indeed, a legitimate target. Otherwise, state action is illegal, immoral, and ultimately ineffective" (Guiora 2013: xi).

In assessing the *legality* of this program a fundamental difficulty arises. As new military technology has been introduced to execute lethal force with fewer constraints across international borders, it has become an open debate among international lawyers and diplomats as to what is the proper body of law to apply in a territory where there is no declared armed conflict. At a minimum, such action engages humanitarian law, human rights law, and the *jus ad bellum* regime, along with domestic criminal and constitutional law. Consequently, the kaleidoscope of legal questions shifts and moves with the specific circumstances of each action.

We know that up until the time of this writing, US drone strikes had taken place in Afghanistan, Iraq, Libya, Pakistan, Yemen, and Somalia (the former three are or were overt zones of armed conflict while the latter three are not) and that the attacks have taken the lives of foreigners and US citizens alike. Such operations are labeled "targeted killings" in international law and are defined as the premeditated use of lethal force against individuals not in the physical custody of the perpetrator (Melzer 2008: 3–5).

The first acknowledgment of such a state policy came from Israel in November 2000, and its High Court of Justice handed down a ruling on its legality in 2006 (*Public Committee against Torture in Israel* v. *Government of Israel*). In his last ruling before leaving the bench, Supreme Court President Aharon Barak presented one of the most comprehensive judicial decisions on the idea of a "war on terror" to date. He wrestled with the difficulties of a war paradigm and concluded that the applicable law in those circumstances stemmed from an international armed conflict with Palestinian militants.

As further indication of the legal difficulty presented, one can look to the study on targeted killings submitted to the Human Rights Council by Philip Alston, the Special Rapporteur on Extrajudicial, Summary or Arbitrary Executions (2010). Although the action of targeted killing may entail crude forms of violence, what has captured many people's attention involves a new technology. Due to the secrecy cloaking this novel drone equipment, the conclusions and recommendations of Alston's study principally pertain to the need for further disclosure of relevant information so that the operations can be legally assessed. Among other conclusions,

Alston recommended that states should publicly identify the rules of international law that are applicable, disclose the reasons why they have chosen to kill rather than to capture, and that if a state carries out such an operation in the territory of another state then that second state should say publicly whether it gave consent.

To fix some of the parameters so as to present a coherent analysis and focus our short examination of these operations we will here concern ourselves with the drone strikes on foreign citizens in the territory of Pakistan. The reasons for this choice are because the majority of such US attacks have taken place in this territory thus far, and the available information is the most complete for this case. Yet, even with this further delineation of the subject, many unanswered questions remain.

Nevertheless, strike data has been aggregated by various NGOs and is frequently cited in a whole range of public reports showing that since 2004 the US has targeted persons in the Federally Administered Tribal Areas of Pakistan along the border with Afghanistan to attack suspected leaders of the Taliban and Al-Qaeda (New America Foundation 2013; Long War Journal 2013; Bureau of Investigative Journalism 2013). What the publicly available data reveals is that there have been well over 300 strikes in Pakistan, with more than 80 percent of them carried out under Obama.

In March 2013, the UN Special Rapporteur on Counter-Terrorism and Human Rights, Ben Emmerson, conducted a three-day visit to Islamabad, Pakistan, and upon his return he issued a statement which is directly consequential for determining the legality of these drone strikes. After Emmerson's visit with the relevant government ministries, he affirmed:

> Officials stated that reports of continuing tacit consent by Pakistan to the use of drones on its territory by any other State are false, and confirmed that a thorough search of Government records had revealed no indication of such consent having been given. Officials also pointed to public statements by Pakistan at the UN emphasizing this position and calling for an immediate end to the use of drones by any other State on the territory of Pakistan.
>
> (Emmerson 2013)

There have indeed been reports that Pakistan has assented to certain strikes, and has even done so in exchange for having enemies of its government targeted (Mazzetti 2013: 103–113). Of course, if Pakistan agrees to the use of such force on its territory, the legality of the operation in international law changes entirely; thus, this is a pivotal question to which one would like definite answers. However, the answer of public diplomacy is clear for citizens inside and outside of Pakistan: consent has not been given.

As for the avenues available for resolving a potential legal dispute, they are limited. In 2002, the US announced that its signature to the Rome

Statute of the International Criminal Court was to have no legal effect. Pakistan is not a state party to the treaty, and a bilateral agreement was signed by the two states agreeing not to surrender Americans to the jurisdiction of the court (Dixon *et al.* 2011: 65). However unlikely, this does not rule out the possibility, within the domestic jurisdiction of Pakistani courts, of pursuing crimes committed on its soil. This possibility appears to have increased since in 2013 the Peshawar High Court declared "US Drone Strikes Illegal" (*The Hindu*, May 9).

Although much of the conventional debate is over whether the proper body of international law to apply in such cases is between humanitarian and human rights law, there is much to be revealed by addressing the questions raised by *jus ad bellum* since drones in this case strike across a new border. Besides the fact that such a tack raises a problem because the US sits with veto power on the UNSC (the body charged with determining an act of aggression under Article 39), one must also recognize that the traditional understanding of the use of force was that it was triggered by another *state*. In this circumstance, the Obama administration has been actively pursuing the shift in understanding which began to take hold after the assault of 2001, allowing that individuals, rather than just states, can act as this trigger.

No doubt, UNSC Resolutions 1368 and 1373 (passed in the wake of 9/11) buttress the interpretation that persons or non-state groups can provoke the right to self-defense by states. Yet what might have initially seemed an insignificant modification was quickly pointed out as having "potentially shattering consequences for international law" (Cassese 2001: 993). Thus, it could be said that the ICJ's ambiguous case law on this question in fact reflects the current unresolved debate on the use of force (Bianchi 2009: 655). Despite dispute over whether individuals can trigger a state's right to self-defense, this does not mean that there are no points of agreement on the use of force.

As we have seen in Chapter 4, there has long been accord on the temporal limits of anticipatory military action that can be seen as a reflection of customary law. Also mentioned in its conclusion was the fact that the Obama administration directly followed its predecessor on the course of reinterpreting the definition of "imminence"; both administrations have submitted that the term must be broadened. Thus, here we build on the research and argument of that chapter to expose that Obama jeopardizes legitimacy in a manner reminiscent of the government that came before his own. In other words, not only does the justification of the drone program compromise lines of *legality*, it does so in a place that overlaps with *morality*.

The first years of the Obama presidency were marked by extremely limited legal explanation of their drone program, even in the face of mounting news and NGO reports. The moment at which this shifted was when a key adviser to the president gave a speech in September 2011, stating that the practical issue for assessing threats in its drone program "turns principally on how you define 'imminence'" (Brennan 2011).

Specific details were not given at that time, but the new administration made clear that it was following the old by expanding the definition of the key term which is meant to circumscribe anticipatory military action to fit into legal and moral understandings.

In February 2013, a Department of Justice White Paper was leaked to the press covering the general legal reasoning behind some of the drone strikes. Most pertinent here, the authors of the OLC memo concluded that "an 'imminent' threat of violent attack against the United States does not require the United States to have clear evidence that a specific attack on US persons and interests will take place in the immediate future" (US Department of Justice 2011: 7). Thus, the administration indeed declared a widening of this term beyond its traditional meaning.

In addition to these sources, one must also look to the speech given by Attorney General Eric Holder in March 2012. In it, you find a perfect coincidence with the leaked White Paper since both were meant to specifically address the circumstance of a targeted and killed US citizen (Anwar al-Awlaki). The precise contours of this new definition are explained as such:

> The evaluation of whether an individual presents an "imminent threat" incorporates considerations of the relevant window of opportunity to act, the possible harm that missing the window would cause to civilians, and the likelihood of heading off future disastrous attacks against the United States.
>
> (Holder 2012)

While there are numerous avenues to pursue in dissecting this three-part test, the scope of this brief examination allows for only a couple points to be illuminated. The first is that the idea of inserting factors for the "relevant window of opportunity to act" flips the question on its head. The standard of "imminence" is meant to spotlight the verifiable actions of a potential aggressor, yet this criterion inverts the focus onto one's own considerations and capabilities. This is backwards. Second, it is hard to understand how the enormously imprecise and subjective measure of "the likelihood of heading off" is meant to limit the use of force in any way.

To further confuse and distort this question of temporal limits, the Attorney General claimed, in a letter to Congress in May 2013, that "lethal force may be used only when a terrorist target poses a *continuing, imminent threat*" (Holder 2012; my emphasis). Unfortunately, the additional term only warps the matter. While more information is necessary to best analyze this change, it appears as though the Obama administration is infusing *jus ad bellum* with standards from humanitarian law. That is, the continuing threat from a (suspected?) combatant is meant to be sufficiently threatening to allow the crossing of a new international border to use lethal force. This is a perilous mix. The risk can be readily discerned if we consider the ramifications if India had characterized the Mumbai attack of 2008 as authorizing the use of force against the Lashkar-e-Taiba group which concealed itself in a nuclear-armed Pakistan (Martin 2012: 242).

Most importantly, what is found in this attempt at redefining a word that already has an agreed-upon meaning is that it is once again reminiscent of the "just feare" standard suggested in the seventeenth century by Francis Bacon. We know that this idea ran into a philosophical dead end and sowed no progeny. Additionally, one can immediately discern that this standard of the Obama administration diverges greatly from that we have seen from Pufendorf ("unless I prevent him, I shall immediately feel his Stroke") or Webster in the *Caroline* incident ("instant, overwhelming and leaving no choice of means and no moment for deliberation"). Thus, it is troubling that in this reading of the law we do not find something similar to the criteria of "immediate and certain" for justified anticipatory action put forward by Hugo Grotius and accepted by a majority of contemporary international jurists.

What also needs to be repeated from Chapters 1 and 4 is that this very question of anticipatory action deals with an important portion of the space of overlap between *morality* and *legality*: the prohibition of unconstrained violence. The key to this understanding turns on being able to focus on the "modest aim of survival," and "[t]his simple thought has in fact very much to do with the characteristics of both law and morals" (Hart 1994: 191). As a result, the association of peoples requires both a legal and moral demarcation of forbearance from attacks based on a "just feare" of future intent. It is difficult to imagine that such an interpretation, which leaves the regulation of violence up to individual members' own discretion, would find favor within the broader diplomatic community.

The final lens of legitimacy is that of *efficacy*. Unfortunately, due to the intense secrecy of the drone program it is enormously difficult, if not impossible, to provide an empirical analysis that does not contain crucial gaps of data leading to potentially false conclusions. Yet this has not dissuaded the administration or its critics from putting forward a host of claims, nearly all of them unverifiable. For example, key adviser to the President, John O. Brennan, gave a speech in 2012 entitled "The Ethics and Efficacy of the President's Counterterrorism Strategy" in which he listed the names of persons killed who were alleged to be "the core al-Qa'ida leadership" (Brennan 2012). Perhaps this is true.

Yet, as we have seen in Chapter 5, the status of some individuals within the organization were wrongfully construed, leading to the torture of the innocent and ill-informed. Moreover, as a result of the Supreme Court's involvement (seen in Chapter 3), we know that only 82 of the 779 people (10.5 percent) who have passed through Guantánamo are meant to be detained until the end of hostilities. In this case, the targeted persons are not even in custody, but rather are primarily assessed from a camera in the sky.

On top of this, further doubts should be raised about whether the undisclosed information being used by the administration to piece together the puzzle in Pakistan is entirely reliable. One account from a local reporter (now a Fellow of Journalism at the University of Harvard) concludes that the story of alliances and enemies is far more complicated in North Waziristan than is presented by the administration. This native to one of the world's most inaccessible regions writes about Obama's drone program: "[W]e know virtually nothing about it. I spent more than half a decade tracking this most secret of wars across northern Pakistan.... Yet even I can say very little for certain about what has happened" (Shah 2012). Another correspondent reported on the constant change and flux, writing that "by 2011, the map of Islamic militancy inside Pakistan had been redrawn, and factions that once had little contact with each other had cemented new alliances to survive the CIA's drone campaign in the western mountains" (Mazzetti 2013: 3). In light of such reporting, it is questionable whether the Obama administration itself has more dependable sources for explaining what is actually happening on the ground in Pakistan and, by extension, whether the drone killing is in fact efficacious in targeting the right people.

As for demonstrably false claims by the Obama administration raising questions of efficacy, one can look to the use of "signature strikes." Although the precision of the strikes and exhaustive review process of who could be targeted was consistently touted in public, intelligence reports reviewed in April 2013 confirmed a worrying account that reverberated through the diplomatic and international law community (Landay 2013). That is, the US has used drones to attack and kill unidentified individuals believed to be associated with terrorist groups because they fit particular behavior patterns. This type of action is differentiated from "personality strikes," in which the target is a known terrorist leader. This dubious practice was first exposed in November 2011, and it was reported that in Pakistan "[t]he bulk of CIA's drone strikes are signature strikes" (Entous *et al.* 2011).

This point is of importance here. As explained in the first half of this conclusion, the use of irrevocable harm exercised by the government based on suspicion can lead to the jeopardizing of legitimacy. Alston also clarified in his UN Special Rapporteur report that one of the requirements of international humanitarian law is that "[t]argeted killings should never be based solely on 'suspicious' conduct or unverified—or unverifiable—information" (2010: 28). What has been exposed with regard to "signature strikes" reveals that this indeed occurred during a one-year period starting in September 2010, when at least 265 of up to 482 people killed by the CIA were not senior Al-Qaeda, but were assessed as "unknown extremists" (Landay 2013). Of course, the efficacy of such action turns entirely on the accuracy of the speculation, or this *targeting on suspicion*.

Nonetheless, this does not mean that nothing can be said more definitively about the efficacy of drone warfare across new borders. To do so it is necessary to move beyond the more conventional assessment of counting the number of enemies killed. As has been cogently explained, "the purpose of the conduct of hostilities is not to *kill* the enemy but to *defeat* him" (Melzer 2008: 427). This brings us to an important question raised by Weber's definition of the state which we have used throughout this book. If the modern state is "a human community that (successfully) claims the *monopoly of the legitimate use of physical force* within a given territory" (Weber 1946: 78; original emphasis), how can the unexplained (and uninvited?) exercise of lethal force within that terrain do anything but undermine the local government? And does this destabilization of the state government assist in defeating non-state enemies or play into their hands? These are important questions of strategic efficacy that need to be considered.

In 2013, at the beginning of his second term, Obama delivered a major speech on counterterrorism and raised an intriguing possibility for how to continue forward. Noting that the authorization for the armed conflict had been passed twelve years earlier, he advocated refining and ultimately repealing the legal authorization for the use of military force (Obama 2013). While this certainly would not be a panacea resolving all of the difficulties raised here, it would likely limit the available tactics for counterterrorism by removing the legal justifications for a wartime footing. In doing so it is conceivable that the excessive policies which jeopardize legitimacy most significantly would be largely taken off the table as options now and for future presidents. It is worthwhile to keep an eye on this proposition.

Finally, it is fitting to return to the epigraph of this conclusion, in which Ignatieff highlights the political requirement of guarding and preserving legitimacy. The attackers of 9/11 were willing to slaughter innocent civilians in total rejection of established laws, norms, and institutions, and it was warned that those who confront them must not do the same. Defensive strategy for counterterrorism must begin by safeguarding legitimacy. Thus, the lenses of *legality, morality,* and *efficacy* will serve us well as analytical tools to assess whether President Obama, or his successors, are living up to the imperative of defending the target of legitimacy.

Bibliography

I Legal sources

a International treaties and UN Security Council Resolutions

Additional Protocol I to the Geneva Conventions of 12 August 1949, Relating to the Protection of Victims of International Armed Conflicts (signed June 8, 1977, entered into force December 7, 1978), 1125 UNTS 3.

Additional Protocol II to the Geneva Conventions of 12 August 1949, Relating to the Protection of Victims of Non-International Armed Conflicts (signed June 8, 1977, entered into force December 7, 1978), 1125 UNTS 609.

African Charter on Human and People's Rights (signed June 27, 1981, entered into force October 21, 1986), OAU Doc. CAB/LEG/67/3 rev. 5, 1520 UNTS 217.

American Convention on Human Rights (signed November 22, 1969, entered into force July 18, 1978), OAS Treaty Series No. 36, 1144 UNTS 123.

Charter of the United Nations (signed June 26, 1945, entered into force October 24, 1945), 9 *Int. Leg.* 327.

Convention against Torture and Other Cruel, Inhuman or Degrading Treatment or Punishment (adopted December 10, 1984, entered into force June 26, 1987), 1465 UNTS 85.

Covenant of the League of Nations, 1919, 1 *Int. Leg.* 1, 7.

Geneva Convention I, Amelioration of the Condition of the Wounded and Sick in Armed Forces in the Field (signed August 12, 1949, entered into force October 21, 1950), 75 UNTS 31.

Geneva Convention II, Amelioration of the Condition of Wounded, Sick and Ship-wrecked Members of Armed Forces at Sea (signed August 12, 1949, entry into force October 21, 1950), 75 UNTS 85.

Geneva Convention III, Relative to the Treatment of Prisoners of War (signed August 12, 1949, entered into force October 21, 1950), 75 UNTS 135.

Geneva Convention IV, Relative to the Protection of Civilian Persons in Time of War (signed August 12, 1949, entered into force October 21, 1950), 75 UNTS 287.

International Convention for the Protection of All Persons from Enforced Disappearance (adopted December 20, 2006, entered into force December 23, 2010), UN Doc. A/RES/61/177 (2006).

International Convention on Civil and Political Rights (signed December 16, 1966, entered into force March 23, 1976), 999 UNTS 171.

Kellogg–Briand Pact of Paris, (1928) General Treaty for Renunciation of War as an Instrument of National Policy, 94 UNTS 57.

St. Petersburg Declaration (December 11, 1868), reprinted in *The American Journal of International Law*, Supplement: Official Documents (April 1907), 1 (2): pp. 95–96.

UN Security Council, Resolution 678, UN Doc. S/RES/678 (1990).

UN Security Council, Resolution 687, UN Doc. S/RES/687 (1991).

UN Security Council, Resolution 1368, UN Doc. S/RES/1368 (2001).

UN Security Council, Resolution 1373, UN Doc. S/RES/1373 (2001).

UN Security Council, Resolution 1377, UN Doc. S/RES/1377 (2001).

UN Security Council, Resolution 1441, UN Doc. S/RES/1441 (2002).

US Reservations, Declarations, and Understandings, Convention Against Torture and Other Cruel, Inhuman or Degrading Treatment or Punishment, Art. I(2), Cong. Rec. S17486–01 (daily ed., October 27, 1990).

Vienna Convention on the Law of Treaties (signed May 23, 1969, entered into force January 27, 1980), 1155 UNTS 331.

b International courts

European Court of Human Rights (1979) *Airey* v. *Ireland*, Application No. 6289/73, October 9.

European Court of Human Rights (1997) *Aydin* v. *Turkey*, 57/1996/676/866, September 25.

International Court of Justice (1986) Military and Paramilitary Activities in and against Nicaragua *(Nicaragua* v. *United States of America)*, Merits, Judgement of June 27, 1986, ICJ Rep. 14.

International Court of Justice (1996) *Advisory Opinion*, "Legality of the Threat or Use of Nuclear Weapons," July 8, 1996, ICJ Reports 1996-I, 226.

International Court of Justice (2004) *Advisory Opinion*, "Legal Consequences of the Construction of a Wall in the Occupied Palestinian Territory," July 9, 2004, ICJ Reports 2004, General List No. 131.

International Criminal Tribunal for Ex-Yugoslavia (1998) *Prosecutor* v. *Zejnil Delalić Zdravko Mucić also known as "Pavo" Hazim Delić Esad Landžo also known as "Zenga,"* Trial Chamber (Celebici Judgment), Case No. IT-96–21-T, November 16.

International Criminal Tribunal for Ex-Yugoslavia (1999) *Prosecutor* v. *Dusko Tadic* Appeals Chamber, Case No. IT-94–1-A, July 15.

International Criminal Tribunal for Ex-Yugoslavia (2001) *Prosecutor* v. *Zejnil Delalić Zdravko Mucić also known as "Pavo" Hazim Delić Esad Landžo also known as "Zenga,"* Appeals Chamber (Celebici Judgment), Case No. IT-96–21-A, February 20.

Special Tribunal for Lebanon Appeals Chamber (2011) Interlocutory Decision on the Applicable Law: Terrorism, Conspiracy, Homicide, Perpetration, Cumulative Charging, Case No. STL-11–01/I, February 16.

c United Nations documents/standard setting

Alston, P. (2010) "Report of the Special Rapporteur on Extrajudicial, Summary or Arbitrary Executions," A/HRC/14/24/Add.6, May 28.

Committee Against Torture (2006), Conclusions and Recommendations: United States, UN Doc CAT/C/USA/CO/2, May 18.

Committee Against Torture (2007), "General Comment no. 2: Implementation of article 2 by States parties," UN Doc CAT/7C/GC/2/CRP.l/Rev.4, November 23.

Lieber Code: General Orders No. 100, Instructions for the Government of Armies of the United States in the Field (April 24, 1863), prepared by Francis Lieber, LL.D., Adjutant General's Office, 1863, Washington 1898: Government Printing Office.

Paris Minimum Standards (1985) "The Paris Minimum Standards of Human Rights Norms in a State of Emergency," International Law Association, 61st Conference.

Permanent Mission of the United Kingdom of Great Britain and Northern Ireland (2001), Letter dated October 7, from the Chargé d'affaires a.i. to the United Nations addressed to the President of the Security Council, UN Doc. S/2001/947.

Permanent Representative of the United States of America (2001) to the United Nations addressed to the President of the Security Council, Letter dated October 7, UN SCOR, 56th Sess., UN Doc. S/2001/946.

Responsibility to Protect (2001), Report of the International Commission on Intervention and State Sovereignty, Co-chairs Gareth Evans and Mohamed Sahnoun, Ottawa, Canada, December.

Turku Declaration (1991), Minimum Humanitarian Standards, E/CN.4/Sub.2/1991/55 or the International Review of the Red Cross, No. 282, May–June 1991, pp. 330–336.

UN General Assembly, Body of Principles for the Protection of All Persons under Any Form of Detention or Imprisonment, Resolution of the General Assembly, 43/173 (concluded December 9, 1988).

UN General Assembly, "Human Rights and Terrorism," 48th Session, UN Doc. A/RES/48/122 (1993); 49th Session, UN Doc. A/RES/49/185 (1994); 50th Session, UN Doc. A/RES/50/186 (1995); 52nd Session, UN Doc. A/RES/52/133 (1997); 56th Session, UN Doc. A/RES/56/160 (2001); 58th Session, UN Doc. A/RES/58/174 (2003).

UN Human Rights Committee (2001), "General Comment No. 29: States of Emergency(Art.4)," ICCPR, Office of the United Nations High Commissioner for Human Rights, Geneva, Switzerland (CCPR/C/21/Rev.1/Add.11), August 31.

UN Human Rights Committee (2004), "General Comment No. 31," ICCPR, Office of the United Nations High Commissioner for Human Rights, Geneva, Switzerland (CCPR/C/21/Rev.1/Add.13), March 29.

UN Office of the High Commissioner of Human Rights, "Protection of Human Rights and Fundamental Freedoms While Countering Terrorism," Resolutions 2001/37, 2003/37, and 2004/44.

Universal Declaration of Human Rights (concluded December 10, 1948), GA res. 217A (III), UN Doc A/810 at 71.

Vienna Declaration (1993), World Conference on Human Rights, Vienna, U.N. Doc. A/CONF.157/24 (Part I), June 14–25.

d US and other domestic court cases and documents

Declaration of Commander James R. Crisfield Jr. (2004), Judge Advocate General Corps, in the case of *Mozzam Begg* v. *Bush*, District Court for the District of Columbia, Civil Action No. 04-CV-1137 (RMC), December 20.

Hertz, M. (2009), "Brief of the United States as *Amicus Curiae*," in the United States Court of Appeals for the Ninth Circuit, *Padilla* v. *Yoo*, 633 F. Supp. 2d 1005 (ND Cal. 2009).

Israeli High Court of Justice, *Public Committee against Torture in Israel* v. *The State of Israel* [1999], HCJ5100/94.

Israeli High Court of Justice, *Public Committee Against Torture in Israel* v. *Government of Israel* (Targeted Killings Case) [2005], HCJ 769/02.

Petitioner's Brief (2006), *Hamdan* v. *Rumsfeld*, 126 S. Ct. 2749 (No. 05–184), January 6.

Petitioners' Brief on the Merits (2004), *Rasul* v. *Bush*, No. 03–334, January 14.

Respondent to *Zayn al Abidin Muhammad Husayn* v. *Gates*, (2009) Civil Action No. 08-cv-1360 (RWR), Respondent's Memorandum of Points and Authorities in Opposition to Petitioner's Motion for Discovery and Petitioner's Motion for Sanctions.

Respondents' Memorandum (2009), Regarding the Government's Detention Authority Relative to Detainees Held at Guantanamo Bay, Guantanamo Bay Detainee Litigation, No. 08–0442 (DDC), filed March 13.

US Court of Appeals, *Al-Adahi* v. *Obama*, 613 F.3d 1102 (DC Circuit 2010).

US Court of Appeals, *Al Maqaleh et al.* v. *Gates*, 605 F.3d 84, 99 (DC Circuit 2010) (slip opinion).

US Court of Appeals, *Hamdan v. Rumsfeld*, 415 F.3d 33 (DC Circuit 2005) (slip opinion).

US Court of Appeals, *Kadic v. Karadzic*, Second Circuit, 70 F.3d 232, (2nd Circuit 1995) (slip opinion).

US Court of Appeals, *Latif* v. *Obama*, 666 F.3d 746 (DC Circuit 2011).

US Court of Appeals, *Padilla* v. *Hanft*, 423 F.3d 386 (4th Circuit 2005).

US Court of Appeals, *Padilla* v. *Yoo*, 633 F. Supp. 2d 1005 (9th Circuit 2009).

US Court of Appeals, *Siderman de Blake* v. *Republic of Argentina*, 965 F. 2d 699 (9th Circuit 1992).

US Court of Appeals, *United States* v. *Lee*, 744 F.2d 1124 (5th Circuit 1983).

US District Court, *Al Maqaleh et al.* v. *Gates*, 604 F. Supp. 2d 205 (DDC 2009).

US District Court, *Farhi Saeed Bin Mohammed et al.* v. *Obama*, 704 F. Supp. 2d 1 (DDC 2009).

US District Court, *Hamdan* v. *Rumsfeld*, 344 F. Supp. 2d 152 (DDC 2004).

US District Court, *Hedges* v. *Obama*, No. 12-CV-331, 2012 WL 1721124 (S.D.N.Y. 2012) (slip opinion).

US District Court, *Padilla* v. *Hanft*, 432 F.3d 582 (2005).

US Supreme Court, *Ahrens* v. *Clark*, 335 US 188 (1948).

US Supreme Court, *Boumediene* v. *Bush*, 553 US 723 (2008).

US Supreme Court, *Braden* v. *30th Judicial Circuit Court of Kentucky*, 410 US 484 (1973).

US Supreme Court, *Ex Parte Quirin*, 317 US 1 (1942).

US Supreme Court, *Foster* v. *Florida*, 537 US 990 (2002).

US Supreme Court, *Hamdan* v. *Rumsfeld*, 548 US 557 (2006).

US Supreme Court, *Hamdi* v. *Rumsfeld*, 542 US 507 (2004).

US Supreme Court, *Johnson* v. *Eisentrager*, 339 US 763 (1950).

US Supreme Court, *Korematsu* v. *US*, 323 US 214 (1944).

US Supreme Court, *Padilla* v. *Hanft*, 126 S.Ct. 1649.

US Supreme Court, *Rasul* v. *Bush*, 542 US 466 (2004).

US Supreme Court, *Roper* v. *Simmons*, 543 US 551 (2005).
US Supreme Court, *Rumsfeld* v. *Padilla*, 542 US 426 (2004).
Zubaydah, A. (2007) Verbatim Transcript of Combatant Status Review Tribunal Hearing for ISN 10016 (March 27, 2007), available at www.defense.gov/news/transcript_ISN10016.pdf (accessed June 2013).

e US domestic statutes

Authorization for Use of Military Force (AUMF) (2001), Public Law 107–40, 115 Stat. 224, September 18.
Detainee Treatment Act of 2005, Pub. Law No. 109–48, Div. A, Tit. X, 119 Stat. 2739.
Military Commission Act of 2006, Public Law No. 109–366, 120 Stat. 2600, October 17, 2006.
National Defense Authorization Act for Fiscal Year 2012, Pub. Law No. 112–81, 125 Stat. 1298, December 31, 2011.
Torture Act, 18 USC. §§2340–2340A.

II Scholarship, government documents, NGO Reports, and other sources

Aaron, D. (2008) *In Their Own Words: Voices of Jihad*, Santa Monica, Calif.: RAND Corporation.
Ackerman, P. and Duvall, J. (2000) *A Force More Powerful: A Century of Nonviolent Conflict*, New York: Palgrave.
Almond, S. (2006) "Condoleezza Rice at Boston College? I Quit," *The Boston Globe*, May 12.
American Bar Association (2006) "Report: Task Force on Presidential Signing Statements and the Separation of Powers Doctrine," August 7–8.
American Law Institute (1987) *Restatement of the Law (Third), The Foreign Relations Law of the United States*, St. Paul, Minn.: American Law Institute.
Aquinas, Thomas (1265–1274) *Summa Theologiæ*, English translation by Fathers of the English Dominican Province (New York: Benziger Bros. 1947).
Arendt, H. (1970) *Crises of the Republic*, New York: Harcourt, Brace & World.
Armstrong, K. (1993) *A History of God: The 4,000-Year Quest of Judaism, Christianity and Islam*, New York: Random House.
Associated Press (2007) "US General: No Evidence Iran Is Arming Iraqis: Pace Contradicts Claims by Other US Military, Administration Officials," *MSNBC*, February 13, available at www.msnbc.msn.com/id/17129144/ns/world_news-mideast/n_africa (accessed June 2013).
Austin, J. (1954) *The Province of Jurisprudence Determined and the Uses of the Study of Jurisprudence*, London: Weidenfeld & Nicolson.
Bacon, F. (1629) "Considerations Touching a Warre with Spaine" (1624), in *Certaine Miscellany Works of the Right Honourable Francis Lord Verulam, Viscount St Alban*, London.
Baker, J. and Hamilton, L. (co-chairs) (2006) *The Iraq Study Group Report*, New York: Vintage Books.
Barak, A. (2003) "The Role of a Supreme Court in a Democracy, and the Fight against Terrorism," *University of Miami Law Review*, 58: 125–141.

Barak, A. (2006) *The Judge in a Democracy*, Princeton, NJ: Princeton University Press.

BBCNews.com (2003) "Anti-War Rally Makes Its Mark," February 19, available at http://news.bbc.co.uk/2/hi/uk_news/2767761.stm (accessed June 2013).

Becker, J. and Shane, S. (2012) "Secret 'Kill List' Proves a Test of Obama's Principles and Will," *New York Times*, May 29.

Beetham, D. (1991) *The Legitimation of Power*, New York: Palgrave Macmillan.

Bennett, B., Burger, T., Donnelly, S., and Novak, V. (2005) "Inside the Interrogation of Detainee 063," *Time Magazine*, June 12.

Benvenisti, E. (1993) "Judicial Misgivings Regarding the Application of International Norms: An Analysis of Attitudes of National Courts," *European Journal of International Law*, 4: 159–183.

Benvenisti, E. (2004) "National Courts and the 'War on Terrorism,'" in A. Bianchi (ed.), *Enforcing International Law Norms Against Terrorism*, Oxford: Hart Publishing, pp. 307–330.

Benvenisti, E. (2008a) "Reclaiming Democracy, The Strategic Uses of Foreign and International Law by National Courts," *American Journal of International Law*, 102 (2): 241–273.

Benvenisti, E. (2008b) "United We Stand: National Courts Reviewing Counterterrorism Measures," in A. Bianchi and A. Keller (eds), *Counterterrorism: Democracy's Challenge*, Oxford: Hart Publishing, pp. 251–276.

Bianchi, A. (2004a) "Dismantling the Wall: The ICJ's Advisory Opinion and Its Likely Impact on International Law," *German Yearbook of International Law*, 47: 343–391.

Bianchi, A. (2004b) "International Law and US Courts: The Myth of Lohengrin Revisited," *European Journal of International Law*, 15 (4): 751–781.

Bianchi, A. (2009) "The International Regulation of the Use of Force: The Politics of Interpretive Method," *Leiden Journal of International Law*, 22 (4): 651–676.

Bianchi, A. and Keller, A. (eds) (2008) *Counterterrorism: Democracy's Challenge*, Oxford: Hart Publishing.

Bilmes, L. and Stiglitz, J. (2008) *The Three Trillion Dollar War: The True Cost of the Iraq Conflict*, New York: W. W. Norton & Company.

Bin Laden, O. (1996) "Declaration of War against the Americans Occupying the Land of the Two Holy Places," *Al Quds Al Arabi*, London, August.

Bin Laden, O. (2001) "Bin Laden Rails against Crusaders and UN," translation on BBCNews.com, November 3, available at http://news.bbc.co.uk/2/hi/world/monitoring/media_reports/1636782.stm (accessed June 2013).

Bin Laden, O. (2002) "Letter to Mullah Mohammed Omar from Osama bin Laden," available at Combating Terrorism Center at Westpoint, Harmony and Disharmony: Exploiting Al-Qa'ida's Organizational Vulnerabilities, Doc ID: AFGP-2002-600321 (unknown date of origin, translation date: June 5, 2002).

Bin Laden, O. (2004) "Message to America," November 1, available at Al-Jazeera. com, www.aljazeera.com/archive/2004/11/200849163336457223.html (accessed June 2013).

Bin Laden, O. (2006) "Letter to Mullah Mohamed Omar," *Washington Post*, September 5.

Box Office Mojo (2013) "Documentary—Political, Total Grosses, 1982–Present," available at www.boxofficemojo.com/genres/chart/?id=politicaldoc.htm (accessed June 2013).

Bradbury, S. (2005a) "Re: Application of 18 USC. §§2340–2340A to Certain Techniques that May Be Used in Interrogation of High Value al Qaeda Detainees," Office of Legal Counsel, May 10.

Bradbury, S. (2005b) "Re: Application of United States Obligations under Article 16 of the Convention against Torture to Certain Techniques that May Be Used in Interrogation of High Value al Qaeda Detainees," Office of Legal Counsel, May 30.

Brennan, J. O. (2011) "Strengthening Our Security by Adhering to Our Values and Laws," Speech at Harvard Law School, Cambridge, Mass., September 16.

Brennan, J. O. (2012) "The Ethics and Efficacy of the President's Counterterrorism Strategy," Speech at Woodrow Wilson International Center for Scholars, Washington, DC, April 30.

Breyer, J. (2003) "Keynote Address at American Society of International Law," Washington, DC, April 4.

Broad, W., Sanger, D., and Bonner, R. (2004) "A Tale of Nuclear Proliferation: How Pakistani Built His Network," *New York Times*, February 12.

Brunnée, J. and Toope, S. (2010) *Legitimacy and Legality in International Law: An Interactional Account*, Cambridge: Cambridge University Press.

Bureau of Investigative Journalism (2013), Covert Drone War, available at www.thebureauinvestigates.com/category/projects/drones (accessed June 2013).

Burke, E. (1999) *Selected Works*, 4 vols., Indianapolis, Ind.: Liberty Fund.

Bush, G. W. (2001a) "Detention, Treatment, and Trial of Certain Non-citizens in the War against Terrorism": Military Order, vol. 66, no. 2, November 13; reprinted in K. Greenberg and J. Dratel (eds.), *The Torture Papers: The Road to Abu Ghraib*, Cambridge: Cambridge University Press, 2005, pp. 25–28.

Bush, G. W. (2001b) "Statement by the President, September 11, 2001."

Bush, G. W. (2002a) "Humane Treatment of al Qaeda and Taliban Detainees," White House Memorandum, (February 7); reprinted in K. Greenberg and J. Dratel (eds), *The Torture Papers: The Road to Abu Ghraib*, Cambridge: Cambridge University Press, 2005, pp. 134–135.

Bush, G. W. (2002b) "The State of the Union Address to Congress and the Nation," Washington, DC, January 30.

Bush, G. W. (2002c) Speech at United States Military Academy at West Point, NY, June 1, available at. www.nytimes.com/2002/06/01/international/02PTEX-WEB.html (accessed June 2013).

Bush, G. W. (2002d) "Text of Iraq Speech to UN: President Urges World Body to Act against Iraq," United Nations General Address, New York, September 12.

Bush, G. W. (2006a) President's Statement on Signing of H.R. 2863, "Department of Defense, Emergency Supplemental Appropriations to Address Hurricanes in the Gulf of Mexico, and Pandemic Influenza Act," available at http://georgewbush-whitehouse.archives.gov/news/releases/2005/12/20051230–8.html (accessed June 2013).

Bush, G. W. (2006b) "Speech on Terrorism," White House, Washington DC September 6.

Bush, G. W. (2010) *Decision Points*, New York: Crown.

Bybee, J. (2002a) "Re: Status of Taliban Forces under Article 4 of the Third Geneva Convention of 1949" (February 7); reprinted in K. Greenberg and J. Dratel (eds), *The Torture Papers: The Road to Abu Ghraib*, Cambridge: Cambridge University Press, 2005, pp. 136–143.

Bybee, J. (2002b) "Re: Standards of Conduct for Interrogation under 18 U.S.C. §§2340–2340A," Bybee Memo, (August 1); reprinted in K. Greenberg and J. Dratel (eds), *The Torture Papers: The Road to Abu Ghraib*, Cambridge: Cambridge University Press, 2005, pp. 172–217.

Bybee, J. (2002c) "Interrogation of al Qaeda Operative," Classified Bybee Memo, (August 1), available at www.fas.org/irp/agency/doj/olc/zubaydah.pdf (accessed June 2013).

Byrd, R. (2003) "Arrogance of Power," Senate Floor Statement, March 19, 108th Congress, 1st Session, Congressional Record 149(43).

Carlson, P. (2006) "Lewis Lapham Lights Up," *Washington Post*, March 21.

Cassese, A. (1989) *Terrorism, Politics and Law*, Cambridge: Polity Press.

Cassese, A. (2001) "Terrorism Is Also Disrupting Some Crucial Legal Categories of International Law," *European Journal of International Law*, 12 (5): 993–1001.

Cassese, A. (2004) "Terrorism as an International Crime," in A. Bianchi (ed.), *Enforcing International Law Norms against Terrorism*, Oxford: Hart Publishing, pp. 213–225.

CBS News (2009) "CBS News/NY Times Poll Finds President Will Leave Office with Lowest Final Approval Rating Ever," January 16, available at www.cbsnews.com/stories/2009/01/16/opinion/polls/main4728399.shtml?source=related_story (accessed June 2013).

Chatterjee, C. (2007) *International Law and Diplomacy*, London and New York: Routledge.

Cheney, R. (2002) "Speech to Veterans of Foreign Wars," National Convention, Nashville, Tenn., August 27.

Cheney, R. (2009) "Remarks before the American Enterprise Institute for Public Policy Research," Washington, DC, May 21.

Church, Vice Admiral A. (2005) *Church Report*, Office of the Secretary of Defense Review of Department of Defense Detention Operations and Detainee Interrogation Techniques, available at www.defense.gov/news/Mar2005/d20050310 exe.pdf (accessed June 2013).

CIA Inspector General (2004) "Counterterrorism Detention and Interrogation Activities, September 2001–October 2003," 2003–7123-IG, May 7.

Cicero (1931) *The Speeches: Pro Milone; In Pisonem; Pro Scauro; Pro Fonteio; Pro Rabirio postumo; Pro Marcello; Pro Ligario; Pro rege Deiotaro*, trans. N. H. Watts, Cambridge, Mass.: Harvard University Press.

Clark, K. (2005) "Ethical Issues Raised by OLC Torture Memorandum," *Journal of National Security Law and Policy*, 1 (2): 455–472.

Clausewitz, K. (2000) "On War," in *The Book of War*, O. J. Matthijs Jolles (trans.), New York: The Modern Library, pp. 249–973.

CNN (2002) Late Edition with Wolf Blitzer, Interview with Condoleezza Rice, September 8, available at http://transcripts.cnn.com/TRANSCRIPTS/0209/08/le.00.html (accessed June 2013).

Coalition for the International Criminal Court (2006), "Status of US Bilateral Immunity Agreements," December, available at www.iccnow.org/documents/CICCFS_BIAstatus_current.pdf (accessed June 2013).

Cole, D. (2008) "Rights over Borders: Transnational Constitutionalism and Guantanamo Bay," *Cato Supreme Court Review*, Georgetown Public Law Research Paper No. 1272202.

Cole, D. (2012) "Where Liberty Lies: Civil Society and Individual Rights after 9/11," *Wayne Law Review*, 57 (4): 1203–1267.

Constitution Project (2013) "The Report of The Constitution Project's Task Force on Detainee Treatment," Washington, DC: The Constitution Project.

Cook, D. (2003) "Legitimacy and Political Violence: A Habermasian Perspective," *Social Justice*, 30 (3): 108–126, available from *Online Questia Library* (accessed June 2013).

Corn, D. (2010) "Obama and GOPers Worked Together to Kill Bush Torture Probe," Mother Jones Online Reporting, Politics, December 1, available at www.motherjones.com/politics/2010/12/wikileaks-cable-obama-quashed-torture-investigation (accessed June 2013).

Crenshaw, M. (1983) *Terrorism, Legitimacy, and Power: The Consequences of Political Violence*, Middletown, Conn.: Wesleyan University Press.

De Londras, F. (2008) "What Human Rights Law Could Do: Lamenting the Absence of an International Human Rights Law Approach in *Boumediene & Al Odah*," *Israel Law Review*, 41 (3): 562–595.

Dean, J. (2005) "The Torture Memo by Judge Jay S. Bybee that Haunted Alberto Gonzales's Confirmation Hearings," *FindLaw*, January 14. Available at http://writ.news.findlaw.com/dean/20050114.html (accessed June 2013).

Denbeaux, M. (2006) "No-Hearing Hearings: CSRT—The Modern Habeas Corpus? An Analysis of the Proceedings of the Government's Combatant Status Review Tribunals at Guantánamo," Seton Hall University Law School's Center for Policy and Research, available at http://law.shu.edu/publications/guantanamoReports/final_no_hearing_hearings_report.pdf (accessed June 2013).

Denbeaux, M. (2012) "No Hearing Habeas: DC Circuit Restricts Meaningful Review," Seton Hall University Law School's Center for Policy and Research, May 1, available at http://law.shu.edu/ProgramsCenters/PublicIntGovServ/policyresearch/upload/hearing-habeas.pdf (accessed June 2013).

Dershowitz, A. (2002) *Why Terrorism Works: Understanding the Threat, Responding to the Challenges*, New Haven, Conn.: Yale University Press.

Deyoung, K. (2007) "Pace Demurs on Accusation of Iran: General Says He Knows Nothing Tying Leaders to Arms in Iraq," *Washington Post*, February 13.

Dinstein, Y. (2001) *War, Aggression, and Self-Defense*, 3rd edn, Cambridge: Cambridge University Press.

Dixon, M., McCorquodale, R., and Williams, S. (2011) *Cases and Materials on International Law*, Oxford: Oxford University Press.

Dunlap, C. (2001) "Law and Military Interventions: Preserving Humanitarian Values in 21st Conflicts," prepared for the Humanitarian Challenges in Military Intervention Conference, Carr Center for Human Rights Policy, Kennedy School of Government, Harvard University, Washington, DC, November 29.

Duquesne, J. (2001) *Pour comprendre la guerre d'Algérie*, Paris: Perrin.

Dwyer, M. (2007) "Former Bush Aide Card Is Booed at UMass," *The Boston Globe*, May 26.

Eban, K. (2007) "Rorschach and Awe," *Vanity Fair*, July 17. Available at www.vanityfair.com/politics/features/2007/07/torture200707 (accessed June 2013).

Elliott, J. (2011) "Bush Cancels Europe Trip Amid Calls for His Arrest," *Salon.com War Room*, February 7, available at www.salon.com/2011/02/07/bush_amnesty_arrest/ (accessed June 2013).

Emmerson, B. (2013) "Statement of the Special Rapporteur Following Meetings in

Pakistan," United Nations Human Rights, Office for the High Commissioner of Human Rights, Islamabad, March 14, available at www.ohchr.org/EN/NewsEvents/Pages/DisplayNews.aspx?NewsID=13146&LangID=E (accessed June 2013).

Entous, A., Gorman, S., and Barnes, J. (2011) "US Tightens Drone Rules," *Wall Street Journal*, November 4.

Evangelicals for Human Rights (2007) "An Evangelical Declaration against Torture: Protecting Human Rights in an Age of Terror," *Review of Faith and International Affairs*, 5 (2): 41–58.

Farer, T. (2008a) *Confronting Global Terrorism and American Neo-Conservatism: The Framework of a Liberal Grand Strategy*, Oxford: Oxford University Press.

Farer, T. (2008b) "Un-just War against Terrorism and the Struggle to Appropriate Human Rights," *Human Rights Quarterly*, 30 (2): 356–403.

FBI Inspector General (2008) "A Review of the FBI's Involvement in and Observations of Detainee Interrogations in Guantánamo Bay, Afghanistan, and Iraq," Federal Bureau of Investigation, May.

Ferrero, G. (1942) *The Principles of Power*, New York: G. P. Putnam's Sons.

Finkelstein, C., Ohlin, J., and Altman, A. (eds) (2012) *Targeted Killing: Law and Morality in an Asymmetrical World*, Oxford: Oxford University Press.

Finn, P. and Warrick, J. (2009) "Detainee's Harsh Treatment Foiled No Plots," *Washington Post*, March 29.

Fletcher, G. and Ohlin, J. (2008) *Defending Humanity: When Force is Justified and Why*, Oxford: Oxford University Press.

FoxNews.com (2007) "Outgoing Joint Chiefs of Staff Chairman Pace Refused to Voluntarily Retire," June 15, available at www.foxnews.com/story/0,2933,282995,00.html (accessed June 2013).

Franck, T. (1990) *The Power of Legitimacy among Nations*, New York: Oxford University Press.

Franck, T. (2002) *Recourse to Force: State Action against Threats and Armed Attacks*, Cambridge: Cambridge University Press.

Fuller, L. (1958) "Positivism and Fidelity to Law: A Reply to Professor Hart," *Harvard Law Review*, 71 (4): 630–672.

Fuller, L. (1964) *The Morality of Law*, New Haven, Conn.: Yale University Press.

Gallup.com (2001–2008), Presidential Approval Ratings, George W. Bush's Job Approval Ratings, available at www.gallup.com/poll/116500/presidential-approval-ratings-george-bush.aspx (accessed June 2013).

Gellman, B. (2008) *Angler: The Cheney Vice Presidency*, New York: Penguin.

Gellman, B. and Becker, J. (2007) "A Different Understanding with the President," *Washington Post*, June 24, A01.

Ginbar, Y. (2008) *Why Not Torture Terrorists?* Oxford: Oxford University Press.

Ginsburg, J. (2006) "A Decent Respect to the Opinions of [Human]kind," Address on the Value of a Comparative Perspective in Constitutional Adjudication to the Constitutional Court of South Africa, February 7.

Goldsmith, J. (2007) *The Terror Presidency: Law and Judgment inside the Bush Administration*, New York: W. W. Norton & Co.

Goldsmith, L. (2003) "Legal Basis for the Use of Force," UK Foreign and Commonwealth Office (March 17); reprinted in *The International and Comparative Law Quarterly*, 52 (3): 811–814.

Greenberg, K. and Dratel, J. (eds) (2005) *The Torture Papers: The Road to Abu Ghraib*, Cambridge: Cambridge University Press.

Grotius, H. (1925) *"De Jure Belli ac Pacis,"* James Brown Scott (ed.), *The Classics of International Law*, Oxford: Clarendon Press.

Guiora, A. (2013) *Legitimate Target: A Criteria-Based Approach to Targeted Killing*, Oxford: Oxford University Press.

Haass, R. (2002) "Reflections a Year after September 11," Remarks to International Institute for Strategic Studies' 2002 Annual Conference, London, September 13.

Habermas, J. (1976) *Legitimation Crisis*, trans. T. McCarthy, London: Heinemann Educational Books.

Hamilton, A., Madison, J., Jay, J., Rossiter, C., and Kesle, C. (2006) *Federalist and Anti-Federalist Papers*, USA: BN Publishing.

Hamilton, B. (1963) *Political Thought in Sixteenth-Century Spain*, Oxford: The Clarendon Press.

Hart, H. L. A. (1954) "Introduction," in J. Austin, *The Province of Jurisprudence Determined and the Uses of the Study of Jurisprudence*, London: Weidenfeld & Nicolson, pp. vii–xxi.

Hart, H. L. A. (1958) "Positivism and the Separation of Law and Morals," *Harvard Law Review*, 71 (4): 593–629.

Hart, H. L. A. (1994) *The Concept of Law*, Oxford: Clarendon Press.

Heintze, H. (2004) "On the Relationship between Human Rights Law Protection and International Humanitarian Law," *International Review of the Red Cross*, 86 (856): 789–803.

Henckaerts, J. and Doswald-Beck, L. (2005) *Customary International Humanitarian Law*, 2 vols., Cambridge: Cambridge University Press.

Heureux-Dubé, C. (1998) "The Importance of Dialogue: Globalization and the International Impact of the Rehnquist Court," *Tulsa Law Journal*, 34 (15): 15–40.

Higham, S. (2004) "Law Experts Condemn US Memos on Torture," *Washington Post*, August 5, A04.

Hobbes, T. (1991) *Leviathan*, (ed. Richard Tuck), Cambridge: Cambridge University Press.

Holder, E. (2012) Attorney General, Speech delivered to Northwestern University School of Law, Chicago, Ill., March 5.

Holder, E. (2013) Attorney General, Letter to Members of Congress, Chairman of the Committee to the Judiciary, May 22, available at www.nytimes.com/interactive/2013/05/23/us/politics/23holder-drone-lettter.html?_r=0 (accessed June 2013).

Hopfl, H. and Thompson, M. (1979) "The History of Contract as Motif in Political Thought," *American History Review*, 84 (4): 919–944.

Horne, A. (1977) *A Savage War of Peace: Algeria 1954–1962*, London: Macmillan.

Horton, S. (2008) "The Case for Impeachment," *Harper's Magazine*, February, available at http://harpers.org/blog/2008/02/the-case-for-impeachment (accessed June 2013).

Human Rights Watch (2003) "Off Target: The Conduct of the War and Civilian Casualties in Iraq," available at www.hrw.org/node/12207/section/2 (accessed June 2013).

Hume, D. (2006) *A Treatise of Human Nature*, Charleston, SC: BiblioBazaar.

Hummel, D. (2007) "BYU Campus Protests Dick Cheney Speech," *The Associated Press*, April 2.

Hurd, I. (2011) "Law and the Practice of Diplomacy," *International Journal*, 66 (3): 581–596.

Ignatieff, M. (2004) *The Lesser Evil: Political Ethics in an Age of Terror*, Princeton, NJ: Princeton University Press.

Independent International Commission on Kosovo (2000) *The Kosovo Report*, Oxford: Oxford University Press.

International Committee of the Red Cross (2004) "Treatment by the Coalition Forces of Prisoners of War and Other Protected Persons by the Geneva Conventions in Iraq during Arrest, Internment and Interrogation," February, available at www.cbsnews.com/htdocs/pdf/redcrossabuse.pdf (accessed June 2013).

International Committee of the Red Cross (2007) "Confidential Report: Treatment of Fourteen 'High Value Detainees,' in CIA Custody," February, available at www.nybooks.com/media/doc/2010/04/22/icrc-report.pdf (accessed June 2013).

Iraq Survey Group (2004) Comprehensive Report of the Special Advisor to the DCI on Iraq's WMD, with Addendums (Duelfer Report), April 25, available at www.gpo.gov/fdsys/search/pagedetails.action?granuleId=&packageId=GPO-DUELFERREPORT&fromBrowse=true (accessed June 2013).

Isikoff, M. (2009) "'We Could Have Done This the Right Way': How Ali Soufan, an FBI agent, got Abu Zubaydah to Talk without Torture," *Newsweek*, May 4, available at www.newsweek.com/id/195089 (accessed June 2013).

Jackson, V. (2004) "Comparative Constitutional Federalism and Transnational Judicial Discourse," *International Journal of Constitutional Law*, 2 (1): 91–138.

Jenkins, B. (1975) "International Terrorism: A New Mode of Conflict," in David Carlton and Carlo Schoerf (eds), *International Terrorism and World Security*, London: Croom Helm, pp. 13–49.

Johnson, J. (2012) "The Conflict against Al Qaeda and Its Affiliates: How Will It End?," Speech delivered at Oxford University, Oxford, November 30.

Johnstone, I. (2011) *The Power of Deliberation: International Law Politics and Organizations*, Oxford: Oxford University Press.

Joseph Loomis, A., "Legitimacy Norms as Change Agents: Examining the Role of the Public Voice" in Falk, R., Juergensmeyer, M., and Popovski, V. (eds) (2012) *Legality and Legitimacy in Global Affairs*, Oxford: Oxford University Press, pp. 72–91.

Jouvenel, B. (1949) *On Power, Its Nature and the History of Its Growth*, trans. J. F. Huntington, New York: Viking Press.

Kant, I. (1991a) "The Metaphysics of Morals: The Theory of Right, Part II—Public Right," in *Political Writings*, ed. Hans Reiss, Cambridge: Cambridge University Press, pp. 131–175.

Kant, I. (1991b) "Perpetual Peace: A Philosophical Sketch," in *Political Writings*, ed. Hans Reiss, Cambridge: Cambridge University Press, pp. 93–130.

Kant, I. (2010) *Fundamental Principles of the Metaphysic of Morals*, trans. Thomas Kingsmill Abbott, University Park, Penn.: Electronic Classic Series Publication.

Kennedy, E. (2002) "Military Consequences of War with Iraq," Senate Floor Statement, October 8, 107th Congress, 2nd Session, Congressional Record 148 (131).

Kilcullen, D. (2009) *The Accidental Guerilla: Fighting Small Wars in the Midst of a Big One*, Oxford: Oxford University Press.

Koh, H. (2013) "How to End the Forever War?" Speech delivered at Oxford University, Oxford, May 7.

Kolb, R. (2004) "Self-Defence and Preventive War at the Beginning of the Millennium," *Zeitschrift für öffentliches Recht*, 59 (2): 111–134.

Krulak, C. and Hoar, J. (2007) "It's Our Cage Too: Torture Betrays Us and Breeds New Enemies," *Washington Post*, May 17.

Kull, S., Ramsey, C., and Lewis, E. (2003/2004) "Misperceptions, the Media, and the Iraq War," *Political Science Quarterly*, 118 (4): 569–598.

Landay, J. (2013) "Obama's Drone War Kills 'Others,' Not Just Al Qaeda Leaders," *McClatchy Newspapers*, April 9.

Lapham, L. (2006) "The Case for Impeachment: Why We Can No Longer Afford George W. Bush," *Harper's Magazine*, March.

Laqueur, W. (1977) *Terrorism*, London: Weidenfeld & Nicolson.

Lemann, N. (2002) "The Next World Order: The Bush Administration May Have a Brand-New Doctrine of Power," *The New Yorker*, April 1, available at www.newyorker.com/archive/2002/04/01/020401fa_FACT1 (accessed June 2013).

Lepsius, O. (2006) "Human Dignity and the Downing of Aircraft: The German Federal Constitutional Court Strikes Down a Prominent Anti-Terrorism Provision in the New Air-Transport Security Act," *German Law Journal*, 7 (9): 761–776.

Leung, R. (2004) "Abuse of Iraqi POWs by GIs Probed: 60 Minutes II Has Exclusive Report on Alleged Mistreatment," April 28, available at www.cbsnews.com/stories/2004/04/27/60ii/main614063.shtml (accessed June 2013).

Liptak, A. (2004) "Legal Scholars Criticize Memos on Torture," *New York Times*, June 25, available at www.nytimes.com/2004/06/25/world/the-reach-of-war-penal-law-legal-scholars-criticize-memos-on-torture.html (accessed June 2013).

Lobe, J. (2006) "POLITICS-US: Most Now Say Iraq Invasion Was a "War of Choice," Inter Press Service News Agency, March 15, available at www.highbeam.com/doc/1P1–119916404.html (accessed June 2013).

Lobel, J. and Ratner, M. (1999) "Bypassing the Security Council: Ambiguous Authorizations to Use Force, Cease-Fires and the Iraqi Inspection Regime," *The American Journal of International Law*, 93 (1): 124–154.

Long War Journal (2013), available at www.longwarjournal.org/about.php (accessed June 2013).

Martin, C. (2012), "Going Medieval: Targeted Killing, Self-Defense and the *Jus as Bellum* Regime," in Finkelstein, C., Ohlin, J., and Altman, A. (eds) *Targeted Killing: Law and Morality in an Asymmetrical World*, Oxford: Oxford University Press, pp. 223–252.

Maris, G. (1967) "International Law and Guantánamo," *The Journal of Politics*, 29 (2): 261–286.

Mayer, J. (2008) *The Dark Side: The Inside Story of How the War on Terror Turned into a War on American Ideals*, New York: Doubleday.

Mazzetti, M. (2013) *The Way of the Knife: The CIA, a Secret Army, and a War at the Ends of the Earth*, New York: Penguin.

McCrudden, C. (2000) "A Common Law of Human Rights? Transnational Judicial Conversations on Constitutional Rights," *Oxford Journal of Legal Studies*, 20 (4): 499–532.

Mead, W. R. (1999/2000) "The Jacksonian Tradition and American Foreign Policy," *The National Interest*, Winter, 58: 5–30.

Melzer, N. (2008) *Targeted Killing in International Law*, Oxford: Oxford University Press.

Mickum, B. (2009) "The Truth about Abu Zubaydah," *The Guardian*, March 30.

Nance, M. (2007) "Waterboarding Is Torture … Period," *Small War Journal*, October 31.

National Intelligence Council (2007), National Intelligence Estimate, "Iran: Nuclear Intentions and Capabilities," November, available at http://graphics8.nytimes.com/packages/pdf/international/20071203_release.pdf (accessed June 2013).

Neuharth, A. (2007) "Mea Culpa to Bush on President's Day: Bush Is Worst President of All-Time," *USA Today*, February 16, p. 15A.

New America Foundation (2013) Year of the Drone Project, available at http://counterterrorism.newamerica.net/drones (accessed June 2013).

Nowak, M. and McArthur, E. (2008) *The United Nations Convention against Torture: A Commentary*, Oxford: Oxford University Press.

Nye, J. (2008) "Public Diplomacy and Soft Power," *Annals of the American Academy of Political and Social Science*, 616 (1): 94–109.

Obama, B. (2002) "Transcript: Obama's Speech against the Iraq War," Federal Plaza, Chicago, October 2.

Obama, B. (2006) "Homeland Security," Senate Floor Statement, September 27, 109th Congress, 2nd Session, Congressional Record 152(123).

Obama, B. (2009a) Executive Order No. 13, 491, 74 Fed. Reg. 4, 893, "Ensuring Lawful Interrogations" (January 22).

Obama, B. (2009b) Executive Order No. 13, 492, 74 Fed. Reg. 4, 897, "Review and Disposition of Individuals Detained at the Guantanamo Naval Base and Closure of Detention Facilities" (January 22).

Obama, B. (2013) "The Future of Our Fight against Terrorism," Speech delivered at National Defense University, Washington, DC, May 23.

Odom, W. (2007) "Bush Has Gone AWOL," Democratic Radio Address, April 28.

O'Driscoll, C. (2008) *Renegotiation of the Just War Tradition and the Right to War in the Twenty-First Century*, New York: Palgrave Macmillan.

Open Society Justice Initiative (2013) "Globalizing Torture: CIA Secret Detention and Extraordinary Rendition," February, available at www.opensocietyfoundations.org/reports/globalizing-torture-cia-secret-detention-and-extraordinary-rendition (accessed June 2013).

Ost, F. and Kerchove, M. (2002) *De la pyramide au réseau? Pour une théorie dialectique du droit*, Brussels: Publications des Facultés Universitaires Saint-Louis.

Pachios, H. (2002) "The New Diplomacy," Remarks to Woodrow Wilson School of Public and International Affairs, Princeton University, Princeton, NJ, April 24.

Packer, G. (2005) *The Assassins Gate: America in Iraq*, New York: Farrar, Straus & Giroux.

Philbin, P. and Yoo, J. (2001) "Re: Possible Habeas Jurisdiction over Aliens Held in Guantánamo Bay, Cuba" (December 28); reprinted in K. Greenberg and J. Dratel (eds), *The Torture Papers: The Road to Abu Ghraib*, Cambridge: Cambridge University Press, 2005, pp. 29–37.

Pictet, J. (1960) *The Geneva Conventions of 12 August 1949, Commentary*, 4 vols., Geneva: International Committee of the Red Cross.

Piirmäe, P. (2002) "Just War in Theory and Practice: The Legitimation of Swedish Intervention in the Thirty Years War," *The Historical Journal*, 45 (3): 499–523.

PollingReport.com (2001–2008) "Bush: Job Rating" and "PRESIDENT BUSH: Overall Job Rating," available at www.pollingreport.com/BushJob1.htm (accessed June 2013).

Pompe, C. A. (1953) *Aggressive War: An International Crime*, The Hague: Martinus Nijhoff.

Popp, R. (2006) "Stumbling Decidedly into the Six-Day War," *Middle East Journal,* 60 (2): 281–309.

Posner, E. and Vermeule, A. (2007) *Terror in the Balance: Security, Liberty, and the Courts,* Oxford: Oxford University Press.

Powell, C. (2002) "Draft Decision Memorandum for the President on the Applicability of the Geneva Convention to the Conflict in Afghanistan" (January 26); reprinted in K. Greenberg and J. Dratel (eds), *The Torture Papers: The Road to Abu Ghraib,* Cambridge: Cambridge University Press, 2005, pp. 122–125.

Powell, C. (2003) "A Policy of Evasion and Deception: Address to the United Nations Security Council," February 5, available at www.guardian.co.uk/world/2003/feb/05/iraq.usa (accessed June 2013).

Pufendorf, S. (1703) *Of the Law of Nature and Nations,* (trans. and ed. Basil Kennet), Oxford: L. Lichfield.

Quainton, A. (1983) "Terrorism and Political Violence: A Permanent Challenge to Governments," in M. Crenshaw, *Terrorism, Legitimacy, and Power: The Consequences of Political Violence,* Middletown, Conn.: Wesleyan University Press, pp. 52–64.

Quinn, P. (2011) Statement on Senate Bill 3539 "Abolishing the Death Penalty in Illinois," March 9, available at www3.illinois.gov/PressReleases/ShowPressRelease.cfm?SubjectID=2&RecNum=9265 (accessed June 2013).

Rawls, J. (1999) *A Theory of Justice,* Cambridge, Mass.: The Belknap Press of Harvard University Press.

RealClearPolitics.com, President Bush Job Approval, available at www.realclearpolitics.com/polls/archive/?poll_id=19#polls (accessed June 2013).

Rehnquist, W. (2002) "Remarks of the Chief Justice to Court of Appeals for the Federal Circuit, 20th Anniversary Judicial Conference," April 8, available at www.supremecourt.gov/publicinfo/speeches/viewspeeches.aspx?Filename=sp_04–08–02a.html (accessed June 2013).

Rejali, D. (2007) *Torture and Democracy,* Princeton, NJ: Princeton University Press.

Repko, A. (2012) *Interdisciplinary Research: Process and Theory,* Thousand Oaks, Calif.: Sage.

Richardson, L. (2006) *What Terrorists Want,* New York: Random House.

Roberts, A. (2003) "International Law and the Iraq War 2003: Memorandum from Professor Sir Adam Roberts," Session 2002–2003, House of Commons, Foreign Affairs Committee Publications, available at www.parliament.the-stationery-office.co.uk/pa/cm200203/cmselect/cmfaff/405/405we20.htm (accessed June 2013).

Roberts, A. (2006) "Just Peace: A Cause Worth Fighting For," in Pierre Allan and Alexis Keller (eds), *What Is a Just Peace?* Oxford: Oxford University Press, pp. 52–89.

Roberts, A. (2007) "Transformative Military Occupation: Applying the Laws of War and Human Rights," in J. Pejic and M. N. Schmitt (eds), *International Law and Armed Conflict: Exploring the Faultlines,* The Netherlands: Koninklijke Brill BV, pp. 439–495.

Roberts, A. (2008) "Countering Terrorism: A Historical Perspective," in A. Bianchi and A. Keller (eds), *Counterterrorism: Democracy's Challenge,* Oxford: Hart Publishing, pp. 3–41.

Rodley, N. with Pollard, M. (2009) *The Treatment of Prisoners under International Law,* 3rd edn, Oxford: Oxford University Press.

Rumble, W. (1965) "Legal Realism, Sociological Jurisprudence and Mr. Justice Holmes," *Journal of the History of Ideas,* October–December, 26(4): 547–566.

Safire, W. (2008) "Waterboarding," *New York Times Magazine*, March 9, available at www.nytimes.com/2008/03/09/magazine/09wwlnSafire-t.html (accessed June 2013).

Sands, P. (2005) *Lawless World: America and the Making and Breaking of Global Rules from FDR's Atlantic Charter to George W. Bush's Illegal War*, New York: Viking.

Sands, P. (2008) *Torture Team: Rumsfeld's Memo and the Betrayal of American Values*, New York: Palgrave Macmillan.

Sauer, M. (2007) "Generals Opposing Iraq War Break with Military Tradition," *San Diego Union Tribune*, September 23.

Savage, C. and Bowley, G. (2012) "US to Retain Role as Jailer in Afghanistan," *New York Times*, September 5.

Schell, J. (2003) *The Unconquerable World: Power Nonviolence, and the Will of the People*, New York: Metropolitan Books.

Schmidt, R. and Furlow, J. (2005) *Schmidt-Furlow Report: Investigation into FBI Allegations of Detainee Abuse at Guantanamo Bay, Cuba Detention Facility*, April 1 (amended June 9).

Scobbie, I. (2008) " 'The Last Refuge of the Tyrant?' Judicial Deference to the Executive in Time of Terror," in A. Bianchi and A. Keller (eds), *Counterterrorism: Democracy's Challenge*, Oxford: Hart Publishing, pp. 277–312.

Scott, J. B. (1934) *The Spanish Origin of International Law: Francisco de Vitoria and His Law of Nations*, Oxford: The Clarendon Press.

Shah, P. Z. (2012) "My Drone War," *Foreign Policy*, March/April, available at. www.foreignpolicy.com/articles/2012/02/27/my_drone_war (accessed June 2013).

Simonson, K. (2003) "The Anti-War Movement: Waging Peace on the Brink of War," (Geneva) Researcher Associate at CASIN, Report for the Programme on NGOs and Civil Society of the Centre for Applied Studies in International Negotiation.

Slaughter, A. (2003) "A Global Community of Courts," *Harvard International Law Journal*, 44 (1): 191–219.

Slaughter, A. (2004) *A New World Order*, Princeton, NJ: Princeton University Press.

Slomanson, W. (2003) *Fundamental Perspectives on International Law*, Belmont, Calif.: Wadsworth/Thompson Learning.

Soufan, A. (2009) Testimony before the US Senate Judicial Committee, Subcommittee on Administrative Oversight and the Courts, "What Went Wrong: Torture and the Office of Legal Counsel in the Bush Administration," May 13, available at http://judiciary.senate.gov/hearings/hearing.cfm?id=3842 (accessed June 2009).

Soufan, A. (2011) *Black Banners: The Inside Story of 9/11 and the War against al-Qaeda*, New York: W. W. Norton & Co.

Statman, D. (1997) "The Absoluteness of the Prohibition against Torture," [Hebrew] *Mishpat u-Mimshal*, 4: 161–198.

Steyn, L. (2004) "Guantanamo Bay: The Legal Black Hole," *International and Comparative Law Quarterly*, 53 (1): 1–15.

Suskind, R. (2006) *The One Percent Doctrine: Deep inside America's Pursuit of Its Enemies since 9/11*, New York: Simon & Schuster.

Taguba, A. (2004) *The Taguba Report: On Treatment of Abu Ghraib Prisoners in Iraq*, "Article 15–16 Investigation of the 800th Military Police Brigade," available at www.npr.org/iraq/2004/prison_abuse_report.pdf (accessed June 2013).

Taguba, A. (2008) "Preface to Broken Laws, Broken Lives," *Report by Physicians for Human Rights*, June, available at http://brokenlives.info/?page_id=23 (accessed June 2013).

Tapper, J. (2007) "Political Punch: General Discontent," May 9, available at http:// abcnews.go.com/blogs/politics/2007/05/general_discont (accessed June 2013).

Thai, J. (2006) "The Law Clerk Who Wrote Rasul v. Bush: John Paul Stevens's Influence from World War II to the War on Terror," *Virginia Law Review*, 92 (3): 501–529.

Thatcher, M. (1985) Speech at Albert Hall, South Kensington, to the American Bar Association, July 15.

Thompson, R. (1966) *Defeating Communist Insurgency: Experiences from Malaya and Vietnam*, London: Chatto & Windus.

Thucydides (1989) *The Peloponnesian War: The Complete Hobbes Translation*, ed. D. Grene, Chicago, Ill.: University of Chicago Press.

Thucydides (1998) *The Landmark Thucydides: A Comprehensive Guide to the Peloponnesian War*, ed. R. Strassler, New York: Touchstone.

Tuck, R. (1999) *The Rights of War and Peace: Political Thought and the International Order from Grotius to Kant*, Oxford: Oxford University Press.

Turner Johnson, J. (1975) *Ideology, Reason and the Limitation of War: Religious and Secular Concepts, 1200–1740*, Princeton, NJ: Princeton University Press.

Turner Johnson, J. (1981) *Just War Tradition and the Restraint of War*, Princeton, NJ: Princeton University Press.

Tyler, P. (2003) "Threats and Responses: News Analysis—A New Power in the Streets," *New York Times*, February 17.

US Army (1992) *Intelligence Interrogation*, Field Manual 34–52, Washington, DC: Department of the Army, available at www.loc.gov/rr/frd/Military_Law/pdf/ intel_interrrogation_sept-1992.pdf (accessed June 2013).

US Army (2006) *Counterinsurgency*, Field Manual 3–24, Washington, DC: Department of the Army, available at www.fas.org/irp/doddir/army/fm3–24.pdf (accessed June 2013).

US Army Personnel (2002–2003), Interrogation Log of Detainee 063, available at www.time.com/time/2006/log/log.pdf (accessed June 2013).

US Department of Defense (2001) *Dictionary of Military and Associated Terms*, Joint Publication 1–02, April 12 (amended October 31, 2009), available at http://jitc. fhu.disa.mil/jitc_dri/pdfs/jp1_02.pdf (accessed June 2013).

US Department of Defense (2010) *Dictionary of Military and Associated Terms*, Joint Publication 1–02, November 8 (amended December 31), available at www.dtic. mil/doctrine/new_pubs/jp1_02.pdf (accessed June 2013).

US Department of Justice (2009) *Investigation into the Office of Legal Counsel's Memoranda Concerning Issues Relating to the Central Intelligence Agency's Use of "Enhanced Interrogation Techniques" on Suspected Terrorists*, Office of Professional Responsibility (Final) Report, July 29.

US Department of Justice (2011) "Lawfulness of a Lethal Operation Directed against a US Citizen Who Is a Senior Operational Leader of Al-Qa'ida or an Associated Force," White Paper, draft copy, Office of Legal Counsel, November 8, available at http://msnbcmedia.msn.com/i/msnbc/sections/news/020413_ DOJ_White_Paper.pdf (accessed June 2013).

US Senate Armed Services Committee (2008) "Inquiry into the Treatment of Detainees in US Custody," November 20, available at www.armed-services.senate. gov/Publications/Detainee%20Report%20Final_April%2022%202009.pdf (accessed June 2013).

US Senate Select Committee on Intelligence (2006), "Postwar Findings about

Iraq's WMD Programs and Links to Terrorism and How They Compare with Prewar Assessments: Together with Additional Views" (September 8), available at www.fas.org/irp/congress/2006_rpt/srpt109-331.pdf (accessed June 2013).

US Senate Select Committee on Intelligence (2008) "Report on Whether Public Statements Regarding Iraq by U.S. Government Officials Were Substantiated by Intelligence Information together with Additional and Minority Views," 110th Congress, 2nd Session, Second Part of Phase II Inquiry, June 2008, available at www.fas.org/irp/congress/2006_rpt/srpt109-331.pdf (accessed June 2013).

US Senate Select Committee on Intelligence (2009) in conjunction with the Justice Department "Release of Declassified Narrative Describing the Department of Justice Office of Legal Counsel's Opinions on the CIA's Detention and Interrogation Program," April 22, available at www.intelligence.senate.gov/pdfs/olcopinion.pdf (accessed June 2013).

Vattel, E. (2003) *The Law of Nations or the Principles of Natural Law in Four Books*, J. Chitty (trans.), Michigan: Lonang Institute.

Wallach, E. (2007) "Drop by Drop: Forgetting the History of Water Torture in US Courts," *Columbia Journal of Transnational Law*, 45 (468): 471–506.

Walzer, M. (1977) *Just and Unjust Wars*, 3rd edn, New York: Basic Books.

Waters, M. (2007) "Creeping Monism: The Judicial Trend toward Interpretive Incorporation of Human Rights Treaties," *Columbia Law Review*, 107 (3): 628–705.

Weber, M. (1946) "Politics as a Vocation," in *From Max Weber: Essays on Sociology*, ed. and trans. H. H. Gerth and C. Wright Mills, Oxford: Oxford University Press, 1946.

Weber, M. (1947) *The Theory of Social and Economic Organization*, trans. A. M. Henderson and T. Parsons, New York: The Free Press.

Weber, M. (1954) *Law in Economy and Society*, ed. M. Rheinstein, Cambridge, Mass.: Harvard University Press.

Webster, D. (1906) US Secretary of State, The *Caroline* Incident (1842), reprinted in *Digest of International Law*, 2: 409–413.

Wedgwood, R. (1998) "The Enforcement of Security Council Resolution 687: The Threat of Force against Iraq's Weapons of Mass Destruction," *The American Journal of International Law*, October, 92 (4): 724–728.

Wheeler, N. (2003) "The Bush Doctrine: The Dangers of American Exceptionalism in a Revolutionary Age," *Asian Perspective*, 27 (4): 183–216.

White House (2002) "The National Security Strategy of the United States of America," September, available at www.state.gov/documents/organization/63562.pdf (accessed June 2013).

Wight, M. (1992) *International Theory: The Three Traditions*, New York: Holmes & Meier.

Wilentz, S. (2006) "The Worst President in History? One of America's Leading Historians Assesses George W. Bush," *Rolling Stone Magazine*, April 19.

Wilson, S. (2009) "'Global War on Terror' Is Given New Name," *The Washington Post* March 25.

Woodward, B. (2009) "Detainee Tortured, Says US Official: Trial Overseer Cites 'Abusive' Methods against 9/11 Suspect," *Washington Post*, January 14, A01.

Xenophon (1994) *Memorabilia*, ed. and trans. A. Bonnette, Ithaca, NY: Cornell University Press.

Yoo, J. (2001) "The President's Constitutional Authority to Conduct Military

Operations against Terrorists and Nations Supporting Them" (September 25); reprinted in K. Greenberg and J. Dratel (eds), *The Torture Papers: The Road to Abu Ghraib*, Cambridge: Cambridge University Press, 2005, pp. 3–24.

Yoo, J. (2004) "Using Force," *University of Chicago Law Review*, 71 (3): 729–797.

Yoo, J. (2006) "Sending a Message: Congress to Courts—Get Out of the War on Terror," Editorial, *The Wall Street Journal*, October 19.

Yoo, J. and Delabunty, R. (2002) "Re: Application of Treaties and Laws to al Qaeda and Taliban Detainees" (January 9); reprinted in K. Greenberg and J. Dratel (eds), *The Torture Papers: The Road to Abu Ghraib*, Cambridge: Cambridge University Press, 2005, pp. 38–79.

Zagorin, A. (2006) "Detainee 063: A Broken Man?," *Time Magazine*, March 2, available at www.time.com/time/nation/article/0,8599,1169310,00.html (accessed June 2013).

Zaharna, R. S. (2004) "From Propaganda to Public Diplomacy in the Information Age," in Nancy Snow and Yahya Kamalipour (eds), *War, Media, and Propaganda: A Global Perspective*, New York: Rowman & Littlefield, pp. 219–225.

Zelikow, P. (2009) "The OLC 'Torture Memos': Thoughts from a Dissenter," *Foreign Policy Magazine*, April 21.

Zhou, K. (2007) "Former Classmates Criticize Gonzales: '82 School Alums Publish Open Letter in *Washington Post*," *The Harvard Crimson*, May 16.

Index

Page numbers in **bold** denote figures.

9/11 63, 73, 75, 89, 114, 143, 175–6,
193, 193n1, 242, 244, 260;
anniversary 128; attacks 3, 7, 48, 65,
67, 90, 142, 152, 180, 216, 219, 257,
264; detainees 198, 214; film 94;
hijacker 236, 239, 245; mastermind
128, 239; post-9/11 world 173, 187,
190; reaction to 2, 23, 191, 252;
ringleader 236; victims 216; wake of
90, 114, 260

Aaron, D. 59, 66–7, 69, 72
Abu Ghraib 137, 198; prisoner-abuse
scandal 97; prison facility 87, 201,
254
advocacy 37, 79, 161
Afghanistan 66, 78–80, 114, 136, 146n3,
226, 259; conflict 125; detainees 111,
121, 130, 137–9, 146n4, 147n13, 198,
215, 232, 236; drone strikes 258;
invasion of 65, 103, 152, 213; military
training camps 228; Soviet forces 70,
228; Taliban regime 74, 77, 173; US
forces in 57; wars against 73, 76
Al-Adahi v. *Obama* 140–1
Algeria 212; war of independence
100–1
al-Libi, Ibn al-Shaykh 197, 213–16, 218,
228–9
al-Qaeda 1, 14, 56, 58–9, 66, 70, 80, 123,
143, 206, 215, 236, 252; attacks 65,
208; cell 219; conflict 125–6, 144;
detainees 114, 124, 140, 146n3–4;
group 72, 77, 125; leaders 128;
Manchester Manual 219, 221, 243;
members 78–9, 84, 112, 214, 218,
226, 238, 263; membership 142;

movement 64; operatives 214, 218,
231; organization 9, 197, 220–1, 223,
227, 233, 240, 242, 256; planning
238; regime 213–14; strategists 67,
69, 72; suspected leaders 259;
terrorists 130, 216, 218; training
camps 74, 228, 232
al Qahtani, M. 197, 219, 236–9, 245
Al Maqaleh et al. v. *Gates* 130–40
Alston, P. 258–9, 263
American Bar Association 205
American Convention on Human
Rights 147n10
American Law Institute 113
Aquinas, T. 43, 156–7, 163
Arendt, H. 16, 20, 27–9
armed conflict 6, 8, 13, 72, 76, 84, 86,
93, 104, 112, 125, 127, 131, 134,
136–7, 141, 144, 146n5, 159, 161,
164, 171, 212, 248, 254–5, 258;
authorization 264; initiation of 162;
international 74, 77–8, 258;
noninternational 74, 240; operations
in Iraq 152; US 126
Austin, J. 38, 40–1, 50, 53
Authorization for Use of Military Force
(AUMF) 74, 135–6, 140–2, 144, 257;
Resolution 231

Bacon, F. 148, 161–3, 166, 174, 176, 262
Barak, A. 48, 258
based on suspicion 199, 220, 224, 235,
249, 256, 263
Becker, J. 145, 257
Beetham, D. 16, 24–6, 37, 39, 89
Benvenisti, E. 104–5, 107, 119–20, 122
Bianchi, A. 68, 103, 250

Bin Laden, O. 56, 59, 65, 70, 227
black site 128, 137, 216, 219–20; prison system 240
bombs 34, 66, 182, 199; bombings 65; cluster 152; dirty 209, 223, 230, 235; dirty bombers 229, 231; radioactive 231; suicide bomber 196; terrorist 62; terrorist plot 213; *USS Cole* 216; *see also* ticking bomb
Boumediene v. *Bush* 80, 104–5, 128–41, 227, 232
Bradbury, S. 202, 206, 208–11, 222, 224–5, 240
Bradbury memos 202, 207–9, 224–5
Brennan, J.O. 193, 261–2
Bureau of Investigative Journalism 259
Bush, G.W. 4–5, 57, 65–6, 70, 73–5, 80, 82, 90, 94–5, 111–12, 124, 128, 144–5, 146n3–5, 173–5, 178–9, 182, 193n1, 197, 204–5, 216, 230, 241–2, 248, 252, 255–6; administration 55, 71, 78, 84, 87, 105, 112, 124, 144, 153, 172, 175, 183, 185, 193, 200–1, 203, 213–14, 247–8, 257; Department of Justice 128; Doctrine 150, 153, 155, 172, 175, 191–2, 255; former officials 248; presidency 205; successor 257; White House 75, 173
Bybee, J. 9, 79–80, 201, 220–2, 227
Bybee memo 9, 86, 201, 205, 208–9, 220–3, 228

Canada 109; Supreme Court of Canada 108
Cassese, A. 1, 4, 45, 62–3, 254, 260
Central Intelligence Agency (CIA) 57; Inspector General 206, 210, 225, 230, 240–2; enhanced interrogation program 224, 226; report 206, 210, 230, 241–2
Chemical and Biological Weapons (CBW) 186, 215
Cheney, R. 76–7, 94, 179, 196–7
Cicero 156, 159–60, 167
Clausewitz, K. 1, 6, 27
CNN 67, 179
Cole, D. 92–3
Combatant Status Review Tribunals (CSRT) 120–1, 135, 228
Constitution Project 198, 247
Convention against Torture and Other Cruel, Inhuman or Degrading Treatment or Punishment (CAT) 9,

86–7, 195, 201–3, 206, 208, 211, 247–8, 252
Cook, D. 13, 18, 20, 23
counterinsurgency (COIN) 7, 14, 57; field manual 7, 13, 57
counterinsurgents 14, 57, 101
counterterrorism 18, 42, 45–6, 105, 111, 137, 193, 257–8; actions 75, 253; CIA team 217; detention 137, 141, 144; efforts 104; information-gathering goals 249; interrogation 195, 220; legislation 142; Obama's speech 145, 264; operation 254; policies 2, 4, 11, 14, 22, 25–6, 46, 56, 61, 68, 74–5, 91, 99, 114, 192, 195–6, 201, 204, 247, 257; President's Strategy 262; program 66; project 175; right-wing reaction 71; strategy 252; US policies 72; validity 25; war 88
Crenshaw, M. 17, 68, 71

Denbeaux, M. 120, 140
Dershowitz, A. 244–5
detainee abuse 87–8, 201; photographs 8788, 198, 201, 254; *see also* images
Detainee Treatment Act of 2005 (DTA) 121, 130, 134–6, 204
diplomatic 92, 191–2; agents 62; community 257, 262–3; debate 8, 150, 178; forum 8–9, 76; implications 5, 107, 144, 182, 191, 247; interaction 23; language 169, 181, 240; missions 76; personnel 11; practice 145; pressure 93; problem 8, 103, 193; proceedings 91; relations 80
diplomats 3, 5, 7, 23, 59, 61, 76, 80, 91, 144, 170, 185, 192, 214, 254, 258; foreign 11, 257
drone 4, 192–3, 257, 259–60; attacks 145; campaign 263; equipment 258; killing 4, 263; program 5, 142–3, 145, 153, 173, 193, 258, 260, 262–3; strikes 258–61, 263

Eastern Europe 29
Eban, K. 217
Emmerson, B. 259
Enhanced Interrogation Techniques (EITs) 196, 198, 206–10, 219, 225, 240–2
European Court of Human Rights 46, 85, 107
Evangelicals for Human Rights 95

Federal Bureau of Investigation (FBI)
201, 215, 236–7, 245; agents 216–17,
219, 229, 232–3, 235–6, 244; Director
219; former agent 223; Inspector
General 198, 219–20, 237–8; team
213, 216–17
Ferrero, G. 6, 12, 16, 27, 31–6, 55, 55n1,
5960, 71, 88, 99, 251
Finn, P. 226
France 5960, 101, 109
Franck, T. 16, 30–1, 184
French Army 100–1; colonial authority
212; former Secretary-General 213;
Revolution 59, 62
Front de Libération Nationale 212
Fuller, L. 43, 51–2

General Security Service (GSS) 47
Geneva Conventions 77–8, 92, 97, 107,
112, 119, 122–4, 129, 137, 157, 202,
252; Additional Protocol I 47, 78;
Commentary 80, 126; Common
Article Three 78–9, 84, 106, 123–7,
137, 204–5; GC-III 112, 146n4, 146n7
German 245; Federal Constitutional
Court 48, 245; Nazi 29; philosopher
169; sociologist 13, 21
Germany 109, 195, 245; Nazi 77
Ginbar, Y. 199
Ginsburg, J. 109
Goldsmith, J. 75, 200–1
Goldsmith, L. 188–9
Grotius, H. 43, 148, 165–9, 172, 174,
262
Guantánamo Bay 8, 42, 77, 91, 107,
111, 119, 121, 128, 134, 138, 143,
255, 257
guerrilla groups 219; action 56; warfare
6, 70

Haass, R. 190–1
Habermas, J. 16, 18, 21–3; theory 100;
view 36, 55n1
Hamdan v. *Rumsfeld* 8, 80, 104, 113,
120–30, 137, 146n5, 204
Hamdi v. *Rumsfeld* 105, 114, 120
Hamilton, A. 131
Hamilton, B. 163–4
Hart, H.L.A. 17, 38, 41, 49–53, 150–1,
162
Henckaerts, J. 10, 74, 126, 254
Heureux-Dubé, C. 102, 108
hijack 94, 246; hijackers 63, 236, 239,
245, 256; plane 56, 62, 242, 245–6

Hobbes, T. 37–8, 43, 58, 177
Holder, E. 143, 147n14 261
Horne, A. 212–13
Horton, S. 94
human rights 71–2, 107, 110, 122, 137,
190; abuses 14, 179; American
Convention 147n10; Commission on
85, 146–7n9; conventions 112;
Council 258; Evangelical Declaration
against Torture 95; European Court
46, 85, 107; groups 248; issues 108;
law 2, 22, 45, 47, 73, 77, 85–6, 92,
105–7, 112, 118, 129, 134, 152, 258,
260; lawyers 94, 118; legal obligation
68; monitoring bodies 61; norms 117,
146–7n9; organizations 97;
perspective 117, 136, 139; Physicians
for 96; question 116, 118; scholar
243; treaties 3, 85, 110, 119; Universal
Declaration 85, 87, 118, 147n10; UN
reports 88; victory 119, 134
Human Rights Committee (HRC) 113,
134, 139, 146n8
Human Rights Watch 34

Ignatieff, M. 68–9, 243–4, 251, 264
ill-treatment 78, 85, 87, 210, 214–15,
227, 229, 237, 240–2, 250n1; based
on suspicion 220, 235; of detainees
10, 84, 129, 198; for intelligence-
gathering 96, 196, 243; in
interrogation 76, 84, 144, 152, 206;
legality 91; legislation 205; program
197, 199, 211, 219, 243, 247, 249,
255–6; prohibition 76, 203; threats
233; victim 248
illegitimacy 5, 14, 73, 89
images 2, 37–8, 66, 201, 254; *see also*
photographs
insurgency 34–5, 57, 100, 212
insurgent 14, 64, 152; control 57;
groups 97, 221; suspected 100
international 3, 5; borders 56, 64,
153–4, 192, 258, 261; Court of Justice
74, 78–9, 125, 260; courts 49, 84, 195,
206, 248; diplomacy 83; legal
obligations 10, 75, 88, 103, 108, 111,
129, 145, 184; organizations 254;
relations 81, 151; scholar 16, 30
International Commission 191;
Responsibility to Protect 189
International Committee of the Red
Cross (ICRC) 10, 198, 232, 240
international community 23, 62, 83, 98,

180, 184, 190, 192; legality 62, 106,
201, 205; norms 22, 31, 104, 111, 122;
society 5, 23, 81, 149, 184, 191
International Convention on Civil and
Political Rights 110, 112–13, 118, 134
International Convention for the
Protection of All Persons from
Enforced Disappearance 240
International Court of Justice 74, 78–9,
125, 260
International Criminal Court 107;
Coalition 248; Rome Statute 248,
259–60
International Criminal Tribunal for
Ex-Yugoslavia 62, 78–9, 84, 86, 124–5
international humanitarian law 3, 8, 10,
74, 7779, 85, 105, 126127, 236, 254,
263
international law 4–5, 10–11, 15, 22–3,
31, 45, 56, 72, 76, 78, 80, 82–3, 88,
92–3, 103–5, 107, 110–11, 122, 127,
131, 136–7, 144, 150–1, 155–7, 164,
169, 178, 183, 186, 200–1, 248, 252,
254, 258, 260; American Society of
109; beginnings of 156, 163, 165,
172, 192, 255; codified 184–5;
community 263; contemporary 154,
159; customary 7, 62, 113, 125–6,
187; defied 97–8; definition of
terrorism 61–3; detainee treatment
77, 84–5, 87; framework 73, 75, 254;
initiators 43; interpretation 83, 89,
123–4; public 3, 109, 185; rules of 2,
259; secularized 161; self-defense
176; on torture 9, 95, 195; use of
force 81; violations 30; of war 8
international lawyers 1, 4–5, 73, 149,
152, 165, 257–8
interrogation 4–5, 54, 88, 98, 201, 210,
214–18, 227–8, 231–5, 241; abusive
54, 87, 96, 103, 144, 152, 199, 202,
205, 213, 229; accounts of 64;
aggressive 237, 239; CIA program 96,
209, 211; coercive 196, 200, 205–7,
211, 229; counterterrorism 195, 208,
220; enhanced program 224, 226;
enhanced techniques 196, 208, 223,
224, 226; illegality of ill-treatment 76,
84; ill-treatment during 152, 206;
legal methods 244, 257; legislation
204–5; methods of 47–8; practices
236; program 203, 206, 209, 217, 224,
226; standards 230; of suspected
terrorists 222; team 221, 224, 238;

techniques 205; treatment during
197; US policies 97; *see also* Enhanced
Interrogation Techniques
Iraq 214, 255; cease-fire agreement
186–7, 189; drone strikes 258;
invasion of 8–9, 34, 57, 65, 82,
149–50, 152, 169, 178–9, 181–2,
184–6, 190–1, 213; military action
against 83, 185; prisoner abuse 198,
201, 254; Survey Group 82, 176; war
66, 73, 256; weapons of mass
destruction 186, 188; weapons
training 215
Iraqi 179; compliance 187; detention
facility 198; government 186; military
34, 180; regime 192, 218
Isikoff, M. 216217, 219
Israel Public Committee against
Torture 47, 258
Israeli High Court of Justice 258

Jackson, V. 107, 145n2
Jenkins, B. 1, 60, 64
jihad 59, 65, 228–9; jihadis 69, 213;
military training 227
jihadist 226; movement 229; prisoners
216
Johnstone, I. 23, 178
Jouvenel, B. 27
Justice 109; Canada 108–9; European
Court of Justice 109; Open Society
Justice Initiative 198; Permanent
Court of International Justice
(PCIJ) 81; Uniform Code of Military
Justice (UCMJ) 77, 97, 123–4, 137;
US Department 75, 128, 138–9,
146n3, 146n5, 206, 209, 228, 247–8,
261
Justices 109–10; Alito 109; Breyer 109;
Chief 108–9; Ginsburg 109; Heureux-
Dubé (Canada) 108; Jackson 145n2;
Judge Robertson 123; Kennedy
109–10, 127, 130–3, 135–6, 139, 230;
Rehnquist 108; Roberts 109;
Rutledge 116, 118; Scalia 109–10,
132; Stevens 114, 116–19, 121, 123,
141, 230; Thomas 109
justification 4, 19, 60, 88, 149, 225, 230,
241, 253, 260; for invasion of Iraq
179, 190; legal 87, 103, 192–3, 225,
252, 264; moral 157, 256; rational 21;
reasonable 208; sanctioned 150; for
self-defense 160; for use of force 171;
of war 159, 161, 164, 166, 192

Kant, I. 44, 169–72; Kantian 48, 245
Kennedy, E. 180
killings 197; enemies killed 264;
    targeted 258, 263
Koh, H. 144, 201
Kosovo Independent International
    Commission 191; NATO intervention
    190–1
Krulak, C. 96, 256
Kull, S. 83, 150

Landay, J. 263
Laqueur, W. 2, 15, 59
Latif v. *Obama* 140–1
League of Nations 81
Lebanon 216; Cedar Revolution 29;
    Special Tribunal Appeals Chamber
    623
legitimacy 2, 4, 13, 19, 24, 28, 33–4, 38,
    41; of authority 27, 91, 99; belief in
    20–2, 25; claims 13, 23; component
    of 6, 29–30, 47, 55n1; concept of 6,
    14–18, 20, 25–6, 32, 36, 39, 98;
    content of 6–7, 15, 23, 36, 49, 54–5;
    critical in terrorism 18, 71; deficit 4,
    13, 35–6, 57, 73, 88–91, 95, 98, 203,
    256; definition of 24, 29; domestic 5;
    government 6, 8, 13, 21, 31, 35, 44–6,
    55, 55n1, 57–8, 80, 88, 94, 99–100,
    191, 243–4, 247, 249–50, 253–4, 256;
    model of 39, 46, 54, 102; moral
    100–1; nature of 7, 26, 39; principles
    of 12, 32, 88; reduced 36; of a regime
    17–18, 20, 26, 151; target 67, 11,
    1516, 31, 36, 87, 243, 251, 264;
    taxonomy of 31, 37; tests 10;
    tripartite structure 25, 39
Lepsius, O. 48, 245–6
Lieber Code 74
Lobel, J. 186–7

Mayer, J. 198, 213, 215–17, 223, 226,
    240
Mazzetti, M. 259, 263
media 3, 9, 67, 185, 222–3, 230, 235;
    accounts 97; attention 68; coverage
    66, 88; French 101; interviews 233;
    leaks 193; mainstream 83, 179; mass
    60; sources 61; US 1; war 70, 72
Melzer, N. 258, 264
Mickum, B. 226–7
Military Commissions Act (MCA)
    128–30, 134–6, 139
Mohamed, B. 197, 230–4, 250n2

Moussaoui, Z. 244–5
Muslim 65–6, 69; community 72;
    groups 226; lands 228; population
    67, 101; religion 217

Nance, M. 222–3
National Defense Authorization Act for
    Fiscal Year 2012 137–8, 141
National Intelligence Council 176
National Security Strategy 83, 175, 193
New America Foundation 259
nongovernmental organizations
    (NGOs) 11, 93, 96, 259; reports 254,
    260
North American Free Trade Agreement
    (NAFTA) 107

Obama, B. 4, 57, 90, 136–7, 139, 141,
    143–5, 180, 193, 220, 257, 259–60,
    264; administration 5, 8, 55, 107, 139,
    140, 142–5, 153, 173, 192–3, 201–3,
    239, 247–8, 257, 260–3;
    counterterrorism speech 145, 264;
    Department of Justice 139; Doctrine
    191–2; drone program 193, 258, 263;
    policies 5, 139; presidency 239, 260
Office of Legal Counsel (OLC) 9, 75,
    80, 206, 221, 252; lawyers 79, 200,
    202, 220, 222; member 201; memos
    78, 87, 205, 220, 242, 248, 257, 261;
    opinions 203; White Paper 193
Office of Professional Responsibility
    205–6
Open Society Justice Initiative 198
Operation Iraqi Freedom 269
opposition 101, 170, 180; crushed 29;
    military 95; party 74; political 179;
    vocal 181
Ost, F. 7, 16, 36–9, 42, 44–6, 49

Pachios, H. 34
Padilla, J. 197, 230–1, 233, 235, 247,
    250n1
Pakistan 231, 239, 242, 260, 263;
    Federally Administered Tribal Areas
    259; law-enforcement officers 215;
    nuclear weapons proliferation 176,
    262; US drone strikes 258–9
Pakistani 233; agents 232; officials 213
Palestine 228; Palestinian 215, 258
Paris Minimum Standards 146–7n9
Permanent Court of International
    Justice 81
Petitioner's Brief 126–7

Philbin, P. 77, 111
Pictet, J. 80, 124, 126
Powell, C. 77, 80, 185, 188, 214–15
power 2, 6, 14, 25, 27–8; to command 5, 12, 26–8, 55, 70; executive 75, 93; foreign 212; government 33, 88, 93, 103, 131, 195, 244, 249; growing 155, 168; judicial 118, 135–6, 138, 204; legitimate 15, 26; major 83; military 163, 168; occupying 57–8; political 7; presidential 92, 111, 205; relations 16, 24–6; separation-of-powers 111, 131–2, 135, 138; in wartime 111, 205
Prague Spring 29
preemptive action 173–5; attack 83, 154–5, 173; force 255; policy 153; war 82, 150, 152–3, 158, 161, 165, 172, 185
preventive war 83, 150, 152–5, 158, 165–7, 169–76, 185, 193
Prisoner of War (POW) 7880, 84, 112, 124
propaganda 66–7, 72, 101
Pufendorf, S. 165, 169, 262

Rasul v. *Bush*, 80, 103, 105, 113–20, 136, 147n11, 230
Reagan, R. 9; administration 201
Rejali, D. 197, 200, 211–13, 219, 244
religion 41–4, 162, 164, 220; Muslim 217
Respondents' Memorandum 142–3
revolution 24, 29, 66; French 59, 62
Richardson, L. 2, 7, 56, 58, 64, 68
right authority 83, 149–50, 153, 158, 165, 181–91
Roberts, A. 56, 58, 75, 185, 188
Rose Revolution 29

St. Petersburg Declaration 74
Sands, P. 84, 88, 237
Saudi Arabia 221, 238; Saudi Arabian 215
Schell, J. 1, 6
Schmidt, R. 198, 237
Schmidt-Furlow Report 198
Scott, J.B. 163–5
self-defense 76, 81, 83, 149, 152, 157, 161–2, 184, 193, 260; anticipatory 153, 167, 176–7; interceptive 154–5; justification for 160, 172; reactive 154
Shaykh Mohammed, K. 197, 216, 233, 239–40, 242
Simonson, K. 180–1

Slaughter, A. 107–9
sleep deprivation 96, 217, 219
Soufan, A. 198, 216–20, 222, 229, 235
sovereignty 38, 111, 136, 165, 192; limits of 190; principle of 189; territorial 132; ultimate 114, 133
Soviet Union 28, 70; occupation 70, 228; Warsaw Pact allies 29
Special Tribunal for Lebanon Appeals Chamber 62–3
Steyn, L. 77, 103
strategy of provocation 2, 15, 56–7, 59, 70
stress positions 96, 237, 242
Survival, Evasion, Resistance, and Escape (SERE) 202; program 210, 217; school 209, 222
suspicion *see* based on suspicion

Taguba, A. 97, 198; Taguba Report 198
Taliban 59, 143; Detainees 78, 80, 114, 140, 146n4–5; fighters 77, 124; Forces 79, 142; members 77–9, 84, 112, 227; militia 79–80; movement 70; regime 74, 125, 130, 173; suspected leaders 259
terrorism 1–3, 6, 11, 21, 35, 59–63, 67–8, 193, 214; affected by 18; aims 71, 90; charges 231; combating 72, 175; consequences of 17; countering 258; defense against 22; employ 13, 15, 17, 35, 65–6, 73, 174; global 83, 192; goals 7; intelligence traffic 226; issues 203; policy 128; strategy 13, 65, 251; strategy of provocation 56; struggle against 174; support 121, 190; suspects 76, 139, 142; tactic of 64; target 16, 21, 31–2, 70, 87, 91, 98; targeted by 37, 196; threat 57; US analysts 215; war against 4, 75, 111
terrorist 2, 17, 59, 207; activities 85, 235, 241; acts 1, 7, 13–14, 36, 61–2, 68, 114, 196, 251; attacks 14, 17, 36, 48, 63, 65–6, 68, 73, 76, 111, 114, 173, 216, 223–4, 227–8, 236, 244, 246, 253; bombing 62; bomb plot 213; connections 179; groups 61, 65, 68, 207, 238, 252, 263; incidents 255; leader 216, 263; literature 65; movements 58, 64; networks 130, 221; operation 227; operatives 215, 219, 240; organizations 18, 59, 193, 219–20, 227, 253, 255; plans 197; plots 223, 241–2; strikes 3, 73;

terrorist *continued*
  suspected 112, 144, 192, 200, 217–18,
    222; tactics 10, 35, 60, 212; target
    261; threat 14, 17, 75, 230; ticking
    bomb 244–5; training camps 74
terrorists 59–60, 64, 66–9, 74, 139, 144,
    196, 215, 249; Al-Qaeda 216, 218;
    Communist 75; detention 241; future
    attacks 208; hijackers 246;
    interrogating 229; legitimacy 17;
    support 231; suspected 192, 200, 218,
    222; target 11, 99
Thai, J. 115–17, 216–17, 219–20
Thailand 216–17, 219–20
Thatcher, M. 60
Thompson, R. 33, 56, 75
Thucydides 160, 167, 177–8
ticking bomb 213; scenario 199, 207,
    243–6, 249; terrorist 244–5
torture 9, 14, 22, 49, 72, 78, 84–5, 87,
    94, 100–1, 194, 199, 202–4, 207, 223,
    228, 230, 232–3, 237, 240, 245–6;
    application of 100, 199, 212, 229;
    authorized 247, 256; borderline 219,
    235; Committee Against 86, 91, **92**,
    248; confessions 226; contracts 219;
    Declaration against 94–5; of
    detainees 10, 129, 152, 198, 239, 256;
    domestic law 76, 197; efficacy 195–6,
    212, 234, 238, 243; illegality 86, 196,
    248; inefficacy 213, 229; of the
    innocent 242, 262; international law
    95, 195; Medical Evidence 96; memos
    9–10, 87–8, 200–1, 205, 219, 221, 223,
    248; permitted 248; policy 215, 247;
    program 88, 213, 235–6, 249;
    prohibition of 9, 85, 195, 243; Public
    Committee against 47, 258; regime
    97; resistance training 209; on
    suspicion 220, 223–5, 243, 250, 253,
    256; techniques 96, 211, 222; threats
    215; Torture Papers 252; UN
    Convention against 76, 85, 97, 202,
    248; use of 85, 88, 97, 195, 211, 236,
    243, 256; US Statute 77; warrants 244
Tuck, R. 43, 156, 159–60, 165, 170
Turku Declaration of Minimum
    Humanitarian Standards 146–7n9
Turner Johnson, J. 149, 157–8, 161,
    165, 183

UK 83, 109, 152, 181, 185–6, 232, 235;
    Attorney General 188; British
    Constitution 132; British resident

231; military and police operation 75;
    Permanent Mission 152
UN 186–8; Charter 3, 8, 73, 76–8, 81–3,
    92, 150, 154, 172, 175, 181, 183–6,
    189–92, 252; Committee Against
    Torture 86, **92**, 248; Human Rights
    Committee 113, 139; Special
    Commission (UNSCOM) 186, 188;
    Special Rapporteur on Counter-
    Terrorism and Human Rights 259;
    UN weapons inspectors 187–8; *see
    also* UN Security Council
Uniform Code of Military Justice
    (UCMJ) 77, 97, 123–4, 137
Universal Declaration of Human Rights
    85, 87, 118, 147n10
UN Security Council 8, 62–3, 76, 81–2,
    150, 152–4, 169, 178, 181–3, 185–7,
    189–90, 192, 214, 260; authorization
    76, 178, 184; *see also* UN Security
    Council resolutions
UN Security Council resolutions 78, 83,
    88, 179, 188, 191; Resolution 678
    185–7, 189; Resolution 687 185–7,
    188; Resolution 1368 63; Resolution
    1373 62, 152, 260; Resolution 1377
    62; Resolution 1441 185, 187, 189
US 65, 70, 72, 87, 98; administration 7,
    56, 83, 146n6, 178, 191; citizens 69,
    71, 82, 88, 91, 94, 105, 114, 145, 182,
    192–3, 204, 230, 248, 257, 261;
    democracy 205; detention 137, 198;
    interrogation policies 97; legitimacy
    56, 58; media 1, 83, 92, 233; national
    court system 124; obligations 9;
    PATRIOT Act 114; political authority
    59; power 66; propaganda machine
    67; State Department 3, 190; territory
    93, 114, 134; Torture Statute 77
US Army 14; Field Manual 7, 13, 22,
    57–8, 100, 204, 218, 229, 236–7,
    256–7; official investigation 97;
    Personnel 239
US Constitution 89, 109–11, 115, 131,
    252; constitutional standard 203;
    constitutional structure 110–11
US courts 8, 111, 115, 117, 123, 125,
    219; Court of Appeals 85, 121, 125;
    Supreme Court 8, 42, 54, 76–8, 88,
    93, 102–9, 111, 113–16, 118, 120–3,
    125–8, 130–1, 133–8, 140–1, 145, 205,
    230–1, 255, 258, 262; *see also* US
    District Courts
US Department of Justice 75, 138,

146n3, 146n5, 206, 209, 228, 247–8;
Bush 128; Obama 139; White Paper
leak 261; *see also* American Bar
Association, American Law Institute
US District Court 122–3, 136, 138;
Columbia 115; jurisdiction 119;
Washington 228
US government 1, 14, 23, 42, 56, 72, 98,
179, 202, 232, 235, 239; Department
of Defense 173–5, 193; Department
of Justice 206, 209, 261; federal 90;
Senate Armed Services Committee
198, 202; Senate Select Committee
on Intelligence 82, 198, 213–15; State
Department 3, 190; system 89, 133
US military 14, 34, 73–4; armed forces
96, 213; base 115; Central Command
57, 96; Commission Act 250n2;
control 147n13; deterrence 69;
dominance 69; facility 107, 111, 114,
139; forces 14, 57, 76, 111, 145;
headquarters 63; ill-treatment of
detainees 198; officers 96; officials
97; troops 57, 97, 186, 214
USSR 29; *see also* Soviet Union

Vattel, E. 165, 169–70
veto 53, 191; power 260
Vienna Convention on the Law of
Treaties 103, 172
violence 20, 27, 29, 32, 36, 47, 49–50,
64, 83, 132, 154, 160, 251, 258, 262;
against noncombatants 255; civilian
74; cross-border 2; enemy 159; free
50, 149, 185; illegal 199; irrational 63;
legitimate 19; mass 155; political
16–18, 22, 28–9, 55, 59–60, 62–3, 68,
71–2, 101; politically motivated 7, 61,
73; public 183; threatened 28, 61; use
of 6, 23, 51, 53, 150, 157, 189, 192;
victims of 62

violent 2, 20; actions 17, 28, 63–4, 157;
armed combat 167; attacks 2, 16, 68,
261; clashes 158; conflict 159;
confrontation 163; dominance 195;
events 251; force 196; injury 83;
power 66; targeting 69

Walzer, M. 151–2, 155, 177–8
war crimes 96–7, 114; Act 77; Tokyo
War Crimes trials 207
war on terror 2, 4, 7–8, 10, 13–15, 23,
39, 42, 54, 71, 73, 75–7, 80, 82, 84,
88–9, 91, 93, 95, 97–9, 103–5, 107,
111–12, 119–20, 122, 127–9, 131, 133,
137–9, 145, 151–2, 174, 192, 197–8,
200–1, 204–5, 211, 213, 222, 229–30,
239, 249, 252–3, 255–6, 258
waterboarding 96, 194, 202–3, 207–11,
218, 222–6, 240–1
weapons of mass destruction 9, 82, 174,
176, 179, 185–8, 192, 214–15
Weber, M. 13, 16, 18–27, 31, 55n1, 71,
75, 98, 253, 264; theory of legitimacy
25
Webster, D. 176–7, 262
Wedgwood, R. 186–7
Wheeler, N. 190, 192
White House 75, 83, 97, 173, 175, 179,
193, 204

Xenophon 4950

Yoo, J. 75, 77–9, 87, 111, 128, 201, 247,
252–3, 255

Zelikow, P. 203–4
Zubaydah, A. 197, 215–17, 219–31, 233,
235, 240

For Product Safety Concerns and Information please contact our EU
representative GPSR@taylorandfrancis.com
Taylor & Francis Verlag GmbH, Kaufingerstraße 24, 80331 München, Germany

www.ingramcontent.com/pod-product-compliance
Lightning Source LLC
Chambersburg PA
CBHW060148280326
41932CB00012B/1685